NAPOLEON AND EUROPE

—— ◆ ——

NAPOLEON AND EUROPE

Edited by
PHILIP G. DWYER

Routledge
Taylor & Francis Group

LONDON AND NEW YORK

First published 2001 by Pearson Education Limited

Published 2014 by Routledge
2 Park Square, Milton Park, Abingdon, Oxon OX14 4RN
711 Third Avenue, New York, NY, 10017, USA

Routledge is an imprint of the Taylor & Francis Group, an informa business

British Library Cataloguing in Publication Data
A CIP catalogue record for this book can be obtained from the British Library

Library of Congress Cataloging in Publication Data
A CIP catalog record for this book can be obtained from the Library of Congress

ISBN: 978-0-5823-1837-3 (pbk)

Typeset in 11.5/14pt Garamond MT by Graphicraft Limited, Hong Kong

CONTENTS

———◆———

Contents

PREFACE

———◆———

Despite the outpouring of works on Napoleon and the First Empire (over 220,000 volumes at the last count), the period has long been regarded as the poor cousin of French history, largely overshadowed by the enormous variety and originality of studies on the event that immediately precedes it, the French Revolution. Regrettably, the two periods are often treated separately, thereby obscuring any continuities that may exist. Traditionally, the Napoleonic era has also been dominated by political, military and diplomatic historians preoccupied with the French conquest of Europe and the foreign-political negotiations that preceded the military campaigns. Even here, however, there has been a relative decline in the output of work based on archival research. It has only been in the last ten years or so that historians have grappled with other, fundamental social and political questions such as how the Napoleonic wars affected the everyday lives of ordinary men and women, the nature of empire, the responses of the European elites to French occupation, and the impact of the French conquest on the political development of individual European states as well as on the European states system. Although strides have been made in these areas, largely by non-Francophone historians whose work French publishers have seemed reluctant to translate, much work still needs to be done.

The Napoleonic Empire, as the essays in this collection clearly demonstrate, was not just an adjunct of the French Revolution. It was also a conflict over the future shape of Europe in which social, economic, political and even intellectual interests were at stake. It was a struggle between modernity and the Ancien Regime, between the old conservative Europe and the new progressive Europe into which it could potentially evolve, even if this is not how the Napoleonic wars were viewed by contemporaries. The First Empire thus embodies, to an even greater extent than the French Revolution, the passage of Ancien Regime Europe to the modern world. In this process, no one is more responsible for dragging Europe kicking and screaming into the modern era than Napoleon. The purpose of this series of essays then is threefold: to place the period within the larger context of French and European history; to explore the impact of the Napoleonic regime on France and Europe; and to present a series of accessible, new studies that are based on either original research or recent historiographical developments. Any historian dealing with Napoleon has to contend with the myths he did so much to create while in exile on St Helena, which continue to distort the historical reality even today. This collection of essays, which brings together some of the leading scholars in the field, will help lay some of those myths to rest.

Like all books of this nature, this one was dependent upon the goodwill and the readiness of the contributors to take time out from their busy schedules to participate in a project that brought them little reward, other than the opportunity to help advance historical research in the field of Napoleonic studies. The end result was a collaborative effort; the demands I placed upon them at times exceeded what is normally expected of contributors to works of this sort. I am truly grateful, therefore, to all the participants, but especially to Charles Esdaile, for their co-operation, patience, advice and suggestions. During the course of this project, I also had the good fortune of corresponding with Harold T. Parker, whose enthusiasm for history and whose readiness to share his ideas epitomise what scholarship is all about. Although we did not always agree, we share a conviction that the study of this period, beyond its inherent interest, is important for an understanding of how Europe worked and evolved. I should also like to acknowledge Andrew McLennan, formerly of Addison Wesley Longman, for allowing me to get this project off the ground when it was only an idea. My thanks also to Rory Muir for his help and advice. Finally, the Research Management Committee at the University of Newcastle, Australia, provided funding that made it possible to write my own contribution. I hope this book goes some way in stimulating interest in a field that is rich in potential for further research.

Philip G. Dwyer

ABOUT THE CONTRIBUTORS

——— ◆ ———

Michael Broers is Reader in European History at the University of Aberdeen. He is the author of three recent books: *Europe under Napoleon, 1799–1815* (London, 1996); *Europe after Napoleon, 1814–1851* (Manchester, 1996); and *Napoleonic Imperialism and the Savoyard Monarchy, 1773–1821. State Building in Piedmont* (Lampeter, 1997). He has also written several articles and chapters on Napoleonic Italy, and most recently on the post-1814 period: 'Sexual politics and political ideology under the Savoyard monarchy, 1814–1821', *English Historical Review* 114 (1999). He is currently working on a study of counter-revolution and cultural imperialism in Napoleonic Italy, to be published by Routledge.

Philip Dwyer is Lecturer in Modern European History at the University of Newcastle, Australia. He is the editor of *The Rise of Prussia, 1700–1830* (London, 2000) and *Modern Prussian History, 1830–1945* (London, 2001), as well as the author of a number of articles on Prussian foreign policy during the Napoleonic era. He is currently completing *Talleyrand* for the Longman's 'Profiles in Power' series, as well as working on a study of Napoleon's youth and rise to power.

Geoffrey Ellis is a Fellow and Tutor in Modern History at Hertford College, Oxford, and Lecturer in French History at the University of Oxford. His earlier published works include *Napoleon's Continental Blockade: The Case of Alsace* (Oxford, 1981), *The Napoleonic Empire* (London, 1991) and *Napoleon* (London, 1997). He has also contributed to other collected volumes on Napoleonic history, and has written a review-article on Marxist interpretations of the French Revolution for the *English Historical Review 93* (1978). He is currently working on an economic history of the French Revolution.

Charles J. Esdaile is Lecturer in History at the University of Liverpool. He has written extensively on the Napoleonic period and is the author of *The Spanish Army in the Peninsular War* (Manchester, 1988), *The Duke of Wellington and the Command of the Spanish Army, 1812–1814* (Basingstoke, 1990), *The Wars of Napoleon* (London, 1995), *Spain in the Liberal Age: From Constitution to Civil*

War, 1808–1939 (London, 2000) and *The French Wars, 1792–1815* (London, 2001). He is currently completing a history of the Peninsular War.

Alan Forrest is Professor of Modern History at the University of York. He has published widely on French revolutionary and Napoleonic history, especially on social history and on the military. His publications include: *Society and Politics in Revolutionary Bordeaux* (Oxford, 1975); *The French Revolution and the Poor* (London, 1981); *Conscripts and Deserters: The Army and French Society during the Revolution and Empire* (Oxford, 1989); *The Soldiers of the French Revolution* (Durham, NC, 1990); and *The Revolution in Provincial France: Aquitaine, 1789–1799* (Oxford, 1996). He has also written a short textbook on *The French Revolution* (London, 1995). He is currently working on a book about the writings of French soldiers during the revolutionary and Napoleonic wars and their value to historians of the period.

Alexander Grab is Professor of History at the University of Maine. He has published widely on the army, law and order, and finances in Napoleonic Italy. His most recent publication is 'From the French Revolution to Napoleon', in John Davis (ed.), *The Risorgimento and Unification 1789–1796* (Oxford, 2000). He is currently working on a book about Europe under Napoleon to be published by Macmillan.

Alexander M. Martin is Associate Professor of Modern European History at Oglethorpe University, Atlanta, Georgia. He is the author of *Romantics, Reformers, Reactionaries: Russian Conservative Thought and Politics in the Reign of Alexander I* (DeKalb, Ill., 1997) and of several articles and chapters published in the United States, Germany and Russia. He is currently working on a study of Moscow from the 1760s to the 1840s.

Harold T. Parker is Professor Emeritus at Duke University. He is the author of *The Cult of Antiquity and the French Revolutionaries* (New York, 1965); *Three Napoleonic Battles* (Durham, NC, 1983); *The Bureau of Commerce in 1781* (Durham, NC, 1979); and *An Administrative Bureau during the Old Regime: the Bureau of Commerce and its Relations to French Industry* (London and Toronto, 1993); as well as numerous articles on the period of the Ancien Regime, the French Revolution, and Napoleon.

Michael Rowe is Lecturer in Modern European History at Queen's University, Belfast. He has published on various aspects of Napoleonic rule in Germany, including most recently 'Between empire and home town: Napoleonic rule on the Rhine, 1799–1814', *The Historical Journal* 42 (1999), and 'The Napoleonic legacy in the Rhineland and the politics of reform in Restoration Prussia', in David Laven and Lucy Riall (eds.), *Napoleon's Legacy: Problems of Government in Restoration Europe* (Oxford and New York, 2000). He is currently completing a monograph on the history of the Rhineland from 1780 to 1830.

Michael Sibalis is Associate Professor of History at Wilfrid Laurier University in Waterloo, Ontario, Canada. He has published numerous articles and essays on the nineteenth-century French labour movement, the Napoleonic police, and the history of French homosexuality. He is currently working on a book on the Napoleonic police state.

Brendan Simms is College Lecturer and Admissions Tutor at Peterhouse, Cambridge, and Newton Sheehy Teaching Fellow in International Relations at the Centre of International Studies, the University of Cambridge. He is the author of *The Impact of Napoleon: Prussian High Politics, Foreign Policy and the Crisis of the Executive, 1797–1806* (Cambridge, 1997); *The Struggle for Mastery in Germany, 1779–1850* (London and New York, 1998); and of numerous articles on Weimar Germany and the Third Reich.

John Lawrence Tone is Associate Professor of History in the School of History, Technology, and Society at the Georgia Institute of Technology in Atlanta. He is the author of *The Fatal Knot: the Guerrilla War in Navarre and the Defeat of Napoleon in Spain* (Chapel Hill, NC, 1994) and *La Guerrilla española y la derrota de Napoleón* (Madrid, 1999). He has written several articles on Spanish and Cuban history. His current project is a history of Spain's war in Cuba from 1895 to 1898.

Isser Woloch is the Moore Collegiate Professor of History at Columbia University. He has published widely on French revolutionary and Napoleonic history, especially on social history. His books include: *Jacobin Legacy: the Democratic Movement under the Directory* (Princeton, NJ, 1970); and *The French Veteran from the Revolution to the Restoration* (Chapel Hill, NC, 1979). *The New Regime: Transformations of the French Civic Order, 1789–1820s* (New York, 1994) won the Leo Gershoy Award of the American Historical Association. His latest book is *Napoleon and his Collaborators: the Making of a Dictatorship* (New York, 2001).

LIST OF TABLES AND MAPS

———◆———

All maps are from C. Esdaile, *The Wars of Napoleon*, Longman (1995) pp. 378–393.

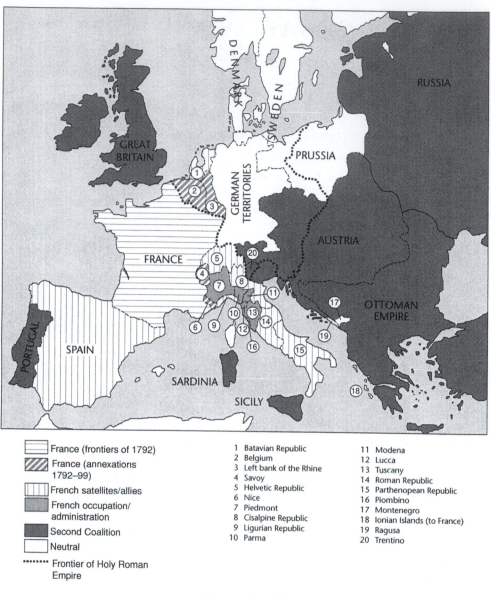

France (frontiers of 1792)	1 Batavian Republic	11 Modena
France (annexations 1792–99)	2 Belgium	12 Lucca
	3 Left bank of the Rhine	13 Tuscany
French satellites/allies	4 Savoy	14 Roman Republic
	5 Helvetic Republic	15 Parthenopean Republic
French occupation/ administration	6 Nice	16 Piombino
	7 Piedmont	17 Montenegro
Second Coalition	8 Cisalpine Republic	18 Ionian Islands (to France)
	9 Ligurian Republic	19 Ragusa
Neutral	10 Parma	20 Trentino
Frontier of Holy Roman Empire		

Europe in 1799

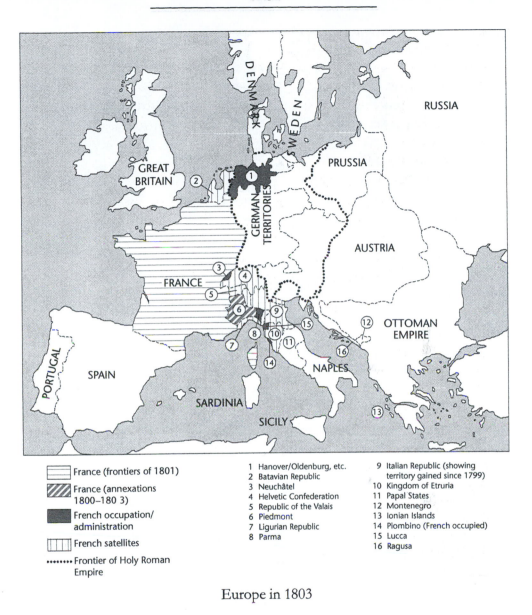

France (frontiers of 1801)	1 Hanover/Oldenburg, etc.	9 Italian Republic (showing territory gained since 1799)
France (annexations 1800–180 3)	2 Batavian Republic	10 Kingdom of Etruria
	3 Neuchâtel	11 Papal States
French occupation/ administration	4 Helvetic Confederation	12 Montenegro
	5 Republic of the Valais	13 Ionian Islands
French satellites	6 Piedmont	14 Piombino (French occupied)
	7 Ligurian Republic	15 Lucca
Frontier of Holy Roman Empire	8 Parma	16 Ragusa

Europe in 1803

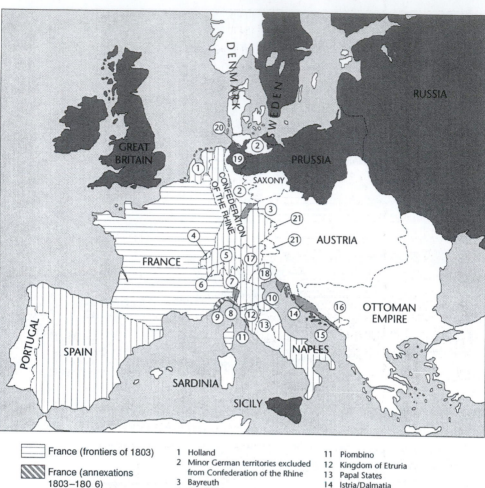

▭ France (frontiers of 1803)	1	Holland	11	Piombino
	2	Minor German territories excluded	12	Kingdom of Etruria
▨ France (annexations 1803–180 6)		from Confederation of the Rhine	13	Papal States
	3	Bayreuth	14	Istria/Dalmatia
	4	Neuchâtel	15	Ragusa
▦ French occupation/ administration	5	Helvetic Confederation	16	Montenegro
	6	Republic of the Valais	17	Tyrol/Vorarlberg (to Bavaria, 1805)
▥ French satellites/allies	7	Kingdom of Italy	18	Venetia (to Kingdom of Italy, 1805)
	8	Parma	19	Hanover (to Prussia, 1806)
▬ Fourth Coalition	9	Ligurian Republic	20	Hamburg
	10	Lucca	21	Salzburg (to Austria, 1805)

Europe in 1806

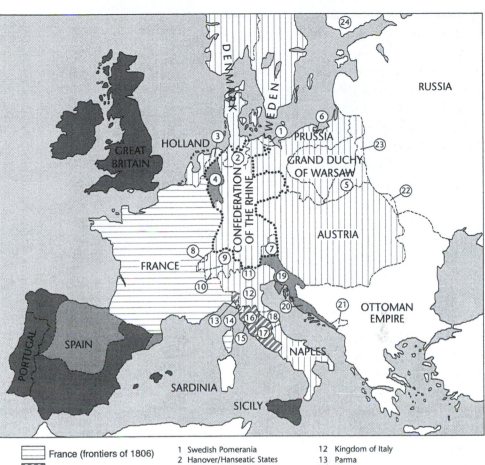

▭ France (frontiers of 1806)	1 Swedish Pomerania	12 Kingdom of Italy
	2 Hanover/Hanseatic States	13 Parma
▨ France (annexations	(to Westphalia, 1810)	14 Lucca
1806–1809)	3 East Friesland (to Holland)	15 Piombino
▤ French occupation/	4 Berg	16 Kingdom of Etruria
administration	5 Western Galicia (to Grand Duchy	17 Rome
▥ French satellites/allies	of Warsaw, 1809)	18 Marches (to Kingdom of Italy, 1808)
	6 Danzig (French occupation)	19 Habsburg territory lost to Illyrian
▦ Great Britain and allies/	7 Salzburg/Ried (to Bavaria, 1809)	Provinces
dependencies	8 Neuchâtel	20 Illyrian Provinces
•••••• Frontier of Confederation	9 Helvetic Confederation	21 Montenegro
of the Rhine	10 Republic of the Valais	22 Tarnopol (to Russia, 1809)
	11 South Tyrol/Trentino	23 Bialystok (to Russia, 1807)
	(to Kingdom of Italy, December	24 Finland (to Russia, 1808)
	1809)	

Europe in 1810

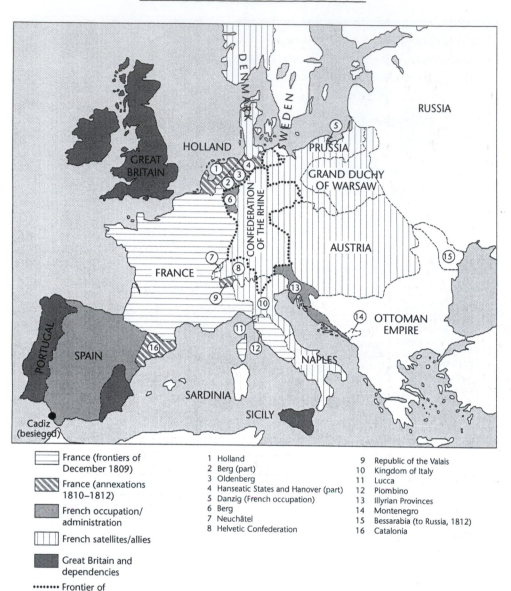

France (frontiers of December 1809)

France (annexations 1810–1812)

French occupation/administration

French satellites/allies

Great Britain and dependencies

•••••• Frontier of Confederation

1 Holland
2 Berg (part)
3 Oldenberg
4 Hanseatic States and Hanover (part)
5 Danzig (French occupation)
6 Berg
7 Neuchâtel
8 Helvetic Confederation

9 Republic of the Valais
10 Kingdom of Italy
11 Lucca
12 Piombino
13 Illyrian Provinces
14 Montenegro
15 Bessarabia (to Russia, 1812)
16 Catalonia

Europe in 1812

Territorial restorations
and acquisitions

■ Prussia

▨ Austria

▥ Russia

▨ Sweden

▤ Other

•••••• Frontier of German Confederation

1 United Netherlands
2 Neuchâtel (to Prussia)
3 Helvetic Confederation
4 Piedmont/Genoa (to Sardinia)
5 Parma
6 Modena
7 Lucca
8 Tuscany

9 Papal States
10 Naples (to Sicily)
11 Tarnopol (to Austria)
12 Montenegro
13 Catalonia
14 Valais (to Helvetic Confederation)
15 Piombino (to Tuscany)

Europe after the Congress of Vienna

INTRODUCTION

——◆——

Philip G. Dwyer

While in exile in 1816 on St Helena, Napoleon, reflecting on the causes surrounding his prodigious rise and fall from power, commented that when he took over the reins of power in 1799:

> all the elements of empire were already there. People were tired of anarchy; they wanted [the Revolution] to be over and done with. If I had not come on the scene it is probable that another would have done the same. France would have finished by conquering the world! . . . a man is nothing more than a man. His resources are nothing if circumstances and [public] opinion do not favour him.[1]

Even in exile, when fate had seemingly abandoned him, Napoleon had an eye to posterity. The narrative he communicated to his entourage through countless hours of monologues and conversations, later conveyed in written form to the world by the four evangelists – Las Cases, Montholon, Gourgaud and Bertrand – was meant to exculpate him from all blame for the wars which bear his name. They were also meant to promote the view that he was a beneficent, enlightened ruler, a lawmaker, who wanted to unify Europe in much the same way as the Roman and Carolingian empires. The deliberate dissemination of a very particular idealised image, which he first had an opportunity to mould during the campaign in Italy in 1796–97, was still being shaped and refined after his fall from power so that when he died his version of events would prevail. Napoleon was effectively rewriting history to fit his own image, and in this he was perhaps the most successful propagandist of all times. Despite some detractors, and despite the existence of a 'black legend' which portrayed Napoleon as an ogre, many of the myths Napoleon helped create have tenaciously endured to the present day.

One of the more important elements of this idealised image was Napoleon's self-portrayal, not as an active agent in history changing and bending the world to his will, but as its instrument and even its victim. He reasoned that what happened was inevitable (he was, after all, a firm believer in destiny). If he had not taken power in 1799, then someone else would have. If he had not introduced the Empire, then it surely would have been introduced anyway since all the elements were already in place. An individual's actions are limited by 'circumstances' over which they have no control, and their decisions are determined necessarily by others or by the weight of mightier forces, like public opinion. 'A man is nothing more than a man.'

Napoleon's account of his own role in history raises fundamental questions about the extent to which the individual can have an impact on the social, political and cultural environment in which they live. If we hold Napoleon responsible for the wars that were fought between 1803 and 1815, as most historians do, then we must also hold Napoleon responsible for the creation and the consequences of the Empire in Europe. Napoleon was, of course, a product of Ancien Regime society, and like many of his contemporaries he found both political and personal expression through the French Revolution. But he also managed to disseminate the Revolution through a policy of expansionism that the revolutionaries could not have conceived, and to bring the French administrative model to places where it would never have otherwise gone.

It would be a mistake, of course, to rehash some sort of 'great man theory' of history, but it would be just as unfortunate to discount entirely the impact of Napoleon as an individual. In any assessment of the period, a balance between his personal qualities and real achievements as general, administrator and lawmaker on the one hand, and the broader political, social and economic forces at play on the other has to be found. It can only be achieved by placing Napoleon as subject – as 'conscious agent' – in historical context. This involves exploring and understanding many different facets of, for want of a better term, the long Napoleonic era (the 1780s to the 1820s): the contours of Corsican society and politics; the military culture of the Ancien Regime; the social and political transformations brought about by the French Revolution; the workings of the European states system and the impact French expansion had on it; the institutions and structures put in place by the French, both at home and in the countries they administered; the responses of the European elites; and the responses of the people of Europe to the experience of French occupation.

NAPOLEON AND FRANCE

Napoleon's immediate context was defined by family life in Corsica, and later during his school days at Brienne in the north of France. Previous investigations of Napoleon's childhood and formative years, and their possible influence on his development as an adult, have obliged historians to pay closer attention to Corsican cultural values, which remained with Napoleon throughout his life.[2] Napoleon was born into a petty noble family whose head, Carlo Buonaparte, had clear political ambitions which were passed on to his sons.[3] The family, and the values that were taught within it, 'had a formative and lasting influence on [Napoleon's] views of himself and on his dynastic ambition'.[4] Just as importantly, the notion of the extended family – the clan – had an extremely important social function in Corsica at the time.[5] It helps explain, if only at a superficial level, later developments in France once Napoleon assumed the reins of power: the swing away from revolutionary egalitarian principles in gender and family relations, the return of patriarchal family values in the Civil Code, the degree to which nepotism governed the division of territories and states during the Empire, and the efforts to found a lasting Bonaparte dynasty.

Another determining influence was, of course, the army and its military culture.[6] Napoleon, raised from the age of 9 to become an officer, was consequently imbued with the military values of the French army of the Ancien Regime – honour, courage, sacrifice and glory. These concepts helped determine the way in which Napoleon perceived and negotiated the world and, Alan Forrest argues, were later imposed on French society – that is, Napoleon equated military values with civic virtues. The degree to which these military values were already present in French society, and the degree to which French society was already militarised, have yet to be fully explored. The army was, nevertheless, always present and not only had an impact on everyday life (through war and conscription), but determined the nature of authoritarian rule instituted after 1800. Napoleon ran France in much the same way as he ran the army; order and obedience were essential, so too was a hierarchy of command with Napoleon at the top.

The army also allowed Napoleon the opportunity to create a particular image of himself through his military victories. Italy and Egypt were the beginnings of a legend that involved not only the print media and the visual arts (prints, paintings and sculptures celebrating his real and imagined feats),[7] but also what today would be referred to as public relations. He was always at pains to appear close to the common soldier, accessible to all, and to make sure he was seen to share their hardship and suffering. In this manner, the soldier could and did identify with him, as the extracts from letters in Forrest's essay testify. The 'leader born of the people' was perhaps the most enduring image of Napoleon in nineteenth-century France and attracted millions of supporters to the Bonapartist cause long after he had died.

The army was also the backdrop to the network of personal relations Napoleon built during the course of campaigning in the south of France, Italy and Egypt, which helped him gain and maintain a position of influence.[8] The coup of Brumaire, after all, was carried out by troops that were largely loyal not to the Directory, but to the person of Napoleon. The events surrounding Brumaire have been discussed in detail elsewhere and can be passed over here. A number of essays in this collection focus instead on the impact of Napoleon on French society, and the direction it took as a result. Napoleon's consolidation of power was neither rapid nor smooth, and was only accomplished through a combination of reconciliation and repression.

1. Reconciliation

This took a number of forms, but essentially Napoleon eliminated the factionalism that had torn the country apart under the revolutionaries, and brought an end to the state's conflict with those sections of French society that had been alienated during the course of the Revolution (Catholics, royalists and émigrés, among others). The introduction of a unified code of law, the Civil Code of 1804 (known as the *Code Napoléon* after 1807), the introduction of monetary and financial reforms (the Bank of France was established in February 1800, three months after the coup of Brumaire), and the Concordat with the Catholic Church in Rome were all designed to create the social, economic and political stability necessary to consolidate and maintain power.

That is also why, in the spring of 1800, there was a massive shift in the reorganisation of the state's administrative and judicial apparatus away from locally elected officials to a highly centralised system of appointed officials (prefects, sub-prefects, mayors and judges).[9] Elections, one of the principles of 1789, were effectively abandoned (except for a few plebiscites that were in any event rigged).[10] Increasingly people were simply administered from Paris and no longer took an active part in national or even local politics. In fairness to Napoleon though, this process of depoliticisation had begun before he came on the scene – the *sans-culottes*, for example, were effectively suppressed as a political force in 1794, while many political clubs were closed down during the Directory – but the trend was compounded during the Consulate.

In short, there was a shift in the political culture away from the people back towards the national and local elites. This shift, according to Isser Woloch, necessarily had important consequences for the way in which

French society organised itself. For example, the concept of free primary education advocated by the revolutionaries was abandoned under Napoleon. Instead, greater emphasis was placed on the establishment of state-run *lycées* (high schools) in order to produce the trained professionals that a highly organised, structured state needed.[11] In other words, the people were neglected while the elite were nurtured, an attitude that was perfectly consistent with Napoleon's background. Despite having flirted with Jacobinism, Napoleon was not a revolutionary in the true sense of the word; he was an Ancien Regime noble with a noble's disdain for the people.

During the Empire, therefore, wealth and property once again took precedence, although not entirely, over talent in the race for careers and positions. This is clear in the studies that have been conducted on the *notables* (new landowners, government officials, army officers, professionals and businessmen).[12] Napoleon actively courted their co-operation; they were, after all, the mainstay of the regime and were, therefore, absolutely necessary to the smooth functioning of the state. However, Napoleon also actively courted the former nobility (which had been abolished in 1790), partly in order to promote social reconciliation, which he did with some degree of success (although many noble families simply refused to rally to the new regime).[13] In 1808, Napoleon even introduced a new nobility which was meant to be based on the principle of meritocracy, in distinction to the Ancien Regime nobility based on birth and privilege. More than one-fifth of the Napoleonic nobility was made up of former Ancien Regime nobles. Another means used by Napoleon to reward those who served the state – that is, the Emperor – was the *Légion d'Honneur* established in 1802. Its primary purpose was to reward military service, and the vast majority who received it during this period were military personnel (that is, 34,000 out of 38,000 recipients were military).[14] Indeed, the new award was defined by a concept that in Napoleon's eyes was quintessentially military – honour – an emphasis that was to remain throughout the Empire.[15]

The whole purpose of courting the *notables*, the old nobility, as well as creating a new nobility and the Legion of Honour, was to establish a generation of high-ranking servitors, schooled in the Empire, 'free of nostalgia for either the Ancien Regime or the Revolution', who would faithfully implement the Emperor's will.[16] The problem for Napoleon, however, was that they supported the regime only as long as their interests were in tune with his. As soon as they fell out, around 1810, even if they did not abandon the regime outright they proved indifferent to its fate.

2. Repression

This was the other means used to bring about political stability and it was especially important in the opening months and years of the Consulate (even though it has not received as much attention from historians as the 'reconciliation' process). The revolutionaries had attempted for years to bring a number of troubled regions (Brittany, Normandy and the Midi) under control, and had used brutal methods in an attempt to crush the enemies of the Republic (the Terror, the drownings at Nantes and the massacres at Lyons). In the process these methods had to a large extent, somewhat ironically, destroyed the new democratic polity.[17] The Directory brought with it a change in attitude. An attempt was made to restore the rule of law with the application of a highly democratic criminal justice system; but faced with generalised banditry, factionalism and open clashes between republicans and royalist/Catholic opponents across the country, it turned increasingly to 'authoritarian means' to solve the problem – that is, the army was increasingly used to restore law and order, and only then was the judiciary brought in to maintain it. The shift occurred after the coup d'état of Fructidor in 1797 and culminated with Napoleon being named First Consul for Life in 1802, during which period 'traditional methods of repression were used on an unprecedented scale to restore order in large areas of endemic lawlessness so that more modern methods of surveillance, policing, and control could maintain order thereafter'.[18] During the Directory, over two hundred communes were placed under a form of martial law known as a 'state of siege' in order to assert state authority over rebellious communes. Military justice was also used in an effort to break the back of brigandage and counter-revolution. From 1798 on, military courts tried hundreds of people accused of highway robbery. By November 1799, 40 per cent of the country was under the jurisdiction of generals who were able to impose the state of siege on any town or village.

The army, then, was the key to restoring the rule of law, and in this the Directory made considerable progress by 1798. Nevertheless, Napoleon inherited a situation of widespread unrest on coming to power. During the last few months of the Directory, conscription, taxation and the transfer of troops from the interior to the frontiers – all in an effort to cope with the war of the Second Coalition – resulted in a sudden increase in anti-republican insurgency. Napoleon exacerbated the situation by deciding to pursue the war aims of the Directory. He could only hope to regain control over areas in rebellion by tipping the 'balance of fear' in his favour.[19] Thus, in his instructions to General Hédouville concerning the Vendée, he spoke of 'extermination' and suggested that it would set a good example to burn down two or three large communes.[20] At the same time, Napoleon continued the Directory's policy of using extra-judicial, military justice as an accompanying means of deliberately instilling terror. Mobile columns, accompanied by Extraordinary Military Commissions, began operating in 1800–1801 to restore order in the Midi and the west of France. However, although their methods seem to have been extremely effective, they soon began to discredit the new regime. In February 1801, Napoleon consequently resurrected Special Tribunals, reminiscent of those created during the Terror; made up of civilian and military judges, they conducted their proceedings in public. In the first six months, 1,200 people, a third of whom were condemned to death, passed through these courts. Special Tribunals ultimately delivered the control the state needed and thus became a permanent feature of the Napoleonic criminal justice system.[21] To this extent, Brown is right in describing the Napoleonic state as 'liberal authoritarian' – that is, the state may have used extra-judicial measures to restore the rule of law, but it was also limited by a liberal legal system. Even under Napoleon, courts required hard evidence before they convicted.

Order and stability, in other words, were brought about and maintained by harsh measures of repression, but there was nothing unusual in this. Any regime would have suppressed unrest in much the same way; the use of mobile columns, extra-judicial military tribunals and the systematic destruction of villages were methods used throughout the Ancien Regime and the French Revolution. The true nature of a police state, argues Michael Sibalis, lies in 'its surveillance of its citizens and the way it manages peaceful political dissent'.[22] Napoleon's police kept him informed about every aspect of imperial society and public opinion. Their reports were placed on his desk daily and represent one of the most informative sources of what ordinary French men and women were thinking and feeling during these times. The mistaken belief that Napoleon's spies and informers were everywhere was perhaps enough to stifle most expressions of discontent in the cafés, taverns and markets across the country. However, those who were unfortunate enough to get carried away by the effects of alcohol and blurt out 'seditious' or 'vile' words against either Napoleon or the army sometimes found themselves under lock and key, a measure of just how sensitive the regime was to public criticism. The Napoleonic police were able to hold people in detention for an indefinite term by *mesure de haute police* (an order from the Ministry of Police).[23] In real terms, however, never more than a couple of hundred political prisoners existed at any one time, and very few people were executed or even deported for political reasons. Indeed, the few political executions that were carried out under Napoleon – such as the duc d'Enghien, the Nuremberg bookseller Palm, and the two Austrian booksellers in Linz – seem to have been knee-jerk reactions and not a part of a premeditated, systematic attempt to eliminate opposition. Despite periodic lapses, the Napoleonic regime was essentially based on the rule of law, and certainly political repression under Napoleon was mild in comparison to the Terror. Internal exile was a much more common punishment than imprisonment or execution.[24]

THE NATURE OF THE EMPIRE

Notions of law, order and stability bring us, in a roundabout way, to the debate on the nature of the Napoleonic Empire. It was only a short time ago that historians assumed the French, following in the footsteps of their victorious armies, simply imposed reforms and their administrative model – which to many Napoleonic functionaries represented the best system elaborated in history – on the peoples they had conquered. They did so in the belief that, now 'united' (*réunis*) to the French nation, it was for the good of the people of Europe. Indeed, the French administrative elites believed they were simply extending French civilisation across the Empire. This was no mere colonisation: conquered territories were incorporated into the French body politic. This was the consequence, Stuart Woolf argues, of a type of 'cultural imperialism', but the purpose of the Empire was to 'integrate' Europe within a model of administrative efficiency.[25]

What was once a given has now been thrown open to contention. The legacy of imperial rule, argues Geoffrey Ellis, varied from country to country depending on a whole range of factors, not the least of which was the amount of time it took for the French model to be accepted and assimilated, if indeed it was ever applied at all.[26] Michael Broers also believes the acceptance of imperial rule had less to do with the amount of time it was applied, and much more to do with whether a particular region possessed the necessary structural preconditions – like a co-operative local government, or deep-seated rivalries between town and country – that made it responsive or not to directives from the centre. Consequently, even regions inside France, such as the Vendée, could be very unresponsive to conscription and taxation, while regions much farther from the centre – like the Duchy of Warsaw, Berg or Westphalia – proved to be fertile ground for the imperial war effort in terms of men and money.

Nor was the Napoleonic administrative system simply imposed on subject peoples. As a general rule, local elites were prepared to serve the French – it was a question of practical co-operation and a lack of loyalty to the ruling house – but they usually did so to further their own interests. In some regions of the Empire where assimilation proved impossible, like Naples or various regions in Spain, the Napoleonic system dissolved itself into the existing indigenous culture.[27] In others, systems that were already in place were simply extended. For the most part, assimilation successfully took place in the large urban centres of northern Italy, western Germany, Belgium and Holland – that is, the inner empire – where Napoleon was usually supported by the local educated elites, even if this did not always prove to be an easy process. In most regions outside the core inner empire, however, and indeed sometimes within it, the French centralising model was often fiercely resisted.

These explanations, which centre on structures, purpose and (as we shall see) consequences, have greatly contributed to our understanding of the Empire, but to the neglect of the role of Napoleon in its creation. It is as though Napoleon still heads the billing outside the playhouse, but his performance has gone unnoticed by the critics in their reviews. Napoleon, of course, did not create an empire by himself; his decisions largely conformed to the material and political interests of the French elite. Indeed, there was a kind of 'ideological consensus' that existed in favour of France's bid for imperial power, at least up until around 1810 when the consensus began to collapse. Moreover, there was a good deal of foreign-political continuity between Ancien Regime, revolutionary and Napoleonic France; Napoleon finalised rather than initiated French imperial expansion in Western Europe.[28] This said, imperial institutions were centred on the person of the Emperor, whose power was not limited by state structures and who was essentially able to take France into directions which had little or nothing to do with traditional French foreign-political interests. It is important, therefore, to try and understand what motivated Napoleon, what impelled him to conquer virtually all of western Europe.

In my own contribution, three facets of Napoleon's character are examined under the loose heading of 'the drive for glory': the creation of an idealised self-image, the role of Napoleon's unbounded imagination, and the apparent need to dominate and humiliate all those who stood in his way.[29] An understanding of these traits makes not only his drive to conquer clearer, but so too his inability to compromise after the disastrous Russian campaign. In 1813–14, anything less than total victory was seen as a weakness and an attack against his self-image. None of this negates the larger forces at play, or the traditional explanations that have been put forward over the years to clarify particular decisions or indeed Napoleonic foreign policy in general. It does, however, relegate them to the background and puts Napoleon back on centre stage, obliging the critics to sit up and take note of his performance and consider how much his character was central to the overall plot. This approach can perhaps best be reduced to the formulation 'No Napoleon, no Empire'. His will, in other words, was decisive. He made the decisions that led to the conquest of Europe; they were not made for him by abstract forces in history.

Whatever motives may have governed Napoleon's actions, his empire was essentially *both* a 'spoils system' designed to reward his associates, *and* a system geared towards the military and economic exploitation of subject peoples, so that the large armies needed to wage war could be maintained. The former meant that large estates in foreign countries were given as rewards, especially to the marshals, in line with the theory that they would fight all the harder to preserve the Empire.[30] The latter meant two things – taxation and conscription – both of which overshadowed just about every other administrative problem in Napoleonic France and Europe. Indeed, one can measure the extent to which the Napoleonic regime had successfully imposed itself (or not) on a region by the extent to which Napoleon was able to extract men and money from his subjects. Thus, in areas where low quotas were the rule, including regions in France, it is evident that the Empire had not struck deep roots, and these could not therefore be relied upon to stand by the regime in the face of revolt or, indeed, against the armies of the coalition.

1. The need for money

Paul Schroeder has suggested that Napoleon's fiscal reforms were both inadequate and indeed, like much else in the Empire, that they constituted a reversion to Ancien Regime practices.[31] This is true up to a point but, as Alexander Grab points out, an 'efficient and lucrative financial system was indispensable for . . . imperial expansion'. After all, no money, no army, no conquests; and yet one is at pains to find a substantial treatment of Napoleon's taxation system or the manner in which he financed his wars. How then did Napoleon do it? It was not so much that the regime introduced new taxes (although new indirect taxes were created; and old ones abolished during the Revolution, like the hated salt tax, were revived), but that it collected existing ones much more efficiently. In this manner at least

Napoleon was able to raise revenues substantially, although almost always never enough to cover the constant increases in military expenditure.

The fact that France alone could not bear the burden of the Napoleonic wars meant that Napoleon was compelled to exact money from both satellite states and those subject to French occupation. Indeed, conquered territories paid more than half of Napoleon's military expenses. In Italy, for example, the financial administration was reformed along the lines of the French model to create an efficient and reliable tax collection hierarchy (which lasted until the First World War). The revenues raised during the latter part of the Consulate and the Empire were largely able to satisfy Napoleon's needs, although their collection placed enormous strains on the Italian social and political fabric. In Holland, on the other hand, the French taxation system was not imposed on the Dutch until the country was incorporated into the Empire in 1810.[32]

Other methods were used to raise money, all designed to make war pay for itself. Booty was one method by which the war effort was if not financed, then at least subsidised. Napoleon was not the first revolutionary general, and certainly not the most reticent in the large-scale plundering of valuable artworks, treasures and money.[33] Another method was simply to impose reparations on countries defeated militarily. Thus Austria in 1805 and again in 1809, and Prussia in 1806, were not only obliged to pay massive indemnities running into hundreds of millions of francs, but were also forced to maintain and pay for large occupation armies. Even so-called allies were obliged to come to the table. The Kingdom of Italy, for example, paid close to 300 million lire for the privilege of maintaining a French army on Italian soil.[34] None of this, of course, takes into account the reality of occupation and the exactions carried out by occupying troops living off the land – the wholesale requisitioning of livestock, pillaging, rape (which was common) and even murder.

2. The need for men

Just as urgent as revenues was the need for men to fill the ranks of Napoleon's armies. As the scope of the Napoleonic wars increased, the demand for young men intensified. From 1806 on, about 80,000 men were conscripted annually, with much higher figures towards the closing years of the Empire. In all, over two million men (French and foreign) were inducted into the *Grande Armée* between 1803 and 1814. Of those, the number who died in battle or as result of wounds, or who went missing, is estimated at around 900,000 – that is, around 48 per cent of effectives, a figure which is much higher than many historians have thought.[35] Napoleon also increasingly relied on allied states to furnish contingents to the *Grande Armée*. Figures are difficult to assess and vary from source to source, but around 718,000 foreign troops were recruited over approximately a ten-year period.[36] Over half of the *Grande Armée* was made up of troops from satellite and allied states.

There were various ways of getting out of the army – marriage, self-mutilation, buying a replacement, draft dodging and desertion – but, interestingly enough, not only in France but also in other parts of the Empire, resistance to conscription declined over the years in the face of the growing effectiveness of the recruitment process. It gave way instead to a grudging compliance as the sustained 'cumulative impact of bureaucratic and coercive pressure' made itself felt.[37] Conscription, according to Isser Woloch, was an important factor in the process of state building. In Italy, for example, it brought people from different regions together under the same flag and in the same uniform, helping break down regional loyalties and developing a nationalist outlook. Although this was by no means a universal response, it was nevertheless the beginning of the process of turning peasants into Italians. The same could be said for France, Germany, Spain and just about any other region where people spoke a common language. In general terms, across Europe conscription became the principal battleground between individuals and local communities on the one hand, and the centralising state on the other. It was the state which eventually won out, so that by the 1820s conscription had become as routine as the local harvest festival or taxation.[38] Before that occurred, however, a great deal of resistance to the state had to be overcome. Conscription caused enormous social disruption among communities and families which often translated into unrest and brigandage (even in areas traditionally loyal to the state), if not open revolt.[39]

3. *Responses to empire*

Historians, especially French historians, have had a tendency to gloss over the social reality of occupation and to mirror the idealist element in Napoleonic propaganda justifying the French conquests – namely, that the French were bringing the principles of the Revolution ('liberty' and 'equality') and enlightened principles of government to essentially backward and superstitious peoples. Instead, one is tempted to draw a parallel between the French soldier in southern Europe during the Napoleonic wars and the

German soldier in eastern Europe during the Second World War; attitudes were determined by ideology (in this case, a belief in the universality of the principles of the Revolution) and a sense of cultural superiority.[40] The demands of the imperial state and the violence committed by French troops on local communities naturally resulted in opposition and resistance to the French.

Indirect passive resistance occurred where local traditions came under attack, or where local populations had little or no affinity with their own collaborating elites. This type of resistance could take the form of boycotting festivals associated with the regime, evading conscription or giving shelter to deserters or refractory priests and nuns. Passive resistance was especially evident in matters of religion where the Concordat was imposed on an unwilling population. Resistance also occurred where the French attempted to impose the *Code Napoléon* on areas where local traditions were deeply entrenched. In these cases, both the French authorities who had come to impose new laws and the local elites who collaborated in attempting to have them enacted were more often than not simply ignored.

Open, active resistance was far less frequent than indirect, passive resistance. Active responses might vary from acts of individual violence against imperial officials to outright revolt. (They do not, however, include traditional acts of collective violence such as pogroms or peasant uprisings which would have taken place no matter who was in power.) Open rebellion against the regime really only took place on a large scale in three areas of the 'outer empire': Calabria in 1806, Spain and Portugal in 1808, and the Tyrol in 1809. Just as the acceptance of imperial rule was dependent on whether a particular region possessed the necessary structural preconditions, so too did certain preconditions have to exist before general unrest translated into open revolt. Generally speaking, revolt occurred in regions where local elites were weak, where independent peasantries predominated, where there were already traditions of conflict or popular military activity (banditry, smuggling and local home-guards) against the centralising forces of the state, where there were social tensions between urban and rural areas, where the influence of the Church made itself felt (most areas of open revolt were profoundly Catholic, although there is not necessarily a correlation between revolt and religion), and where of course the terrain was suitable (mountainous and inaccessible regions are obviously more likely to promote guerrilla warfare than open plains). There were also within these revolts, as Charles Esdaile points out, 'sub-texts' like hatred of authority or a desire for revenge against the propertied classes.[41] In some areas where these conditions were not met, such as northern Germany, deliberate attempts made by local elites in 1813 to encourage the people to revolt against the French fell on deaf ears.

In those cases where taxation and conscription elicited acts of resistance, the response from the Napoleonic state was categorical: a policy of pacification was vigorously pursued. Usually, the army was used as an agency of law enforcement, dispersing illegal gatherings, arresting offenders, fighting brigandage and pursuing deserters and draft dodgers. This applied as much to areas inside France, like the Vendée, as to provinces within the Empire comprised largely of non-French-speaking people. Action was taken as much to win support for the regime from local populations (who often feared brigands as much as the troops sent to suppress them) as to enable the regime to exploit the region more efficiently. It was only when areas were relatively calm that a return to more 'normal' administrative processes occurred: law enforcement by police, judgment by civilian courts, rule by mayors and prefects and departmental administration.

One of the most important tools in this process of pacification was the Gendarmerie. Michael Broers ranks it as 'the major advance made by the state into the lives of ordinary people' during the Napoleonic era. Napoleon's reorganisation of the Gendarmerie had much to do with his promise to restore law and order after years of upheaval caused by the Revolution, but it was also meant to create the stable conditions necessary to implement conscription in such a way that the imperial army could always be regularly supplied with peasant troops.[42] Consequently, the chief job of the Gendarmerie became, even if that was not what it was originally intended for, the collection of conscripts. Although there were occasions when individual gendarmes colluded with local communities to avoid conscription, or accepted bribes, or turned a blind eye, more often than not – especially in the more remote regions of France and the Empire – conscription brought with it confrontation and sometimes violent clashes between the gendarmes and local communities.[43] Unlike the mobile columns used during the Directory and the Consulate to combat unrest, however, the Gendarmerie established itself as a fixture among local rural communities, thereby becoming the permanent representatives of the state at the local level. In this respect, the Gendarmerie was probably the most influential of Napoleonic institutions and was, indeed, so successful that even those rulers who had been most opposed to Napoleon (in Russia, Prussia, Austria, Spain and even Britain) set about creating paramilitary police forces based on the French model after 1814.[44]

NAPOLEON AND EUROPE

It would be tempting but nevertheless simplistic to argue that the whole process of empire building, centred as it was on the collection of men and money, had but one objective – the defeat of Britain and its allies. Certainly, the conflict with Britain is at the heart of any approach to the period although,[45] where once upon a time it engendered debates about the responsibility for the resumption of war in 1803, the tendency today is to lay the blame squarely at Napoleon's feet. If a recent study suggests the wars were largely a result of misconceptions, and that Britain and France went to war only reluctantly in 1803,[46] Brendan Simms is in no doubt about who was to blame for their continuation. The British government would have come to an arrangement with Napoleon, he argues, if it were not for Napoleon's unlimited ambition, which made any lasting agreement impossible.[47] Napoleon's strategic ambitions were, in the first years of the Empire at least, hardly out of keeping with the French foreign-policy ambitions of the Ancien Regime. Indeed, some historians see the Napoleonic wars as the last phase of the 'Second Hundred Years War'.[48] The only difference, considerable though it might be, was that Napoleon gave up on overseas conquests, one of the driving forces behind Ancien Regime foreign policy, and concentrated instead on continental victories and exclusion of Britain from its markets in Europe (the Continental Blockade). Commercial warfare was the only means by which Napoleon could hope to defeat Britain.

The British had the choice of a number of policy options in their fight against France and attempted them all at various stages of the Napoleonic wars. Britain could promote royalist insurrections in France (although this policy was not really pursued after 1803). It could capture overseas colonies, thus giving the war a global dimension, and in the process conduct its own commercial war against France. It could attempt an invasion of the Continent, which it did on five occasions between 1799 and 1809 (Holland in 1799, northern Germany in 1805–1806, southern Italy in 1805, Stralsund in 1807, and the Walcheren expedition in 1809), all of which were failures. It only succeeded in gaining a solid foothold in Portugal and consequently Spain after 1808. Finally, it could reinforce its continental allies through money and arms.[49] This policy was pursued so vigorously that Britain laid itself open to the criticism of being willing to fight Napoleon down to the last Austrian, Prussian, Russian and so on. Europe's statesmen were consequently extremely suspicious of Britain's motives and, at least before

1808–1809, were more often than not convinced that Britain, rather than Napoleon and France, posed a threat to Europe.[50]

The almost uninterrupted conflict with France after 1803 necessarily had an impact, even if limited, on British domestic politics and society. If the 'nation' was by no means united in its opposition – the conduct of the war was always strongly contested in the House of Commons, and there were successive waves of peace agitation among the middle classes – the requisition of large numbers of men for service in the army, the navy and militia formations was one of the highest in the world. About one-sixth of the population was made available for service of one sort or another, a rate that was greater than France and comparable only to Prussia. This need for manpower necessarily had an impact on societal structures and attitudes, even if it was not as profound as in other European states.[51] At government levels too, the experience of the French wars underlined the need for radical change, even if it was not always forthcoming. Indeed, every state in Europe was affected by the wars to one degree or another. Napoleon's constant campaigning forced other states if not to reform radically, then at least to adapt – sometimes successfully, as in the case of many of the German states; sometimes not, as in the case of Russia and Spain.

This brings us to the debate about the extent to which Napoleon left his mark on Europe.[52] In one corner, we have those who believe that the benefits of the Napoleonic Empire – modernisation, centralisation, the rationalisation of politics and public administration, the advances made in social and legal equality, the contribution made to nationalism and state building – far outweigh the short-term horrors that war brought with it to Europe.[53] In the opposite corner are those who believe that Napoleonic reforms made little or no lasting impact on large parts of Europe under nominal French rule, and in some instances even hindered the process of modernisation by reinforcing the hold of the local feudal elites over the peasantry.[54] Michael Broers, for example, insists that the Napoleonic state in Italy was essentially rapacious and culturally disruptive, creating a new governing elite, but alienating key elements of Italian society in the process.[55] It seems clear from the contributions in this collection that the Empire was a mixed blessing.

This is nowhere better illustrated than in Germany. The abolition of the old Holy Roman Empire, the absorption of smaller territories into larger state entities and the shock of military defeat in the face of superior French forces proved a remarkable impetus for reform. In countries that aligned themselves with France, like Bavaria and Baden, state structures were completely overhauled by a small group of professional bureaucrats. Indeed, the

Napoleonic administrative system served as a model and was largely adopted, albeit with modifications. In countries which suffered from defeat and occupation, like Prussia, the French model served as an impetus to internal reform, although largely in an attempt to reorganise the state's resources in such a way as to enable it to resume the fight against Napoleon more effectively at a later date. For the most part, Napoleonic rule in Germany had a positive, modernising influence. Even conscription and taxation, for all the suffering that they may have caused individuals, encouraged the development of the state's administrative structures. If in the short term the Napoleonic demand for men and, especially, money resulted only in increased bureaucratic absolutism at the expense of the old estates (which in many places had shown signs of revival in the 1780s and 1790s), in the long run it unintentionally encouraged the emergence of constitutional government.[56] After all, financial institutions were only prepared to meet the state's demands for huge loans if there were constitutional structures in place to provide adequate guarantees for their repayment.

Of course, there were areas of Germany, those that happened to lie farthest geographically from France like Mecklenburg and Saxony, where little or no reform was undertaken. In Austria, unlike Prussia, the defeat of 1809 discredited the whole reform agenda, at least in the eyes of Francis II.[57] There were other areas where the French presence promoted some of the more pernicious aspects of Ancien Regime rule – princely absolutism, bureaucratic control and the continued domination of the ruling elites. In the supposedly model state of Westphalia, for example, the nobility were rewarded for helping Napoleon consolidate his power by having their feudal rights left virtually intact. In other states, where feudalism was abolished in the wake of the French armies, peasants were often worse off than before because they could now be evicted or forced to carry greater burdens for their lords. The French themselves found it difficult to introduce uniform laws in societies dominated by so many different local institutions and administrations,[58] and had a tendency not to implement the *Code Napoléon* in areas where it provoked resistance. The French administrative model was never simply transposed; it was negotiated and adapted to local circumstances in order to extract men and money better from the regions they controlled. Since reform in the Empire was carried out with one purpose in mind – to facilitate exploitation and domination[59] – resistance that made exploitation difficult often resulted in reform being simply abandoned. Put simply, reforms were only by-products of the need to acquire resources for the *Grande Armée* and for the endowment of Napoleon's imperial nobility.[60]

If one accepts this interpretation, then the notion of a liberal empire needs to be reviewed if not rejected entirely because it is predicated upon the myth of Napoleon's good intentions. Moreover, such an interpretation downplays both the reform programmes implemented under the Ancien Regime and the argument that the impact of the French Revolution and Napoleon was to discredit reform in the eyes of central Europe's elite. That elite went from being pro-reform in the eighteenth century to become conservative and reactionary in the nineteenth, with disastrous consequences.

Although different from the German example, the histories of Spain and Portugal are testimony to the persistence of that myth – that is, of Napoleon as beneficent, modernising force. Part of the problem is that resistance to the French in Spain and Portugal is seen as being carried out by reactionary elements opposing change as much as the French invader. As John Tone points out, however – and this is valid for all of Europe – resisting France was not the same thing as resisting modernity.

Previously, Spanish responses to the French occupation were believed to be relatively uniform throughout the satellite kingdom and to be a patriotic/religious response to both the overthrow of the old monarchy and the extraordinarily tactless treatment of the Catholic Church by hardened, cynical French soldiers. French revolutionary anti-clericalism, therefore, combined with a certain amount of loyalty on the part of the people to the Spanish House of Bourbon, helps explain, but only incidentally, the origins of the guerrilla movement. Also, the idea of a war of national liberation fought by the Spanish people against the French invader was a nineteenth-century construct that had nothing to do with the reality of occupation. The Spanish people did not rise *en masse* to oppose the French, while the Spanish *notables*, like those in the rest of Europe, usually either rallied to the French cause or remained indifferent to the fate of the Spanish monarchy. Indeed, in some regions enthusiasm for the war was non-existent, even in areas occupied by the French.

Much more important as an explanation for the guerrilla movement are regional, rather than national, loyalties. Indeed, *la guerrilla* (or 'little war') was fought more to protect homes and families than 'king and country', and was often initiated by French exactions in a village. Once the French had left or had been cleared from a particular province, the guerrillas would simply return to their villages. The localism of the movement was one of the reasons why there was never any intra-regional co-operation among the guerrilla leaders, and why they always maintained a close contact with their own rural base. Far from being a disadvantage, however, as one might suspect, Tone argues that it was precisely the local quality of the movement that defeated Napoleon.[61]

There is another aspect to the guerrilla movement, however, that needs mentioning, and that is its association with traditional banditry. Some so-called guerrilla leaders, under cover of a war against the French, were simply pursuing their careers as bandits. Their followers, moreover, who sometimes comprised deserters from both the French and the British armies, were more interested in pillage than anything else. The guerrillas, like the French, lived off the Spanish people and were just as ruthless in their use of terror against their own people as the French. Indeed, there are clear signs that *la guerrilla* was rooted in rural poverty and that in some regions a war was being waged against property.[62] No matter what the origins of the guerrilla movement, however, the bottom line is that it was essentially a struggle over resources. The French needed taxes, conscripts, horses and, of course, collaborators to help them acquire these things; whereas the guerrillas, by eventually control-ling the countryside, prevented the French from gaining any of them.[63]

Russia was another country that Napoleon was never able to dominate completely or to defeat. Like Austria and Prussia, it too had engaged in a vigorous state-building process since the 1770s. That was accelerated under Paul I and Alexander I by the creation of central ministries to oversee the sprawling administration. As well, there were sustained efforts to strengthen commerce, improve the legal position of the working classes, and promote secondary and higher education. Reform received a powerful impetus in the early years of Alexander I's reign – he came to the throne in 1801 after the assassination of his father, Paul I – partly in response to the French chal-lenge. However, it proved to be so slow and so difficult that by the time rela-tions between Russia and France had deteriorated to the point of the Third Coalition in 1805, reform had been virtually abandoned.[64] To make matters worse, Alexander's foreign policy was so disastrous – the battles of Austerlitz, Eylau, Friedland and the treaty of Tilsit were all seen as humili-ations by the Russian nobility – that he could count on little support at home. The tsar, in fact, was caught between a rock and a hard place. Military defeat meant that reform was necessary and was once again attempted after Tilsit, but defeat was never disastrous enough to make reform absolutely necessary. Certainly, attempts were made to introduce change – which led to some minor improvements, especially in the functioning of government – but an unwillingness on the part of Alexander to push things through, in the face of the opposition that change automatically aroused among Russia's traditional elites, meant that reform never amounted to very much.[65] As relations between Alexander and Napoleon soured after Tilsit, the nobility worked to discredit reform, which they associated with the French model. It was only when Napoleon attacked Russia, and Alexander made assurances about upholding the traditional social order, that the nobility rallied to the throne.

The response of the Russians to the French invasion was perhaps like no other in Europe – people simply fled rather than collaborate or resist. But the French presence, no matter how brief (less than six months in total), and Russia's role in the defeat of Napoleon, elicited a number of responses.[66] The educated classes believed it was time the old institutions in Russia were replaced with new, more liberal institutions that would enable them to participate in public life. Conservative nobles and bureaucrats, on the other hand, saw the victory over Napoleon as a vindication of the system to which they belonged – absolutism, serfdom and noble privileges. As in the rest of Restoration Europe, therefore, Alexander faced two possible alternatives: the liberalisation of society or a return to the old order. Faced with the possibility of enormous social and political tensions, Alexander chose a third way – gradual, evolutionary change in the mantle of Christian piety. In the end, however, this programme failed too, stymied by the same forces of opposition that had seen previous reform programmes fail. Russia, like other European countries, had missed the opportunity to modernise.

CONCLUSION

In some respects Napoleon was an evil necessity, the foreign-political and social equivalent of an enema; never very pleasant, it can help clean out the system. The Napoleonic wars did exactly that; they helped expurgate the European system by eliminating many small, but non-viable states; expanding others; and consolidating yet others. Also, the wars gave many (but not all) European countries the necessary impetus to introduce reforms that modernised the state administrative machinery. Not only did Napoleon implant, through bureaucratic routine and coercion, a new civil order in France which the Bourbons inherited when they returned to power, but the Napoleonic state provided a model for other European powers to follow. In most European states, even those that suffered the horrors of occupation, contact with the French proved beneficial in the long run. The methods of organising and running the state (taxation, recruitment, police and justice) were largely maintained by Restoration governments, despite some notable exceptions where efforts were made to turn back the clock. In some states there was even an expansion of Napoleonic administrative practices.[67]

Just as important, however, was the states system put into place at Vienna in 1814–15, which was a direct consequence of the Napoleonic wars. Power politics was no longer perceived in the same way, wars were no longer fought for relatively minor territorial compensations as they were in the past. Europe after Napoleon was better equipped to deal with the international problems that it had to confront, and usually did so in a spirit of conciliation and co-operation. The post-Napoleonic states system remained largely in place until the unifications of Germany and Italy in the later nineteenth century. It is ironic that after fighting so many battles, and after causing so much suffering, Napoleon proved to be the impetus for a long period of relative peace and stability in Europe.

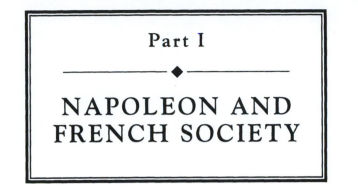

Part I

NAPOLEON AND
FRENCH SOCIETY

Chapter 1

NAPOLEON'S YOUTH AND RISE TO POWER

Harold T. Parker

CORSICA AND CORSICANS

To understand Napoleon we must first try to understand the Corsicans of the eighteenth century among whom he spent his early years. Corsica, before it was spoiled by modern technology and tourism, was an enchanted island of bewitching beauty, a giant granite rock rising out of the sea to wooded foothills and snow-capped mountains, sparsely populated in 1769 by about 130,000 people. There were then three Corsicas: the rugged mountainous interior of hardy shepherds and subsistence-farming villagers; the small port towns, whose shopkeepers, merchants, lawyers and administrators were subject to the broadening influences of outside contacts; and Corsica abroad, made up of Corsicans whose extra energy and initiative had propelled them to leave the claustrophobic, shut-in life at home and seek their fortune abroad.

In all three Corsicas fidelity to the family was the dominant loyalty. In the eighteenth century a Corsican child was born into an elementary nuclear family. To the family and to the promotion of its interests they owed time, energy, loyalty and trust. There may have been sibling rivalries for attention, influence and position (in his own family Napoleon was an irrepressible climber), but the members of the family could trust each other not to cheat or lie to one another. The child was also a member of an extended family, to the fourth cousins perhaps. Within the extended family, there might be litigation, chiefly over property claims, but in a crisis they could count on each other for practical support. No wonder the wealth of a marriageable young

· 25 ·

woman was counted not only in property but also in how many cousins she had. Unrelated families and, more generally, the outside world were regarded with distrust and might be treated with calculated ruse, deceit and guile.

Violence was endemic in Corsican society. Relations between families were governed in principle by a strict honour code. Breaking the honour code by infringing upon property or violating a woman's honour was punished in the interior of the island by private, remorseless stalking and killing of the transgressor – blood vengeance that could grow into a vendetta lasting for generations. One thousand such murders, it is estimated, occurred each year. Like a public war between nations, the vendetta as a private war was institutionalised violence, legitimised killing of human beings by other human beings, governed in theory by honour. Corsicans accepted the obligations of the vendetta with a sense of being controlled by an inexorable destiny that was stronger than God, a belief that yielded impassive courage while sustaining self-assertive initiatives. In the port towns clan rivalry and violence took the form of frequent and prolonged litigation.

In addition to violence generated natively, Corsicans had been subjected for millennia to waves of foreign conquerors: the Etruscans, ancient Greeks, Romans, Vandals, Saracens, Aragonese, Pisans, Genoese and most recently the French. In 1768–69 the last named had bloodily crushed resistance in the latest episode of a violent history.

The French also ended a Corsican experiment in republican government that was far ahead of its time. It had arisen in this way. Except for the inhabitants of the few port towns, the Corsicans lived mostly in the interior, in villages whose natives were linked by ties of kinship and the Catholic religion and by acceptance of the leadership of the local chief. In their agricultural/pastoral culture much of the property was held communally: the gardens, vineyards and orchards immediately around the village were communally held by the village; the pasturages used by the shepherds in the forested uplands during the summer and in the plain during the winter were communally held by groups of villages. The Corsican insurrection against Genoa in 1729 had been triggered by the Genoese attempt to declare as private property land that had been communally held for centuries. As the uprising spread until Genoa retained tenuously only a few port towns, a Corsican central representative assembly drafted a written constitution in 1735. Modified in 1755 by Pasquale Paoli, a hero-statesman, in the light of his reading of Montesquieu and the practical need for a stronger executive, the document granted Corsica a representative constitutional government that guaranteed liberty and legal equality, recognised by implication the sovereignty of the people, and accorded with the basic customs of the people. The Corsicans did not need an enlightened Bourbon monarchy or even a French revolutionary assembly to endow them with a progressive, enlightened liberal government. They had one of their own, with its own flag, national hymn, coinage, army and navy, elective executive and legislature, and university.[1]

A CORSICAN CHILDHOOD

The Bonaparte clan stood nowhere near the top in Ajaccio, a Corsican port town of nearly four thousand people. Ever since their remote ancestor had migrated from Tuscany (Italy) in the sixteenth century, the Bonapartes had been content to acquire a house, a vineyard or two, and other bits of land, and to serve modestly as members of the Ajaccio municipal council of Anciens. Meanwhile rival families were pulling ahead. The Peraldis, for example, were gaining control of the coral-fishing fleet, the basis of the Ajaccian economy, and the Pozzo di Borgos were acquiring a fortune in land and a substantial house in Ajaccio. However, in Charles Bonaparte, Napoleon's father, the Bonapartes acquired an ambitious and resourceful climber. Born in 1746, he grew up to be a superbly handsome young man, with a gift for charming influential and powerful men. In obedience to clan calculations he married in 1764 not the woman he loved but Letizia Bonaparte, a local beauty of not quite 14 years who brought a satisfactory dowry and the not unimportant consideration of fifty cousins.[2]

After a playboy year in Rome, Charles enrolled in the University of Corte, which Paoli had founded in his mountain capital to win Corsican young men to the national republican ideal. Charles invited Letizia to join him. Together, they charmed Paoli, and Charles became his part-time secretary. In this idyllic dream of republican idealism, Letizia gave birth on 7 January 1768 to their first child to live, Joseph, a pretty and amiable baby who smiled at everyone and at whom everyone smiled back.

However, the republican dream was broken when on 15 May 1768 Genoa ceded to the French monarchy its rights over Corsica. To be sure, Corsican militia would defeat a contingent of invading French troops at the battle of Borgo on 7 October. In the joyful aftermath of that moment Charles and Letizia conceived Napoleon, during early November. But the next spring the French monarchy returned with an overwhelming force of 22,000 regular soldiers. Commanded by the comte de Vaux, an able general and administrator, they crushed the brave Corsican fighters at the battle of Ponte Novo on

9 May 1769. After accompanying the fleeing Paoli to an English frigate that departed Corsica on 13 June, Charles Bonaparte returned to Corte to conduct Letizia across the mountains of central Corsica to Ajaccio, while the French were still mopping up pockets of Corsican resistance. It was a terrible journey. Walking or riding on muleback up and down rocky mountain trails, crossing a swollen stream, sleeping in a cave, carrying one child (Joseph) and bearing another in her womb (Napoleon), who was kicking to get out, Letizia survived but never forgot the trip's ordeal. When finally, at Ajaccio, her time came, she gave birth to Napoleon on 15 August 1769. A scrawny baby with spindly legs and a disproportionately large head, he repelled those who viewed him. Letizia tried to nurse him but for the first and only time her milk failed, and he was committed to a wet-nurse and slept with her in a back room. From her other children Letizia knew the mutual tenderness and bonding that develops between a nursing mother and a suckling infant, but not from Napoleon.[3]

Today, in an age when pregnant women are warned to choose with care their television programmes because the infant in the womb is listening too and when psychologists speak of the individualising innate temperament (emotionality, activity level, sociability and impulsivity) of each newborn baby, we may be permitted to speculate that Napoleon's hard ride in the womb may have been the most significant event in his life. It may have affected his physique, his unimpressive appearance, and his hyper-energetic, hyper-active, always-on-the-move personality before there was a chance for sibling rivalry or Oedipus complex. At the end of his life, on St Helena, reflecting on what had gone wrong and why, he remarked: 'J'ai trop d'ambition, et un esprit enflammé' – 'I have too much ambition and a spirit afire.' His fantasising ambition, as we shall see, expanded with opportunity and age, but his inner intensity was there from the start.

Corsica was a clan-oriented society, and each clan had its own inner dramas. The ambivalent relationships within the Bonaparte family were to be reflected in the developing complexity of Napoleon's personality. Essential was his trustful relationship with the wet-nurse, Camille Ilari, who loved him and gave the infant Napoleon a fundamental self-assurance that would sustain him in later events. When after two years she weaned him and he entered the full life of the family, he discovered that the Bonaparte house was filled with a crowd of women – grandmothers, aunts and servants – who came and went, and who doted on the two boys, Joseph and Napoleon. Later, when he was away at school or on garrison duty, he always remembered them with affection. To him they were home.

However, at 2 years old he also had discovered that he was a member of two triangles (Napoleon, Letizia, Joseph; Napoleon, Letizia, Charles) in which Letizia, the beauteous mother, had a warm and close relationship with Joseph and with Charles of the type from which Napoleon was excluded. In this situation Letizia was the key figure. By Corsican clan custom the father conducted the 'foreign' relations of the family, whereas the mother was in complete charge at home. Charles loved his children and pampered them when he was at home, but he was often away and it is difficult to discern what influence, if any, he had on Napoleon. But Letizia took her domestic duties seriously. She curtailed her time at religious festivities because, she said, as the responsible chief of the family she was needed at home to serve as a check (*frein*) and keep the children in line.[4] Joseph, a quiet, obedient little boy, presented no difficulty. According to Corsican custom he as eldest son enjoyed special consideration. During the two years that Napoleon was relegated to the back room, Joseph continued to sleep in the parents' room. Napoleon, in contrast, was a problem child. Whether it was because of the hard ride over the mountains, or the withdrawal of the mother's milk, or the final weaning from the wet-nurse, or the special privileges of Joseph, or all four, he came out into household society bellicose and fighting. In 1813 the Emperor Napoleon smilingly chided his 2-year-old son: 'Lazybones, when I was your age I was already beating up Joseph.' In 1817 on St Helena he recalled how he had been the terror of his elementary school's playground. Observing the 'tenacity' of young Bertrand, the son of an aide, he remarked:

> I was as stubborn as he at his age; nothing stopped or disconcerted me. I was a quarreller, a fighter; I feared nobody, beating one, scratching another, making myself redoubtable to all. It was my brother Joseph who most often had to suffer. He was slapped, bitten, scolded, and I had already complained against him before he had time to recover himself. But my quickness was to no avail with Mama Letizia, who soon repressed my bellicose humour. . . . She was both tender and severe; she punished wrongdoing and rewarded good conduct; she recognised impartially our good and bad actions. . . . She was all her life an excellent woman, and as a mother was without an equal.[5]

These are richly revealing passages about the young Napoleon – quick, active, aggressive, creating by his aggressions challenging situations and then violently and deceptively fighting them; for him deception was a technique, amorally applied, to get his way and enjoy the pleasures of victorious domination. The passages also suggest much about Letizia and her allies, the teaching nuns, who together were innovative and resourceful in channelling Napoleon's aggressive drives into socially acceptable forms. When the nuns discovered his analytical gift for arithmetic, they dubbed him 'the mathematician' and rewarded him with treats of jam. As a good Corsican mother Letizia whipped him for the slightest transgression (beatings that the child Napoleon accepted without a whimper or cry), but she also in his eighth year built for him on the family's terrace a special, private bower where he could work in proud seclusion. In addition, she applauded him when, on one of his walks, 'he observed with great attention the functioning of a watermill. Having noted how much grain was milled in an hour he dumbfounded the farmer by calculating how much he could expect in a day and a week.'[6] Analytical thinking and zeal for work were to be two of the salient traits of Napoleon's evolving personality. However, Letizia, truthful herself, was never able to curb Napoleon's inveterate lying. That, too, was becoming one of the enduring features of his character.

Letizia, obviously, was an important factor in Napoleon's growth. Was Joseph? Let us think about that. Napoleon's sense of rivalry with Joseph did continue. When in 1804 Camille Ilari, the wet-nurse, attended the imperial coronation in Paris she let slip the remark: 'Joseph était un joli enfant.'[7] The Emperor, now master of France and certainly ahead of Joseph, blackened with rage. Yet even in childhood the two siblings had become close friends. The story was told that when in Ajaccio the two boys were attending a Jesuit primary school, the master divided the class into Romans and Carthaginians. He naturally placed the elder brother Joseph with the Romans. The little Napoleon stormed that *he* had to be on the winning side. Joseph amiably yielded and sat on the Carthaginian bench. To him it was no big deal. But afterwards on the way home the little Napoleon was deeply upset by the thought that he had been unfair to Joseph, whom he now liked.[8] The story suggests that Joseph, mild, amiable and charming, was too different for Napoleon to learn anything from him and still be Napoleon. Yet later the difference helped Napoleon to define himself in contrast: 'Joseph can't be a good artillery officer – he won't work, but I do.' 'I have the habit of command. I was born with it. Joseph does not have it.' Joseph 'likes to cajole people and obey their ideas; *Moi*, I want them to please me and obey mine.'

A FRENCH EDUCATION

When we think of education, schools and books usually come to mind. But there is also an education that comes with experience as we pass through events. That was true of the young Napoleon. Before he ever attended a French school, events at home educated him in how to deal with a conquered people. 'I learned how to handle a conquered people through having been a member of a conquered society.'

To subjugate the Corsicans the French Bourbon monarchy appealed to fear and to self-interest, two motives that were later to be at the core of Napoleon's policy. The French royal government also employed specific procedures that Napoleon was to use. It brought in the overwhelming force of regular soldiers. After the stunning defeat of the Corsican raw militia at Ponte Novo it sent out mobile columns to hunt down and execute last-ditch resisters, until not a village was unaware of French military power and terror. In each village the inhabitants were disarmed and their oaths of loyalty and obedience to the king were accepted. A strong French garrison, 7,744 men in all, was permanently stationed in the island. Later, in 1774, when revolt flared in the Niolo district, the French and military snuffed it out brutally: families of individual rebels were held hostage; rebels, when caught, were shot, hanged or broken on the wheel; on the principle of collective responsibility, hundreds of Corsicans who had aided them were imprisoned in France or sent to the galleys; entire villages were burned to the ground and their crops destroyed. Bourbon terror became legendary in the memory of Corsicans, including the Bonapartes, Charles, Letizia, Joseph and Napoleon.

Meanwhile, the royal government was introducing improved French institutions. It deliberately did this in such a way as to involve Corsicans in their operations and thus to open careers and favours to the ambitious, to co-opt them for the regime, and in time to assimilate them to French culture and ways of doing things. To promote assimilation of French customs, to reward those parents loyal to the regime, and quietly to hold them hostage to the conqueror (calculations were always multiple), a few children (boys and girls) from a few Corsican families were awarded scholarships in French schools.[9]

For twenty years, until 1789, the Bonaparte family was on the receiving end of these French policies and thus became educated in French methods by participation. Charles and Letizia chose to collaborate with the French. As they had charmed Paoli, they now charmed the comte de Marbeuf, the French commander and effective governor, for the favours he had the power to give. Marbeuf, in turn, needed Corsican supporters of the French regime and responded. Charles was accorded a certificate of nobility, was repeatedly elected a noble representative to the Corsican Assemblée des états, and one year served as one of its delegates to Versailles. He was appointed *assesseur* to the judge in the royal tribunal in Ajaccio. His sons, Napoleon, Joseph and Lucien, received scholarships at mainland French *collèges* or preparatory schools, as did his daughter Elisa at the elegant young girls' school of Saint-Cyr. Charles and Letizia were granted by the royal administration a subsidy to grow mulberry trees for the nourishment of silkworms. Thus the Bonapartes, a striving, pushing clan, achieved contact with every instrument of government that France opened to Corsicans: legislature, judiciary, schools and bureaucracy – and, soon, the military.

On the young Napoleon the twenty-year experience of French rule had immediate effects and left a lasting impression. As a child he hobnobbed with the French soldiers garrisoned at Ajaccio; he traded his mother's white bread for their black ration, believing he needed to learn how to endure a soldier's lot. He attended the semi-military *collège* of Brienne and graduated to the French Sandhurst or West Point, the Royal Military School, and then to the French army. More profoundly – and this is the reason for telling all this – when it became time for him to be a conqueror and to rule, the twenty-year experience as a subject gave him many of the procedures he used. His aggressive, combative drives were then exercised and fulfilled not in a void but along lines of force and by adroit techniques that he had observed and absorbed in his youth.

When Joseph and Napoleon sailed from Corsica on 15 December 1778 for enrolment in mainland French schools, they were implementing the calculations of the rising Bonaparte clan that someday the smooth, smiling Joseph would be a perfect bishop and the combative Napoleon an able army officer. The children understood and accepted those roles.

Joseph, not only smooth but able, was quietly assimilated into the French student body at the *collège* of Autun, and by sheer talent won his school prizes. The little Napoleon found life difficult at the *collège* of Brienne. The French Minister of War, Saint-Germain, had decided that 650 young gentlemen, poor but noble, would be educated at the king's expense in twelve *collèges*. The most gifted graduates would then be promoted to the Royal Military School in Paris. In many respects Brienne, with 110 students, was a typical French boarding school, taught by the Catholic teaching order of Minimes. Instruction in Latin was stressed, but other subjects were taught: French composition, mathematics, German, geography and history. Discipline was military and strict. A uniform was prescribed. Each boy was assigned a cell, sparsely furnished with a camp bed, jug and basin, and a single blanket, even in winter. The days were regulated by an unyielding timetable from 6 a.m., when the boys were awakened, to 10 p.m., when they were locked into their cells. Food was wholesome if austere; for example, bread and water with fruit for breakfast. For six years no boy could leave the school grounds. There were no trips away. Visits by parents were restricted.

For Napoleon, a child of 9, small and slight for his size, treated as a person of importance at home by a warm and affectionate family, Brienne was a shock. He was a Corsican, a member of a conquered people; he was scorned and derided by his French fellow students. He was by French standards a poor, provincial noble; the sons of French aristocrats snubbed, taunted and teased him. To a degree he provoked the developing combative situation. A new kid on the block, with a Corsican chip on his shoulder, he provoked merciless tormenting by the disdainful young scions of the French nobility.

Resourceful, he developed mechanisms of defence that enabled him psychologically to keep going and to emerge stronger for the experience. In the face of opposition he turned to those measures of sublimation of his aggressive drives that had brought him distinction at Ajaccio: work and analytical mathematical thinking. Over two or three summers he built a garden and arranged the plants, vegetation and palisades to form a bower of seclusion. There he worked at those subjects that interested him, mathematics, history and geography. There he also read, borrowing book after book from the school library. Work paid off in knowledge, a developing maturity of judgement, a growing sense of accomplishment, and prestige. At successive annual exhibitions when the best students were put on display, he was publicly quizzed first on arithmetic, then on geometry and algebra, and finally on trigonometry and conic sections. He came to be known as the ablest mathematician of the school and its most indefatigable reader.

He worked, and he also dreamed and planned. He accepted the Corsican identity thrust upon him by his tormentors. 'Yes, I am Corsican, and I am proud of it; today we are vanquished, but tomorrow we shall be free.' Paoli was his hero. 'Paoli will return,' he cried one day, 'and if he cannot break our chains, I shall go to his aid as soon as I am strong enough and perhaps the two of us together will deliver Corsica from the odious yoke it bears.' This was egocentric, extravagant fantasising, a salient Napoleonic trait. What followed was also Napoleonic: he began rationally to plan the implementation of his dream. In his last year at Brienne he asked his father to send him James Boswell's *History of Corsica* as well as other materials useful for writing a projected history of his people.[10]

From Brienne he was promoted in November 1784 to the Royal Military School in Paris, where he again became known as the ablest mathematician of the school. After completing two years' work in one, he was dispatched in September 1785 to the artillery regiment of La Fère, then stationed in Valence, where he was commissioned lieutenant in the third degree in the Royal Army.

'THE HAPPIEST DAYS OF MY LIFE', 1785–1789

Napoleon at St Helena had good reason to remember the years 1785 to 1789 as the happiest of his life – in fact several good reasons.[11]

First, he had proven himself to be worthy of the trust his family had placed in him. After seven years of arduous, stressful schooling he had been commissioned in the French Royal Army. He could now proudly sign his letters 'Buonaparte, Officier'; never lieutenant in the third and lowest degree, but 'Officier'.

Second, the schooling had disciplined his character, strengthened his powers of analytical thinking, and indoctrinated him in the values of the French Royal Army. In childhood he had played at being a soldier and had absorbed almost without thinking the Corsican code of honour of loyalty to the clan and of impassive courage in a violent world. Now these values were not displaced but rather were absorbed into the code of the French military: courage at all times, bravery and disdain for death under fire, and stoic endurance of suffering; devotion to one's comrades; obedience to superior officers; work-oriented competence in the performance of one's duties; loyalty to France and to its king; and glory in deeds of valour and victory – all subsumed under an all-embracing concept of honour. By craft and force the army tried to do as much damage as possible to the enemy.[12] Except for his dubious loyalty to France and to its king, the young Bonaparte accepted the code without question. He never deviated from it. He never flinched from a fight. It gave him a socially acceptable status and provided a reinforcing endorsement to his basic aggressive and combative drives. Later, when he became a commander, he could use it to inspire and control and, thus, to command his troops.

Third, as a hard-working intelligent and obedient subordinate officer, Bonaparte was now introduced to a new way of making war which utilised infantry, cavalry, artillery, soldiers, modern technology and new ideas in combined operations designed to overwhelm the enemy. To implement the new military doctrine of organised dispersion, mobility and swift concentration of separate units, Jean-Baptiste Vaquette de Gribeauval, inspector-general of the artillery of the French army, had invented in 1765 a completely new system of mobile guns, gun carriages, limbers, ammunition chests and servicing tools that could travel with the infantry. First at Valence, from October 1785 to September 1786, and then from June 1788 to September 1789 at Auxonne – the finest artillery camp in the world – Bonaparte enjoyably participated in exercises that explored the potentialities of the new guns. He was singled out for special assignment and gratifying praise by the baron du Teil, Auxonne's commandant. Through good fortune and his own habits of work and analytical thinking he was acquiring the basic and advanced techniques of his profession.

Fourth, in September 1786 he returned to Ajaccio, a young lieutenant of 17, short, dark and energetic. After nearly eight years of exile he revelled in being amidst an affectionate and admiring family. His mother, Letizia, at 36 was a vital southern beauty and widow who needed his aid. He resumed relations with Joseph, who had completed a French education at the *collège* of Autun and returned to Corsica in 1785. As the oldest son, Joseph was now the head of the family; but Napoleon, with the prestige of a French commission, had drawn even with him. Affectionately they together declaimed the tragedies of Corneille, Racine and Voltaire. Probably it was during this first Corsican visit that the brothers were most closely together. 'Oh,' exclaimed Joseph when the Napoleonic Empire was at its height, 'the glorious Emperor will never indemnify me for the loss of that Napoleon whom I loved so dearly, whom I should like to see again as I knew him in 1786.'[13]

Fifth, whether in garrison in France or at home in Ajaccio, Napoleon was still living in a dream about himself: that he would some day lead his people to freedom and independence, perhaps in association with Paoli. His reading of history, a favourite subject, helped him to interpret his role. In an essay written in November 1787 he contrasted two moralities: the love of glory – that is, the love of the esteem of men – and the love of country. 'Open', he wrote, 'the annals of the monarchies. Doubtless our soul catches fire upon reading of the actions of Philip [of Macedon], Alexander, Charlemagne, Turenne, Condé, Machiavelli and of so many other illustrious men who, in their heroic career, had for guide the esteem of men.' Illustrious, no doubt, but compare Condé and Turenne, who turned against their country, with Leonidas and his three hundred Spartans at Thermopylae, Aristides, Themistocles, Cincinnatus, Fabius, Cato and two Corsican heroes, Gaffory and Paoli, who in self-denial served their *patrie*. Who will question that the palm of virtue belongs to the patriotic, freedom-loving heroes, with whom the adolescent Bonaparte sympathised?[14]

His reading of Boswell's interview of Paoli led him to perceive that a patriotic leader must be prepared to exercise two functions, military and political. Service in the French army, he thought, was preparing him for military leadership of his people, if the opportunity ever came. Paoli's example of prior self-cultivation led him to undertake a sustained self-selected, self-assigned and self-executed programme of reading that would give him the background for political action. Driven by his dream, he rose each morning at 4.30 a.m. to read Plato; universal history (Voltaire), ancient history (Rollin), history of European expansion (Raynal); histories of Florence (Machiavelli), Venice, France (Mably), the Sorbonne, England, Frederick the Great and the Arabs; natural history (Buffon); Rousseau; and brochures on French financial administration. His detailed notes reveal a mind which was oriented toward action and which recognised that for swift, analytical, efficient operation it needed precise facts – places, dates, statistics, terms, institutions and persons.[15] This remarkable adventure in adult self-education at the university level had consequences beyond what he intended; it brought him into the universe of discourse of western thought, disposed him towards the progressive, utilitarian solutions of the Enlightenment, and nurtured an appetite for knowledge that never left him. Meanwhile he was collecting materials for a projected history of Corsica that would remind his people of their freedom-loving, freedom-fighting past.

THE DREAM BROKEN, 1789–1793

By May 1789 Bonaparte was leading a relatively tranquil, patterned existence – on garrison duty in France or in his study amidst an admiring and affectionate family in Ajaccio; in both locations reading, writing and dreaming of Corsica's liberation with himself and Paoli as leaders. Then came the French Revolution, whose tumultuous events swept him into undreamed turbulence, turmoil and potentially educative opportunities. Psychologically speaking, it greatly enlarged the number, variety and intensity of inter-personal encounters.

For the Corsicans the first major liberating event was the decree of the French Constituent Assembly that on 30 November 1789 declared Corsica was no longer to be treated as a conquered province. Instead, it announced that 'Corsica was an integral part of the French Empire and its inhabitants would be governed by the same Constitution as other Frenchmen'. Also enacted on the same day was a decree that accorded 'an amnesty for all Corsican fugitives who had not committed capital crimes'. In accord with these decrees Paoli left his exile in London in April 1790. He was honoured in Paris as a heroic fighter for liberty, and in July he was deliriously welcomed in Corsica.

Starting in January 1790, the Constituent Assembly reorganised French local government in decrees that also applied to Corsica. France was divided into eighty-three *départements* (Corsica formed one). Departments were subdivided into districts (Corsica had nine) and municipalities (Corsica had six). At each level, municipal, district and departmental, there was an elective council, an elective executive director and elective executive officials. There were also elective judges, and (as it turned out) elective officers of the battalions of the local National Guard.

In Corsica there were thus many elective offices to be filled, all at once, but even more bright young men who were avid for office and for the prestige, power and spoils it would bring. Each young man was backed by his clan. Elections became clan fights, with charges and counter-charges, guile, deceit, intrigues, deals, bribery and sometimes physical violence. Each candidate sought the favour of Paoli, whose prestige and influence were still considerable.[16]

In this frenetic hardball politicking, where was Napoleon? Mostly in Corsica. From September 1789 to June 1793 he spent only seven months with his regiment (February to September 1791). Except for three and a half months in Paris (28 May to 9 September 1792) he spent the rest of the time in his native land. His attitudes were complex. To him a liberty-loving France that admitted Corsica to a legal equality as a French department and recalled Paoli was far more acceptable than Bourbon authoritarianism, but he still hoped the Corsican situation would evolve toward complete independence. Nor was this hope unrealistic; as late as February 1793 there was a strong move in the French Convention to divest France of Corsica as an expensive, troublesome liability. As a Plutarchian lover of his *patrie* (Corsica), he burned and worked to establish liberal institutions in his native land, but he wanted himself and his clan to be number one. So, too young for office, he was yet deep in the political game, attending political clubs, writing manifestos, aiding his brother Joseph in his run for elective office and, not least, courting Paoli.[17]

The ensuing story is too intricate to be told here, but in general over four years to June 1793 the Bonapartes lost out both at the clan level and in Paoli's favour. Before the French Revolution the Bonapartes and the Pozzo di Borgos and the Peraldis in Ajaccio had been allies, Charles André di Borgo even being their lawyer. But after 1789 competition for office turned them first into rivals and eventually into enemies. To borrow an idiom from present-day basketball, Joseph was always one step slower than Charles André, who was five years older and more mature. For example, in 1790, when Charles André was elected to the executive directory of the *département* of Corsica, Joseph was elected to the directory of the district of Ajaccio. Only when in 1792 Charles André was elected Corsican deputy to the French Legislative Assembly meeting in Paris was Joseph elected to the departmental directory. When Charles André returned to Corsica in 1793 to be elected the executive director (*procureur-syndic*) of the Corsican department, Joseph had failed in his bid to succeed him as deputy in Paris and held no office.

Upon his arrival in Corsica Paoli was at first friendly to the Bonapartes, as he was to everyone. He gave Joseph a card from his father, Charles. He praised Napoleon: 'You are on the antique model. You are one of Plutarch's characters.' But for some reason he soured on the Bonapartes. Thus, when the Patriotic Club of Ajaccio in January 1791 authorised the printing of Napoleon's *Letter to Buttafoco*, an eloquent defence of Paoli against the calumnies of an enemy, and when Napoleon proudly sent Paoli a copy of his first publication, the Corsican leader coolly brushed him off; such calumnies, Paoli wrote, had best be left unanswered. For six years Napoleon had been working on a history of Corsica; it was the major project of his life. His first draft of several chapters had been carefully read and taken seriously by his history teacher, Father Dupuy, and by the celebrated author the abbé Raynal. Yet when in 1791 he asked Paoli for documents to complete his history, Paoli replied that he was too busy and tired to ransack his archives and, besides, writing history was not for young people.

A hardball electoral contest aggravated the rivalry between the Bonapartes and the Peraldis, and the Pozzo di Borgos. What happened is worth study. On 14 January 1792 Napoleon became adjutant of one of the battalions of the National Guard, stationed in Ajaccio, thinking he could hold both his lieutenancy in the regular army and a post in the local battalion. In March he was informed that he could do this only if he were elected one of the two lieutenant-colonels of the battalion. The election by members of the battalion was set for 1 April. If Bonaparte lost he would be cashiered from the French regular army and lose out in the National Guard as well.

The five leading candidates were a Peraldi, a Pozzo di Borgo, a local magnate named Quenza, his brother-in-law Perretti, and Bonaparte. In desperation Bonaparte resorted to the tactics already used by others in several other Corsican elections:

Deceit: He let it be known that Paoli favoured his candidacy, which was a lie.
Dealing: To overcome the preponderance of the Peraldi/di Borgo clans within the town of Ajaccio, Bonaparte arranged to bring in his country cousins and friends from the northern highlands of the district of Ajaccio to support Quenza for first lieutenant-colonel; Quenza and his clan would support Bonaparte for second lieutenant-colonel.
Bribery: While the Peraldis bribed electors openly, Bonaparte kept an open house for his followers, with wine and conversation flowing.
Physical violence: When one of the official supervisors of the election was lodged with the Peraldis and winning voters, Bonaparte sent in an armed

country partisan to kidnap him at gunpoint and bring him to the Bonaparte house.

At the electoral assembly the next morning, when the Peraldi candidate (Mathieu Pozzo di Borgo) attempted to protest the brutal illegality of Bonaparte's action, he was shouted down and hustled out of the meeting. The prearranged election of Quenza and Bonaparte was then achieved.[18]

The contemporary comment of Napoleon's younger brother, Lucien, was acute. In a letter to Joseph (24 June 1792) he wrote: 'I have always distinguished in Napoleon an ambition not entirely altogether egoist but one which surpasses in him his love for the public good; I really believe that in a free state he would be a dangerous man.'[19] The comment was also prescient. Later, in 1799 during the coup d'état of 18 Brumaire, Bonaparte employed his techniques of ruthless fusion of craft and force to gain control of the French central government. On St Helena he observed to an aide on his notorious procedures: 'When a conspiracy is in progress, one has the right to do anything.' In other words: 'The end justifies the means' and 'Necessity knows no law'. He could have learned that in any European country, but the point is that he learned it in Corsica, where the competitive and often combative clan culture harmonised with his own competitive and combative drive to succeed.

In succeeding months several clan fights escalated. They involved the French Convention and unfairly rendered Paoli's loyalty suspect. At a time when Napoleon was still trying to win Paoli's favour, his hothead brother Lucien in March 1793 in a Marseilles political club wildly denounced the Corsican leader as a traitor. Assuming he was speaking for the entire Bonaparte family, the Corsican central assembly condemned them to Corsican execration and drove them into exile in June. After that Napoleon, with the death of his adolescent dream of leading a free Corsica, became a resilient survivor; a careerist officer in the French army; a supporter of his family but otherwise an outsider using other men for a rise in fortune. That quality of distance between himself and the reality in which he was moving became another of his lasting characteristics.

DREAMING AND ACCOMPLISHING IN ANOTHER ZONE, 1793–1799

A student of Napoleon's youth continues to be amazed at the 'lucky' accidents that marked it: to suffer the rough ride in Letizia's womb, which may have shaped his physique and personality; to have so excellent a mother as Letizia, who taught him to sublimate his competitive drives in work; to live in a place newly conquered by France, which offered the opportunity not only to attain an enlightening education but also to gain entrance into the French army when it was progressively reforming its military doctrine and gun power; and now to be expelled from Corsica and liberated from the thraldom of its constricting local feuds at a time when France was at war and badly needed professional artillerymen – all this was sheer good fortune. Of course, what Bonaparte made of the lucky chances was important too.

As Bonaparte's opportunities for advancement were closing down in Corsica they were opening up in France. On 21 April 1792, France had declared war on Austria with an army that was unready. During the Revolution thousands of its aristocratic officers had emigrated, leaving it with a shortage of professionally qualified leaders. So, when in May 1792 Bonaparte found it prudent to leave Ajaccio for a three-month stay in Paris, he was not only reinstated in the French army, he was promoted to captain. He was treated as a young man of promise. When he spent several days with his mentor, the baron du Teil, poring over large maps and discussing military strategy, the baron remarked to his daughter: 'This is a man of great ability who will be heard of.'

By the time of Bonaparte's final expulsion from Corsica in June 1793, King Louis XVI had been executed by the French Convention and the list of France's declared enemies had expanded to include Austria, Prussia, Great Britain, Holland, Spain, Piedmont–Sardinia and Naples. Every major power, except Russia, was arrayed against France. On land it was invaded by six armies, while at sea all along the coast the British fleet watched and blockaded. Civil war compounded the desperate situation: revolts against the Convention by the province of the Vendée in the west and by the major cities – Lyons, Marseilles, Bordeaux and the great naval base of Toulon where a British fleet gave support. In the French republican army that re-covered Toulon Bonaparte was in effective charge of the artillery. His intense hard work (he even slept with his guns), professional knowledge and competence, analytic discernment, personal bravery and ability to inspire his men by his example and appeals to honour caught the attention of the chevalier du Teil, brother of his mentor at the artillery camp of Auxonne: 'Words fail me', the chevalier wrote to the Minister of War, Bouchotte, 'to describe Bonaparte's merits. He has plenty of knowledge, and as much intelligence and courage; and that is no more than a first sketch of the virtues of this exceptional officer.' Toulon surrendered to the French army on

18 December 1793. Four days later Captain Bonaparte was promoted to brigadier-general.

After a series of improbable events he saved the republican Convention in Paris by gunning down an assaulting royalist crowd (13 Vendémiaire; 5 October 1795). For that service he was promoted to major-general and later appointed commander of the French army that was poised to invade the Piedmontese Alps.

With the intoxication, responsibilities and cares of his first overall command he entered a new zone of operation and feeling. Almost from the start he insisted that he was in sole charge of a combined operation whose elements were inter-related, inter-supportive and co-ordinated: the conduct of a military campaign, management of conquered peoples, diplomatic negotiation and securing financial resources. The victorious army, deployed along the lines he had learned at Auxonne, gave the power needed to manage conquered peoples; that management, in turn, gave the financial resources to sustain the army. Usable French revolutionary reforms, such as equality before the law, were fused with Bourbon policies with regard to Corsica to create in each conquered province a stable base for the army and a counter for diplomatic negotiation. Crafty negotiations, backed by force, formed alliances and obtained and nailed down what the army and management had won. As he pragmatically and dexterously evolved policies and applied them to northern Italy, Malta and Egypt, Napoleon drew on previous experiences – his schooling, his reading, his professional army training, his observation of Bourbon policies in Corsica, and his agitation in Corsican and French Jacobin clubs. It was as if his entire life had been a preparation for this moment of command.

When the north Italians proved indifferent to his offer of liberty, the greatest gift within the power of the French Republic to bestow, Bonaparte drew upon his knowledge of the sequential strategies and procedures of the Bourbon occupation of Corsica – appearance with overwhelming military force; instruction to his soldiers to observe an exact discipline and to abstain from pillage; an order to the Lombard communes to submit within twenty-four hours their 'act of submission and their oath of obedience to the [French] Republic'; an order for general disarmament; a provisional continuance of civil and criminal courts until they could be reorganised on a French model; and the co-optation of leading citizens for service in municipal councils. When he imposed heavy requisitions to pay for the costs of the French occupation and when Milan and other Lombard towns and villages revolted, Bonaparte resorted to the practices of Bourbon terror and governed by fear.

Milanese caught arms in hand were summarily killed; their leaders were tried by military commission and executed within twenty-four hours; hundreds of hostages were transported to France; a mobile French column burned and destroyed the rebellious village of Binasco, and other disaffected villages were threatened with a similar fate; two mobile columns, eight hundred strong, continued to patrol the countryside until not a single town or village was unaware of French power. Once the north Italians were within his grip, he incorporated them into a Cisalpine republic with its own legislative executive, judicial and military institutions. Activity within this institutional framework, he hoped, would in time mould the Lombards into an active and valorous citizenry.

The early successes of the Italian campaign when combined with his interpretation of the history of past heroes reawakened his dormant powers of egocentric fantasising. On St Helena he confided to Montholon: 'It was only on the evening after [the spectacular little battle of] Lodi (10 May 1796) that I believed myself to be a superior person and that the ambition came to me of performing the great things which hitherto had filled my thoughts only as a fantastic dream.'[20] The French, he continued later, are not fit for a republic. They do not understand liberty. They need glory and the satisfactions of vanity. They need a chief, illustrious by glory, who will lead them. For Bonaparte his vision of himself after Lodi was an illuminating and luminous moment. Psychologically, his traits, his values, his knowledge, his techniques and his self-image (identity) were now fused into a unitary, integrated personality. Since Brienne his concept of leadership had been the same. Wherever he was, *he* would be the chief, both military and political, whether in Corsica, France or anywhere in the world and, of course, in history. He accepted the role with a sense of destiny: 'the career I am to traverse'.[21]

At the coup d'état of 18–19 Brumaire (9–10 November 1799) he seized power in France by an improved version of the methods he had employed to secure election as a lieutenant-colonel of the Ajaccian National Guard: deceit, prior dealing, bribery, presence and exercise of armed force, and in addition an appeal to plebiscite – a method that was later studied by Napoleon III, Mussolini and Hitler. He then imposed a 'phoney' constitution that was a republic in form but a dictatorship in fact. As the abbé Sieyès, a French constitution-maker, observed: 'Gentlemen, you have got yourself a master – a man who knows everything, wants everything and can do everything.'

Chapter 2

◆

THE MILITARY CULTURE OF NAPOLEONIC FRANCE

Alan Forrest

OFFICER OF THE REVOLUTION

The Napoleon who has passed down to posterity was first and foremost a soldier, the young revolutionary general who conquered northern Italy before staging his bid for political power with the military coup d'état of 18 Brumaire.[1] In spite of his undeniable achievements in civilian life during the years that followed, as First Consul and then as Emperor – whether in reforming local administration, codifying the laws, extending educational opportunity or ending the rift between Church and state – it is for his military exploits that Bonaparte would be principally remembered. Future generations would be dazzled by the scale of his success and by the glory he brought to France by building an empire which at one point stretched across the European Continent. In the course of his career he fought all of sixty battles, and he emerged victorious in almost all of them; the only notable exceptions were Aspern-Essling, Leipzig and Waterloo.[2] But there was more to his reputation than success on the battlefield. Napoleon would be remembered by his soldiers as a commander of genius with a gift for quick thinking and incisive action, as an innovative leader who was prepared to trust his own instincts rather than follow the rule-book, as a general whose presence on the battlefield, as Wellington memorably remarked, 'made a difference of 40,000 men'.[3] He prepared his strategy with a precise, almost mathematical exactitude, leaving little to chance, and he understood more than any general of his generation the importance of rapid movement and the benefit to be reaped from surprise tactics. Above all, perhaps, he won the respect of his men because he knew how to motivate them and to inspire them with a sense of their own worth. They recognised in him a talented commander capable of bold improvisation on the battlefield, a general who not only brought them the fruits of victory but helped to build up their status and self-respect. Napoleon managed to retain a reputation with the troops for being on their side, speaking up for their rights, understanding their hopes and anxieties. He had risen to the top through merit and had not had to depend, like so many before him, on privilege or birthright. To that extent they could recognise him as one of themselves.

In a sense he was. He may have been a petty nobleman in Corsica – his father was, in David Chandler's words, 'an impecunious lawyer of minor aristocratic connections but immense social and literary aspirations'[4] – but as such he enjoyed none of the privileges that were reserved for the French aristocracy in the Ancien Regime army. Indeed, he chose to make his career not in the infantry or the cavalry, but – like Lazare Carnot and so many other ambitious sons of bourgeois stock[5] – in the artillery, precisely because it was the one branch of the army where military science and not aristocratic ancestry was the key to promotion. And he entered at the bottom. He attended the military school at Brienne from the age of 9 before moving to the Ecole Militaire in Paris in 1784, the first Corsican to do so. Here he performed with flying colours, emerging at the age of only 16 with the rank of sub-lieutenant. He was promoted to lieutenant before the onset of revolution in 1789; thereafter he took advantage of the resignation and emigration of many noble officers in the first years of the Revolution to secure his own rapid advancement. And rapid that rise was, as he repeatedly attracted the attention of his superiors with his intelligence and flair. By 1793 he had attained the rank of captain when he attracted national attention by leading the force that brought federalist Toulon to its knees. Here he demonstrated that he was an officer who could be entrusted with delicate political missions. In October 1795 we find him once again in a prominent political role, leading the government's forces against its own civilians to put down the royalist insurrection of Vendémiaire in Paris. Bonaparte showed by this action that he did not hesitate to use the army against his fellow Frenchmen in what was essentially a counter-insurgency role; he also proved his loyalty to the directorial regime, a loyalty that would be rewarded by the trust and friendship of one of the new directors, Paul Barras and, very rapidly, by promotion – first to the command of the Army of the Interior and then, in February 1796, to that of the Army of Italy, where he succeeded the incompetent Scherer. This was a bold appointment, which represented a quite astonishing rise to prominence for a young artillery officer still only 26 years old.[6]

Bonaparte had arrived in this position of power through the army, and it was the army and its culture which he understood best and in which he arguably felt most at home. But it would be facile to dismiss him as being simply a soldier, whose experience was limited to the battlefield and the bivouac. That might be the image that Napoleon himself frequently liked to portray. It was a useful tool when he sought to present himself as a man of the people, an army officer who had risen by talent alone, often in the face of privilege and adversity. But it was also a rather deceptive image. From the very beginning of the Revolution in Corsica the Bonaparte family had clear political ambitions, with Joseph Bonaparte prominent in Ajaccio city politics, and Napoleon himself tending to identify with the more explicitly pro-Jacobin factions on the island. It may be no accident, therefore, that Napoleon was soon singled out as one of the more political of the revolutionary generals, to be entrusted in turn with the delicate missions of quelling the federalist rebellion in Toulon in 1793 and turning his 'whiff of grapeshot' on the Paris crowd in 1795. Napoleon seemed pleased to be identified with the Jacobin cause, and he would use his political associations to advance his career. He had, for instance, attracted the attention of his political masters in 1793 not only by his triumphant success over Toulon but also through the publication of a pamphlet, the *Souper de Beaucaire*, in which he pinned his colours firmly to the republican mast. Even before this he had shown some literary ambitions, writing a history of his native Corsica when he was only 20 and submitting a philosophical essay for consideration by the Academy of Lyons two years later.[7] But the *Souper de Beaucaire* was much more overtly political in its content. It is a drama set in the south-east at the height of the federalist revolt and taking the form of a conversation between a soldier in General Carteaux's army – the hero of the piece – and three men from the region affected by the temptations of federalism. To the soldier falls the duty of explaining the Jacobin line and with it the national interest. The revolts, he explains, are destroying national unity and distracting the army from its principal duty on the frontiers; they therefore cannot be tolerated.[8] In this clear, uncomplicated message, Napoleon neatly merges the twin calls of patriotism and loyalty to the regime of the moment.

SOLDIERS AND CIVILIANS

If Napoleon understood something of revolutionary politics, he also nurtured political ambitions of his own, and was not inclined to leave political leadership to civilians. In the French revolutionary armies, after all, the dividing line between soldiers and civilians had been redrawn, with soldiers redefined as citizens, even if it was recognised that in the service of their country they had to accept the rigours of military discipline. But, the Jacobins believed, the fact that a man had agreed to serve his country should not deprive him of his basic human rights; and in 1794 the citizen-soldier was encouraged to vote, to discuss the current political agenda, to sing revolutionary songs, to read the radical press, to attend patriotic plays at the theatre, and even to join political clubs in his regiment or in the town where he was garrisoned. The Jacobins believed that the army was an institution well suited to teaching the young to identify with the cause for which they were fighting. It became the focus of political indoctrination or, in Jean-Paul Bertaud's phrase, 'une école du jacobinisme',[9] where the soldier would listen to patriotic speeches, read papers circulated by the Ministry of War, and sing anthems from state-funded song-books around the campfire after supper. This ritual had a purpose, of course: to mould a French citizen with loyalty to his country and his republic – from the sons of shopkeepers and journeymen, peasants and fishermen, brought together from towns and villages across the various provinces which now made up the French state. It was a purpose that would be conveyed in festivals and celebrations across France, where soldiers and civilians were symbolically united into a single, indivisible whole. Under the Republic the soldier enjoyed a new respect from the community which he served and of which he remained a part.

That status would be maintained even after the ideological fervour of the Jacobins had been consigned to memory, and with it the insistence that army officers should share the political priorities of their masters. For the revolutionary army was not a static construct, impervious to the political changes around it. It had continued to evolve, in its recruitment and promotion, its tactics and organisation, throughout the revolutionary decade, to the point where the high command had rejected any idea of the army as a seed-bed of revolutionary ideology, insisting instead on discipline and training, exercises and drill. Under the Directory in particular, there was a new emphasis on obedience, with the powers of superior officers reinforced and the imposition of military law more rigorous. The army of the Year II, with its idealism and bravado, was gradually giving way to a more professional war machine, where officers and men would be judged by their capacity and military knowledge rather than by their political ideas. Gone were the days when disgruntled soldiers were encouraged to denounce their superior officers to political commissars, and when those so denounced might find themselves before a military commission or even a firing squad. The emphasis now was on obedience. In 1795 a much stricter system of military police was introduced, with a new military code which prescribed the death penalty for a wide range of crimes and offences against military discipline. The hierarchy of the armies was reasserted, with soldiers once again judged by their superior officers rather than by military tribunals.[10] Gone, too, was the pretence that a major European war could be fought with an army of volunteers, those brave or patriotic or foolhardy enough to step forward to defend the frontiers. Already the great levies of 1793 had introduced a powerful element of compulsion, the *levée en masse* of August placing the entire population on a state of readiness for war. If systematic annual conscription was not introduced until the Loi Jourdan of 1799, the principle that citizenship implied clear obligations, including the obligation of the young and the single to provide military service, was already accepted. The armies of the Directory which helped expand the *Grande Nation* beyond its frontiers were already highly professionalised in both their ambition and their composition. In no sense could they be seen as armies of revolutionary militants, even though considerable numbers of committed Jacobins had migrated to the military after Thermidor, when their political services were no longer welcome.

Napoleon clearly endorsed this change and encouraged the military values which the armies inculcated, often equating them with those of civic virtue and of true support for the Republic. From the Army of Italy, indeed, his had been one of the most audible voices in support of the Directory, making it clear that the military would not stand idly by while the country drifted back to royalism or political reaction. One particularly effective propaganda mechanism, spread through the military press and in petitions and dispatches back to Paris, was the circulation of the toasts which were being drunk by army officers at their patriotic banquets in northern Italy – toasts that were quite politically explicit, like 'To the re-emigration of the émigrés' or 'To the unity of French republicans: may they follow the Army of Italy's example and, supported by it, regain that energy which is fitting for the leading nation on Earth!'[11] Here Napoleon was stressing the value of military qualities as well as of republican beliefs; the 'energy' of the soldier is, by implication, combating the weakness or lethargy of the political leadership. He believed in the value of military service and military training for inculcating martial values in the young, for making them strong and resolute, and for binding them to codes of honour and masculinity. Honour was of the essence here, the value which more than any other inspired and lubricated the military. Though he held firmly to the principle of a conscript army in which all were bound to serve – and those who shirked that service were condemned as cowardly and effeminate – his was an army inspired by rewards and promotions, by honours and privileges, rather than by abstract values like citizenship and civic obligation.[12] It was a masculine society bound by masculine values of courage and sacrifice, inspired by images of gallantry and honour.

This was the society which the young General Bonaparte knew in Italy, the kind of army which he had himself been responsible for forging during his years in the field. It was a society which he understood and whose values he shared – the same values, in large measure, which he would try to impose on civil society after the successful military putsch which brought him to power on 18 Brumaire. That *journée* was, after all, carried out with and by units close to Bonaparte, men who knew him well, veterans of his campaigns in Italy and in Egypt. Their loyalty to their commanders, and by extension to the institution of the army itself, was total, and swept away any concerns that may have lingered about their duty to the existing regime. For the army was now confident of its abilities and of its place in the polity; this was not the first attempted military coup of the directorial years. One might almost say that the soldiers simply obeyed their general's orders as they had been trained to do, confident that he could make a better job of governing than a corrupt and largely discredited Directory. But there was more to it than that. Discontent was heightened in the summer of 1799 by the combined impact of internal upheaval and the threat of invasion from the outside, which further undermined the Constitution of the Year III and made a gradualist approach to reform seem irrelevant. Once again, the war proved decisive in the course of the Revolution, undermining the case for legitimacy and passing supreme power to a soldier.[13] Almost symbolically, at the very gates of the capital, Napoleon posed this central question of authority and legality when he shouted to a group of soldiers whom he spotted in the crowd:

> Grenadiers . . . soldiers. . . . If any speaker in the pay of foreign powers dares to pronounce against your general the word 'outlaw', may he be instantly struck down by the thunderbolt of war. Always remember that I march accompanied by the god of war and the god of good fortune.[14]

There was no hint of demurral; the soldiers cheered.

TRUST AND RAPPORT

There is no doubting that Napoleon understood his troops and was in turn understood by them. That he had a gift for public relations with his army is hardly in doubt, and he would seem to have had an immediate effect on the men with whom he came in contact. Ordinary soldiers may have expressed little ideological commitment to the regime, but they appeared to show a real affection for Napoleon personally, as their commander in Italy and later as First Consul and Emperor. He was accessible, unpretentious, concerned for their welfare. He granted them honours; he came to the front to review his troops in person; and he never forgot the material concerns which were so dominant in the ranks, the shortages of food and clothing, the lack of bedding and firewood. Some admitted to being dazzled by his style and his presence, or by the sheer melodrama created by his arrival in their midst. As one soldier wrote home to his parents, 'the Emperor, surrounded by several of his marshals, passed along the line of our army; he was escorted by a host of soldiers who had straw torches which in the distance lit up the whole scene magnificently'.[15] His soldiers held him in awe for his feats on the battlefield, a sense that he was their saviour, the one man capable of leading them to victory and, with victory, to the peace they so deeply craved. Being in his presence caused a flurry of excitement which, soldiers avowed, was shared by both officers and ranks. Their sense of identification was well summed up by one young man from the Oise in an eloquent paean of praise of Napoleon written to his uncle in 1807. From Italy he notes:

> Finally we have enjoyed the presence of our sovereign which had been promised us for so long; he inspected our division at Palma-Nuova in the midst of rain, mud and snow; I don't think I have ever been as cold as I was that day, and I do not know how the Emperor could put up with it; the soldiers were scarcely able to handle their weapons; but it seemed that his presence warmed us up; repeated shouts of 'Long live the Emperor' must have told him how much he is appreciated. The weather did not permit him to pass through all the ranks; he talked only with the officers.[16]

But – and here again Napoleon demonstrates his common touch – the letter continues 'those soldiers who wanted to say something to him could approach him with confidence, sure that they would be warmly welcomed'. Spontaneously, it would appear, this young soldier reinforced the image so carefully fostered by Napoleon himself, of the commander who listened to his men and who was accessible to all, even the humblest new recruit, in his armies.

It was an image which Napoleon sought to impress both on his contemporaries and on posterity, an image that was to play a key role in the myth which he was careful to construct for himself, both during his years of power and later, in exile on St Helena. He had to be seen to be on the side of the people while standing firmly outside the political arena, and the army was to prove an ideal instrument for projecting this image – a forum where he could be seen to champion the little man and reward the contribution of the ordinary infantryman while at the same time satisfying his lust for military glory and bringing to fruition the directorial dream of *la Grande Nation*. The image of the Emperor that would prove most persistent in the popular consciousness and that would convert millions to the Bonapartism of the nineteenth century was that of a caring military leader, born of the people and consistently mindful of the interests of the people. As supreme commander of the army, he took care to be represented as being at one with his army, a general who shared their fears and their most basic deprivations, who knew at first hand the reality of the sacrifices which they were asked to make in his name. When he appeared among them it was as one of them; his own uniform was that of a colonel of the Imperial Guard cavalry (1st *chasseurs à cheval*); and he made a fetish of always appearing before his troops in the same familiar green coat.[17] Bernard Ménager, in the introduction to his study of the clientele for the Bonapartist cause, notes the twin appeal of popular Bonapartism – a form of authoritarian democracy that embraced both civil equality and military glory – and quotes approvingly the words with which Goguelat ends his speech in Balzac's *Médecin de campagne*: 'Long live Napoleon, father of the people and of the soldier'.[18] The soldier here is not an afterthought, so much were Bonaparte's image and reputation linked to military glory and tactical brilliance in the field. But he was a key link – perhaps *the* key link – between the common man and an imperial court that was becoming increasingly reminiscent of the Bourbons at Versailles.

This role is stressed in many of Napoleon's own writings, whether in official decrees and letters to his ministers, in private correspondence, or in the *Mémorial de Sainte-Hélène*, the carefully sanitised *souvenirs* which he dictated to Las Cases during his long months of exile. He is at pains to express his respect for the noble character of the French soldier, his courage and fighting qualities and his devotion to the cause of the French nation. At times, indeed, he may seem to get carried away by his own eloquence, ascribing to the soldiers qualities of which they would surely scarcely have been capable. His observations on pillage, for instance, seem somewhat utopian at a time when every army in Europe was accustomed to enjoy its share of booty and after a decade in which the French had gained an unenviable reputation across Europe for seizing whatever plunder they could find, in some cases at the behest of the state itself. Napoleon contends that he no longer allowed French troops the freedom of a city after a successful siege, not because of the impact on France's reputation with the civilian population, serious though that might be, but because of the effect on the army itself. 'A soldier no longer has any discipline from the moment when he can pillage, and if by pillaging he has enriched himself, he immediately becomes a bad soldier who no longer has any appetite for fighting.'[19] But if his principal reason for the prohibition was to maintain army discipline, he significantly went on to explain that he could enforce this regulation without any difficulty because pillage was not in the nature of the French soldier. Twenty-four hours of licence of the kind that had been common throughout Europe would be unthinkable in the case of his French battalions. And why? Because of their nature, their character, their innate horror of injustice. Abusing authority in such a way, Napoleon mused, was simply not French; 'looting is not part of our French way of life'.

AN ARMY OF HONOUR

Honour, on the other hand, constituted a major part of what Napoleon saw as the motivation of his soldiers, which perhaps explains why he went to such lengths to reward them for their service and why even civil office in Napoleonic France was endowed with a profoundly military culture. Napoleon's own experience when he became First Consul was, of course, dominated by the military, and when he looked for deserving candidates for promotion to the highest offices in the land, he instinctively turned to the men who led his armies, rewarding them with both substantial *primes* in cash and in kind and with lavish social honours. From the Year VIII arms of honour were bestowed upon military men who had distinguished themselves by some notable exploit or action. More prominently, when the *Légion d'Honneur* was created as a national merit award, Napoleon quite explicitly defined it as a reward for the qualities of honourable service which he wished to recognise; he defined the Legion as 'the mainspring of that honour to which the French nation is so powerfully attached'.[20] And honour, in Napoleon's eyes, was quintessentially military; indeed, when he proposed the establishment of the Legion to the Conseil d'Etat in 1802, he justified it as a means of 'regularising the system of military rewards'.[21]

All those who had previously received the arms of honour were incorporated into the Legion at its inception, and the military emphasis within it would remain constant throughout the Empire. At the ceremony at the Boulogne camp in 1804, for instance, where Napoleon decorated 2,000 members of the Legion, all but a dozen were soldiers; ten years later, of its 32,000 members, only 1,500 were civilians.[22] And it was not only in the Legion that the precedence of army officers was demonstrable. The eighteen marshals of France appointed in 1804 were selected from among Napoleon's most trusted generals, while army officers were an important constituency among those chosen for the Senate. So amongst the nobility of the Empire, army officers were most prominent. Of the 3,263 men who became nobles between 1808 and 1814, Jean-Paul Bertaud has calculated that 59 per cent came from the army, as against 22 per cent from high officials of the state and a further 17 per cent from the *notables*. All marshals and the majority of lieutenants-general and brigadiers-general were counts or barons, while 387 colonels also obtained letters of barony.[23] Honour, in other words, was a quality which Napoleon continued to equate with the military, though cynics might note that honours came with more material rewards attached. Membership of the Legion of Honour, for instance, came with a salary, while military commanders could expect to receive very large gratifications, large enough to allow the holder to aspire to the trappings of a noble lifestyle. Berthier and Davout were awarded *rentes* of 300,000 francs apiece; Ney, a colossal 800,000 francs. In all, Napoleon made 1,261 gifts, many of them in land, to no fewer than 824 different officers in recognition of the service they had rendered. Their total value amounted to more than 16 million francs.[24]

CREATING THE LEGEND

If the most lavish honours were reserved for the military high command, they were not alone in basking in imperial approval or in wrapping themselves in the trappings of glory. From the outset, indeed, Napoleon was careful to avoid any return to the Ancien Regime army where the officers alone enjoyed status and where the ranks were filled by the have-nots of society. He sought to confer status on all, even on those in the ranks, and to involve all classes of society in his military ventures. He did this in a number of ways, many of them highly imaginative and innovative, like the involvement of the social elites in the army through the creation of the largely symbolic *gardes d'honneur*,[25] or the incorporation of scholars – archaeologists, botanists, specialists in classical art and languages – with the army in Egypt in a campaign whose aims were tied in with the preservation of civilisation itself.[26] Throughout his life the Emperor took care to show respect for his men, recognising the extent of their sacrifice. Again and again he returned to this theme in his proclamations and in the *ordres du jour* he had read to the troops. The soldiers were characteristically open, generous and loyal. Typical is this paean of praise from Lützen during the German campaign of 1813, addressed, directly and typically, to the troops themselves: 'Soldiers, I am pleased with you! You have fulfilled my every expectation! You have compensated for everything through your good will and your gallantry!'[27] Here as in so many of his proclamations, Napoleon acknowledged the courage and devotion of his men. But he was always aware that their interest did not stop with victory, or even glory; they sighed for peace and an honourable return to civilian life. And so, encouragingly, did Napoleon. After crossing the Alps in June 1800, at the start of the second Italian campaign, he was already looking forward to the peace that would follow, to that result of all their efforts which would be 'unclouded glory and lasting peace'[28] – a peace which they could enjoy, admired and respected by their fellows as men who had dreamed, and fought and conquered. In his dealings with his men, Bonaparte did not confine himself to the material or the prosaic; he encouraged them to forget the misery they saw around them and to dream a little. For who could forget the uplifting words of his first proclamation, made to a sadly demoralised army on the eve of their departure for Italy in March 1796:

> Soldiers, you are naked and undernourished; the government owes you a great deal, yet can give you nothing. .... I will lead you into the most fertile plains in the world. .... Rich provinces and great cities are within your grasp, and there you will find honour, glory and wealth. Soldiers of Italy, will you be wanting in courage or in resolve?[29]

The speech may have been apocryphal; but it was the stuff of the Bonapartist legend of the nineteenth century.

Just as the Emperor was anxious to appear to care for his men in the field, so he sought to reward them once their active service was over, effectively reserving various forms of state employment for veterans. That, at least, was the image he wished to create, that of a grateful head of state providing for the welfare of those on whom the security of his empire depended. On St Helena Las Cases recalls Napoleon's musings on the care he had taken of veterans and on the privileges he had sought for them. In June 1816 he expressed his wish that the state provide special facilities for veterans, reserving for them those posts in the customs and excise service which were in the public gift. Challenged on the legality of such favouritism, Napoleon had made no attempt to hide his intentions: 'The Constitution gave me the right to nominate to all these posts, and it seemed to me only just that those who had suffered most should have the greatest right to compensation.' Napoleon went on to harangue those who opposed this as special pleading and who, from the comfort of their benches in the Conseil d'Etat, dared suggest that he was drawing an unwarranted distinction between soldiers and civilians. He insisted on that distinction, and he had, he implied, the right to make it precisely because he had first-hand experience of the conditions of military life:

> Gentlemen, war is not a bed of roses; you know it, here on the benches where you sit, only from reading about it in the bulletins or in accounts of our triumphs. You do not know our bivouacs, our forced marches, the privations which we undergo or the sufferings which we endure. I do know them, because I observe them and from time to time I share in them.[30]

Here he not only identified with his men, as any general might, but identified his deprivations and physical sufferings with theirs.

He also liked to claim that he was heir to the more democratic instincts of the Revolution in the medical provision that he made for his troops, presenting himself as a caring leader who valued the lives of his soldiers, providing field ambulances to tend their wounds on the battlefield and welcoming the broken and wounded to a dignified retirement in the Invalides. Napoleon was not only a brilliant strategist; he administered to the sick and showed compassion to the dying. Perhaps the most memorable representation of this aspect of Napoleon is the scene in Gros's famous painting of him visiting the plague victims of Jaffa, which shows a tender and compassionate figure surrounded by the sick, reaching out his hands to them in a healing gesture reminiscent of the miracle healing of the Bourbon kings of old. There is, as Timothy Wilson-Smith remarks, something 'Christ-like' in this vision of Bonaparte, the leader administering to the humblest of men around him.[31] Like all such claims, it does, of course, hold a grain of truth. Napoleon did not revert to the social and legal inequities of the Ancien Regime. The Invalides, in particular, remained open to all on the basis of need and sacrifice rather than as a reward for rank, as it had been under the Ancien Regime. And Napoleon gave great freedom and prominence to a few star practitioners, like Percy and Larrey, around whom much of the Napoleonic myth was constructed. But we should not allow ourselves to be deluded by Napoleonic discourse here. It was the Revolution rather than the Consulate or Empire which made the greatest advances in military medicine, introducing large numbers of new military *officiers de santé* to care for the troops and conscripting civilian doctors to complement them. By Year III the revolutionaries had restored military teaching hospitals in an attempt to raise medical standards in the armies, while the establishment of the Military Health Council in Year II offered army doctors the autonomy they craved in the administration of health care. Napoleon was far less innovative, and medical expenditure was not one of his top priorities. Larrey, it is true, developed his 'flying ambulances' to remove the wounded rapidly from the battlefield and give them treatment. But there his innovation largely ceased. The *officiers de santé* of the revolutionary years were discharged; the military teaching hospitals closed. Percy wrote damningly that the result was a severe impoverishment of the standard of care that could be offered. He added that the government must bear a heavy responsibility for this. 'Considering the indifference and lethargy of all the men in power when one speaks to them about hospitals, it would seem as if the sick and wounded cease to be human beings when they can no longer be soldiers.'[32]

IMAGES AND REPRESENTATIONS

Part of Bonaparte's purpose was, of course, to improve army morale, to convince the soldiers that they were well looked after and that they would be cared for if they should fall sick or suffer serious injury. But it was also more fundamental – a desire to build on the propagandist work of the Revolution in persuading the French public that the troops were valued for their efforts and that they enjoyed the esteem that properly accrued to the most patriotic of citizens. The symbolism of these years emphasised the heroism of the soldier and the glory of the cause, lionising the person of Napoleon and linking the battlefield of the Napoleonic wars to images of the heroic in antiquity and in classical mythology. The evolution of the popular festival after Brumaire provides an excellent instance of this use of the symbolic. Popular spontaneity was immediately downgraded, and with it the role played by the common people. All images of the crowd, of popular justice, of violence and retribution were removed, and the balance between civilian and military figures in the representation of the nation began to shift in the direction of the military. Themes were carefully selected to buttress the authority of the regime. The festival of 1er Vendémiaire VIII gives an excellent idea of the tone of these typically Napoleonic festivities. The festival, celebrated throughout France, was devised with a clear military theme: to praise one of France's past military heroes by celebrating the removal of the remains of

Turenne for reburial in the Invalides. There was to be a military commemoration and loud military music, and it was requested that the festival be celebrated 'with all the dazzling display which the memorable period being celebrated might merit'. But the participation of the people was far less general and far from democratically organised, with three administrators to be chosen by each department to represent the people in Paris. In contrast, the contribution of the army was central, with the singing of *Te Deums* and the involvement of the military both imposing some degree of hierarchy on the celebration and imposing on onlookers a sense of the solemnity of the occasion.[33] The military presence, it is true, had been steadily increasing in the various *fêtes* ordered by the Directory, but what is striking under Napoleon is the clear focus of public celebration, its use to reinforce the authority of the state. That purpose had never been clearly evinced by the directors. In Lille in 1799, for instance, if the military presence had been notable in the five festivals ordered during the year, the subjects celebrated were a curious and rather inchoate jumble of the solemn and the revolutionary: three of the principal events of the Revolution (the abolition of the monarchy on 10 August, the execution of Louis XVI on 21 January and the overthrow of Robespierre on 27 July), along with funeral services to commemorate the martyrs of Rastadt (8 June) and General Joubert, recently killed on the battlefield (1 October).[34]

Napoleon was keenly aware of the power of visual images, as can be seen in the monumental legacy of his years in the streets and squares of Paris, from the Châtelet to the Pyramides and Concorde – and to the Louvre. In particular, the French history rooms of the Louvre provide an object lesson in the use of art in support of his regime, especially the great canvases of Gros and David, Boilly and Géricault, who linger on voluptuous images of military splendour that would help create the lasting legend of the *Grande Armée*. Napoleon held that the real people of France were to be found in the army; people and military, leader and led were as one. This identification, notes Christopher Prendergast, is repeated time and time again in the *salon* painting of the Empire, principally through the use of four recurring themes – 'the allocution and the harangue, pre- or post-victory; the eve-of-battle visit to the bivouacked troops; patriotic support for conscription; above all, the wounded overcoming physical pain in euphoric acclamation of their general'.[35] Napoleon was more than an interested bystander. If, as art historians seem agreed, he had little artistic taste as such, he was fascinated by the detail of a work, took a personal interest in judging the Paris *salons*, and rewarded artists in whom he saw especial merit. Above all, he understood the potential of art to project his imperial image and to win over public opinion; he followed the Bourbons in seeking to give artists work, and he made sure that they worked for him, using their art to provide a record of his military triumphs. 'Bonapartist artists of the future might dwell on the retreat from Moscow or Napoleon's farewell to the Guard in the Cour des Adieux at Fontainebleau. His artists did no such thing – he was unmoved by pathos.'[36]

If the world of the Napoleonic soldier was dramatically preserved in art and high culture, so it was in the popular prints which were the cultural mainstay of the poor, those bright, often gaudily coloured *images d'Epinal* which circulated in their millions throughout rural France. Traditionally, these pictures had generally been religious in theme, depicting saints and scenes from the life of Christ, targeted at the devout Catholic peasant as much as at the parish priest. But from the early nineteenth century Jean-Charles Pellerin, owner of the most important printing firm in Epinal, saw a tempting market opportunity open up before him as he sought to exploit popular militarism and Napoleonic nostalgia in large parts of the French countryside, and he took advantage of improved inks and printing techniques to diversify his product range. His preferred subject matter was the imperial army, the soldiers of the Emperor in their bright uniforms appealing to each succeeding generation of young men who grew up with these images and longed to serve in their turn. What these pictures presented in the name of portraiture was more a series of symbols, idealised images of simple military virtues, personified in those who fought in the *Grande Armée*. More often than not, they glorified ordinary soldiers and identified with the common man as high culture signally failed to do – not ordinary soldiers as individuals, but rather as stereotypes, presented in groups and huddles, and always including those more glamorous figures with whom the young and their parents could identify – the *sapeur*, the *tambour-major*, the *cantinière*. The features might be anonymous, but the uniforms spoke eloquently. That is what made them so popular, the fact that for one or two *sous* families could buy images that could so easily be their son, their brother, their neighbour. In the words of René Perrout in his analysis of Pellerin's art, they appealed to a widely diffuse clientele: 'While pleasing to the soldier, the picture also pleases the people. When they examine the uniforms, they are really admiring themselves.'[37] It was not that Napoleonic soldiers were presented as being without failings; they knew too many real soldiers to be deceived in that way. It was rather that the soldier was perceived as a man of the people, a man like themselves, with all their faults and appetites, but who had been swept up to serve in a great national adventure. That was what excited emulation and brought the soldiers' world close to their own.

MILITARY CULTURE AND THE STATE

What all these different media helped create was a strong image of the military culture with which Napoleon sought to identify and which would be central to the legend he left behind. But they were not only about image; they also help explain the nature of the authoritarian rule which he progressively instituted in the years after 1800, as he became First Consul under the Constitution of Year VIII, then Consul for Life in 1802, before having himself crowned Emperor in 1804. That is not to infer that Napoleonic rule was based on a military dictatorship, even though with France at war for most of the Napoleonic years it was perhaps inevitable that the military agenda was prominent and that army officers achieved a peculiar prominence in the affairs of state. Napoleon's was a government of civilians ratified by plebiscite – but a civilian government of a hierarchical and authoritarian kind, where administration was highly centralised, where representative institutions were stripped of much of their authority, and where Napoleon himself was assumed to embody in his person the sovereignty of the French nation.[38] If the Emperor retained an appearance of parliamentary institutions, it was little more than a sham. The principle of election so much vaunted by the revolutionaries was largely rejected in favour of clear lines of authority. Napoleonic France, in a manner reminiscent of the military, was a highly centralist state, in which everyone reported up to the ministries and the ministers in turn reported to Napoleon. Little was left to local consultation. Administration and justice were highly centralised, with a common system of local government for all of France and a comprehensive codification of the law. Authority was maintained in the provinces by the institution of prefects in 1800, with each prefect appointed at the centre and answerable to the Minister of the Interior. Authority in religious matters was assured by the Ministry of Religious Affairs and by the imposition on the Catholic Church of the Concordat of 1802. Social hierarchy was strengthened by the assimilation of the old nobility and the creation of a new nobility based on merit. State service was lavishly and publicly rewarded, with the granting of honours facilitating Napoleon's desire for social manipulation. And Napoleonic educational policy, based on the *lycées* and the University of France,[39] guaranteed not only a common curriculum but also the means of producing the meritocratic society on which Napoleonic institutions were so dependent. The army was, of course, ever present, with its spiralling demands for conscripts and a seemingly insatiable appetite for supplies. Conscription, indeed, soon 'overshadowed every problem of administration in Napoleonic France', and became the litmus test by which the success of ministers, prefects and sub-prefects was judged.[40] For ordinary Frenchmen it became the dominant, lowering image of the regime as it became increasingly onerous, increasingly resented and increasingly policed. For many in the villages and hamlets of provincial France – as, indeed, in those of the territories which France conquered and annexed – this was the moment when their loyalties were most severely tested, when they were forced to choose between the well-being of their families and the demands of the state.[41] It was also the moment when the true character of the Napoleonic regime was most forcibly brought home to ordinary civilians.

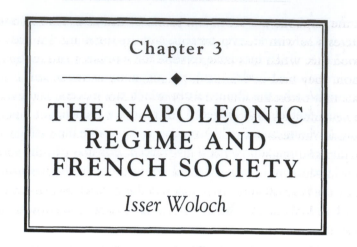

Chapter 3

◆

THE NAPOLEONIC REGIME AND FRENCH SOCIETY

Isser Woloch

By most definitions, the study of social history must be long durational and one can scarcely expect to see dramatic social transformation during the relatively brief 'Napoleonic episode', as some French historians aptly call it. Even had General Bonaparte never made it back from Egypt in 1799, the distribution of landed property, the relations of social classes, the contours of family life and the demographic characteristics of French society would have been unlikely to change fundamentally over the ensuing decades. Yet activist regimes like the successive revolutionary and Napoleonic governments did nurture social visions, and could not help but touch the deep structures of society as well as the rhythms of daily life, above and beyond the obvious vicissitudes of politics and war.

Over time, explicitly or implicitly, the Napoleonic regime sifted what it had inherited in 1799 and either rejected altogether, modified or consolidated the innovations of the French Revolution. Simultaneously, in ways both subtle and obvious, Napoleon gradually resuscitated some of the Ancien Regime's habitudes and values. Institutional reforms and government policies under Napoleon often carried significant social ramifications.

DEPOLITICISATION: BENEFITS AND COSTS

Arguably by 1799 the French Republic had disillusioned large swathes of its own population. While the Republic sustained a passionate commitment among small minorities of politically engaged citizens, it had not sunk deep roots or achieved any kind of consensus in society at large. What broad support the Republic did command probably had as much to do with tangible interests as with ideological appeals. Napoleon and his collaborators understood this. When they pledged repeatedly to safeguard the gains of the Revolution, they held to a limited, pragmatic sense of what this signified. Above all, they offered assurance that the Bourbons would never return and that the new interests created by the Revolution would therefore be secure. These broad interests included civil equality, the abolition of seigneurial overlordship and seigneurial dues, and the suppression of the church tithe. Narrower in scope but equally part of this agenda were guarantees for the transfer of the *biens nationaux* (nationalised church and émigré property sold by the state to individuals), and opportunities to rise in the officer corps and the civilian administration.

If, as the Revolution unfortunately demonstrated, civil strife is one of the worst fates that can befall a society, then the suppression of armed rebellion, political brigandage and murderous factional conflict might easily appear as the most obvious blessing conferred by the advent of Napoleon.[1] The price, however, would be considerable. The Consulate promoted social peace by depoliticising France and reinforcing the powers of the executive. From its inception, the Consulate eliminated genuine elections and effective representative government in favour of co-option. Immediately as well it curtailed the classic public liberties of 1789 almost to the vanishing point by such practices as the prohibition of political clubs, press censorship and preventive detention.

The Napoleonic regime nurtured an image of domestic tranquillity in which people turned away from politics and got back to real life, as it were. 'The department of Seine Inférieure', boasted its prefect in 1802, 'has an excellent public spirit, because there reigns here a great political immobility and a great movement toward domestic concerns. When a people has made a wise and serious delegation of public powers [i.e. to Napoleon Bonaparte], it has nothing better to do than to occupy itself with other matters.'[2] To be sure, this picture of a contented, depoliticised country can easily be overdrawn. The embers of revolutionary factionalism and victimisation still smouldered beneath the surface in many localities, and in some departments a kind of low-intensity warfare of mutual fear and disdain persisted. But no longer did such passions erupt openly or with regularity as they had, thanks to the Directory's routine of annual elections and frequent purges.[3]

Depoliticisation, a hallmark of the Napoleonic regime, had important if indirect social consequences. If the basic poles of social history are wealth, status and power, then the French Revolution's electoral democracy had introduced entirely new routes to power for both individuals and groups. By eliminating those novel electoral paths to political power, the Napoleonic regime was not simply interring the French Revolution's nascent democratic political culture. It was solidifying the overwhelming advantages of wealth and local status by eliminating a new, open-ended variable in the way society might organise itself.

To be sure, this change was less stark in the countryside than in the towns. It is worth recalling that in its first phase (1789–91) the Revolution not only empowered various non-noble elements of the elite on both national and local levels of government, but also brought French peasants onto the political stage. Starting in 1789 with a traditional repertoire of direct, sometimes violent action, peasants quickly adapted to their new judicial and political rights as citizens. As Jean-Pierre Jessenne has shown for the Artois, the new electoral system allowed the emergence in almost all the region's villages of an oligarchy of larger farmers (a *fermocratie*), who now displaced the lord's agents as the principal local power-brokers. With the consent of less fortunate peasants, and with a rotation in office that mitigated entrenched local tyrannies, this change proved durable. Even after the Consulate eliminated elections in favour of appointing village mayors and members of the municipal council, who together planned local budgets, the *fermocratie* retained its position. Its power was diluted, however, since village budgets now had to be approved by the prefect and could be modified by that distant official. The potential for communal autonomy and initiative that the Revolution had unlocked now contracted.[4]

In urban society, the Revolution brought far more dramatic change in the social bases of political power. With the fall of the monarchy in 1792, urban revolutionary militants known as the *sans-culottes* assumed unprecedented importance in Paris and many other towns. Local businessmen, master artisans, shopkeepers, journeymen, white-collar employees – such ordinary people became the backbone of the Revolution's participatory political culture in its radical phase. The *sans-culottes* filled the ranks of the political clubs (*sociétés populaires*), revolutionary committees and paramilitary battalions that flourished in 1793–94, promoting and implementing the Reign of Terror. For this they would pay dearly, once the survivors among the Terror's victims regained the upper hand after the fall of Robespierre in Thermidor (July 1794). But the *sans-culottes* also left a more positive legacy with their egalitarian and populist ardour.

After Thermidor, the Republic tried to free itself from the influence of the *sans-culottes*. It stigmatised them as bloodthirsty anarchists, purged them from public life, and often threw them into jail. But in late 1795 the Directory regime was inaugurated with a general amnesty, and the egalitarian ideals of the *sans-culottes* could again be articulated, albeit in far more muted form. During the electoral campaigns of 1798 and 1799, democratic-republicans (or neo-Jacobins, as they were sometimes called) advocated the revival of political clubs, progressive taxation, public welfare entitlements, a bonus for war veterans, and universal free primary schooling. But the Brumaire coup put an end to any possibility of popular political participation or such egalitarian social policies.[5] In effect, the Napoleonic regime finally expelled the *sans-culottes* from public life once and for all, demonising them into the bargain as nothing more than fanatical terrorists who had to be exorcised. In 1800, the Revolution's earlier promise of popular, democratic politics was banished to the realm of memory.

To illustrate this process let us consider a basic plank of the democratic project: the ideal of universal, free public education organised by the Republic. At the height of its egalitarian revolutionary enthusiasm, the National Convention repeatedly attempted to translate this compelling vision into reality. Having banished the clergy at least formally from responsibility for primary education, the Convention hoped to fill the void with a national system of free public education for boys and girls. This was an incredibly ambitious notion, since schooling had traditionally depended on the will and resources of local communities. The Convention debated and voted several plans that did not work, until in late 1794 it finally adopted an artfully crafted proposal known as the Lakanal Law. This legislation authorised the employment of state-salaried teachers, male and female, in every community with a population over 1,000, thus eliminating the need of parents or local communities to pay for tuition. But a scarcity of qualified teachers and hyper-inflation – which destroyed the Revolution's currency and thus rendered the salaries of these teachers worthless – combined to derail the plan, and it was abandoned after two years of valiant local efforts.[6]

The directorial Constitution persisted with a vague reference about the need for public schools, and it stipulated that after several years the right to vote would entail a requirement for literacy. In 1798–99 a new debate began in the legislature on how to establish and fund public schools across the land, but Brumaire terminated this debate before it could be resolved. The question then remained: would the Consulate and Empire take up this effort? In fact, the Napoleonic regime renounced the cause of free public primary schooling in the countryside. Instead it reverted to the old system of local community initiative and tuition, a hands-off attitude by the state and a *de facto* reversion to the clergy of their dominant role in supervising local primary schooling.

Not that the Napoleonic regime was indifferent to education. On the contrary, much was done to advance secondary education, with the establishment of high-quality state-run *lycées*. In addition the state revived higher education, especially for the professional training that would produce engineers, scientists, doctors and barristers. The regime, in other words, nurtured the upper or elite tracks of education but effectively severed them from the base of popular education. Universal primary schooling and mass literacy were no longer deemed necessary for French society.[7]

RELIGIOUS LIBERTY AND CONSCRIPTION

Beyond promoting social peace, stability and an end to bitter factionalism, Brumaire almost immediately produced a striking change in the quality of daily life, for the Consulate tacitly pulled back from the Directory's ill-considered campaign against Catholic traditionalism. In 1798 the Directory had rallied around the republican calendar, first created in 1793 as a new way of dividing time by a system of ten-day weeks, with the months renamed to reflect the seasons. On its face the republican calendar challenged the cycle of Catholic traditions embodied in the Gregorian calendar. But instead of letting this radical innovation lapse, the Directory began to enforce observance of the *décadi* or tenth day of the republican week as a day of rest, and to prevent church worship on Sunday. It also reinforced an earlier prohibition against the ringing of church bells, and at the extreme local authorities closed church buildings altogether. With such policies, an otherwise anti-Jacobin Directory effectively resurrected the secularising drive of 1793–94 and seriously eroded religious liberty.[8]

Citizens who resented these policies seized on Brumaire as a signal to disregard such repressive laws and local decrees. As historians have documented for at least three departments (the Var, the Pas-de-Calais and the Aisne), citizens aggressively reclaimed their religious liberty: they ignored the *décadi*, forced open church buildings, observed Sunday worship, and rang church bells in the accustomed fashion. Formally, the republican calendar survived in official usage as a way of recording dates until the establishment of the Empire in 1804. But by informal agreement, the Napoleonic regime ceased enforcement of the *décadi* with dramatic results. After Brumaire in the Artois, 'village cohesion reconstituted itself on the basis of the aspiration for autonomy and religious engagement'. And in the Var, as Maurice Agulhon put it, 'it all seemed as if the fall of the Directory, interpreted by the notables as a promise of order, was understood by the popular masses as the announcement of a return to normal life'.[9]

Ultimately, normal life for the French people under Napoleon also came to include subjection to military conscription. When one considers the strenuous objections in the *cahiers* or grievance petitions of 1789 to the *milice* – the relatively limited intrusion of the state since Louis XIV's time, which supplemented its standing army of long-term professional volunteers by forced levies among the peasants – then one can begin to judge how objectionable Napoleon's unrelenting demand for military service might have seemed. In theory Napoleonic conscription applied to all male citizens when they turned 18 or 19, although in practice annual lotteries to fill quotas did not require all eligible conscripts to serve in most years, while up to a third avoided the draft legally by being physically or medically unfit. Moreover, wealthy families of various kinds had the option of hiring a substitute or replacement, albeit under tightly regulated and increasingly expensive conditions. (It is estimated that 7–10 per cent of conscripts from wealthy families availed themselves of this opportunity to avoid induction.)[10]

The battle over conscription was the great domestic drama of the Napoleonic era. As annual troop levies became routine, then grew progressively harsher in frequency and size, draft evasion among citizens in certain regions was endemic, with a pattern of collusion among the draftees, their families and their villages. But even in adamantly resistant regions, officials persisted and gradually wore down this opposition, making draft evasion a futile response to the demands of the state. The Napoleonic regime won this struggle by a combination of official zeal, fine tuning of its bureaucratic procedures, and the use of increasingly coercive sanctions. As the final confrontation between Napoleon and his European foes began in 1813 after the Russian debacle, the imperial conscription machine was still operating at peak efficiency. But once the imperial armies began to lose consistently and Napoleon's demand for more bodies reached ludicrous levels, the system collapsed completely towards the end of that year.[11]

In this atmosphere, the Bourbons scored propaganda points by promising to end military conscription, and after the Restoration they did so for all of three years. By 1818 a modified system of conscription was back in place, far more modest in scale, to be sure, and with most previous restrictions on hiring replacements lifted, so that the traffic in replacements became a respectable business instead of a clandestine practice as it had been during the Napoleonic years. But the fact remains that conscription emerged out of the revolutionary-Napoleonic experience as a transforming innovation, an unsurpassed intrusion by the state into society, not only in France but by example in much of Europe. Two centuries earlier, the French monarchy's relentless expansion of its taxing powers had met staunch resistance, which it eventually overcame. The absolute monarchy thus began turning peasants into (tax-paying) Frenchmen. Now the revolutionary-Napoleonic conscription experience became another huge step in this process of state building and the forced integration of citizens into a national community.

As Napoleonic conscription spread through society at large, a sub-plot was unfolding within the ranks of the elites, centred around the Napoleonic officer corps. While (as already mentioned) up to 10 per cent of families – wealthy peasants, landed proprietors, professionals and business families – opted out of military service by purchasing costly replacements or substitutes for their sons, others recognised that family strategy and ambition might best be served in Napoleonic France by joining the military establishment. The extremely ambitious Roederer family, for example, which previously made its careers in the courts and in business, sent one son into the officer corps. And even Napoleon's Second Consul and close adviser Cambacérès, a quintessential civilian man of the law and a confirmed bachelor, was not hurt by the fact that one step-brother served as a general in the imperial army.

The potential for prestige, wealth, glamour or adventure as a military officer formed a heady brew in the years of imperial expansion and battlefield victories. But beyond the obvious potential for material and social rewards, an officer's career also entailed a morally attractive sense of discipline, service and sacrifice, all subsumed under the notion of 'honour', which Napoleon personally exalted.[12] Once, 'honour' had been the leading self-ascribed attribute and value of the aristocracy, but it was now a virtue accessible to any worthy son of France in the army. Young men who might never have thought for a moment of a military career before 1789 could easily be enticed by this career path in the Napoleonic years. The nostalgia of Stendhal for the excitement of the *Grande Armée* is only the most famous testimony to this outlook. After the demobilisations of 1814 and 1815, however, and with the Bourbon preference for old-line nobles in conferring new officer commissions, the military career must have lost this attraction, thereby creating a sharp discontinuity in elite ambitions that historians have yet to explore.

LOCAL ELITES: THE EMERGENCE OF
THE NOTABLES

The most well-studied social phenomena of the Napoleonic era, on the other hand, are surely the lists of *notables* compiled by the regime at various stages. At the outset, the Consulate wished to know who really counted in local society as reflected in how much individuals paid in property taxes. The government therefore requested lists of the 600 largest taxpayers in each department. Subsequently prefects were asked for more detailed profiles of the top names on these lists. Such information was vital for the regime in organising patronage and in trying to co-opt prominent individuals. Thus in June 1802, Roederer, a counsellor of state charged by Bonaparte with overseeing education and *esprit public* (public spirit), requested information from all prefects on the leading taxpayers of each district, and on the sixty *plus imposés* of each department. He wanted this information 'in order to establish certain ideas about the civil existence of the largest proprietors in the nation. Because it is they who, by the triple influence of example, discourse, and expenditures, determine (when times are calm) general opinions and dispositions.' While he claimed not to be asking about their political opinions, however, he cautioned the prefects 'that it would be wise to avoid any publicity getting out about your inquiry'.[13]

For the historian, the most useful source for studying the era's official elites is the membership lists, compiled in 1810, of the permanent electoral colleges established in each department and *arrondissement*. Ostensibly, these electoral colleges were to designate individuals from time to time for consideration by the Emperor for nomination to the Senate or by the Senate for appointment to the parliament. But this function was exercised only once every few years and entailed no real power to speak of. When it was a department's turn to propose two possible candidates for a Senate vacancy, the electoral college usually selected one local *notable* and one national *notable* who hailed from that department, since the regulations dictated that only one of the two nominees could himself be a member of the electoral college. After 1802, for each vacancy due to be filled by the Senate, Napoleon would choose only three names from the dozens of that year's departmental nominations, and forward them to the Senate for its final choice. Usually he chose individuals who had received the higher number of votes in an electoral college's choice of its two nominees, but not always. Thus in 1804 he recommended one of his favourites, Sémonville, currently an ambassador, who had received only 86 out of 163 votes cast in the electoral college of his native

Ardennes, while Bachiocchi, the president of the college, had received 146 out of 156 votes cast.[14] Besides making such nominations for final selection by the Senate, Napoleon was also empowered by the constitution of the life consulate to designate up to forty senators directly.

The electors were named by a convoluted system combining designation of some by cantonal assemblies of citizens and appointment of others by the regime. With exceptions, members of the departmental colleges were to be drawn from the 600 largest taxpayers, while those in the lesser *arrondissement* colleges need not be.[15] But if lifetime membership in an electoral college carried little actual political power, it was a definite honour, a badge of local status and recognition. In effect the state was saying: 'You are an important person in the eyes of the government.'

These lists of electors (totalling around 70,000) are replete with information about age, profession in 1789 and in 1810, and levels of landed income – ideal material for the kind of statistical analysis that was all the rage in French historiography of the 1960s. They are the point of departure for numerous monographs on local Napoleonic *notables*, and have been skilfully used for a provisional synthesis by Louis Bergeron and Guy Chaussinand-Nogaret. These historians describe the *notables* as the social 'granite masses' constituted by Napoleon alongside his institutional 'granite masses' – such creations as the prefectorial system, the Civil Code, the Bank of France and the centralised university, which all endured as foundations for nineteenth-century French society. Unlike such institutions, however, the Napoleonic *notables* do not reflect much in the way of creativity by the regime. Rather, these lists simply identify a durable post-revolutionary upper crust of local citizens whose prominence and wealth had developed before most had even heard of Napoleon Bonaparte.[16]

While the Napoleonic regime did create a new kind of titled elite at the national level, as we shall see, it did not, then, transform or create new elites at the local level. Instead it codified local elite status, and formally enshrined it in the electoral colleges. The government hoped to flatter these prominent local citizens into a harmonious relationship with the regime. It assumed that these *notables* had networks of dependants (tenants, employees, relatives and tradesmen) whom they could in turn influence favourably toward Napoleon. Large landed proprietors – including cultivators as well as those who owned but did not work the land themselves – naturally constituted the leading social category (see table 3.1). While acquisition of *biens nationaux* in the 1790s had consolidated the position of many such landowners, those were

Table 3.1 Known occupations of the *notables* in 1810 (63,683)[17]

Occupation	Percentage
Landed proprietors	24.6
Local administrators	18.1
State functionaries	15.8
Liberal professions	14.4
Commerce	10.8
Cultivators	8.2
Armed forces	2.3
Clergy	1.2

not necessarily the key element of their holdings. The ranks of local *notables* also included local officials, businessmen, professionals and high state functionaries who now resided in Paris. Under-represented were military officers and also what the French call *les talents*, including intellectuals, artists and the like. But the Legion of Honour had already been formed to honour deserving military officers as well as civilian state functionaries. To a certain extent the emergence of the Napoleonic *notables* realised the vision held by Sieyès and the liberal 'patriots' of 1789 that wealth and talent should take their place beside the inherited status of birth to constitute a new, open elite. This modern, progressive elite would leave behind the exclusivism, privilege and extreme social pretension that had bedevilled the late Ancien Regime, when the line separating the second and third estates had become extremely porous yet surprisingly tenacious. Along with state officials, members of the pre-revolutionary liberal professions turn up in appreciable numbers, most having survived the radical reorganisation and deregulation that briefly swept across the professions in the revolutionary decade.

The composite profile of these Napoleonic *notables* unmistakably reveals the over-riding importance of landed property, regardless of profession, in the configuration of the local post-revolutionary elites. The process of social selection or designation of these 70,000 local electors (who did very little in the way of electing) was narrow yet not really rigid. As Bergeron and Chaussinand-Nogaret conclude: 'within a system founded on the ease procured by the ownership of land [l'aisance que procure la terre], a large spectrum was present that did not exclude modest levels of wealth', and which went beyond the plutocracy of the 600 largest taxpayers in each department. 'It was a society of middle classes, a prefiguring of the Balzacian world . . .

which [however] embodied a disdain for the common people.' In the world of the local Napoleonic *notables*, wealth and property trumped other considerations, including traditional hierarchies of hereditary status and also sheer talent. 'The principle was simultaneously revolutionary and sterile. It precluded the reconstitution of a society of orders, but it held back, by its inertial force, the dynamic of ascent by means of hard work and merit.'[18]

A NEW NATIONAL ELITE: THE NAPOLEONIC NOBILITY

All Ancien Regime nobles lost their titles and their seigneurial rights during the Revolution, but those who survived the Terror without emigrating did not lose their land. Many laid low during the Revolution and had little reason to greet the Brumaire coup with any enthusiasm, no doubt seeing young Bonaparte as the leading general of a republic most of them despised. But the First Consul believed that the stability of post-revolutionary France required an accommodation of some sort with the former nobility. The Consulate therefore allowed the émigrés to return, provided that they renounced any overt opposition to the regime and any public gestures on behalf of the Bourbons. It was also made clear to them that if the property confiscated when they emigrated had already been sold (which was most often the case), the transfer was irrevocable. Gradually Napoleon won a grudging submission from many ex-nobles, whose names often filled the top ranks on the lists of the largest departmental taxpayers.[19] Later, after he ascended the imperial throne, Napoleon aggressively courted distinguished ex-noble families. He was particularly interested in employing the scions of families such as the Molés and the Pasquiers (renowned members of the old *parlementaire* or judicial nobility), who indeed entered his service as young men and rose meteorically to the highest levels of office.[20] At the same time Napoleon still depended on the administrative and legislative abilities of his original ex-revolutionary supporters, and his loyalty to them never flagged. Both tendencies were inscribed in the imperial nobility that he launched in 1808.

Proponents of the Napoleonic nobility depicted it as a codification of meritocracy, which fused the imperatives of service, wealth and social distinction, and was perfectly consistent with modern notions of equal opportunity. As Rafe Blaufarb reminds us, certain key Napoleonic officials had personally observed the conflicting claims of service versus wealth in the creation of new nobles during the late Ancien Regime. 'The central problem of elite formation [in the late Ancien Regime]', Blaufarb observes, 'was how to preserve the traditional value of service within a society where wealth was becoming increasingly important. . . . The solution [that the Empire] ultimately found, a nobility originating in service but perpetuated through wealth, was intended to . . . transcend the divisions which had shattered the unity of the Ancien Regime elites.'[21]

When Napoleon's right-hand man Cambacérès presented the legislation to the Senate in 1808 establishing new titles of duke, count, baron and chevalier of the Empire, he emphatically portrayed them as the reward for exceptional service:

> The pre-eminence that such an institution establishes, the ranks that it sets out, the memories that it transmits are the sustenance of honour. . . . Such titles will henceforth serve only to mark for public recognition those already noted for their services, for their devotion to the prince and the fatherland.[22]

Such titles, he added, were the best means 'to extirpate the last roots of a tree that the hand of time has toppled' – meaning the prestige of the old, presumably non-meritocratic, privileged nobility. Nor did this close off opportunity and recompense in the future: 'Careers still remain open to virtues and useful talents; the advantages that [the new titles] accord to proven merit are in no way inimical to merit as yet undemonstrated.'

Yet while these titles were personal in the first instance, they could become hereditary providing that the recipient guaranteed it by a *majorat* or entail, whose amount varied according to the title; in the Napoleonic social order no titles were transmissible without a guaranteed level of wealth to sustain their dignity. Moreover, the transmission to an heir could occur only if the proposed *majorat* was approved after close scrutiny by the Conseil des Sceau des Titres chaired by Arch-Chancellor Cambacérès. It seemed vital to avoid the presence of poor nobles that plagued such European societies in the Ancien Regime as Spain and Hungary, as well as France itself. Although the term 'nobility' was not formally used to describe the Napoleonic titles, the accompanying certification of a coat of arms testified that the Emperor was indeed creating a new nobility.[23]

In 1808 Napoleon bestowed 740 titles. After this first promotion of his veteran collaborators, the Emperor granted hundreds of new titles each year, with a peak of 1,085 in 1810. By 1814, 3,263 citizens across the Empire had received titles. The lion's share of 59 per cent went to military men; 22 per cent went to high functionaries such as prefects, senators, counsellors of state and bishops, while men of achievement in the arts or in business had scant representation. Napoleon's attempt to woo families from the old-regime nobility bore some success, and 22 per cent of all the new titles went to such old names. But, as historian Jean Tulard argues in his comprehensive study of the Napoleonic nobility, this new emphasis did not quite bear the fruit that Napoleon had wished. Many old families refused to rally, no matter what the inducements, and among those that did bend their knee, many did so for opportunistic reasons combined perhaps with a sense of duty to France that implied no serious loyalty to the new dynasty. [24]

At the pinnacle of the new nobility stood a small number of princes and dukes (only 34 altogether at the end of the Empire) drawn from a handful of early imperial dignitaries such as Napoleon's brothers Joseph and Louis; his brother-in-law Murat; the former Second and Third Consuls, Cambacérès and Lebrun; long-serving ministers like Talleyrand, Fouché, Gaudin and Regnier; and twenty marshals.[25] Between these grandees and the lesser categories of barons and chevaliers of the Empire came the counts. This prestigious title went not only to a host of favoured generals and virtually all senators but to the long-term members of the Council of State, some twenty-five in number by 1808, including not only former republicans but even regicides such as Berlier, Merlin de Douai and Thibaudeau. These prominent ex-revolutionaries were now to be addressed as 'count', with the possibility of arranging for the hereditary transmission of their titles to their eldest sons.

This was an odd state of affairs for men who had helped abolish all noble titles in the National Assembly or who treated former nobles with hostility later in the decade. The former regicide member of the Convention, now counsellor of state, Théophile Berlier reflected wryly on his experience in his memoirs:

> What a singular destiny was mine! In 1802 I had combatted the establishment of the Legion of Honour; and when it became law I was called to become part of it with the rank of commander. [Then in 1808] I found myself enrolled in a new nobility by virtue of the functions that I exercised [in the Council of State]![26]

Everything changed around him, he continued uneasily, 'and, caught up in the general movement, I yielded to it, but without renouncing either the liberal ideas that remained compatible with the new institutions or my [previous] amicable relations'.

As if the title of count were not discomfiting enough, Berlier faced the question of establishing the *majorat* or entail required for transmitting the title to his son. He did not have the resources to establish a *majorat* that would 'favour one of my children to the prejudice of the others', he recalled, and would have been disinclined to do so out of principle even if he had been wealthy enough. For the former deputy to the Convention, the ground-breaking equal inheritance law of 1793 was an article of faith, notwithstanding the restoration of a limited testamentary discretion to fathers in the Napoleonic Civil Code (see below). But Napoleon understood the problem faced by the likes of Berlier and he solved it 'by personally providing to [certain] title holders the capital necessary to establish their *majorats* from the immense reservoir of his *domaine extraordinaire*'. From the far corners of the Empire Berlier received an endowment (*dotation*) that comprised assets in Swedish Pomerania producing an estimated 10,000 francs annually; mines, foundries, *rentes* and rural properties in the Illyrian provinces yielding 4,000 francs a year; and four shares in the Canal du Midi paying 2,000 francs.[27]

FORMING THE NEXT GENERATION OF SERVITORS

Back in 1804, as Napoleon prepared to assume the imperial throne, his servitor P.-L. Roederer had urged him to make the Senate a hereditary body as well. This, he believed, would establish a future phalanx of loyalists rooted in the families of his original collaborators.[28] Napoleon had disdainfully spurned this advice. And when the Emperor established a new hierarchy of inheritable titles in 1808, which initially favoured those present at the creation of the regime, he was certainly not creating the hereditary body that Roederer advocated, nor did he share the senator's belief that the original men of Brumaire promised the highest order of loyalty compared to the newcomers who would inevitably join their ranks in the future. On the contrary, with a misplaced confidence, Napoleon now actively courted new collaborators among the aristocratic families of the old regime and, as we have seen, 22 per cent of the Napoleonic nobility came from their ranks. But the Emperor's highest priority was to nurture a future generation of high-ranking servitors.[29] Although he remained comfortable with the men of Brumaire and the Consulate, he relished the prospect of moulding young men in the 'school of the Empire', men relatively free of nostalgia for either the Ancien Regime or the Revolution. The corps of *auditeurs* in the Council of State would be his principal instrument.

Conceived more modestly by Second Consul Cambacérès in 1803, the *auditeurs* were meant to provide assistance to an overburdened Council of State and government ministries, and to train young men for high administrative careers in the future. 'From another perspective', Cambacérès added in his unpublished memoirs, 'those same personages [i.e. current high-level officials] rightly ask that a career be opened for those of their children whom they destine for the civil order. . . . Bonaparte saw in this a means of founding a school in which future magistrates could be formed, just as generals are formed in the military schools.' Practical administrative needs, training and nepotism all entered into the original conception of this new position, which began informally with a mere sixteen young men. Gradually, however, the *auditeurs* grew into a veritable corps, numbering 400 by 1809.[30]

> The purpose of the institution (Napoleon explained to the Council of State in that year) is to bring under the Emperor's wing men of the elite who are sincerely devoted to him, who have sworn an oath between his hands, whom he will observe closely enough to appreciate their zeal and their talents. They will be formed, so to speak, in his school, and he will be able to employ them wherever the needs of his service will make them useful. From this will emerge veritable magistrates and administrators. . . . His Majesty's intention is [also] that the *auditeurs* be received at court, so that if they are on the one hand trained in work, they will on the other hand develop urbanity, the good taste and usages of society, which will be necessary in the places where they might be assigned.[31]

As initial hurdles for consideration at this juncture, candidates had to meet two formal qualifications. First, they had to prove that they had satisfied the conscription laws. Like prospective state-certified attorneys (*avoués*) who faced the same requirement, the vast majority did so without actually having served in the army. Either they were not called, having drawn a low number in the lottery for their local contingent that placed them outside its quota, or (at considerable expense) their family had hired a replacement when they had drawn a high number. Second, aspirants for the post of *auditeur* had to demonstrate that they commanded a minimum income of 6,000 francs annually. A third condition, starting in 1812, would require a university degree in law or science.[32]

For a sample group of 120 candidates from 1809, the dossiers included comments on the status of the candidates' families (some from 'revolutionary' families, more from old-line families); the full extent of the family's property; and recommendations by highly placed persons – including in some cases ministers, generals, senators or counsellors of state. Often the local prefect and mayor lent their support as witnesses for the notarised documents submitted for the dossier. Some candidates had to cobble together the capital for a 6,000-franc annual income, but most of the aspirants, typically in their mid-20s, already possessed substantial wealth. Families usually met the income qualification by settling property on a younger child earlier than usual, but some older children had already become family heirs. In either case these families usually ranked among the 600 highest taxpayers in their department.

Real property – that marker of both wealth and status – was the *sine qua non* for entry to this corps of *auditeurs*, but family reputation counted heavily as well.[33]

The corps was intended as the seed-bed for second-generation civilian servitors of the Empire, and candidates were screened by experienced officials before winning an appointment. Most spent a probationary period seconded to a section of the Council of State or a government ministry, and some occasionally served as couriers over the vast distances between Paris and the Emperor's camp when he was out on campaign. After passing muster in their apprenticeship, *auditeurs* would usually reach the next rung as sub-prefects, ministerial functionaries or aides in the satellite kingdoms. From there they could aspire to appointment as *maîtres de réquêtes* (associates) in the Council of State, and finally as prefects.

LEGAL CODIFICATION

Looking back during his exile on St Helena, Napoleon considered his role as lawmaker to be the most durable element of his legacy. (Waterloo, he expected, would efface the renown of his numerous military victories and conquests.) As a lawmaker he was joined at the hip to his hand-picked Council of State, comprised in the main of lawyers, judges, administrators and legislators whose careers extended back to the Ancien Regime and through the Revolution. From different positions on the political spectrum, they combined learning, practical experience and dedication to public service. The Council of State drafted the government's laws and decrees at Napoleon's behest, reviewed countless administrative matters, and scrutinised all local initiatives originating in towns and villages. Its most significant mission, however, was the work of legal codification.

Napoleon intended to consummate a project begun without success no fewer than three times during the revolutionary decade. The challenge was to integrate and unify the multiple bodies of extant legal doctrine: the Ancien Regime's various systems of customary law, found primarily in northern France; the traditional written-law system based on Roman models operative in the south during the Ancien Regime; and finally the mass of legislation passed helter-skelter by the National Assembly, the National Convention and the directorial legislatures. Napoleon shared the French Revolution's vision of national uniformity and integration. France (and later the Empire) must have a single, consistent body of legal doctrine – a systematic legal code or, as it was known, a civil code.[34]

During his first year in power Bonaparte began this monumental task by appointing a four-man committee of legal experts to sift previous attempts at codification, and to propose a preliminary outline for a new code. After review by the country's leading magistrates and revision by committees in the Council of State, drafts of various sections went before the full Council of State for final debate. Bonaparte presided over 57 of 102 such plenary sessions himself, the others being led by Second Consul Cambacérès, who had attempted the same task during the Convention. Napoleon proved a quick study, participated actively in the debates, and on certain issues insistently pressed his generally conservative positions. More important, he energised the whole process, and demanded that contentious issues be resolved despite the propensity of his legal experts to debate indefinitely. For the social development of France, no undertaking of the regime was more important than the 2,281 articles of the Civil Code. Its last sections were approved by the legislature in 1804 and in 1807 it was rebaptised as *Le Code Napoléon*.

While Napoleon's Concordat with the papacy restored the main features of traditional religious life in France, the Civil Code ratified the Revolution's secularisation of civil identity by vesting state officials rather than the clergy with keeping records of births, deaths and marriages – known in France as the *état civil*. The code also spelled out definitions of citizenship and how foreigners might attain it. Much of the code concerned property relations and contracts. The code reflected the abolition of all aspects of seigneurialism, and provided instead for contractual relations that did not depend on social status. Landowning peasants particularly valued the assertion in article 544 of 'the right to enjoy and dispose of property in the most absolute fashion, provided that one does not engage in usages prohibited by law'. Workers, on the other hand, found that doctrines of economic individualism deprived them of the freedom to form trade unions or to strike, while authorising employers to demand labour passports (*livrets*) that gave them substantial leverage over the movement of workers. In support of private transactions that individuals might wish to make, but whose details the nation's laws could not anticipate, the code stipulated that private contracts freely engaged would have the same standing as formal law.

The thorniest issues faced by the drafters centred on the family. Here the pull of tradition and the diversity of customary practices ran headlong into the Revolution's sweeping assertion of individual rights and equality within the family. By 1800 there was a consensus that the Revolution had gone too far in that direction. Napoleon and most of his counsellors viewed the traditional patriarchal family more favourably. They deplored the atomisation of family relations under the Revolution's egalitarian doctrine, which undercut both traditional emotional bonds and economic arrangements. The Civil Code therefore restored the patriarchal authority of the head of the family – the husband and father. In the process wives lost almost all the rights they had gained during the Revolution to control their own property, to share in control of communal property, to enter contracts and to testify in court. In short, they were subordinated to the control of their husbands legally and economically. Children up to the age of 25 were also subjected to stringent paternal discipline and authority. As for illegitimate children, who had been granted virtually equal rights to consideration and property by revolutionary legislation, the code stripped them of these rights and returned them to their dispossessed status – a poignant case of how revolutionary idealism could not survive this backlash of traditional values.[35]

The Revolution's most striking innovations in family relations concerned inheritance and divorce. Under the inheritance law of the National Convention, each child, male or female, was entitled to an equal share of the family estate, leaving the father virtually no discretion in the matter. The arguments in favour of such equality were compelling, but the disruption of customary arrangements touched off by equal inheritance (especially since it was made retroactive) produced a good deal of contention, litigation and complaint. During the Directory certain legislators already began to argue that the father's discretion and leverage over his children would serve their collective interest as an ongoing unit. The Civil Code restored a degree of testamentary discretion to the father, while still maintaining the right of each child to a portion of the estate. It should be noted, however, that regardless of what the law dictated, whether in 1793 or 1804, families could still follow traditional practices that favoured eldest sons by means of various sub-terfuges, although the law now made it possible to contest such arrangements when one of the parties felt sufficiently aggrieved.[36]

The Revolution's radical divorce legislation of 1792 derived from the view that marriage should not be regarded as a Catholic sacrament, unbreakable to the end of one's days, but simply as a contract freely entered into by a man and woman, who were therefore free to terminate their arrangement either by mutual consent or for cause. The list of possible causes, including incompatibility as well as abandonment or physical abuse, made divorce quite easy[37] – far too easy, in the view of more conservative opinion, including that of Napoleon, who considered easy divorce a corrosive practice that undermined the family. The Council of State did not have a religious interest in reverting to a blanket prohibition of divorce, such as occurred under church auspices after 1815, but it did wish to curtail divorce drastically, particularly on the part of women. As a result, an extraordinary double standard found its way into the Civil Code (articles 229 and 230) over the question of divorce for cause: 'The husband may demand a divorce on the ground of his wife's adultery. The wife may demand divorce on the ground of adultery in her husband, [only] when he shall have brought his concubine into their common residence.'

The Civil Code was only one of six codes that the Council of State hoped to produce, although by far the most important. It was followed by the new Penal Code, which echoed the revolutionary penal code of 1791 in maintaining capital punishment and long prison sentences with hard labour. Then came the companion Code of Criminal Procedure, which retained revolutionary innovations such as the right to defence counsel and trial by jury of felonies, but scaled back their latitude and put more discretion into the hands of prosecutors and judges. The Code of Civil Procedure represented yet another melding of revolutionary innovation and Ancien Regime practice. Among other things it restored some of the procedural complexities of civil trials that revolutionary legislation had eliminated, and made the services of an attorney once again obligatory for a civil litigant. But the new codes maintained the most popular judicial innovation of the Revolution – the *juge de paix* or justice of the peace, who brought expeditious and inexpensive dispute resolution to town and country, particularly by offering mediation in place of costly formal litigation.[38]

After considerable labour, the Council of State also produced the Commercial Code to deal with issues such as credit instruments, bankruptcy law, imprisonment for debt and dispute resolution among merchants through special commercial tribunals.[39] The government hoped to achieve the same type of codification for the special needs of rural society – to create systematic and uniform rules that would govern the details of husbandry and agrarian life in all regions. But the Napoleonic regime could not complete the Rural Code. The officials who worked on it were stymied by the enormous variety of local practice, and by the impossibility of imposing individualist doctrine on the collective practices of French cultivators, such as their use of village common land and communal grazing on harvested fields (vacant pasture). With good reason, one historian has referred to this project as 'the impossible code'.[40] Indeed, the Empire's failure to produce a definitive rural code is an apt note on which to conclude this chapter, since it underscores the limits of what any regime could hope to do in shaping, let alone transforming, *la France profonde*.

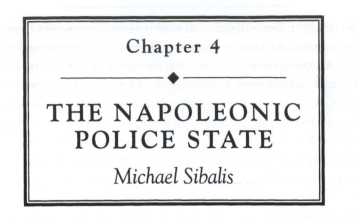

Chapter 4

♦

THE NAPOLEONIC POLICE STATE

Michael Sibalis

Napoleon's France was a police state. Of course, it cannot compare for ruthlessness and horror with twentieth-century police states, like Stalin's Soviet Union, Hitler's Germany or even Pinochet's Chile. No jack-booted policemen broke down doors in the middle of the night to haul people off to concentration camps; the army did not 'disappear' political opponents by kidnapping, torturing and killing them in secret; in short, terror was never a tool of Napoleonic government. Napoleon's police nevertheless did exercise tight control over all public expressions of opinion, did pay a network of secret agents to keep the nation under surveillance, and did detain the regime's enemies in special state prisons without charge or trial. In short, they regularly ignored proper judicial procedures and systematically violated the civil rights that the French Revolution had proclaimed with such high hopes in 1789 to end centuries of so-called 'monarchical despotism'.

Howard Brown, seeking to avoid 'the exaggerated connotations of "police state"', has recently coined the phrase *liberal authoritarianism* for regimes like Napoleon's, in which 'hard-won civil and political rights would not stand in the way of preserving the social order in time of crisis', but in which a liberal legal system placed some (albeit in reality few) limits on the police apparatus. Brown prefers to call Napoleonic France a *security state*, 'because [security state] emphasises the importance of surveillance and regulatory control in maintaining public order, rather than the use of coercive force to restore it'. The term also emphasises one of the principal justifications for the regime: the maintenance of political and social order after a decade of revolutionary

upheaval.[1] Despite Brown's well-founded reservations, however, *police state* is too much a part of our daily language to discard quite so readily. Moreover, it underlines the power and influence that the Minister of General Police exercised in the day-to-day workings of the Napoleonic government.

THE MINISTRY OF POLICE

Charles-Maurice de Talleyrand, Napoleon's Minister for Foreign Affairs, once quipped that 'a Minister of Police is a man who minds his own business and then minds other people's'.[2] Two such busybodies served Napoleon during his fifteen years in power. The first of them, Joseph Fouché (1759–1820), had been an Oratorian monk and then a Jacobin deputy to the National Convention (1792–95). When the Directory named him Minister of General Police in July 1799, he was the ninth man to hold the office since the creation of the police ministry three and a half years earlier in January 1796 'in order to ensure the execution of the laws relative to the general police, the security and the internal peace of the Republic'. Fouché immediately betrayed the Directory by supporting Napoleon's coup d'état in November 1799. Except for a nineteen-month interval during which Napoleon, having temporarily abolished the police ministry, transferred its responsibilities to the Ministry of Justice (September 1802–June 1804), Fouché held the office until June 1810, when his independent spirit and political intrigues finally lost him the Emperor's confidence.[3] Fouché has left behind an infamous (and certainly exaggerated) reputation 'as the clever, cunning, infinitely intelligent and suave police minister, the begetter of the modern police system, and the father of the Gestapo [of Nazi Germany]'.[4] His successor was Anne-Jean-Marie-René Savary (1774–1833), duke of Rovigo, a career cavalry officer and former commander of Napoleon's personal guard.[5] People feared yet admired Fouché; they merely despised Savary as an unimaginative and unscrupulous toady who was totally subservient to the Emperor. Napoleon reappointed Fouché during the Hundred Days in the spring of 1815, which gave the inveterate conspirator the opportunity to engineer the return of Louis XVIII after Napoleon's defeat at Waterloo.

The Minister of General Police had under his orders a large and experienced body of civil servants headquartered on the Quai Malaquais, just across the river Seine from the Louvre.[6] In 1813, the ministerial staff numbered 124 men with total annual salaries of about 360,000 francs. The general secretary earned 22,700 francs a year; the most junior clerk a mere 300. Forty per cent of the ministry's employees already worked there before Napoleon's

coup d'état.[7] Here as elsewhere, then, the Napoleonic government used a bureaucratic machine largely inherited from the Directory (1795–99), although in this instance one reorganised and perfected by Fouché. The prefects, sub-prefects and mayors exercised police functions in their departments and communes under the supervision of the police ministry. In addition, the ministry appointed general police commissioners in the most important or strategically located cities – twenty of them by 1810. Most towns and cities, too, had local police commissioners who reported to the mayor. In Paris there were forty-eight police commissioners, one for each quarter of the city, under the prefect of police. In some sense, then, the entire state bureaucracy worked directly or indirectly for the Ministry of General Police. As the prefect of the Gers explained in a circular to the officials in his department: 'The police should know everything and be acquainted with everything. Consequently, it is from you that it expects information and news, because you are its vigilant sentinels.'[8]

To facilitate policing, the Ministry of General Police divided the entire French Empire into four police districts in 1804. The first district, the largest and most important, comprised northern, western and part of eastern France. The second district encompassed the south and part of the east. The Empire's Italian departments made up the third district. The three councillors of state placed in charge of these first three districts – respectively, Pierre-François Réal (1757–1834), Jean Pelet de la Lozère (1759–1852) and Jules-Jean-Baptiste Anglès (1778–1828) – had offices at the ministry and worked under the eye of the minister. Things were different for the fourth district: Paris and its suburbs. Because of the capital's immense political importance, the decree of 16 February 1800 endowed it with a prefecture of police, an autonomous bureaucracy on the rue de Jerusalem in central Paris headed by a prefect of police. Although nominally subordinate to the Minister of General Police, the prefect – Louis-Nicolas Dubois (1758–1847) from March 1800 to October 1810, Etienne-Denis Pasquier (1767–1862) from October 1810 to May 1814, and Pierre-François Réal during the Hundred Days – enjoyed considerable independence from his nominal superior and reported directly to Napoleon. He therefore tended to be the minister's bureaucratic rival and a politically useful check on his power.[9]

The primary purpose of the Ministry of General Police was the maintenance of public and political order by repressing crime and protecting the government against subversion. This implied much more than merely enforcing the law. Fouché explained his broad conception of policing in a letter written to Napoleon in 1799: 'The police, as I see it, ought to be established to forestall and prevent crime, to restrain and stop what the laws have not foreseen. It is a *discretionary* authority in the government's hands.'[10] In other words, the police should take preventive measures against anticipated problems at the sole discretion of the government, even in instances where the law happened to be silent.

REPRESSION AND SURVEILLANCE

Fouché once reportedly remarked: 'There are three sorts of conspiracies: by the people who complain, by the people who write, by the people who take action. There is nothing to fear from the first group, [but] the two others are more dangerous.'[11] This was a very loose definition of conspiracy indeed. In fact, as we shall see, the police were always very much concerned about people who complained and assiduously maintained a close watch on every manifestation of public opinion. As for those who wrote, the Ministry of General Police exercised tight censorship over every kind of publication, including books and especially newspapers, even after the government created a distinct national agency to regulate publishers in 1810. As Napoleon declared shortly after he came to power, 'If I gave the press free rein, I would not stay in power for three months.'[12]

By people who took action, Fouché meant principally those who plotted against the government or engaged in brigandage. Over the years there were quite a number of plots to overthrow the government by republican militants or by royalists who regretted the toppling of the Bourbon dynasty in 1792, and sometimes, rather bizarrely, by both groups working together. There was a series of mostly minor attempts to assassinate Napoleon in 1800–1801, but which included the almost successful attempt to blow him up with a bomb placed in a cart on the Rue Saint-Nicaise on Christmas Eve 1800. There were conspiracies like the 'Conspiracy of the Butter Pots' or 'Conspiracy of the Lampoons' in 1802, when republican army officers in Rouen distributed across France pamphlets attacking Napoleon; the Cadoudal conspiracy to kidnap or kill Napoleon in 1804; the two Malet conspiracies of 1808 and 1812 (in the latter instance, General Claude-François Malet almost pulled off a coup d'état in Paris while Napoleon was campaigning in Russia); and the 'Conspiracy of the Midi' (1809–13), involving efforts to raise a popular insurrection in southern France.[13] There was also the permanent threat from fanatical lone assassins. On the whole, the police proved adept at snuffing out plots and protecting Napoleon's life, although their spectacular failure to anticipate and prevent Malet's coup d'état raised some doubts as to their capabilities and competence. (In the aftermath Parisian wits joked: 'Have you heard anything? No? Then you must be a policeman.')

Brigandage, which combined criminal motives with political discontent, was a serious and endemic problem for the regime down to 1814, but particularly acute in the first years of the Consulate. Armed bands of brigands roamed the countryside in the north, west and especially the south, preying on travellers, isolated farmhouses and in particular mail coaches transporting government funds. Many bands were made up of royalist sympathisers, while others recruited draft dodgers who had taken to the hills to avoid serving in Napoleon's armies. In the recently annexed region around Nice, the *barbets*, inspired by both hatred of the French conquerors and social grievances, attacked representatives of the French state as well as local landowners.[14]

But any regime, no matter how democratic and how committed to civil rights, would have had to repress conspiracy and brigandage. The true measure of a police state is its surveillance of its citizens and the way in which it manages peaceful political dissent. One can get some idea of the extent of police surveillance under Napoleon from the 'police bulletins' that the Emperor received daily from 1804 to 1814, whether he was in France or abroad on campaign. These summarised the information gathered by the Ministry of General Police from across the Empire. In the words of one of their modern editors (they are still in the course of publication), the police bulletins kept Napoleon abreast of:

> society in general and public opinion (festivities, social gatherings, marriages, entertainment, public and private educational establishments), the maintenance of order (rumours, strikes, riots, acts of rebellion, brigandage, measures of the superior police), religious police (relations with the Sovereign Pontiff, measures taken against refractory clergy and Catholic priests, surveillance of pilgrimages, sermons and spiritual retreats), the struggle against smuggling, the analysis of intercepted correspondence.[15]

Moreover, the Ministry of General Police was only one, though by far the most important, of France's police forces. Napoleon could also count on his personal palace guard; the military police; and the gendarmerie, a semi-military police force that took its orders from the Minister of War. The gendarmerie comprised 16,000 to 20,000 gendarmes (often former soldiers), stationed in small groups throughout the countryside, who enforced the law in rural communities. Napoleon called them 'the elite of the army, to which I owe the re-establishment of order in France' and rather ungratefully told Fouché, 'It is only by [the gendarmerie] that I am informed accurately and clearly of what is going on in France.' Rivalry among all these police forces undoubtedly hindered their efficiency, as both Fouché at the police ministry and Pasquier at the prefecture of police observed in their memoirs. Fouché wrote that 'the Machiavellian maxim "divide and rule" having prevailed, there were soon four distinct police agencies; . . . I was nothing more than a counter-balance in the government machine', while Pasquier complained that 'one of the greatest difficulties that I had to overcome derived from the perpetual supervision [of France] by five or six police forces, several of which worked and acted in rivalry with the others'. In addition, Napoleon privately salaried several informants to send him confidential reports on the state of public opinion, while the 'dark chamber' (*cabinet noir*) run by General Lavallette at the post office opened, read and resealed every year thousands of letters, including those written by Napoleon's ministers and family.[16]

THE SURVEILLANCE OF PUBLIC OPINION

When Admiral Decrès, Minister of the Navy, once entertained Fouché at dinner, his guest remarked that the admiral employed an extraordinary number of servants. 'I can afford to have many, my dear sir,' Decrès supposedly replied, 'I don't pay them, because it seems that you do.'[17] This anecdote testifies to the widespread belief at the time that the Ministry of General Police had its spies everywhere, even (and perhaps especially) among one's own domestic servants. Fouché thought this a politically useful fear, and actually boasted in his memoirs (published in 1824) that 'I was certainly shrewd to spread it about and have people believe that wherever four people met together, there were present and in my pay eyes to see and ears to hear.' Yet anxious at the same time to escape any blame for the system, Fouché nevertheless criticised 'these paid informers' as unreliable and added: 'This odious and secret militia was inherent to the system put in place and maintained by perhaps the most easily offended and most mistrustful man who ever lived,' by which, of course, he meant not himself, but Napoleon.[18]

Secret agents are essential to any effective police state. 'It's . . . by means of secret agents that the administration is informed accurately of everything touching on state security and public opinion,' wrote the prefect of the Aude in 1806. 'A warning given and received in time can sometimes destroy a plot or prevent great misfortunes, crimes and misdemeanours.'[19] The police also used a number of unpaid informers, who denounced others to curry favour with the authorities or out of gratitude to the regime, like one 59-year-old former army officer, who wrote to the police in 1804:

> As I see a lot of people, I can sometimes provide you with information with no other
> motive than my gratitude toward His Imperial Majesty who, since he so gloriously

took hold of the reins of government, has provided honest people with peace of body and mind and paid on time bond-holders and pensioners, of which I am one.[20]

In general, however, as one departmental prefect explained in 1813, 'as far as policing is concerned, I need zealous, intelligent and loyal scouts, whom one can procure only by paying'.[21]

The funds for secret agents available from the Ministry of General Police always fell short of demand and the prefects sometimes reached into their own pockets to find the necessary money. Especially in the final years of the Empire, when public dissatisfaction was on the rise, the prefects repeatedly asked the police ministry for more funding for their agents, while the ministry, hit by budget cuts – which in 1811 limited its total expenditure for secret police to 75,000 francs for all of France – either refused them outright or gave them only partial satisfaction. For instance, the prefect of the Seine-et-Oise received only 500 francs to spend on the secret police for all of 1813; his predecessor had received 2,000 francs for 1802, at a time when he claimed to need 6,000 francs.[22]

Officials employed secret agents on a wide variety of tasks in their fight against criminality, espionage and dissent. According to the prefect of the Loiret in 1811, 'The secret police is necessary everywhere; and especially in a large city [like Orléans], within easy reach of the capital, where consequently vagrants, suspects, intriguers and swindlers abound more than elsewhere.'[23] In 1804 the police of Toulon wanted to hire a secret agent at 200 francs a month to watch the Mediterranean coast between Toulon and Antibes for English spies.[24] In 1812 the prefect of the Puy-de-Dôme in central France had his agents track false rumours and 'bad opinions' propagated by travellers from the south or from nearby Lyons who crossed the region,[25] while the prefect of the Isère in the south-east used his to combat brigandage in this mountainous district.[26] The prefect of the Doubs in eastern France put secret agents on the border to intercept smugglers in 1809. In 1812 this same prefect observed that the high grain prices threatened to provoke disturbances and that 'one of the surest means of preventing disorder is to establish in advance a precise surveillance of those unruly or ill-intentioned individuals who are always ready to incite trouble'. He assigned agents to follow such men about and to take down what they said, 'so that at the first signal [for revolt], they can be immediately arrested and handed over to the courts'.[27] In 1813 the prefect of the Meurthe in eastern France paid a secret agent 50 francs a month to attend meetings of the recruitment councils: 'This man, mingling with the crowd, listens to and reports on everything that is said and tries to observe whether there is not some ploy being used to incite the conscripts or the National Guards to disobedience.' On other days, 'this man's assignment is to scour the public squares, market-places, cabarets and everywhere that the people gather in order also to give an account of public opinion manifested there, conversations that take place there, &c'.[28]

Listening in on conversations in cafés and taverns was one of the key missions entrusted to secret agents. For example, one agent frequented the Tour d'Argent on the rue de la Ferronerie in Paris 'at various times' in late February and early March 1807 and turned in reports on what the porters, cabbies and market-women were saying there: 'the conversations were trivial, a few complaints about the inactivity of commerce; but no remarks were heard that indicated malevolence'.[29] The police also expected café owners to spy on customers. In November 1810, a police commissioner warned the owners of the fashionable cafés along the boulevard des Italiens in Paris that 'false and alarming news ... was originating in their cafés' and that they 'had the greatest interest' in reporting the guilty parties ('I instructed them to exercise there, and to have exercised by waiters whom they can trust, a surveillance such that they might hear all the remarks and speeches intended to circulate among the public rumours that are alarming, danger-ous and likely to undermine the obedience and respect owed to the govern-ment'); otherwise, he threatened, he would close their establishments. The situation was similar in the provinces. In 1804 the prefect shut down a café in Sancerre after a drunken customer criticised the government and declared 'that he didn't give a damn ... about Emperor Bonaparte', because the owner 'did not oppose the indecent remarks ... and did not silence the [customer]'. The mayor of Nîmes closed three cafés for similar reasons in June 1809: 'I thought that ... the regular customers would thereby be punished and that fear would make them more circumspect.' He promised to reopen the cafés if and when the owners agreed to inform on their customers.[30]

As their use of spies demonstrates, the police were always on the look-out for expressions of hostility to the regime. What they called 'seditious words' were in fact quite common, especially by men or women who had been drinking in taverns or cafés, whether motivated politically by royalism or republicanism or more simply by anger at conscription, high taxes and eco-nomic crisis. Most offenders claimed afterwards that they had been too drunk to remember what they had said, but this could not attenuate guilt in the eyes of the police: 'it can be presumed that at such time words are an expression of the heart; [when drunk] one speaks the way one thinks'.[31]

Nevertheless, the authorities were usually careful not to over-react. They sometimes did no more than issue a warning to be more discreet in the future; occasionally they imprisoned offenders for a few weeks or exiled them to another town. For example, in a café in Metz in 1809, a disabled ex-soldier 'spoke with contempt of the glory of our armies, with regret of the Bourbons, with outrage of the Emperor, and carried his indignation to the point of spitting on a snuffbox . . . on which was embossed the Emperor's portrait'. The prefect incarcerated him for three months.[32]

In contrast, it was virtually impossible to discover and punish the authors of the 'incendiary posters' stuck up at night on buildings in city and town or on trees along country roads; sometimes, too, malcontents chalked or painted their hostile comments on a handy wall. Police files hold hundreds of examples of such acts of defiance against the regime. In August 1806 a crudely written poster in Limoges called for popular insurrection: 'People, rise up against the tyrant; it is not a crime.' In October 1810 someone in Marseilles – tired of war, a stagnant economy and unemployment – posted 'a small piece of paper' on a tree in a public square: 'Long live peace, give us bread, open the port.' Early one morning in October 1813, the police commissioner for Nantes found the following scrawled with charcoal on the wall of a public garden: 'Cowardly French Senate, are you still supporting the plans of that monster Bonaparte?'[33]

The authorities also tracked the spread of rumours, which were good indicators of public concerns and worries. They either blamed rumours on the 'malevolence' of the regime's opponents or on English agents, or more usually attributed them to the French people's 'imbecility', 'credulity', 'ignorance' or 'fear'. As the general police commissioner for Marseilles wrote in October 1800, 'There is no foolishness that the idlers in a big city do not make up, there are no absurd tales that people in the cafés don't listen to, and the police must hear everything, while to a certain extent appearing not to do so.'[34] From time to time persistent rumours circulated of military defeat or foreign invasion, new (and higher) taxes, an impending devaluation of coinage or the printing of paper money (in disrepute ever since the paper *assignats* of the French Revolution fuelled hyper-inflation in the 1790s), rural or urban insurrections, a new and heavier levy of men for the army, an assassination attempt against the Emperor, sometimes even his death. False news of this kind – brought by strangers passing through town, village or countryside and then diffused by gossip in cafés and market-places – threatened to undermine public confidence in a 'beloved sovereign' and his government. Local officials therefore spent a great deal of time and effort recording these stories, which they scrupulously reported to Paris, and trying (almost always unsuccessfully) to discover their source.

The police also kept an eye on theatrical productions. They banned plays on controversial subjects and worried about audience reaction at performances. In December 1804, for example, the Ministry of General Police instructed the prefect to forbid a second performance in Angers of a play about Henry IV, founder of the Bourbon dynasty, because it threatened 'to rekindle Bourbon fanaticism at the moment that the will of the nation has just established a new dynasty'. And in July 1812, during Napoleon's invasion of Russia, the ministry banned three plays about Russia 'and any other work that might contain passages favourable to Russia or its rulers'.[35] Audiences, moreover, often expressed their political opinions by means of their applause. For instance, in 1809 in Bordeaux (a port city whose overseas trade was hard hit by the Napoleonic wars), the police noted that the spectators at *Mohammed* showed far too much enthusiasm in applauding the lines: 'Great God, wipe off the earth's face/Whoever delights to spill the blood of the human race.'[36]

REPRESSING DISSIDENTS

If arrested by the police, a political dissident faced any one of a number of possible punishments. The most dangerous conspirators – those who tried to assassinate Napoleon (like Cadoudal in 1804) or to overthrow him in a coup d'état (like Malet in 1812) – could expect a trial or court martial, usually followed by execution by guillotine or firing squad, along with their leading accomplices. In some cases, however, Napoleon pardoned men implicated in conspiracies against him (especially those of aristocratic birth), but that generally meant incarceration in a state prison until the regime collapsed in 1814.

Otherwise, the best-known victims of political repression in Napoleonic France are probably the deportees of the Year IX (1800–1801). After a particularly bloody attempt on Napoleon's life on Christmas Eve 1800, when a bomb placed in the open street missed its target but killed several bystanders, the government blamed republican conspirators and rounded up a large number of former revolutionary militants. On 4 January 1801, the Senate voted a decree of deportation against 130 of these men and the authorities eventually shipped 94 overseas to the Seychelles Islands in the Indian Ocean or to Cayenne in South America, where almost all of them eventually died. Although Fouché proved shortly after the arrests that royalists had in fact planted the bomb, the deportations went ahead anyway.[37] It was a clear signal of the regime's determination not only to punish actual conspirators, but to purge the nation of any potential political threat.

With deportations difficult in later years, because Britain controlled the seas, the government turned to state prisons and internal exile to manage dissent. The police held political opponents (and even certain suspected criminals) in prison for an indefinite term by an 'act of the superior police' (*mesure de haute police*), a simple order emanating from or approved by the Minister of General Police. Technically illegal, because the Constitution of 1804 required the release of even suspected conspirators after ten days unless the government laid charges and sent them to trial, this practice recalled the infamous *lettres de cachet* of pre-revolutionary France, by which the government exiled or incarcerated people at 'the king's pleasure'. The Decree of 3 March 1810 finally regularised the system by setting up formal procedures by which the Emperor's privy council (*conseil privé*) could authorise the detention of 'state prisoners' without trial in eight fortresses specially designated as state prisons.[38]

It is difficult to know how many people were affected by the decree of 1810. A ledger compiled by two councillors of state charged with visiting the prisons in late 1811 and early 1812 gives 304 names (279 men and 25 women), only three-quarters of whom (218) were political prisoners in the truest sense of the word, which is to say people whose activities had political implications. They were agents and spies for foreign powers or for the Bourbons who still claimed the French throne, priests who supported the Pope in his quarrel with Napoleon, former Chouans (royalist rebels in western France who had once taken up arms against the revolutionary or Napoleonic government), conspirators of all stripes against the regime, foreign nationalists who resisted French rule in their homeland, and so on. The remaining 86 were criminals, swindlers, the insane, and ordinary men and women incarcerated at the request of their own families. The councillors did not even bother with another 570 people locked up in departmental and municipal prisons on an order of the superior police, but it seems that all of them were suspected criminals.[39]

This arbitrary treatment of six hundred suspected criminals has nothing to do with political repression, but it is indicative of general police attitudes. Courts required hard evidence to convict; the police, on the other hand, regularly took action on the basis of mere suspicion, quite outside the law and in violation of the principle of 'innocent until proven guilty'. When François Marin complained to the Senatorial Commission for Individual Liberty in 1808 that the police had locked him up 'without any interrogation or [court] judgment whatsoever', the Minister of General Police explained that '[Marin] is detained . . . for complicity in theft, and if he has escaped justice, it has only been because of a lack of material proof'.[40] In some cases, judges and juries called for police intervention when they felt legally obliged to acquit a defendant whom they nonetheless believed to be guilty. For example, Jean Louis Gachot had been charged with slander and harassment, but the case against him was too weak for conviction. The jury, 'which could not touch [Gachot], but which considered him too dangerous a man to be released', simply asked the police to prolong his incarceration.[41]

As for political prisoners, if few were totally innocent and some were a very real threat to state security, the majority were relatively insignificant opponents of the regime whose prolonged detention without trial was, by any reasonable measure of justice, way out of proportion to their offences. The Chouans still in prison in 1811 included several former leaders of some importance, but also nine obscure Breton farmers and rural artisans who did not even speak French, the remnant of a batch rounded up in late 1801 and described vaguely in 1807 as 'the most prominent by their excesses . . . and whose tendencies and habits are to be feared'. Their imprisonment, as a precaution against future troubles, made some sense when the Consulate was new and their opposition recent, but could it reasonably be justified ten years later?[42] Other political prisoners included Joseph Coney, who denounced imaginary conspiracies to the police for the reward money; Joseph de Caamano, a priest arrested in Chambéry in 1808 on suspicion of intriguing with the Pope because he was headed for Italy with a passport for Paris; and a mysterious stranger arrested in Bordeaux in 1806 because 'he is hiding under the false name François Dumont and obstinately refuses to give information that can identify him'. (Held without charge or trial until 1814, Dumont eventually turned out to be a minor swindler named Simon Fossey.)[43] These are not atypical cases. The dossiers of the political police bulge with reports in which innuendo and conjecture outweigh hard evidence of wrong-doing.

The writer Antoine François Eve, known as Démaillot, who was detained without trial as a political prisoner from 1808 to 1814, claimed, with some exaggeration, that while common criminals in France 'have mattresses and sheets for bedding, meat twice a week, and vegetables every day', political prisoners like himself 'were reduced to consuming their sorrow on the straw that served as bedding and to having as the whole of their sustenance only bread and water and a soup as unwholesome as it was disgusting'.[44] In fact, the government extended to political prisoners various privileges denied to common criminals: better accommodations, better food and even a daily allowance for those truly in need. (State prisoners had the right to buy food from outside and could even rent more comfortable cells – if they had the means to pay.) Of course, political prisoners did complain continually to the authorities: their prison cells were too cold and uncomfortable, their food was inadequate and unappetising, their physical and mental health required more daily exercise outdoors and more regular contact with their fellow prisoners. Official reports indicate that poor conditions, which certainly did exist in the state prisons, were not the result of any vindictiveness on the part of the administrators, but occurred simply because police and prison officials were indifferent or preoccupied or (most often) lacked the necessary funds. The authorities, for all their faults, did not treat political prisoners with any deliberate pettiness or cruelty.

An important exception was Toussaint Louverture (1743–1803), leader of the slave revolt in Haiti, whom the authorities wanted to punish for 'his crimes, his odious behaviour and his tyranny over the [white] Europeans'. Louverture was arrested in Haiti in March 1802, transferred to France and incarcerated from August 1802 until his death in April 1803 in the fortress of Joux in a mountainous region on the Swiss border. Although the government saw to it that he was decently clothed and well fed and supplied him with wood for his fireplace (Louverture complained continually of the unaccustomed cold), it refused to permit him any sort of military uniform and denied him the title of general ('his name is Toussaint; it's the only appellation he ought to be given'), required that he surrender his money and even his watch ('the castle clock whose chimes he can hear in his room is enough for him'), forced him to shave in the presence of the commandant of the fortress and to hand over his razor immediately afterwards (so that he couldn't use it to commit suicide), took away his pen and paper to put a stop to his petitions for better treatment, and rationed his sugar although he ordinarily sweetened everything he drank. As for medical care, the commandant declared that 'since the anatomy of Negroes in no way resembles that of Europeans, I do not feel obliged to provide him with either a doctor or a surgeon, who would be useless to him'.[45]

The claim that the Napoleonic police had certain opponents certified insane and interned them in mental hospitals in order to humiliate and discredit them is a persistent myth that appears to have little basis in fact. Nevertheless, in May 1807, after a farmer named Jean Alloix uttered 'very indiscreet remarks against the government' in a café in Gap, the prefect declared that 'I have considered a man who speaks badly of the Emperor to be insane', and signed an order incarcerating Alloix in the local prison (the department lacked a madhouse) on the spurious grounds that 'such excessive dementia could degenerate into a rage and become harmful to society and to Alloix himself'. He released Alloix after six weeks in prison.[46]

Internal exile, another common form of punishment, meant banishing people from their usual place of residence to some other town or village to live under the supervision of local authorities (prefect, mayor, police or gendarmes). The assigned residence was usually fairly distant from both Paris and the coast in order to keep the capital free of political undesirables and the coast clear of unreliable exiles who might make contact with English spies. Police records provide no figures for the total number of internal exiles, but at least three or four thousand men and women must have been affected at one time or another under Napoleon's rule by an order of banishment. At most only about half of these had committed some sort of political offence; the remainder were criminals (convicted or merely suspected), swindlers, lunatics, drunkards, libertines, prostitutes or labour militants.[47]

The police considered internal exile a convenient, inexpensive and relatively lenient way of dealing with offenders. Exile punished political dissidents for what they had said or done, served as a warning for them to behave better in the future, and above all put them in a place where they could do no harm. In December 1810, for instance, the police expelled a former Jacobin radical named Villefumade from the town of Périgueux where he had allegedly 'awakened the old revolutionary quarrels, [and] he spread rumours, both true and false', ordering him to live instead in Riberac. This village was only 30 kilometres from Périgueux, but public opinion there favoured the regime and Villefumade found himself cut off from his usual friends and acquaintances. Presumably having learned his lesson, he was allowed to return home in September 1812.[48] Villefumade had family and property in Riberac, but most internal exiles, without independent means, found life very difficult indeed in their new home. Although the government intended them to be self-supporting, they found work hard to get because locals feared compromising themselves by employing or even fraternising with someone under police supervision. Louis Caillebot de la Salle, 'a pronounced enemy of the First Consul', who spent ten years in internal exile at Châtillon-sur-Seine, was able to live well on his private income and even managed to socialise with the best people in town, but Claude Lenoble was more typical of such exiles. A former Chouan, Lenoble was working peaceably in Paris as a clerk when in 1804 his 'more than indiscreet remarks' came to the attention of the police, who exiled him to Beaune. Unable to get work and on the verge of suicide, Lenoble appealed to the prefect, who persuaded the Ministry of General

Police to pay him a small allowance. When the ministry cancelled this as an economy measure in 1810, Lenoble survived – but barely – by giving private lessons to local children. The fall of Napoleon allowed him to return to Paris in May 1814, after ten years of hardship in exile.[49]

CONCLUSION

Antoine François Eve, Jean Alloix, Claude Lenoble and all the others mentioned above – obscure and forgotten victims of the Napoleonic police state – represent thousands of men and women who, like them, also ran afoul of the regime and found themselves imprisoned or exiled without trial, sometimes for real acts of opposition, sometimes for no more than critical remarks and sometimes merely on suspicion of wrong-doing. What happened to them must, of course, be understood within the context of the period. Antoine-Clair Thibaudeau (1765–1854), who served the regime loyally but without sycophancy as prefect of the Bouche-du-Rhône from 1803 to 1814, wrote what is perhaps the best justification of the Napoleonic police and their handling of dissidence. His comments are all the more striking for coming from a man of liberal convictions:

> The imperial police has been slandered. It was arbitrary, that was in its nature; that's why in free countries people disapprove of a so-called [ministry of] general police. . . . For my part, I can guarantee that, in all the ministerial correspondence, I never saw anything that could offend the conscience of an honest man, and I often found there liberal principles that would vindicate, if that were possible, an institution condemned at all times by public opinion. . . . If one considers the obstacles and the perils that ceaselessly threatened the Emperor and the Empire, I can guarantee that in terms of arbitrary actions the imperial police remained far inferior to the police in states that were more solidly established.[50]

Respectable men like Thibaudeau, traumatised by the revolutionary upheaval of the 1790s, put a very high value (perhaps too high a value) on political stability and the maintenance of internal peace, law and good order. If this meant that at times the police had to ignore hard-won civil rights, they were ready and willing to pay that price. Thibaudeau certainly regretted the regime's excesses – he thought, for example, that state prisons only gave the regime a reputation for despotism 'to no good purpose'[51] – but he refused to condemn as unwarranted the systematic surveillance of France and the police repression of all manifestations of political opposition. Napoleon's police were generally efficient, sometimes ruthless and occasionally heartless, but never deliberately cruel. All things considered, a few hundred political prisoners and a few thousand internal exiles in an empire of 30 millions was hardly excessive in comparison to the far more severe repression that France had experienced in the 1790s during the French Revolution, or would experience again in 1851–52 under Louis-Napoleon Bonaparte or in 1871 when the army crushed the Paris Commune. Of course, the victims of Napoleon's political police undoubtedly had a somewhat different view of things.

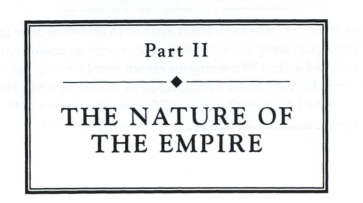

Part II

THE NATURE OF THE EMPIRE

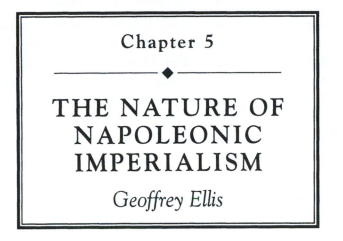

Chapter 5

◆

THE NATURE OF NAPOLEONIC IMPERIALISM

Geoffrey Ellis

THE HEROIC MYTH

The 'classic' accounts of Napoleonic imperialism were constructed mainly by French writers during the period from 1815 to the Second World War, and have been well outlined in Pieter Geyl's survey, *Napoleon: For and Against*, first published in 1949.[1] Although there were many variants of the genre, most of those early accounts had one thing in common: they sought to explain Napoleon's imperial ambition in terms of a major binding theme, or 'grand idea'. The most colourful of these reconstructions celebrated him in some way as the embodiment of the Roman imperial past, a motif which had already been lavishly embellished in the visual arts of the Napoleonic Empire,[2] and which was then transformed into a powerful legend after the publication of the *Mémorial de Sainte-Hélène* by Count Emmanuel de Las Cases in 1823. Some variants of that particular genre made analogies with the empires of Constantine and Theodosius, in which the caesaro-papist theme was predominant, or with Justinian's empire, where the emphasis lay more on Napoleon's achievements as a great lawgiver; while others preferred to stress his own grandiloquent and flamboyant espousal of the Carolingian past. Whatever the image so portrayed, Napoleonic imperialism was construed in retrospective terms, essentially as the consummation of an ancient and glorious heritage. Its historical significance thus looked backwards, to a past dimly remembered and easily distorted, and always closely associated with a personalised heroic cult.[3] It is of course necessary to add here that earlier perceptions of Napoleonic imperialism were not always heroic. The 'black legend' of Napoleon was recounted in a long line of writers stretching from Mme de Staël, Benjamin Constant and Chateaubriand during or shortly after the First Empire to Edgar Quinet, Pierre Lanfrey, the comte d'Haussonville, Jules Michelet and Hippolyte Taine later in the nineteenth century. The image of Napoleon which emerges in their works is associated much more with his brutal repression and incessant war-mongering, with his tyrannical destruction of civil liberties in France and systematic despoliation of conquered peoples beyond her frontiers, with his monstrous ambition and pitiless methods. In short, they saw him as a demoniacal creature who had presided over a new age of barbarism in European history.

Yet in spite of such discordant voices, heroic variants of the 'grand idea' in those earlier approaches to Napoleonic imperialism remained the dominant ones. At the same time, they raise a number of fundamental difficulties for readers reared on the harder empirical evidence of more recent Napoleonic studies. First, they assimilated what had been imperial systems of long duration, extending over centuries, to what in Napoleon's case was a relatively short-lived one – just fifteen years, at most. Second, in their more fanciful constructions of his pursuit of a global empire, whether in the Mediterranean, or in an oriental emporium spread out across the Levant, or indeed in the wider world across the seas, they presupposed a French naval capacity which Napoleon never in fact had at his disposal. Third, they were all much too trusting of his own utterances and symbolical rituals, of the elaborate heraldry and symbolism of his Empire, and too inclined to accept that what he said was what he intended, and that what he intended was what he actually achieved. There is, then, a basic problem with the main primary source for a study of Napoleonic imperialism: the Emperor himself. Even in more recent accounts, authors have often regarded one or other of his particular recorded utterances, one or other of his official pronouncements to his ministers or to the public bodies of the Consulate and Empire, one or other of his 32,000 letters, as somehow encapsulating the essence of his imperial vision.

A closer analysis of all these major sources quickly reveals the pitfalls of such an approach. Napoleon was *not* consistent in what he said. His words were often contradictory, just as his moods were often mercurial. It is true, of course, that his Corsican upbringing had a formative and lasting influence on his view of himself and on his dynastic ambition. Frédéric Masson, in a monumental study of Napoleon's relations with his family published a century ago, elaborated the central theme that his Corsican 'clan spirit' was the underlying motivation of his whole pursuit and exercise of power.[4] Whatever the merits or weaknesses of that argument, it is clear that Napoleon always made much of what he called his 'destiny'. But if he did so at various times during his youth and early training as a soldier, during his years of power, and not least during his final exile on St Helena, the hard evidence for this apparently compelling instinct within him rests on a motley collection of remarks, in which his concepts of destiny, ambition and power were jumbled together in highly idiosyncratic terms.

Only a few examples must suffice here to illustrate the point. In a conversation with Benjamin Constant on 10 April 1815, with only a fragile hold on power during the Hundred Days, Napoleon reportedly said that 'I wanted to rule the world, and in order to do this I needed unlimited power. . . . The world begged me to govern it; sovereigns and nations vied with one another in throwing themselves under my scepter.'[5] Yet in 1804, the very year in which his Empire was proclaimed on the basis of real power, he had remarked to Roederer, one of his councillors of state, that 'as far as I am concerned, I have no ambition – or, if I have any, it is so natural to me, so innate, so intimately linked with my existence that it is like the blood that circulates in my veins, like the air I breathe'.[6] Or, again, his celebrated pronouncement to Las Cases on St Helena that 'I am of the race that founds empires' is so vague that its allusions to 'race' and 'empires' could mean almost anything.[7] Ambitious Corsicans had always dreamed dreams, no doubt, but for centuries their island had actually been more remarkable for its history of successive conquests by other peoples, most recently by the French in 1769, only a few months before Napoleon was born. Or finally, in another conversation recounted by Las Cases on 1 May 1816, Napoleon asked 'shall I be blamed for my ambition?' and then continued:

> This passion I must doubtless to be allowed to have possessed, and that in no small degree; but, at the same time, my ambition was of the highest and noblest kind that ever, perhaps, existed! . . . That of establishing and of consecrating the Empire of reason, and the full exercise and complete enjoyment of all the human faculties![8]

This image of Napoleon as a pacific imperialist, driven to fight defensive wars against the enemies of reason, is perhaps the most absurd conceit in the early historiography of the subject. The rambling reminiscences of the St Helena record, in particular, were in large part a self-justifying fabrication – powerful and fascinating as a myth in its own right, but hazardous as a guide to historical facts.

This essay starts from the assumption that there was no particular utterance or letter or public gesture of Napoleon that encapsulates the essence of his imperial vision. The most massive of all the extant primary sources, the thirty-two volumes of his official *Correspondance* published at the behest of Napoleon III under the Second Empire,[9] are much more notable for their discordances and contradictions than for any consistent theme or 'grand design', unless it be the force of Napoleon's own personality, his imperious attitude to all around him, the belief that he was always right – in other words, his unbridled egotism. When set against the test of his deeds, nothing Napoleon said was actually written in tablets of stone. There were no Ten Commandments of the Empire. There was no carefully formulated Political Testament, no elaborate theory of statecraft, to subsume Napoleon's actions. Instead, we find an assortment of stated aims, often repetitive, usually directed at his immediate audience or correspondents, and designed to provoke the response he wanted. There was always an element of self-interested calculation in his most controversial actions – military deception, diplomatic high-handedness, ruthless atrocities and all. To get his way, as Harold T. Parker has reminded us, Napoleon was prepared to cheat and lie, to use guile and trickery, to threaten and bully, as he thought the occasion demanded.[10] To understand the nature of Napoleonic imperialism, it seems to me, we need to concentrate on what Napoleon actually *did*, and see how far this helps us to establish any clear aim and pattern in his rule.

THE LIMITATIONS OF 'UNIFORMITY' AND 'MODERNITY'

The prospective image of Napoleon as the architect of the modern state started to gain currency only in the more obviously academic, or what it is now fashionable to think of as 'structuralist' or 'revisionist', studies which have appeared since the 1960s. Mindful perhaps of the problems inherent in the most familiar primary sources, a number of more recent scholars have sought to argue the case for a consistent imperial plan by shifting the focus from Napoleon himself to the men who manned his burgeoning civil administration or who operated his military system, as the 'Grand Empire' was forged over the years from 1805 to 1812. We thus have the wider evidence of some thousands of individuals who, at different times, served as the everyday technicians of his state. This approach has the considerable merit of depersonalising the heroic myth, and of focusing more squarely on the aims and effects of Napoleon's rule on his subjects. Here, it would appear, the true nature of his regime may be gleaned from the records of administrators and military commanders who were actually responsible for implementing his policies where they mattered most to the subject peoples, at regional or local level. The most challenging of these recent accounts is that of Stuart Woolf, who speaks pointedly of 'Napoleon's integration of Europe', and argues that his imperial rule incorporated a 'model' of administrative statecraft.[11] Besides its obviously authoritarian and highly centralised character, this 'model' was at once 'uniform' in concept and 'modern' in its historical structures, although the same author acknowledges that it met fierce resistance and ultimately produced no lasting institutional legacy in many of the conquered lands. It owed something to the administrative reforms of the French revolutionary state, not least to the official gathering of statistics and other classifiable data. Indeed, Woolf even suggests that it may have had some roots back in the Cameralist theory (*Kameralwissenschaft*) of eighteenth-century German states.[12]

The problem with this latter suggestion, at least, is that it flies in the face of so much of what Napoleon and his officials apparently thought and said about the Germans, their intellectual life, their cultural sensibilities and their statecraft. The public condemnation and banning in 1810 of Madame de Staël's *De l'Allemagne*, a Romantic *tour de force* aimed at extolling the virtues of German aesthetics to French readers, illustrates the objection nicely. That Napoleon and his officials believed in the value of gathering statistics as the basis for a new science of administration is not in doubt. The data sometimes referred to generically as the *Statistique de l'Empire* were the product of a massive exercise, towards the end so relentless and demanding that many prefects complained that they simply did not have the time or resources to provide the information required of them, a reaction which of course vitiated the accuracy of the statistics themselves. The significant point here, however, is that the *Statistique* was conceived as a French exercise, following French precepts and methods, and as evidence of the superiority of French statecraft.

I imagine that Woolf would readily concede the point, since in a seminal article on the nature of French 'civilization' in the Napoleonic era he takes it much further.[13] Recognising that the word itself had entered the French language only in the 1760s, he argues here for a related concept of French 'ethnicity' which, during the revolutionary and Napoleonic wars of territorial expansion, was systematically honed into an instrument of 'cultural imperialism' by the hegemonic elites of the conquering power. This 'cultural imperialism' eventually extended well beyond what had once been thought of as the 'natural frontiers' of France – the Pyrenees, the Alps and the Rhine. As the revolutionary and then the Napoleonic regimes annexed large areas beyond the old frontiers of France, so French administrative forms were imposed on the new subject peoples. The official rhetoric used to justify the process stressed the benefits of such 'uniformization' for all subjects.[14] The prefects, auditors and sub-prefects in the field, as Woolf puts it, 'had no doubt that the Napoleonic achievement represented administratively the reverse side of the coin of civilization, namely the best (as the most rational) system elaborated in the course of history; and hence the most suitable to export for the benefit of the peoples now "reunited" to the French nation'.[15] Under the Empire, this value-system progressively lost the ethnological curiosity of the *savants* who had originally sponsored it; but, conversely, its practical and utilitarian aims as an administrative 'model' were increasingly sharpened. In this way, one might add, the adoption of 'enlightened' forms of government and a rational system of legal codes would more obviously vindicate the 'cultural imperialism' of a superior French 'ethnicity' than the notorious depredations of the revolutionary armies in the conquered territories during the 1790s had ever done.

That, at least, was the theory of it all. In practice, the results often fell far short of the 'model', and for a number of reasons. For a start, the chronology of imperial conquest and political subjugation was an uneven and staggered process. The various annexed territories were not brought under direct French rule at the same time, and their exposure to French administrative practices was not therefore of equal duration. The earliest annexations – of Avignon and the Comtat Venaissin (14 September 1791), of Savoy (27 November 1792), of Nice (31 January 1793), of Belgium and Luxembourg (30 September 1795), of the German left bank of the Rhine (effectively in January 1798, although its full incorporation was not completed until the treaty of Lunéville on 9 February 1801) and of Geneva and its environs (26 April 1798) – all very clearly took place before Napoleon's assumption of power by the Brumaire coup on 9–10 November 1799. The formal annexation of the six new Piedmontese departments (later reduced to five) occurred on 11 September 1802, while France under the Consulate was still officially a constitutional republic, and during the only short period of general peace throughout the Napoleonic period, following the treaty of Amiens (25 March 1802). At that stage the extended French Republic consisted of 104 departments, 21 having been added to the 83 departments of 'old France' originally formed in 1790.

It should be abundantly clear from these basic facts that much of the territorial expansion of France so often associated with Napoleon's wars of conquest actually preceded the formal inauguration of his hereditary Empire on 18 May 1804, and that the whole process owed much to the military dynamic of his revolutionary inheritance. In this technical sense, it is proper to speak of his 'Imperial' annexations only after that date, and they too came in stages. The lands of the former Ligurian Republic, centred on the port of Genoa, were transformed into three new Imperial departments on 30 June 1805. Parma and the Kingdom of Etruria were similarly annexed in May 1808, then reconstituted in the following year as the Grand Duchy of Tuscany, which was entrusted to the rule of Napoleon's sister Elisa and her husband, Prince Bacciochi. What remained of the truncated Papal States, already placed under French military occupation since February 1808, was also annexed on 17 May 1809, and Rome itself was to become 'the second city of the Empire' on 17 February 1810. Meanwhile, after his victory over the Austrians at Wagram on 5–6 July 1809, Napoleon detached the whole of Istria (including the ports of Trieste and Fiume) and Dalmatia, along with parts of Carniola, Carinthia and Croatia from the Habsburg Empire by the terms of the treaty of Schönbrunn (14 October 1809). These now formed the so-called 'Illyrian Provinces of the Empire', nominally subject to direct annexation, although most scholars now believe that they never in fact attained that status under the governance of Marshal Marmont and later Generals Bertrand and Junot. Finally, at various times during the great spate of expansion of 1810–11, further new Imperial departments were formed by the direct annexation of Holland, part of Hanover, the Hanse towns (Hamburg, Bremen and Lübeck), and the Grand Duchy of Oldenburg. At its territorial height in 1812, the formal French Empire had 130 departments, with a total population of some 44 million subjects.

The significant point in this brief history of the official annexations under the Empire is that a good many of the lands in question were brought under immediate French rule comparatively late in the day. By the time of Napoleon's first abdication on 6 April 1814, the Tuscan, Papal, Dutch and north German departments had been directly exposed to French administrative practices for only a few years, rather too short a time for those practices to take firm root and have any lasting constructive impact there. Much the same could be said of the 'Illyrian Provinces', with the possible exception of Slovenia. Conversely, French administrative forms took firmest root and left their most enduring legacy in the territories which lay closest to France itself and which had been annexed early: Belgium and Luxembourg, the German left bank of the Rhine and Piedmont–Liguria most notably. In these areas, the process of assimilation to French administrative and legal procedures had run a longer course by 1814. It had actually fostered the growth of local elites prepared to collaborate with the French, notwithstanding the resistance of devout Catholics to the secularising ways of their new rulers.

It bears repeating here that we have been dealing thus far with the lands which, at one time or another, were brought under *direct* French rule, and which together marked the full territorial extent of the formal French Empire. As such, they were governed, nominally at least, as integral parts of its organic life. This implied their official assimilation, however briefly, to the administrative structures of the core French state: that is, to the system of departments (with their prefects, advisory prefectoral councils, departmental councils, and receivers-general), *arrondissements* (with their sub-prefects, advisory *arrondissement* councils, and receivers-particular), cantons (electoral and judicial units), and communes (with their mayors, advisory municipal councils, and police commissioners). It also implied their official assimilation to the refashioned electoral colleges which dated from August 1802, to the treasury inspectorates, to the Imperial judicial system and the five Napoleonic legal codes promulgated between 1804 and 1810, to the Imperial Gendarmerie, to the network of military stage-roads (*routes d'étapes*) as from 1805, to the whole edifice of the 'Imperial University' formally decreed in March 1808, to the advisory chambers of commerce set up as from 1802 to 1803, and so on.[16] More controversially, it implied their assimilation to the structure and regulation of the concordatory Church first officially promulgated in April 1802. It implied their adherence to Napoleon's Continental Blockade against Britain, after the proclamation of his Berlin decree (21 November 1806) and Milan decrees (23 November and 17 December 1807). And, perhaps most controversially of all, it implied their assimilation to the French system of military divisions, of which there were thirty-two by 1811, along with a further six in the Kingdom of Italy, through whose sub-divisions the all-important recruitment of soldiers for the Grand Army operated. In so far as the administrative 'model' of 'uniformity' and 'modernity' was effectively extended beyond the frontiers of 'old France' under Napoleon, it was here, in the so-called *pays réunis* (that is, the directly annexed lands), that French 'cultural imperialism' was most resolutely pursued.

Elsewhere, however, the particular forms of French rule were somewhat different, and the results a good deal patchier. Michael Broers, in elaborating his thematic distinction between an 'inner empire' (the lands acquired up to 1807), an 'outer empire' (those gained later) and various 'intermediate zones', offers one interesting explanation of the regional variations in the efficacy of Napoleonic government.[17] If that is a latter-day formula of differentiation, another useful distinction, actually drawn from the technical language of the time, may be made between the *pays alliés* (allied countries) and the *pays conquis* (conquered lands). The former were states allied to France, in some cases enhanced in status and territorially enlarged by Napoleon's favours, and nominally ruled by their native sovereigns. The *pays conquis*, as distinct from the *pays réunis*, were subject or satellite states not directly annexed to the formal French Empire. Most of them were nevertheless entrusted to French rulers, including members of Napoleon's own family and certain high-ranking officers. In some cases, their earliest roots lay back in the satellite 'sister republics' of France formed during the wars of conquest under the late National Convention and more especially under the Directory: the Batavian (Dutch) Republic in May 1795, the expanded Cisalpine Republic (June 1797), the reconstituted Ligurian Republic (June 1797), the Helvetic Republic (May 1798), the Roman Republic (February 1798), the Parthenopean (Neapolitan) Republic (January–June 1799) and several others. Of these, only the Cisalpine Republic, centred on Lombardy, had been directly fashioned by Napoleon himself, following his victories over the Austrians in the first Italian campaign of 1796–97. Later, in December 1801, he transformed it into the Republic of Italy, whose effective government was headed by Count Melzi d'Eril, its vice-president. Within fifteen months Napoleon had also intervened in the Helvetic Republic, which in February 1803 took new form as an enlarged Swiss Confederation, and appointed himself as its official 'Mediator'. However, all the other 'sister republics', with the exception of the Batavian and the Ligurian, had turned out to be short-lived affairs.

After the proclamation of the Empire, the pattern of subjugation changed, and so did the nomenclature, a sign that Napoleon's imperial ambition was evolving from the earlier republican forms into a much larger dynastic system. The process by which he forged his 'Grand Empire' beyond the frontiers of the formal French Empire began in 1805, some two years after the rupture of the Amiens peace. In March that year the Republic of Italy became a new satellite kingdom, with Napoleon as its titular sovereign, and its effective government soon passed to a viceroy, his stepson Eugène de Beauharnais. Its lands already included the papal Legations of Bologna, Ferrara and Ravenna; and by the end of the year were also to incorporate the whole of Venetia. Further political changes in the Italian peninsula were to come with Napoleon's major series of decrees issued on 30 March 1806. In one fell swoop he then followed up his victories of the previous year over the Austrian and Russian armies at Ulm (20 October) and Austerlitz (2 December), and his reduction of Austria through the ensuing treaty of Pressburg (26 December), by creating both the satellite Kingdom of Naples and what became known as the twenty-two 'ducal grand-fiefs of the Empire'. Twelve of these latter were carved out of recent Venetian accessions to the Kingdom of Italy, six more from dispossessed lands in the new Kingdom of Naples itself, and the rest were formed at Massa-Carrara, Parma and Piacenza. They were to be convertible into hereditary estates (*majorats*) under French law by male primogeniture, and were awarded mainly to his top military commanders, chiefly the marshals, while at Naples Napoleon installed his elder brother Joseph as king. At the same time Napoleon established his sister Pauline and her husband, Prince Borghese, as the rulers of the Principality of Guastalla. The concentrated imperial expansion of 30 March 1806 also extended into the Rhineland, where Joachim Murat, one of the marshals and the husband of Caroline Bonaparte, became the duke of Cleves and Berg, and later (12 July 1806) the elevated grand duke of Berg. In June of the same year Napoleon finally did away with the Batavian Republic, appointing his brother Louis as the sovereign of the new satellite Kingdom of Holland.

With Switzerland, most of Italy, and Holland thus apparently secured as subject states, Napoleon was able to turn his main attention to Germany, in the wake of Austria's withdrawal from the Third Allied Coalition. In fact, the process of subjugation there had started more than three years earlier, on 25 February 1803, when an act (*Reichsdeputationshauptschluss*) adopted at a special 'recess' of the German Diet had detached over a hundred small secular and ecclesiastical states from Austrian suzerainty. The process of what had then officially been termed their 'mediatisation' was as yet not fully determined; but in any event Napoleon's purpose had plainly been to re-align them with the states which in due course became his new *pays alliés* across the Rhine. At the turn of the year 1805–1806 Bavaria and Württemberg had been elevated to the status of kingdoms, nominally governed by their native sovereigns, Max Joseph and Frederick I respectively. Both had already received significant territorial gains, mostly at the expense of Austria, and were to be further rewarded during the following months. This prepared the way for Napoleon's major reconstruction of subject Germany, which duly followed when a constitutional Act of 12 July 1806 formally inaugurated the Confederation of the Rhine (*Rheinbund*), and named him as its official 'Protector'. Among the other prominent beneficiaries of his favours was Charles Frederick of Baden, whose title of margrave had already been promoted to that of elector at the time of the 1803 'recess', and whose state was now declared a grand duchy. On the following 6 August the historic Holy Roman Empire (*Reich*) was officially abolished by the Emperor Francis II.

Consisting initially of sixteen states on the right bank of the Rhine, all committed in varying degrees to providing troops for the service of France, the new Confederation was later enlarged by two important accessions. First,

Saxony joined in January 1807, its former elector Frederick Augustus having been raised to the status of king in the previous month. Then, in July 1807, following the French victories over the Prussians at Jena and Auerstädt (14 October 1806) and over the Russians at Friedland (14 June 1807), Napoleon's two treaties of Tilsit provided for a major redistribution of the spoils of conquest. While Tsar Alexander I in effect retreated, officially as an ally of Napoleon, to further his own territorial designs in eastern Europe, the Kingdom of Prussia was virtually cut in half. The dispossessed lands in the west were added to other subject territories to form the satellite Kingdom of Westphalia. Jérôme, the Emperor's youngest brother, now became its sovereign, and soon afterwards the dynastic ties with Germany were further strengthened through his (second) marriage to Catherine of Württemberg. Jérôme's kingdom, originally conceived of as a 'model' state, a flagship of Napoleonic statecraft in the 'Grand Empire', immediately joined the Rhenish Confederation. At the same time, the lands seized from Prussia farther east were joined with the core of Poland to form the new Duchy of Warsaw, whose government Napoleon entrusted to Frederick Augustus of Saxony. Its territory was to be augmented by Austrian Galicia under the terms of the treaty of Schönbrunn some two years later, after Napoleon's victorious Wagram campaign.

The year 1808 marked the extension of Napoleonic imperialism into the Iberian peninsula, a move which had an obvious territorial logic about it and which, potentially at least, offered a vast potential for conquest. Portugal had long been a British ally and trading partner, while Spain was also strategically well placed for a strike at Britain's naval access to the Mediterranean by Gibraltar. In the event, Napoleon's designs on both countries got off to a troubled start, and their subsequent subjugation to French rule was more nominal than real. The appointment of General Junot as governor-general of Portugal in February 1808 presupposed a French victory which had not yet been achieved, a point underlined soon enough by his defeat at Vimiero on 21 August that year. Thereafter, Portugal remained a constant thorn in the side of Napoleon's western front south of the Pyrenees, and a major breach in the cordon of his Continental Blockade against Britain in southern Europe. The creation of the satellite Kingdom of Spain had its origins in the high-handed manner by which Napoleon, with the help of a hand-picked Junta, engineered the deposition of the Bourbon monarch Ferdinand VII, who had just recently forced the abdication of his father, Charles IV. Following this strategem, sometimes referred to as 'the ambush of Bayonne' (May–July 1808), Joseph Bonaparte was appointed as king, his place at

Naples being taken by Joachim Murat and Caroline Bonaparte. Murat indeed, as Napoleon's lieutenant-general in Spain since the preceding February, had already set the tone of the French subjugation there by his notorious fusillade of captured insurgents in Madrid on 2 and 3 May, an atrocity immortalised in two stunning paintings by Goya. This brutal act proved portentous, as the Spanish resistance gathered strength during the following year, encouraged by General Dupont's defeat at Baylen on 21 July 1808, a battle which itself proved significant in dispelling the myth of French military invincibility.

What followed was six years of attrition, as the British committed more troops and resources to the Peninsular War, made use of both the guerrillas and the Spanish regular troops who remained loyal to the revolutionary Cortes of Cádiz established in 1810, and finally turned the tide of the war against the French during the course of 1812 and 1813. Given the strategic importance of Spain, it is surprising that Napoleon did not show more personal determination in securing his military base there. His brief intervention in 1808–1809 was indecisive, while the commanders he left behind to act in his stead proved ineffectual. In the end, the institutional legacy of French rule in the satellite Kingdom of Spain, under its changing avatars, was nugatory. In spite of King Joseph's good intentions, as witnessed not least in his support for the liberal Constitution of Bayonne of 1808, neither he nor his native collaborators (*afrancesados*) ever managed to win over sufficient support among the social elites who still dominated the provinces of Spain. They singularly failed to tame the large and influential Spanish clergy, the main inspiration behind popular resistance to the French, especially after Napoleon's anticlerical and anti-seigneurial amendments to the Constitution of Bayonne in 1809. Of all the territories of Napoleon's 'Grand Empire', which at its height in 1812 numbered around 84 million subjects, Spain perhaps best represents the case against the efficacy of French 'cultural imperialism'.

'CULTURAL IMPERIALISM' OR 'SPOILS SYSTEM'?

Even if allowances are made for that exceptional case, however, one might still question the concept of French 'cultural imperialism' in the 'Grand Empire' in a more fundamental sense. The varying time-lags through which the conquered lands were exposed to French rule, and the different forms of that rule which applied in them, have already been noted. They prompt what seems to me the crucial question here: how long does it take for any 'cultural imperialism' to become manifest in the affairs of nations? If one measure is the major thesis elaborated in Edward Said's *Culture & Imperialism*,[18] for instance, the chronological disparities become only too plain. In that case, it is easy to confuse a cultural process which Said very clearly identifies in a long experience of imperial rule with one that lasted for no more than a quarter of a century. Assimilation to an official language, to administrative and legal forms, to foreign cultural models, to a sense of shared commercial and industrial interests, and to a perception of a common military and strategic security – all take time to evolve. The evidence now available suggests that, by 1814, much of conquered Europe had failed the test. For example, the French system of military conscription was deeply resented by the Dutch, among other peoples, who had no such tradition of their own. The commercial and industrial prohibitions of the Continental Blockade (1806–13) were no less irksome to them, a reaction also evident in most other parts of the 'Grand Empire', and in many departments of the formal Empire itself for that matter, as the ubiquitous incidence of smuggling shows.[19] Indeed, many more Imperial subjects expressed their disobedience to Napoleonic rule through smuggling, or by handling contraband goods in some way, than through the more obvious forms of military desertion and draft evasion.

Even in subject states where there was no major armed rebellion against Napoleon, indirect passive resistance by the local populations was often enough to vitiate his civil government. While such resistance took various forms, there is space here for only two of the most common among them to serve as illustrations. One, germane in all conquered territories where the influence of the Catholic Church was still strong, might be described as a silent revolution against the secularising thrust of French rule, itself conspicuous in the confiscation of ecclesiastical property, in the suppression of the regular orders, in the abolition of traditional festivals and rituals, in the attack on clerical courts and educational institutions, and in other such measures. The peasantry who formed the mass of the subject populations took comparatively little part in the sale of secularised Church property, and had little affinity with or liking for those of the collaborating elites (mostly the landed gentry, urban patriciates and high-ranking civil officials or military officers) who engrossed the sales to their own personal advantage. If this was evident even in the directly annexed departments of relatively long duration – that is in Belgium, the German left bank of the Rhine, and Piedmont – how much more would it have been so in the satellite Kingdoms of Italy and of Naples, or in the Papal States themselves? The rupture in Church–State relations presented the Catholic faithful with a stark conflict of loyalties, and the rough treatment of Pope Pius VII during his enforced exile at Savona and then

Fontainebleau (1809–14) ultimately undermined the aims of Napoleon's Concordat with the papacy. In the particularly revealing case of Italy, Michael Broers goes so far as to speak of 'a pattern of resistance best expressed as a *Kulturkampf* between the "enlightened" Napoleonic state and what might be termed the "baroque" nature of much of Italian culture'.[20]

Second, the same sort of passive resistance was evident in the opposition of secular as well as ecclesiastical elites to the provisions for civil marriage and divorce, or for the whole process of 'defeudalisation' itself, enshrined in the French Civil Code. In fact, the whole reception of the Civil Code of 1804, or *Code Napoléon* as it became known for 'export' purposes as from 1807, well testifies to the patchy results of French 'cultural imperialism' in the 'Grand Empire' as a whole. In France itself, the remnants of what was still called 'feudalism', which in practice meant surviving seigneurial rights and privileges, had been abolished officially during the Revolution by a series of decrees from August 1789 to July 1793. In that sense, the Napoleonic Civil Code was much less a major innovation than a monumental work of recapitulation and consolidation. We need not doubt that it marked the final, definitive legal extinction of 'feudalism' in all its forms in France, above all perhaps in the case of the revolutionary laws abolishing personal dues and of those governing property inheritance. But in subject states where feudal practices were still deeply entrenched, no such claims could be made for the impact of the *Code Napoléon*. The pioneering work of Elisabeth Fehrenbach on the application of the Code in the states of the Confederation of the Rhine, for example, shows that feudal lords often simply ignored, or when necessary found ways of evading, the strict terms of the Code.[21] There were simply not enough French-trained jurists to enforce them. As a result serfdom, including all the seigneurial dues and enforced labour services it implied, survived the Napoleonic hegemony largely intact. If anything, the old feudal lords may even have increased their social, economic and judicial authority over their peasantry. Outside of the Grand Duchy of Berg, where the abolition of labour services in 1811 does seem to have had some lasting effect, subject Germany east of the Rhine remained relatively untouched by the Code at the fall of Napoleon. To borrow Fehrenbach's striking metaphor, the Code then bore the aspect of a truncated 'torso' in most states of the Confederation. Yet these were lands not so very far away from the much more receptive annexed departments of the Rhenish left bank, whose social and professional elites successfully pressed for the retention of the *Code Napoléon*, and so also opposed the alternative *Allgemeines Landrecht* of 1794, when that area came under Prussian rule at the peace.[22]

Fehrenbach's broad conclusions about the social effects of French rule in the 'Grand Empire' are amply supported by the work of Helmut Berding on the Kingdom of Westphalia,[23] and by that of Monika Senkowska-Gluck on the Duchy of Warsaw.[24] With some regional exceptions, rather similar findings were communicated by several scholars at an international symposium in Trier in October 1992, which was devoted mainly to comparative studies of the impact of Napoleonic rule on administration and justice in Germany and Italy.[25] In the light of such research, it is not surprising that the Allied statesmen at the Congress of Vienna in 1814–15 were able to restore much of the old social order east of the Rhine. *Mutatis mutandis*, the same could be said of the Kingdom of Naples (which was then restored to Bourbon rule, along with Sicily) and of the Duchy of Warsaw (which now became the Congress Kingdom of Poland under the aegis of Russia).

Perhaps the greatest irony of all is that, so far from pursuing the process of rationalisation, 'defeudalisation' and 'modernisation' in the subject states of the 'Grand Empire' under the terms of the Code, Napoleon's treatment of them actually hampered its implementation. His own immediate interest was always in their material resources – soldiers, money and supplies – rather than in social altruism. As his imperial and dynastic ambitions grew in the critical years of conquest from 1805 to 1809, so he turned increasingly to the states of the 'Grand Empire' for the wherewithal with which to further his 'politics of grandeur'. This alone testifies to the finality of the revolutionary land settlement in France itself, in other words to the fact that he had not the resources within the national domain for the endowment of his Imperial nobility. At the start of the process in March 1806, as we have seen, the honorific principalities and the twenty-two 'ducal grand-fiefs of the Empire' then created nearly all lay in Italy. The very language used to identify them suggests a practical compromise with feudal nomenclature. As from March 1808, when the new titles of count, baron and chevalier of the Empire were inaugurated, and on a much grander scale, the accompanying land-gifts (*dotations*) to recipients (*donataires*) were carved out from conquered territories in Germany and Poland as well as Italy. The assets were derived mainly from Napoleon's claim to as much as half the income of the domain lands seized from the feudal lords in the Kingdom of Westphalia, and in Poland from the nationalised royal domain lands. By January 1810, the Kingdom of Westphalia and the annexed parts of Hanover together provided well over half (10.5 million francs) of the total annual income of the *dotations* (18.2 million) then enjoyed by over 4,000 *donataires*. The loss of such resources seriously undermined earlier plans to turn Jérôme's kingdom into a 'model' of 'enlightened' rule.[26] By the end of the Empire, there were nearly 6,000 *donataires*, and the total value of their *dotations* amounted to some 30 million francs a year, in nominal terms at least.

To extract those 'feudal' revenues, even at the best of times, Napoleon needed the co-operation of the local seigneurs, and to gain that co-operation he turned a blind eye to the strict enforcement of his Code. There were, of course, pecuniary advantages for himself in doing so. After the creation of his so-called 'Extraordinary Domain' (*Domaine extraordinaire*) in January 1810, a sizeable part of the revenues from the subject states was siphoned off for his own immediate use. Taken as a whole, his spoils system in the subject states certainly amounted to a form of 'imperialism'. But there was nothing definitively 'cultural' about it; nor could it be construed as a mark of the enlightened 'modernity' of his administrative 'model'. On the contrary, his spoils system is more reminiscent of the rack-renting of earlier warrior-kings. It was an improvised and unprincipled form of exploitation, a system of enforced cash levies – a kind of *Napoleongeld*, as it were. It was always dependent on his military power, and it quickly fell apart when that power finally faltered.

One last connotation of the notion of French 'cultural imperialism' in the Napoleonic period needs to be addressed. The whole concept of a superior French 'ethnicity', in which the Napoleonic administrators and jurists apparently had such an impelling belief, ultimately presupposes a civilising mission which transcended the idiosyncrasies of the Emperor himself. While this again has the merit of directing our attention from Napoleon's own grandiloquent rhetoric to the underlying structures of his 'Grand Empire', it does not of course follow that he had much conviction in making the distinction himself. It is true that one will find, yet again, a whole assortment of remarks which suggest otherwise. In a conversation with Roederer in 1809, for example, Napoleon professed that 'I am wholly French by attachment as well as by duty. I do nothing except from duty and from love of France. . . . I had no other aim but the glory and the power of France.'[27] Four years earlier, in an exchange with Bourrienne, in terms which suggest a rather lop-sided view of European 'integration', he had expostulated: 'there is not enough sameness among the nations of Europe. European society needs a regeneration. There must be a superior power which dominates all the other powers, with enough authority to force them to live in harmony with one another – and France is best placed for that purpose.'[28] Copious extracts from the St Helena record might similarly be cited in superficial support of his selfless service to France and respect for her civilisation, as well as of his wish to create a united states of Europe under French tutelage.[29]

On closer inspection, however, such bold asseverations seldom add up to much. The hard evidence of Napoleon's actions suggests rather that he came in time to see, first France, then the formal Empire, and finally the 'Grand Empire', as extensions of himself, legitimised by the ineluctable force of his destiny. He evidently believed that he was the personification, the individual summation, of all those domains, rather than the servant of a higher French civilisation, the mere instrument of its dissemination across Europe. He was notoriously possessive of his conquests and imperious in his instructions on how they should be governed, as his brothers and sisters and many of his military commanders and administrators learnt to their cost. His assertion in a letter to Eugène de Beauharnais of 23 August 1810 that 'my principle is: France first' (*la France avant tout*) is typical of so many other declarations of that sort.[30] For, as that particular correspondent well knew, he – the Emperor Napoleon – would define the advertised priority in his own terms. Any suggestion that his administrators wished to impose and were capable of imposing a superior 'model' of French 'ethnicity' on the conquered peoples *independently* of Napoleon, or perhaps even *in spite* of him, would seem to me perverse.

TOWARDS A DEFINITION

My purpose in the concluding part of this essay is to identify what was distinctive about Napoleonic imperialism, and to compare it with other imperial systems in history. The first and most obvious feature is that it was relatively short. Even if one includes the revolutionary wars, which started the process of territorial expansion towards the 'natural frontiers' of France, the whole imperial experience lasted for only some twenty years. It does not, then, naturally lend itself to comparisons with other, much more enduring empires, such as the Greek, the Roman, the Byzantine and the Ottoman, or (in more modern times) with the overseas colonial empires of Britain, Spain, Portugal or indeed France itself. In terms of historical time, the nearest analogy to Napoleonic imperialism is Hitler's Third Reich, although the present author has no wish to push the analogy further, as some earlier writers have done.

Second, Napoleonic imperialism was more or less a wholly *continental* process, confined that is to the Continent of Europe, or more accurately to its western and central half. Napoleon's Empire was land-based, indeed, yet at the same time land-locked. As Bertrand de Jouvenel once put it, 'Napoleon was master in Europe, but he was also a prisoner there.'[31] The maritime eclipse of France was already quite far advanced by the time of the Brumaire coup. After the battle of Trafalgar (21 October 1805) the French navy was effectively driven off the high seas, while the plight of French colonial trade intensified. Clearly, then, Napoleonic imperialism never developed the wider maritime dimension we associate with other, more global forms of imperialism. It is now fashionable to approach the latter through the reaction of the indigenous peoples to the imperial powers. Such an approach to Napoleonic imperialism would confront us, not for example with the slaves of the Caribbean and the American South, nor with the pagan tribes of black Africa, nor with the caste Hindu of India, but with Belgian, Dutch, German, Swiss, Italian, Spanish, Polish and Balkan peoples – all located in relative proximity to France, and all long since christianised. It is a simple fact that Napoleon never managed to effect the short Channel crossing to England. In the years before he seized power, he had indeed led an expedition to Egypt (1798–99), but this soon proved an unsustainable operation, as the eventual evacuation of the French forces on British terms during the summer of 1801 was to demonstrate. The expedition left a major cultural and scientific legacy, thanks to the 157 *savants* who had accompanied it. In the end, however, Napoleon's so-called 'Army of the Orient' had won its most famous battles at the Institute in Paris, not on the distant sands of Egypt.

Third, Napoleonic imperialism was geared towards the exploitation of the subject peoples in both a military and an economic sense; indeed, one might say in a cultural sense, too, given the plunder of so many art treasures in Italy and in some other conquered lands. As his ambition grew, Napoleon came to regard military conquest more and more as 'a good thing' (*une bonne affaire*), and its financial spoils had their own obvious attractions for him. Quite apart from the punitive indemnities he imposed on defeated enemies, he came to rely increasingly on the resources of the subject states for the routine upkeep of his Imperial system.[32] Before the massive levies of 1813–14, the Grand Army usually numbered between 500,000 and 600,000 officers and men during the wars of the Empire. We now know that at least three-fifths, possibly as much as two-thirds, of that total were made up by non-French contingents, whether from the annexed departments or from auxiliaries recruited in the subject and allied states. Similarly, when Napoleon set about the dynastic advancement of the Bonaparte clan, or the endowment of his Imperial nobility more widely, he turned to the subject states of the 'Grand Empire' for the financial lubrication he needed. And when it came to the erratic application of his Continental Blockade against Britain, he rode roughshod over the commercial and industrial interests of those same subject peoples. What all this adds up to is a strong case against the idea of his 'integration of Europe'.

Throughout, he wanted loyal and subservient subjects rather than independent partners in the 'Grand Empire'.

Fourth, Napoleonic imperialism was more the result of pragmatic opportunism, of *Realpolitik*, than the systematic working out of a preconceived 'master-plan' or 'grand design'. It is tempting to think that the creation of the formal Empire and then the 'Grand Empire' had a predictable logic about it. Yet often enough, in fact, the full consequences had not been clearly planned or even foreseen; they owed more to a gradual process of *ad hoc* improvisation on Napoleon's part. In the event, his methods of government in the 'Grand Empire' were also pragmatic. He was largely indifferent to the wishes and condition of the popular classes, preferring instead to rule with the co-operation of native elites. In lands where feudal custom was still strong, notably in Germany east of the Rhine, in Poland and in southern Italy, the old nobility was the class whose collaboration he chiefly sought, but did not always get. In other territories like Belgium, Holland, the German left bank of the Rhine, Switzerland and northern Italy, he aimed to attract – and to some extent *did* attract – the services of native elites across wider social and professional strata. Most prominent among the latter were the lesser gentry, the urban patriciates, men of the legal profession and local government, former radicals or patriots and freemasons, and wealthy merchants, all of whom had to accept that the price of service was their political subservience. In general, Napoleonic administration was most effective in areas where such local elites had material incentives to work within its framework, and where their social and professional development was receptive to the secular models of their political masters.

All this in turn leads on to one last question, perhaps in the end the most important of all. What *was* the legacy of Napoleonic imperialism after 1815? The short answer is that it had little to do with the overriding military might and aggrandisement of France in any lasting sense. In strictly territorial terms, the second treaty of Paris (20 November 1815) marked the total obliteration of everything Napoleon himself had ever won through military conquest. France was then cut back to her frontiers of 1789, and also lost her claims to even those parts of her 'natural frontiers' which had been gained during the revolutionary wars. None of Napoleon's own annexations survived the final Vienna Settlement, and all the lands annexed before 1799, with the exception of Avignon, the Comtat Venaissin and Mulhouse in upper Alsace, had to be surrendered as well. Not surprisingly, France was deprived of all her subject states, some of which were restored to their former dynastic rulers, while others were re-aligned into new forms of political legitimacy, more especially in the German Confederation (*Bund*) of 1815. The Napoleonic spoils system, already in disarray during the desperate campaigns of 1813–14, thus came to an ignominious end, along with all the titles of the Imperial nobility and the accompanying *dotations*. Powerful memories of *la gloire* and *la grandeur* lived on in the Napoleonic legend, of course, but their real episode in history had ended in 1815.

In the final analysis, the legacy which actually survived the collapse of the Napoleonic Empire lay almost entirely in the structures of the French *civil* state. If one thinks of the Bank of France (1800), the whole system of state centralism implied by the prefectures of 1800, the Concordat with the Catholic Church (1801), the state secondary schools or *lycées* (1802), the early fiscal reforms and bimetallic monetary standard of 1803, and the consolidation of the revolutionary land settlement enshrined in the Civil Code of 1804 – all achievements of the Consular Republic rather than of the hereditary Empire – that legacy was monumental by any standards. All these measures, along with the later legal codes, were to leave their mark on the subsequent institutional history of France, in several cases to the present day.

With important qualifications, one may say the same of the legacy of Napoleonic imperialism beyond French frontiers. The most recent research, not least by the scholars who debated this whole issue at a conference held at the Institute of Historical Research in London in April 1997, suggests that a broad consensus is now forming on a number of major points.[33] It is agreed that Napoleon's long-term impact varied considerably across the annexed departments and the subject or allied states. As the Restoration governments came to terms with these diverse effects, they had to recognise that his methods of raising taxes, harnessing ecclesiastical resources, recruiting soldiers, applying regular justice and maintaining a mobile local gendarmerie, had all been more efficient instruments of executive state centralism than earlier systems in force in their own lands. In more receptive states, such as Bavaria, Württemberg and Baden, Napoleonic models of government had certainly been emulated. Indeed, they had given a new lease of life to the secular reforms of some earlier rulers under the old regime. Even in lands where French rule had met with a hostile reaction, its very shock had had repercussions among the local elites. So, too, sovereign states like Prussia and Austria, which had never been an integral part of Napoleon's 'Grand Empire', had been driven to internal reforms in response to the traumatic experience of their conquest by France. The Catholic Church may have recovered its spiritual and ideological authority at the Vienna Congress, along with the Papal States in Italy, but its material base had shrunk significantly. The secularisation of much of its property and educational institutions, including a good many universities in the former 'Grand Empire', could not be undone. In a wider perspective, the political geography of western and central Europe in 1815 did not – could not – mark a wholesale return to that of 1789. The fragmented complexity of German states (*Kleinstaaterei*) under the old regime had been swept away, and the Holy Roman Empire had been abolished once and for all. Elsewhere, smaller historical entities like the old republics of Genoa and of Venice had disappeared, never to return.

On the other hand, all due allowance has to be made for those hallmarks of Napoleonic rule which were not 'modern', or rational, or constructive, and for those conquered territories where 'integration' with the French administrative and legal practices proved to be a fond chimera. This was especially the case in the years after 1807, when Napoleon's 'politics of grandeur' and Imperial spoils system reached their apogee. Nearly thirty years ago Louis Bergeron perceptively observed that 'paradoxically, Napoleon was both behind and ahead of his time, the last of the enlightened despots, and a prophet of the modern State'.[34] The point was made specifically in relation to France; yet it would, I think, apply just as well to the lands of the 'Grand Empire'.

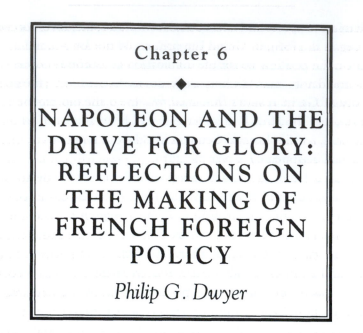

Chapter 6

◆

NAPOLEON AND THE DRIVE FOR GLORY: REFLECTIONS ON THE MAKING OF FRENCH FOREIGN POLICY

Philip G. Dwyer

Although many aspects of the period can be understood without much reference to Napoleon, no account of the wars that took place between 1803 and 1815 can neglect his role in them. Without him, it is difficult if not impossible to imagine the major French military and foreign political undertakings during this period. The conquest of northern Italy in 1796–97, the expedition to Egypt in 1798–99, the intervention in Spain in 1808 and the invasion of Russia in 1812 are all associated with his name. Indeed, the wars that took place during this period are the only wars in the modern era named after the man held responsible for them. However, the debate about the relationship between larger structural impersonal forces and the role of the individual in the formation of foreign policy is noticeably lacking for the Napoleonic era, unlike other periods of modern European history.

The French conquest of Europe has always been at the centre of the historiographical debates surrounding the period. Indeed, it is dominated by multi-volume studies entirely dedicated to the details of diplomatic and military operations. Generally speaking, historians attempting to explain the wars of Napoleon can be roughly divided into two schools of thought (I use that term very loosely), although the two are not mutually exclusive.

The first school of thought emphasises the larger, impersonal socio-economic forces at play. Those who adhere to it place the Napoleonic wars either within the more immediate context of the French revolutionary wars (which began in 1792), or within the context of the long-standing struggle between Britain and France for the domination of Europe and the world. It was a theme that was first taken up by Napoleon at St Helena; the goal of the various coalitions, he always maintained, was the dismemberment of France and the re-establishment of the Ancien Regime.[1] Napoleon thus placed his own wars within the continuity of the French revolutionary wars. The refrain has since been repeated by almost all the major French diplomatic historians. Albert Sorel, for example, argues that when Napoleon came to power in 1799 he simply inherited a foreign political situation that was not of his own making and one that he attempted to resolve by fighting to acquire France's 'natural frontiers'.[2] For Sorel, the wars of Napoleon were fought in legitim-ate defence against monarchical Europe, which continually renewed the coalitions against France. His thesis has been mirrored by François Furet, who argued that the campaigns of Napoleon had their roots in the war begun by the Girondins in 1792 during the Legislative Assembly.[3]

Other historians, however, go back even further than the Revolution. French foreign policy attitudes towards Britain during this period, it has been argued, were no more and no less a continuation of the long struggle between these two powers for the domination of Europe and indeed of the world. Marcel Dunan was perhaps the first to emphasise the political continu-ity of the Napoleonic wars with the past, while François Crouzet has gone so far as to describe the conflict as the 'Second Hundred Years' War'.[4] France lost the upper hand, he argues, despite the brief triumph against Britain during the American War of Independence, well before the Revolution wrought havoc on its proto-industrial and mercantile interests. Similarly, Paul Kennedy argues that the Napoleonic wars were the last round of the seven major Anglo–French wars fought between 1689 and 1815.[5] Paul Schroeder, in his magisterial but sometimes provocative analysis of the European states system, has proposed a variation on this theme. He argues that it was not a competition between France and Britain, nor between France and the rest of Europe, but rather between three hegemonic powers – France, Britain *and* Russia – over who would control and exploit the countries in between.[6] To sum up these views into a somewhat simplistic aphorism, Napoleon's foreign policy was essentially French foreign policy.

This brings us to the second school of thought, in which greater emphasis is placed on the role of the individual in the making of foreign policy. A num-ber of historians, while pointing to the existence of systemic factors that would have made war likely even without Napoleon, nevertheless do not hesitate to lay the blame for the wars fought after 1803 squarely at Napoleon's feet. Thus, Charles Esdaile categorically states that the responsibility for the wars was Napoleon's, and Napoleon's alone. He reasons that 'there was no hope of co-operation with Napoleon on an equal basis, *his personality simply being impossible to accommodate within any normal framework of international relations*'.[7] Gunther Rothenberg believes that Napoleon caused all the wars, which were the result of 'the will of the individual [that is, Napoleon's], rather than external or internal circumstances'.[8] Even Schroeder cannot help reverting now and then to the importance of the individual actor in the formulation of foreign policy: 'just as 1939 was Hitler's war, in the sense that he willed it and made it possible, so all the wars after 1802 were Bonaparte's wars'. Napoleon's foreign policy is thus dismissed as a 'criminal enterprise' with Napoleon behaving little better than a *condottiere*. To Schroeder, there is little point in asking questions about why Napoleon did certain things and not others: 'Napoleon', he argues, 'did what he did because he was Napoleon.'[9]

Underlying this approach – that is, willingness to ascribe the chief responsibility for the wars to Napoleon – is the assumption that there was some sort of fundamental character flaw that prevented him from coming to a working arrangement with the other European powers. There was no such thing as enough; Napoleon was unable to 'see the jugular without going for it', and constantly opted for short-term solutions without taking into consideration the long-term consequences.[10] He did not start out as a 'normal' politician who only later went to extremes; his inability to accept the existence of independent buffer states, his treatment of allies as enemies, his quest for further military victories, his total disregard for the lives of others, were there from the very start, built into his personality. Consequently, 'always very clear in his own mind that he wanted to dominate Europe', Napoleon set out to conquer as much territory as he could.[11]

Almost inadvertently historians keep coming back to the role of personality. The problem is, however, that they seem to have mistaken the symptoms for the illness. If, as the above examples illustrate, historians are prepared to take into account personality as a factor in explaining the Napoleonic wars, then it is essential to examine, over and above the structural deficiencies of eighteenth-century balance-of-power politics, what motivated Napoleon to continually make war; what underlying personality features compelled him to dominate, conquer, bully, refuse compromise and strive after an empire; what indeed lay behind his restless drive for glory. History, after all, is not made uniquely by state structures and social institutions, but by the people who run them. An examination of Napoleon and how he related to the diplomatic structures and values of the day is, therefore, fundamental to understanding why he set out down the path that ultimately led him to conquer most of Europe and also why it ultimately led to his downfall. This emphasis on Napoleon's character is not to downplay other explanations of foreign policy. Napoleon's personal ambition does not alone explain French expansion and conquest; its germ may be found in the ambitious foreign-policy projects of the revolutionaries. It is, however, to argue that Napoleon made a difference.

THE POLITICS OF EXPANSIONISM

Before examining aspects of Napoleon's character that helped shape French foreign policy, it is worth looking at some of the broader forces at play. Napoleon was restricted in his foreign-policy choices by a variety of factors: the consequences of his own upbringing, the values and interests he inherited as a soldier, the attitudes and perceptions prevalent in Ancien Regime society, the geo-political factors he inherited when he came to power; as well as the state of the French navy. The observations which follow are generalisations, but these are necessary if one is to avoid getting bogged down in the intricacies of the diplomatico-political and military manoeuvrings leading to one war or the other.

1. The continuity of French foreign policy

Perhaps the most important point to make is that Napoleon's empire had its roots in the policies of the Revolution. In principle, the French revolutionaries had determined on a policy of expansion to France's natural frontiers – the Rhine in the north and the east, the Alps and the Pyrenees in the south and south-east – which was never anything more than a thinly veiled pretext for expansionist aims. The resulting occupation of the Austrian Netherlands and eventually the Low Countries was a part of this extension and from that time on became a stumbling-block to peace with Britain. Their evacuation was to be a constant British demand throughout the period. If that were not bad enough, individual revolutionary generals soon started taking things into their own hands by creating 'sister republics' outside the areas considered to fall within France's natural frontiers – the Cispadane Republic (1796) later transformed into the Cisalpine Republic (1797, a private initiative on the part of Bonaparte), the Cisrhenan Republic (1797, an initiative by General Hoche that was quickly killed off), the Roman Republic (1798–99) and the Parthenopean Republic (1799). This was one of the reasons why peace was not possible during the revolutionary era; the government in Paris could not control its generals in the field. Moreover, the expansionist tendencies of various French generals were an indication that the revolutionary governments in Paris had no coherent policy, largely a reflection of the internal conflict raging between those who wanted to expand to France's 'natural frontiers' and those who wanted to expand elsewhere (Germany, Switzerland, northern Italy).[12] Large sections of the revolutionary governments were nevertheless complicit in expansionism beyond France's natural frontiers, as can be seen in the creation of the Batavian (1795), Ligurian (1797) and Helvetic Republics (1798). 'Sister republics' were nominally independent but of course little better than puppet regimes.

After Austria was finally knocked out of the war of the First Coalition in 1797–98, largely as a result of Napoleon's victories in northern Italy, and after the invasion of the only country left in the war – Britain – was called off in 1798, the French revolutionaries had one of two foreign-policy choices to make, both aimed at bringing Britain to heel and consequently at bringing the war to an end.

The first option was to strike at British commercial interests. This was done in northern Europe by invading the Electorate of Hanover (nominally ruled by George III of England) and the city of Hamburg in 1803, and in southern Europe by invading the Kingdom of Naples in 1806 and Portugal in 1807. The economic blockade, which the Committee of Public Safety introduced in August 1795, was thereby intensified and taken to its logical conclusion. To follow this policy, however, was to launch into an indefinite expansionist programme in order to plug the breaches of the blockade against British commerce. This is eventually, some historians would argue, the policy that was adopted and relentlessly pursued by Napoleon, and can be seen in French attempts to gain more ships to acquire strong naval partners (Holland, Denmark, Portugal, Spain and even Russia).

The desire to defeat Britain economically also helps explain the French rapprochement with Russia. The two countries had flirted with each other briefly while Paul I was still alive in 1800. However, it was not until the defeat of the Russians at Austerlitz (2 December 1805) and again at Friedland (14 June 1807) that an arrangement between the two countries was worked out at Tilsit in July 1807. Tilsit, in some respects at least, was more about implementing Napoleon's Continental System and less about bringing Britain to its knees.[13] The traditional view on French foreign policy during this

period has it that Russia, and for that matter Spain and Portugal, was fundamental if the Continental Blockade was ever to be effective; that is, if France
was to exclude British trade from the Continent. In reality, however, Spain
was not in breach of the Blockade and Russia was only to a limited extent.
In economic/political terms, the reason why Napoleon decided to invade
Spain in 1808 and Russia in 1812 had less to do with enforcing the Blockade
and much more to do with bringing both countries within the System. It is
worth emphasising, however, that Napoleon only formalised a system and
an approach that he inherited from the Revolution. It was not the primary
motive for continued conquest.

The second option open to the revolutionaries, which in some respects
was an extension of the first, was to threaten Britain and its empire at its most
vulnerable points. This was a policy pursued during the Directory; it resulted
in the expedition to Ireland in 1796 and again in 1798, a planned expedition
to England in 1797–98 and again in 1804–1805, and the expedition to Egypt
in 1798–99. Though the expedition to Egypt might seem like a peculiarly
Bonapartist initiative, the whole scheme was in fact perfectly consistent with
Ancien Regime notions of geo-politics and indeed was based upon plans that
had been accumulated at the Ministry of Foreign Affairs over the preceding
three decades.[14] The expedition failed for reasons that cannot be explored
fully here, but the most important was the inability of the French navy to
maintain the supply routes from France to Egypt and to contend with the
British navy. So when Napoleon returned to Paris in 1799, the French found
themselves back at square one. A number of attempts were made to pursue
this option; plans were made to resupply and reinforce French troops in
Egypt at the end of 1800 and the beginning of 1801 and to attack the Cape
in 1805, India came back on the agenda in 1807–1808, and a naval-building
programme was stepped up to a projected 150 ships of the line in the years
after Trafalgar (October 1805). But as long as France was unable to compete
effectively upon the high seas, the only practical solution to the defeat of
Britain lay in an expansionist policy on the Continent. This was evident even
before Trafalgar. The French inability to come to grips with Britain on the
high seas was one of the main reasons why the Berlin decrees formalising
the Continental Blockade were implemented one year after Trafalgar on
21 November 1806. In other words, it appears as though Napoleon's foreign policy – including the introduction of the Continental Blockade and
the establishment of an empire – was the logical outcome of policies whose
seeds had been planted in the 1790s by the French revolutionaries whose
antecedents lay in turn in the eighteenth-century European states system.

Orville T. Murphy has argued that Louis XVI's commercial policies of exclusion against England might also have led to the Continental System, if pushed to the utmost.[15] Napoleon, in short, inherited a situation that was not of his making (even though his role in northern Italy (1796–97) and Egypt (1798–99) helped create it), and instituted solutions that were largely in keeping with previous regimes' responses. To an extent, then, Napoleon was caught up in wars whose structural causes were beyond his control and beyond his comprehension.

2. The lack of defined, specific objectives

Within this very broad schema, there are a number of observations to be made. First, Napoleon had no long-term goals other than the defeat of Britain and, more importantly, the aggrandisement of his own power and glory.[16] Both became inextricably linked and inevitably the primary motivating factor behind almost all Napoleon's foreign-political decisions. What was to come after that, however, no one – certainly not Napoleon – knew.[17] No one during the whole revolutionary and Napoleonic period even contemplated the consequences of French hegemony on the Continent, or at least never framed it in the shape of a memoir or a policy paper. On only one occasion during the Empire was there an attempt to formulate a programme that would keep France within certain limits and that recognised the place of Austria and Russia in Europe. The plan, impractical in its outlook, was formulated by Napoleon's foreign minister, Charles-Maurice de Talleyrand, and rejected by Napoleon shortly before the battle of Austerlitz in 1805.[18] Nor did Napoleon ever develop specific policies towards many European powers; this was especially the case for Austria and Prussia, although less so for Russia and Britain.

Foreign policy was carried out in much the same way as finances, from day to day, from one event to the other. This is clear from a reading of the diplomatic dispatches of some of the foreign ambassadors to Paris throughout the revolutionary and Napoleonic periods. Time and again they complain of a lack of system.[19]

Towards the end of the Empire, Count Molé, who was conceited enough to believe he had penetrated Napoleon's mind, declared: 'I never perceived the slightest preoccupation with edifying an imperishable edifice.'[20] This was partly because Napoleon never knew what kind of conditions he was going to impose on the vanquished – something that was blatantly obvious in Russia when Napoleon, once in Moscow, desperately sought a means of bringing

Alexander to the negotiating table, but without having first formulated any ideas about what kind of peace he wanted. On the contrary, he put out feelers to know what kind of peace would be acceptable to Alexander.[21]

If there was any direction in Napoleon's foreign-political thinking, then it only started to be introduced in a systematic fashion from about 1806 onwards in the shape of the Continental System, but it never became a governing principle. The traditional historical view is that Napoleon's foreign policy was subordinated to the strategic necessity of implementing the Continental System. He had to oblige all of Europe to submit to it in order to make it work, which is why he invaded Portugal in 1807, Spain in 1808 (repeatedly reducing the authority of his brother, Joseph, during the course of the occupation), annexed Holland and large portions of Westphalia, imposed direct rule in Berg, and invaded Russia in 1812. In fact, a distinction has to be made between the objectives of the Continental System on the one hand and the manner in which it was implemented on the other. The Continental System was much more an attempt to bring Europe under French economic subjugation and far less an attempt to defeat Britain. Napoleon knew that the Blockade against British goods was not working and had, for all intents and purposes, abandoned it as a means of defeating Britain well before the decision was made to invade Russia.[22] If one accepts this argument, then Napoleon's justification for invading northern Germany, southern Italy, Spain, Portugal and especially Russia becomes incomprehensible except as part of a general pattern of conquest and expansion.

3. An ideological consensus

Another generalisation worth making is that Napoleon's foreign-political decisions conformed to the material and political interests of the new elite which he represented (the *notables*), while many of the traditional elite (nobles who had 'rallied' to the regime) identified with his goals. A kind of 'ideological consensus' existed in favour of France's bid for imperial power in the late eighteenth and early nineteenth century.[23] If there was a persistent debate between annexationists and anti-annexationists in revolutionary Paris, it had for all intents and purposes ceased by the time Napoleon came to power in 1799. True, even under Napoleon a peace party was intermittently active (in 1802–1803 during negotiations with Britain, and again in 1806) but Napoleon's determination to exclude Britain from the Continent, or not to make the concessions that might have led to a durable peace, made any effort on the part of those in favour of peace pointless.[24] Moreover, there were too many vested interests at stake. The need for military victory and the fiscal benefits associated with expansionism, which were often the primary motive for launching upon annexationist wars, had seen to it that those against annexation were soon marginalised. Between about 1799 and 1810, the extension of French power on the Continent was regarded not only as understandable but as desirable by virtually all those who had some say in foreign policy – ministers, generals, admirals, diplomats, foreign ministry officials, journalists, bankers, businessmen – whose unanimity on this issue points to larger, impersonal forces at work.[25] This is not to say that the Napoleonic regime was militaristic in nature and that it required war, but that Napoleon always found allies ready to support his expansionist wars.

There was, of course, criticism of Napoleon's foreign policy but it was often limited to private grumbling among Napoleon's generals, to resignations among his ministers, and to a few anonymous – usually royalist or Jacobin – opposition pamphlets. Talleyrand, for example, who had diverged on matters of policy from Napoleon ever since 1803, resigned after Tilsit in August 1807. From about 1808–14, he became a rallying point at court for all those who were discontented with either Napoleon or his policies. This type of high-political opposition, however, although it needs to be studied further, does not seem to have been terribly widespread and never proved to be an effective bulwark against Napoleon's ambitions. The lack of high-political opposition to, and domestic criticism of, an aggressive expansionist foreign policy before 1810, however, leads one to conclude that there was an ideological coherence that was remarkably uniform. This suggests that some attention should be given to the perceptions and prejudices of the statesmen and officials who advised Napoleon – the prevalence of hostile attitudes towards Britain in French society, for example – as well as to the perceptions and prejudices of Napoleon himself.

4. The 'monarchical' character of the Napoleonic regime

The final point to be made is that the edifice of the imperial system was built around the person of Napoleon. Even before the Empire was founded in 1804, there had been a massive reorganisation of the administrative and judicial system away from the elective principle towards a highly centralised system of appointments from the top. All the important decisions were left for Napoleon, as were many of the minor details of the running of empire, a trend which increased with time. There were, for example, no mechanisms in place for the running of affairs in the absence of the Emperor.[26] At the highest levels of government, diplomats, officials, officers and members of court society were thus condemned to try and enlist the favour of the Emperor in order to maintain their position or gain new ones. Moreover, officials were often selected purely on the basis of Napoleon's personal inclinations. As such, Napoleonic officials can be said to represent, in general terms, the institutionalisation of the Emperor's personality. Ministers were consequently often no more than *grand commis* (high civil servants) who carried out the orders of the Emperor. Even personalities such as Talleyrand and Fouché became mere executors of their imperial master's will, (largely) dutiful technocrats, who had few if any long-term views on the place of France in Europe. He appointed the generals, he controlled the finances and, more importantly, he decided war and peace. Although the illusion of representative assemblies was maintained through the Senate, the *Corps Législatif* and the Tribunate, their power was negligible. On the other hand, there were no real controls over the executive. In fact, Napoleon possessed powers and prerogatives that resembled more those of the eastern absolutist rulers than those of the constitutional monarch George III.

Napoleon's dual role as head of state and chief of the armed forces meant that the formulation and adoption of operational war-plans entirely revolved around his person. During the French revolutionary wars, there were several, uncoordinated theatres of operation with several, independent armies. Under Napoleon, the material potential (in manpower and resources) that France enjoyed was transformed into a much more potent force when he reorganised the command structure of the army so that he was in total control of operations and planning. Indeed, the entire conduct of the army and of foreign policy was in Napoleon's hands. In other European states, where war-plans were also laid before monarchs for their approval, there was both a civilian and a military chain of command that ended with the sovereign, who could then balance the two spheres and thus act as a check on the military (when necessary). The opposite, of course, could sometimes happen. It was only at the insistence of Alexander I, against the advice of the Russian commander, Kutuzov, that Russian forces continued into Germany after the French retreat in 1812.[27] But in Napoleon, more than any other monarch, the two spheres were confounded. Indeed, he held the military sphere to be superior to civilian matters.

These are some of the factors that have to be taken into consideration when analysing French foreign policy during this era. Whatever differences in interpretation may exist, there is always a basic general consideration: Napoleon may have inherited a foreign-political situation that was not of his own making, but he was also the primary cause of all the wars fought after 1803. This is a given that few historians would dispute. Napoleon, in other words, was a historical force. He profoundly altered the environment in which he acted; his decisions had a tremendous impact not only on the lives of other people, but on the international system and the way it functioned; he made choices for war rather than peace. Given this, it makes sense to try and understand what motivated Napoleon, to attempt to catch a glimpse, however difficult the task, of the inner man. Great powers do not conquer simply because they can, even in eighteenth-century Europe. Their rulers had to have the will to conquer and Napoleon had it in abundance.

THE DRIVE FOR GLORY

There are a number of character traits that were always present in Napoleon in varying degrees of intensity throughout his career. Three in particular are worthy of consideration: Napoleon's construction of an idealised self-image, his unbounded imagination, and the vindictive nature of his behaviour. These elements form the basis of what one could loosely term a 'drive for glory'.[28]

1. The construction of an idealised image

The process towards the 'drive for glory' was initiated by a few relatively harmless fantasies in which Napoleon pictured himself in the glamorous role of, first, saviour of his people (Corsica), and then as the warrior hero who was to eventually save France. During this period (from his teens to his late 20s) he created an idealised image of what he could become or could accomplish. The most decisive step in this process occurred during the first Italian campaign. Utilising the media available at the time (newspapers, prints, paintings and sculptures), he represented himself through a whole repertory of posturing and symbolism.[29] The image portrayed was that of a young, dynamic conqueror; a hero; a selfless benefactor who not only brought peace to Italy, but whose virtues were extolled and contrasted with the corruption associated with the Directory. (Note the title of one of Napoleon's newspapers, the *Journal de Bonaparte et des hommes vertueux* ('Bonaparte and virtuous men'), in circulation for a short time in Paris at the beginning of 1797.) By this means Napoleon both asserted and maintained his power over the troops he led (who were loyal to him rather than to the state), and the peoples he conquered. In other words, it was an astute use of propaganda for political purposes, but it was also the beginning of a kind of personality cult, which later came to play a central role in the creation of the Empire. By 1804, the notion of the hero, the saviour of France, was embedded in the public imagination. At the same time, however, Napoleon was inviting the public's participation in his fantasies; they were to identify with him as leader, states-man and man of action.

There are two aspects of this process of self-idealisation that have been relatively neglected by historians: its implications for Napoleon's behaviour on the international scene; and the role of 'destiny' in the formation of the idealised self. The written and visual representations of Napoleon, which became more sophisticated as the regime progressed, were essentially a reflection not of how Napoleon saw himself, but of how he wanted to be perceived. We can also safely assume that the psychological forces which impelled the young Napoleon to form a heroic identity during his first cam-paign in Italy, even if it was an exercise in political propaganda, remained active and perhaps even intensified in later years. Indeed, it is likely that Napoleon came to identify with his own idealised image to the point where it began to govern the way he ran his life and how he related to others. More importantly, though, as far as his behaviour on the foreign-political scene is concerned, it prevented him from accepting himself on any other terms (I shall come back to this point in a moment). The image, moreover, was not only self-reinforcing but also self-perpetuating. Artists and writers were only too happy to contribute to the construction of the myth of Napoleon as great man. The image Napoleon projected of himself was blurred with the image flatterers and toadies were sending back to him. In short, the complex inter-relation between Napoleon's projected image and the French people's reception of it is crucial to an understanding of his motives, and warrants a good deal more study before any authoritative conclusions are drawn. For the purposes of this essay, however, one can safely assume that it helped shape Napoleon's political choices by obliging him to conform to that initial projected image.

This idealised image-building was also partly based upon Napoleon's unshakeable belief in 'destiny'.[30] This belief was there from the start – the words *au destin* were inscribed, for example, in the wedding ring he gave Josephine – but the thought that fate had reserved something special for him first dawned on him after the battle of Lodi (10 May 1796): 'I already saw the world flee before me [*fuir sous moi*], as if I were being carried in the air.'[31] By the time he was in Egypt it had become an accepted part of the image: 'Is there a man blind enough to not see,' he declared to the people of Egypt, 'that destiny directs all my operations? Is there anyone incredulous enough to doubt that everything in this vast universe is subordinated to the empire of fate?'[32] These utterances have to be taken with a grain of salt since they were often made during his exile on St Helena where Napoleon was primarily concerned with remaking history in his own image, but I think we can safely assume that he was egotistic enough to believe that he was a special individual. The idea that his star was ineluctably rising was reinforced by victories like Marengo (June 1800), which he normally should have lost; and Austerlitz (December 1805), which he won where another general might easily have been defeated. Continued victories enhanced his belief not only that he was a superior being, a Charlemagne,[33] but also that he controlled the world about him. This feeling of mastery was based upon the notion that there was nothing that he could not do, and no campaign that he could not win. He eventually became the man of destiny, the conqueror, the great giver of laws – that is, he fulfilled his own ideal.

This unquestioned belief in his greatness and uniqueness, which developed and intensified over time, is an important key to understanding Napoleon's behaviour. As a young man, Napoleon had created a kind of fantasy world in which he was the hero, and to an extent he had lived out that fantasy in Italy and Egypt. But this was the rub. In order to live up to his own imagined self, he had to prove himself constantly in action. Hence the constant need for further victory on the battlefield. One of the reasons why Napoleon intervened in the Iberian peninsula, for example, was the need to find fresh opportunities to display his military might after Tilsit. The idealised image he had built of himself was based on a desire, conscious or not, to overcome every material obstacle, to resolve every difficult situation. This was his fate.

2. A vision of unlimited possibilities

The second most striking characteristic of Napoleon's drive for glory was his imagination. Napoleon's mind often wandered into the realm of the fantastic or of unlimited possibilities. No matter how much Napoleon prided himself on being a realist, and no matter how realistic his march towards success, his imagination constantly made him mistake a mirage for the real thing. 'An unbounded imagination, that is the cause, the source of all of humanity's misfortunes. It causes us to wander from sea to sea, from fantasy to fantasy, and if it finally calms down, if its glamour finally abandons us, . . . the hour has come and man dies detesting life.'[34] Imagination, in other words, was intimately tied in with Napoleon's ambition, which as a consequence knew no bounds. He was thinking, for example, of the conquest of the Orient, or the mastery of Europe, while he was still fighting his first campaign in Italy.[35] He later admitted that it was in Egypt that 'the ambition came to [me] of executing the great things which so far had been occupying my thoughts only as a fantastic dream'.[36] Each conquest brought with it the possibility of further conquests. Thus, shortly after the invasion of Spain, which he was always at pains to justify, he began to formulate plans to conquer South America, Havana, Mexico, the Philippines and even the Dutch East Indies. There were also plans to march to Constantinople and India, as well as Persia.[37] A recent study has shown that coronation gear was found in the French baggage train by the Russians during the retreat from Moscow and concludes, somewhat speculatively, that Napoleon had wanted to proclaim the universal monarchy.[38]

None of this means, of course, that Napoleon ever seriously considered conquering these countries or that he was intent on dominating the world. It is even doubtful, in spite of the rhetoric, that Napoleon set out to establish a Roman- or Carolingian-type empire. The very fact, however, that he imagined or simply contemplated vast conquests is significant. It means that he did not realistically consider there were any limits to his power. If the opportunity presented itself, and the means were available, Napoleon would let himself be taken in that direction. The interesting thing about Napoleon's unbounded imagination is that, because he was able to make his projects appear perfectly rational, he was able to appeal to the self-interest of those involved in carrying out his plans. The two most obvious examples are the expedition to Egypt in 1798–99 and the invasion of Russia in 1812. Both examples demonstrate that Napoleon was able to adapt his imagination to the demands of reality. They were, nevertheless, grandiose, and one might even argue fundamentally irrational, because they did not fit within any patterns that could be associated with traditional French foreign-policy behaviour.

The expedition to Egypt is a good example of the correspondence between historical circumstances and the individual that can lead to momentous events. If we put aside for one moment the intellectual and geo-political origins of the expedition, and the dubious notion that the Directory wanted to be rid of a cumbersome general, then we are left with Napoleon as *the* motivating force. The idea of the expedition had been bandied around, inspiring little or no interest, over the previous three or four decades – until Napoleon came along. Without wanting to go into what some historians have described as his 'oriental complex' – that is, his desire to imitate figures

like Alexander and Caesar – there can be no doubt that Napoleon's organising energy, and more importantly his fascination with the idea that conquests
in the Orient would bring him glory, was at the centre of the expedition.
(Talleyrand played a secondary role that facilitated Napoleon's access to the
Directory.)

Important, too, was the role Egypt played in the continued development
of Napoleon's unbounded imagination. Despite the disastrous consequences
of the expedition in military terms, Egypt fed rather than quenched
Napoleon's vision of unlimited possibilities. After the battle of the Pyramids
and the capture of Cairo (21 and 24 July 1798), he realised he could abandon
himself 'to the most brilliant dreams'. Freed from the inhibitions placed on
him in France and Europe, he fantasised about founding his own religion,
and about marching into Asia on top of an elephant with a turban on his
head and a 'new' Koran in his hand.[39]

As for the Russian campaign, if anyone had suggested it to, say, Louis XIV,
Louis XVI or even the French revolutionaries, the idea would simply have
been regarded as 'silly'.[40] In 1810–11, however, it was a sign that Napoleon,
and indeed French foreign policy, had taken a direction that was unimagin-
able under any previous French government. Everyone knows that
Napoleon completely ignored the exhortations of his entourage not to
undertake the invasion. He simply disregarded the evidence, which he chose
not to see. 'He listened only to flatterers; all contradiction was unbearable to
him. He had reached a point where he no longer tolerated the truth, even
in figures.'[41] However, the real reason why Napoleon invaded Russia has
nothing to do with international politics or the Continental System. It was
because he could not tolerate another power acting independently of him.[42]
Russia presented an obstacle to his will that had to be overcome; he was
going to teach it a lesson in the same way that he had taught Prussia in 1806
and Austria in 1809 a lesson and make sure that it would be cowed into com-
pliant submission. Napoleon admitted as much when he instructed his
ambassador in St Petersburg, Lauriston, to place Russia 'back in the situation
of inferiority in which she was' at the time of Tilsit.[43] This brings me to the
third trait in Napoleon's character.

3. The need for a 'vindictive triumph'

The drive for glory was closely linked to a more destructive element, the
drive towards a 'vindictive triumph', often expressed as anger or the need to
defeat and humiliate others. Thus Naples, which was nominally neutral

during the war of the Third Coalition, but which had nevertheless allied with Russia and Britain, was invaded in 1805 and the ruling House of Bourbon overthrown. Even more telling, the Pope, who had dared to protest against the French occupation of Ancona in 1805, ended up having the entire Adriatic and Tyrrhenian coast occupied for his trouble. 'I expect the pope to accommodate his conduct to my requirements,' Napoleon wrote to his ambassador in Rome, Cardinal Fesch. 'If he behaves well, I shall make no outward changes; if not, I shall reduce him to the status of bishop of Rome.'[44] Even France's satellite states and allies were exploited, while other European powers were either threatened or, if they presented an obstacle to his will, simply brushed aside.

This type of behaviour can also be seen in his relations with those in his immediate entourage. 'The arbitrariness of his despotism', wrote the comtesse de Boigne, 'was felt even in the domestic sphere.'[45] Every foreign diplomat at the court of Paris was aware that Napoleon was extremely sensitive to criticism or the slightest bit of opposition to his views.[46] He could, to use a modern idiom, 'lose it' and rant and rave against a poor diplomat who had incurred his displeasure, as happened with Schweitzer in 1801, Whitworth in 1803, Markov in 1802 and again in 1805, Metternich in 1808 and Kurakin in 1811.[47] These outbursts could sometimes lead to acts of physical violence. In Egypt, during the retreat from St Jean of Acre, Napoleon hit his equerry with his riding whip.[48] At Fontainebleau, the Pope not only had to tolerate verbal abuse, but at one stage during the negotiations Napoleon supposedly gripped him by his soutane and pushed him to and fro as he drove home his arguments. On another occasion, furious at the Pope's intractability, he smashed a priceless set of Sèvres porcelain.[49] Napoleon later stated that his rages, and indeed his blows, had always been calculated but this view should be treated with a healthy dose of scepticism.[50]

Many other examples of Napoleon's 'vindictive' behaviour could be given: massacres were ordered; rebellious peoples were brutally suppressed; 'torrents of blood' were sometimes demanded and sometimes exacted; troublemakers were shot; orders to consume towns like Frankfurt and Munich in flames were given, although never carried out.[51] The fact that Napoleon had difficulty controlling his emotions, or that he sometimes physically lashed out at those in his entourage, is *prima facie* not a particularly interesting point to make, especially since the link between Napoleon's behaviour and the foreign-policy decisions he made would at this level appear tenuous. His behaviour is, in any event, as much a cultural time-specific phenomenon as it is a reflection of personality – that is, most eighteenth-century European monarchs issued orders at various stages of their reigns to eliminate rebellious subjects, some with greater zeal than others; some physically abused those in their entourage; and certainly very few showed remorse at the loss of either civilian or military life. Moreover, the danger in focusing on these types of examples is to conclude, like Schroeder, that Napoleon did what he did because he was Napoleon.

More difficult, but more important, is to understand that these were the symptoms of a much more profound illness exacerbated under very specific circumstances; namely, when he was under great pressure to live up to his idealised self, or when he found that his destiny was being frustrated by external forces. Thus, it was only in times of crisis, when there was a discrepancy between Napoleon's self-image and the external forces preventing him from achieving his destiny, that he reacted in such a violent manner. Increasingly there was a blurring of the boundary between fantasy and reality, ideas and people, actions and dreams. This is why in 1813–14, after the disastrous results of the Russian campaign, which would have brought another monarch back to a more realistic assessment of his limitations, Napoleon desperately clung on to the Empire he had constructed, and refused a compromise peace that might have given him a breathing space to re-group and recuperate. To compromise was seen as a weakness and an attack against his self-image. Only by fighting to keep the Empire could he maintain the fiction that destiny had reserved a special fate for him. To admit that it had not was to admit that his glorified self had feet of clay. This was one of the reasons why his drive for glory was ultimately self-destructive.

CONCLUSION

On the international scene, Napoleon conducted himself in much the same way as any other European statesman of the time. The unwillingness to accept compromise, the desire to re-mould Europe that ignored the realities of everyday people, the cynical exploitation of allies, and the reliance on the politics of annexations and expropriations are all attitudes to be found in eighteenth- and nineteenth-century great-power relations. After all, Napoleon was not the only ruler to conquer and suppress other states by the use of bullying tactics, manipulation and extortion; or to bludgeon and threaten other countries into becoming friends and allies. Frederick the Great, Catherine the Great, Joseph II and Gustav III all used the same tactics. Louis XIV also wanted to dominate his neighbours and Europe. The difference between Napoleon and other eighteenth-century rulers is that they often had specific, limited goals (with the exception perhaps of Louis XIV), while Napoleon had none.

This conclusion echoes Paul Schroeder's remark that Napoleon was a corsair and a half compared to everybody else's half a corsair. Granted, the only thing stopping Napoleon from securing a stable position of hegemony for France on the Continent was Napoleon.[52] However, all attempts to date to explain Napoleon's behaviour through an analysis of the European states system, or by reverting to labels like *condottiere*, or by simply laying the blame for the wars at his feet, ultimately fall short of the mark. Without denying the importance of the international system and of the larger impersonal forces at play, without denying the degree to which Napoleon's foreign policy was largely inherited, one simply cannot ignore Napoleon's deliberate decisions and actions, the result of unconscious processes that had little to do with French foreign policy, French security interests or the Anglo–French–Russian struggle for the domination of the Continent. Ultimately, the notions of conquest, expansion and even empire were also political expressions of Napoleon's personality.

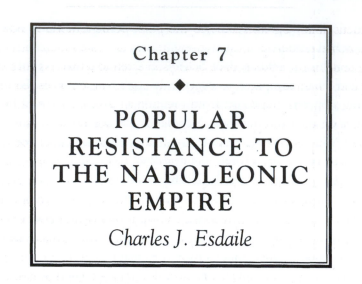

Chapter 7

◆

POPULAR RESISTANCE TO THE NAPOLEONIC EMPIRE

Charles J. Esdaile

Ten years ago I was asked to contribute a volume on the Napoleonic wars to a new Longman series entitled 'Modern Wars in Perspective'. Published in 1995 as *The Wars of Napoleon*, the result included a chapter on popular resistance that mostly remains as valid now as when it was first written.[1] For all that, however, time has moved on. While fresh perspectives on resistance have been offered by Broers in his seminal *Europe under Napoleon*, for example, extensive archival research has persuaded me that the whole subject is open to extensive revision.[2]

BACKGROUND TO REVOLT

The Napoleonic Empire was in no sense a popular institution. Consciously administered by and for elite groups, for the populace it constituted a wearisome burden: taxation and conscription were heavy, and the imperial forces frequently rapacious and badly behaved. At the same time, of course, it was also highly intrusive, often being visibly alien and accompanied by changes that overturned established patterns of life and threatened age-old certainties. Already vividly demonstrated in the revolutionary period, these tensions led to much resistance in the Napoleonic era. The most dramatic examples of this tendency are the revolts that broke out in Calabria in 1806, Iberia in 1808 and the Tyrol in 1809, but – as was again the case in the 1790s – across much of the Empire various forms of low-level resistance also flourished and were in some instances never totally suppressed.

To focus solely on resistance to the Napoleonic Empire is not entirely helpful, however. Between the mid-eighteenth and late nineteenth centuries the whole of Europe was progressively subjected to a process that encapsulated the emergence of both the modern state and the market economy. In that process the Emperor and, before him, the French Revolution were major protagonists, but they were not the only protagonists – as witness the example of Spain, which experienced a series of riots, tumults and civil wars that began in 1766 and did not end until 1839. It is therefore likely that there would have been serious disorders even had Napoleon never been born. From this follow other considerations. Thus, while the revolts often presented the imperial forces with considerable problems, they contained within them sub-texts – hatred of authority or a desire for revenge against the propertied classes – that undermined their military efficacy. Furthermore, outright rebellion was a relatively isolated phenomenon; if Spain, the Tyrol and part of Italy rose in revolt, Germany as a whole did not, the moral being that certain preconditions had to exist for general unrest to be translated into open revolt.

Whatever the reasons that may be ascribed to it, the relative infrequency of armed revolt is superficially somewhat surprising, for it is immediately apparent that the popular experience of empire was universally negative. Let us first take the question of conscription. Though compulsory military service had existed in many parts of eighteenth-century Europe, in practice few men had actually been taken. Not only were there numerous social, occupational and geographical exemptions, but the need for general conscription was reduced by the recruitment of volunteers, foreigners, criminals and vagrants, the result being that conscription might not be employed at all for long periods. Even if a man was called up he was not necessarily called upon to leave his home – in several states conscripts were only expected to put in a short period of training each year, otherwise remaining in their home villages to till the land. Even then military service was not popular, armies generally being seen as sinks of iniquity.[3] Though service with the imperial armies may have been attractive to the occasional plough boy or apprentice – or, more commonly perhaps, to the unemployed and desperate – volunteers do not seem to have come forward in any numbers, the result being that compulsion was inevitable. Despite attempts to palliate the situation by impressing criminals or buying the services of mercenaries, the impact was still enormous. Men invariably disappeared for years at a time, while a very high proportion never came home at all; of 52,000 Westphalian troops who served in the *Grande Armée*, only 18,000 survived, while for Baden the figures are 17,000 out of 29,000. Small wonder, then, that Napoleon increasingly came to be seen as a bloodthirsty ogre, that men literally had to be torn away from their families, and that conscripts were often marched away roped together and under heavy guard.[4]

In addition to conscription, the Empire also signified impoverishment. In the first place, the passage of the French armies across the Continent was immensely disruptive. Convinced of their political and cultural superiority, the French were inclined to regard Belgians, Dutchmen, Germans, Italians and Spaniards alike as backward, superstitious, priest-ridden and uncouth. Meanwhile, the troops were also brutalised, long years of service away from their homes not only habituating them to violence but making them indifferent and even hostile towards civilians. And, last but not least, with its constant stress upon emulation and competition, the Napoleonic army encouraged – nay, expected – bullying, bluster and braggadocio. Despite more-or-less genuine efforts to maintain discipline, the soldiers therefore supplemented their rations by living off the country; fed their campfires with furniture, window frames, doors and fencing; and added to their pay by seizing a wide variety of valuables and trinkets of all sorts. Not even friendly territory was spared, while in extreme cases the result could be wholesale devastation. Nor was the plundering solely unofficial. On the contrary, French occupation was everywhere accompanied by the levying of immense fines known euphemistically as war contributions, as well as by the wholesale requisitioning of horses, draught animals, livestock, and foodstuffs of all sorts.[5]

Meanwhile, war was accompanied by economic disruption. Agriculture was subjected to a variety of strains, while the combination of the Continental Blockade and the British naval stranglehold paralysed trade, reduced many ports to ruin and undermined the many industries which had depended on maritime markets. Nor were matters helped by Napoleon's efforts at economic manipulation, whether it was his attempt to seize the smuggling trade for France in 1810, or his plans to turn the whole of Europe into a combination of captured market and plantation economy. Some areas of what might be termed greater France – the Rhineland, Belgium and Flanders – benefited enormously, certainly, while others succeeded in capitalising on local advantages so as to establish themselves as industrial centres, but on the whole the picture was bleak indeed, while even those areas that did well experienced a severe depression in the period 1810–12.[6]

In a development that was felt all the more for being accompanied by the introduction of new land registers and more efficient fiscal mechanisms, meanwhile, taxation rose dramatically. In Holland, for example, the already crushing burden represented by ordinary taxation, extraordinary levies and forced loans was augmented in 1806 by a series of financial reforms that increased ordinary revenue from around 30 million florins in 1805 to nearly 50 million in 1809, even this increase having to be joined by a further forced loan of 40 million florins in 1807. To add insult to injury, moreover, when Napoleon finally annexed Holland in 1810, he arbitrarily liquidated two-thirds of the enormous Dutch national debt, thereby depriving numerous landowners, merchants and businessmen of much of their income. Meanwhile, in Berg revenue more than tripled between 1808 and 1813, while in Naples it rose by 50 per cent in the first three years of Murat's reign alone, similar examples offering themselves *ad infinitum*.[7]

To all this must be added the impact of the social, political and economic reform by which Napoleonic rule was characterised. Often portrayed as a liberating force, this in fact had alarming implications. Thus, the abolition of feudalism frequently made the position of the peasantry more burdensome than ever, while the suppression of the monasteries and of large numbers of petty political units deprived numerous office-holders and dependants of all sorts of their livelihood and dealt a heavy blow to the local economies which they had sustained. At the same time, too, the suppression of the religious orders stripped away much of such infrastructure as had existed for the relief of poverty. To impoverishment, meanwhile, was added humiliation. All too often the poor were criminalised – beggars, for example, were rounded up and forced into armies or workhouses – while the authorities everywhere introduced police regulations that were aimed at restricting popular entertainments and ensuring that work was the normal order of the day.[8]

Humiliation was not just economic and social. Not all imperial soldiers were brutes, but it is nevertheless clear that the presence of the *Grande Armée* was anything but pleasant. In addition to the incessant looting, the troops were all too often drunken and badly behaved; brawling and duelling were common, while the civilian population were treated in a manner that ranged from the merely boisterous to the downright brutal. And, of course, women were a perennial bone of contention, veterans of the *Grande Armée* boasting that large numbers of girls were all too eager to throw themselves into the arms of the first dashing soldier who came their way. Irritating enough as this was, there was in any case a darker side to the question: economic hardship forced large numbers of women into prostitution, rape was clearly common, and many girls were seduced by promises of marriage only to be left to bear the consequences. And for cuckolding a continent, the Empire paid a heavy price. As one veteran observed, 'The hate which the Germans have for us should not be too surprising. They cannot pardon us for having for twenty years caressed their wives and daughters before their very faces.'[9]

French domination was also offensive in other respects. Despite recent challenges, the Catholic Church remained central to the lives of millions of Europeans. While its teachings provided explanation and consolation for death, disease and natural disaster, its rituals, customs and festivals were integral to daily life and a symbol of communal pride and identity. Each town, village and guild had a patron saint whose feast day would be celebrated with all due ceremony. Shrines and statues, too, were deeply venerated, their presence bringing with it an added measure of protection and prestige. Interference with the Church at the official level might matter little – to the inhabitant of a small German or Spanish village the question of who should appoint his bishop was probably immaterial – but attacks on popular religion were likely to prove calamitous. Yet it was precisely such an attack that the French Revolution had unleashed – hence in part the unrest that had swept France in the 1790s – and largely through the medium of the *Grande Armée* this was now translated to Napoleonic Europe. While the higher levels of government, administration and military command were often prepared to tolerate 'superstition' as a means of keeping the populace quiet or even openly to propitiate the Catholic Church, many soldiers retained a strong allegiance to the violent anti-clericalism of the Republic, as did the erstwhile Jacobins who often actually staffed local, departmental and national government in the satellite states and annexed territories. As a result, disrespect for the clergy and acts of sacrilege remained common, matters not being rendered any better by the Empire's more-or-less favourable treatment of the Jews.[10]

Impoverished, offended and harassed, the lower classes also had to endure the spectacle of the elites who had always dominated their lives being wooed by the French and in many cases profiting from their rule. This is not the place to discuss collaboration, but in every part of the Empire the Napoleonic regime depended on the support of landed property – whether noble or bourgeois – the arts and sciences, and officialdom. The constant attempts that were made to secure such support were not always successful – many nobles, for example, simply withdrew into their estates for the duration – but for those who were prepared to participate in the structures of the regime or simply to benefit from its policies, the advantages were considerable. They lay in the purchase of the large amounts of land that came onto the market as a result of the expropriation of the estates of the Church, the award of one of the 285 titles of nobility granted to citizens of the annexed territories or satellite states, the pursuit of fame and fortune in the Napoleonic armies, and the occupation of posts in the local administration.[11]

THE NORM: RECALCITRANCE, EVASION AND RIOT

Thus emerged a climate of popular hostility that was not primarily political but rather economic, social and cultural. That said, however, resentment is not the same as revolt, the fact being that the latter was very much atypical as a response to Napoleonic rule. Far more common, in fact, were a variety of forms of low-level opposition. At the very lowest level we have what today would be described as passive resistance. Thus, 'state' Catholicism was frequently boycotted; ribbons were worn in colours associated with regimes overthrown by the French; orders to illuminate cities in honour of French victories were defied, or houses decorated with rags instead of bunting; assistance was given to refractories (see below) and monks and nuns who had been turned out of their religious houses; and efforts to enforce collaboration were dodged or otherwise short-circuited.[12]

Increasingly desperate as they were, however, the population also turned to violence. Thus, setting aside brigandage, of which more below, intimidation of various sorts was widespread; while officials, town councillors, army officers and individuals perceived to be guilty of collaboration were occasionally set upon or even murdered. Alongside such more-or-less individual acts of revenge, meanwhile, could be found traditional forms of collective protest: Frankfurt in January 1807 witnessed an anti-Jewish pogrom; in northern Italy a variety of factors combined to produce a series of peasant risings in 1805 and then again in 1809; in Westphalia disputes over feudal dues occasioned disturbances among the peasantry; and in Oldenburg fishermen rioted when the French sought to curb smuggling and register them for service at sea.[13]

Of all the activities of the Napoleonic state, however, none was more hated than conscription, this being a subject that elicited resistance of almost every sort. Forced to live from day to day with the prospect of the ballot, humble families strove every nerve to collect the ever-growing sums of money that were needed to purchase the substitutes that could be sent in lieu of any man who was conscripted; while the young men involved mutilated themselves, simulated the most terrible diseases, contracted marriages of greater or lesser degrees of convenience, or fled their homes rather than risk being called up. Every year, meanwhile, particularly in those areas where it had but recently been introduced, the actual imposition of the draft was accompanied by serious violence, as was, for example, the case in Holland between 1811 and 1813. Finally, amongst those men whose lot it was deemed to be to march away, both draft evasion and desertion were frequent. With regard to the former, in Belgium, for example, over 42 per cent of conscripts absconded in the period 1805–1809, while the rate of absenteeism when conscription was first imposed in Rome in 1810 was one-third. As for desertion, by 1809 a total of 18,000 men, or over one-third of its current strength, had deserted from the army of the Kingdom of Italy, while the imperial forces suffered so many deserters in the Peninsular War that Wellington was ultimately able to maintain no fewer than ten foreign infantry battalions.[14]

For much of the time the thousands of draft evaders lived quietly in or near their homes with the aid of friends and family, while they were often able to find some form of employment. As time wore on, however, the state became not only more and more efficient but more and more ruthless in punishing those who were suspected to be in any way assisting them. As a result many refractories, as they were known, were eventually forced to take to the roads, whereupon they drifted rapidly into vagrancy and, sooner or later, crime. In this, of course, they were joined by the thousands of deserters who had left their regiments far from home and yet had no mind to find shelter in the armies of Napoleon's enemies. Reinforced by deserters from those same armies, not to mention the tens of thousands of men who had already been eking out a living from banditry long since or were forced into such an occupation out of poverty and despair, the whole mass came to terrorise large areas of the Empire. Much progress was achieved in the imposition of order, true; but even in France there were pockets of territory that were never wholly subdued.[15]

THE EXCEPTION: ARMED REBELLION

For all this unrest, however, in only three areas – Calabria, the Iberian peninsula and the Tyrol – do we see full-scale popular insurrections. Clearly, then, rebellion needed very special circumstances: even in the highly auspicious conditions of 1809, five successive attempts to raise a revolt in Westphalia were almost completely ignored by the peasantry. Essentially, these preconditions were threefold, the first being discontent with the dynasty supplanted by Napoleonic rule, the second social tension, and the third traditions of popular military activity. This is not to say that other factors – Catholicism, rugged terrain and geographical isolation – were not of importance, but it should be pointed out that they applied to many areas that did not rise *en masse* in the same style. Taking each of our three preconditions in turn, we find that both Calabria and the Tyrol had been alienated by royal policy, and that in both Spain and Portugal the ruling dynasties had become utterly discredited. Immense, as we shall see, in Spain, Portugal and Calabria, even in the more homogeneous Tyrol – essentially an area of free peasant farmers – there was friction between town and countryside. And, above all, there was a widespread habituation to the use of arms. In Spain, Portugal and Calabria banditry and smuggling were a common feature of the rural economy, and frequently involved large-scale skirmishes with the security forces (by the same token Spain maintained a wide variety of irregular police units that provided a further source of quasi-military experience). Meanwhile, Spain, Portugal and the Tyrol all possessed traditions of popular mobilisation encapsulated in a variety of local home-guards.

1. Calabria: the Ruffians

In each of the three areas under discussion, then, revolt found a ready basis. Taking Calabria first, although resistance broke out in the immediate aftermath of the French invasion of Naples early in 1806, there had been little reason to expect any great display of loyalty. If Calabria had risen against the French in 1799 under the leadership of Cardinal Ruffo, the so-called 'Army of the Holy Faith' – the original ruffians – had chiefly been encouraged by the promise of lower taxation and loot. As for attitudes to the dynasty, they could hardly have been worse. Using a terrible earthquake that had hit the province in 1783 as a pretext (it was claimed that the proceeds were to help the victims), Ferdinand IV had set about the dissolution of the monasteries but had then done nothing to prevent the nobility from securing the lion's share of the land that was thereby thrown upon the market, the peasantry being left worse off than they had been before. Restored to power with the fall of the short-lived Parthenopean Republic, Ferdinand IV and his queen, Maria Carolina, did little to improve matters, reneging on Ruffo's promises and initiating large-scale recruitment to the army. When British and Russian troops landed in Naples in November 1805, they therefore received at best a tepid welcome from the populace. Indifference then turned to hostility, for the large contingent of Albanian mercenaries attached to the Russian forces ravaged the countryside without mercy. In consequence, the queen's desperate efforts to whip up support came to nothing; only a few thousand men came forward, and even these dispersed without resistance when the French crossed the border, while the populace refused to provide the defenders with supplies and even began actively to harass them.[16]

Naples, then, was occupied and the court forced to flee to Sicily, it being only at this point that trouble erupted. Thus, within a short time the invaders' forced requisitioning and disorderly behaviour had produced riots at Nicastro, Soveria and Fiume Freddo in the remote and backward province of Calabria, the French responding with wholesale burnings and executions. Reprisal now led to counter-reprisal, the British lending a hand as well by sending arms, supplies and money and temporarily disembarking a small expeditionary force. With fewer than 10,000 troops, the invaders were power-less, the entire region soon becoming over-run with bands of brigands who harassed the French, terrorised anyone who was suspected of collaboration, and established headquarters in such towns as Amantea. Nevertheless, ser-ious doubts exist as to the nature of the uprising. Even British accounts insist that the insurgents were bandits interested in little more than pillage, while a short-lived royal invasion of the mainland received no support whatsoever. Although fighting raged unabated for years, what kept the revolt alive was not devotion to the monarchy or even the Catholic Church (even though some elements of this preached revolt) but rather reprisals, traditions of vendetta and sheer destitution. Equally provocative, however, were the actions of the new regime (with the departure of the Bourbons, Naples was transformed into a satellite kingdom ruled first by Joseph Bonaparte and then by Joachim Murat). An area characterised by the brutal exploitation of the mass of the populace by feudal overlords and urban *rentiers* alike – thanks to such French-inspired reforms as emancipation, the sale of the lands of the Church and the municipalities and the transformation of local government – Calabria now saw the position of the peasantry become even worse: access to grazing land and watercourses disappeared, the Church could no longer pro-vide charity, village democracy was broken, the local *notables* acquired more land and filled the ranks of the administration, many peasants were reduced to the status of landless labourers, and last but not least 1809 witnessed the introduction of conscription.[17]

2. Spain: the Guerrillas

In short, what we have in Calabria is a *jacquerie* that was precipitated by Napoleonic occupation rather than being specifically aimed at its overthrow. If our picture of events there is a muddy one, that of events in Iberia is even muddier. So much ink has been expended on the origins of the great revolt that broke out in Spain and Portugal in the early summer of 1808 following their partial occupation by the French that there is little need to fill in the background now. However, as in Calabria, it is quite clear that the notion of devotion to the old order is not enough to explain the situation. Thus, taking the case of Spain first of all, we find that in 1808 it was in the grip of a multiple social, political and economic crisis whose most important features for our purposes are in the first place the terrible sufferings being experienced by considerable elements of the population; in the second the manner in which these were being blamed upon the erstwhile royal favourite and chief minister, Manuel de Godoy; and in the third the belief that the recent accession to the throne of the young Ferdinand VII would usher in an age of peace and prosperity in which all Spain's ills would be put to rights. Orchestrated though the rising had been by a variety of elite groups with aims that ranged from the defence of the Church and the nobility against the advance of enlightened absolutism, through the preservation of the rights and policies of the existing monarchy, to the initiation of a thorough-going liberal revolution, its rank and file were instead concerned by other issues while at the same time being utterly indifferent to the war of national liberation in which they had unwittingly involved themselves. Cry their loyalty to Ferdinand VII though they did, they therefore did so as a cover for hurling themselves on a variety of objects of popular hatred – whether they were the landed classes, the tithes owed to the Church, the representatives of the army, or officials and other figures particularly associated with the policies of Manuel de Godoy – matters being much simplified in this respect by the fact that the civil, religious and military authorities had all for the most part been urging them not to oppose the French. Riot and murder therefore abounded, while there were a variety of disturbances on the land as well as a widespread refusal to pay the tithe (in an augury of things to come, isolated examples can even be found of attacks on churches).[18]

What, however, of the war against the French? In those very limited parts of the country actually occupied by the invaders, elements of the populace had soon taken up arms and begun to engage in irregular operations of some efficacy, while attempts to take such towns as Zaragoza were met with desperate resistance. Yet elsewhere enthusiasm for the war was almost non-existent. Desperate for a wage of any sort, plenty of volunteers could be found for the new regiments that had to be organised hastily on all sides, but there seems to have been a general belief, first, that these units would be expected only to mount guard upon their own towns and cities and, second, that the French would be overcome without a fight (rumours abounded, for example, that Napoleon had been, or was about to be, overthrown). Within a very short space of time, however, it became apparent that the new regiments would be expected to march away to war and that there was to be general conscription. Stimulated by the fact that the juntas which headed the uprising were everywhere dominated by the same *notables* who had monopolised local government prior to 1808 and that the propertied classes were attempting by a variety of means to ensure that the brunt of the struggle fell upon the poor, the populace responded with considerable anger. Desertion immediately soared, the flow of volunteers dried up, and conscription was resisted with precisely the same evasion, riot and subterfuge that had made themselves so much felt in France and her satellite states. As pressure increased on the part of the authorities, meanwhile, the disorders that had accompanied the insurrection intensified, with a number of cities experiencing serious risings and the whole country being over-run by gangs of bandits and deserters.[19]

Dozens of insurgent bands were soon in operation against the French, but comparatively few conform to the traditional stereotype of groups of outraged patriots sallying forth to do battle with the foe. Many were formed on the basis of traditional home-guards such as the Galician *alarma* and the Catalan *somatén*, or consisted of new units of volunteers and conscripts raised during and after the uprising.[20] Still others, meanwhile, had been raised by the agents of the various Patriot juntas that were established inside the zone of French occupation, or by *comisionados* dispatched for the purpose by the Junta Central (the new central government that eventually emerged from the chaos of the uprising). This is not to say that cases in the traditional mould did not exist – examples include Juan Palarea, Jerónimo Merino and the two Minas – but many of the *cabecillas* who emerged on their own initiative prove in practice to have been bandits bent on carrying on their careers of brigandage under the guise of fighting the French or deserters whose only means of survival was, in effect, a life of crime (it did not help in this respect that in December 1808 the Junta Central decreed that the personal effects of the French and their collaborators were legitimate booty). And, even when the commanders of the bands were genuinely patriotic, serious questions must be asked of the motivation of their followers. Many of them were to all intents and purposes conscripts, whilst the rest were in large part deserters, men on the run from conscription to the regular army, or day labourers, peasants and artisans driven from their homes by hunger and despair. In a very few instances a degree of ideological commitment may be found: in northern Navarre, for example, the populace was sufficiently prosperous for it to have a genuine stake in defending *dios, rey y patria*, whilst there was always a smattering, and sometimes entire bands, of defrocked friars eager to smite the 'impious' French. Equally, men who had seen their livelihoods ruined and their families murdered or reduced to starvation might well hate the French. But for all too many their essential motives were pillage, survival, avoiding military service *per se*, and, just possibly, avenging themselves on the propertied classes.[21]

As the war went on, despite much resistance – in Catalonia, for example, the *somatenes* would not countenance attempts to transform them into a permanent militia, let alone a regular army – some order did eventually emerge from the chaos. Assisted by units of regulars that had been detached for the purpose, a number of army officers succeeded in establishing 'flying columns' that eventually posed a real menace to the French, while their example was copied by a number of chieftains who saw militarisation as a means of gaining access to the military estate, cementing their authority over their men, securing the patronage of the government, eliminating dangerous rivals, and even of fighting the French more effectively. Amongst their men, however, enthusiasm for such schemes was evidently limited, many of the guerrilla bands themselves beginning to experience serious desertion and occasionally engaging in outright mutiny, while no sooner had the French started to be driven from their conquests (which, guerrillas or no guerrillas, had in the interim expanded to include almost the whole of the peninsula) than band after band all but abandoned the struggle and settled down to live off the already exhausted countryside. By this stage, meanwhile, the whole issue had been still further complicated by the impact of the work of the national parliament, or *cortès*, that met in Cádiz in 1810, this having in reality done almost nothing to address the social problem. So alarming did the situation become, indeed, that – in line with a variety of local initiatives that had already seen the light of day in various parts of Spain – in November 1813 the *cortès* authorised the formation of a paramilitary police force from men who could afford to equip themselves at their own cost.[22]

At this point it will doubtless be objected that to view the Spanish guerrillas as bandits is to miss the point. Bandits though many of them may have been, as bandits they preyed upon the propertied classes, and in doing so made war upon collaboration, the fact being that in most parts of occupied Spain the *notables* showed little hesitation in either rallying to the French cause or at the very least affording it a measure of passive acquiescence. To argue in this fashion is facile in the extreme, however. Pillage was not a phenomenon that was experienced by the propertied classes alone, while as time went on the guerrillas not only came more and more to live off the people rather than amongst them but also showed themselves to be as ruthless in their use of terror as the invaders. That being the case, it is hardly surprising that the Spanish authorities were deluged by protests and pleas for aid, or that the French were able to form a number of urban militias.[23]

Gradually, then, a very different picture is starting to emerge of the Spanish war. Thus, the mass of the population can be seen to have been 'decidedly inimical to the French' but at the same time prepared to do no more than murmur 'under the oppression and tyranny which it suffers without exerting itself to remove or diminish what it complains of'.[24] To put it another way, indeed, 'Had they been permitted to live in peace, it would have been the greatest indifference to them whether their king was Joseph, Ferdinand or the ghost of Don Quijote.'[25] In certain circumstances the populace were prepared to defend their homes and their families, but, despite a campaign of propaganda so intensive that it rivalled the efforts of the Jacobins in the French Revolution, they were hostile to attempts to mobilise them for war and uninterested in harassing the invader except to the extent that it legitimised time-honoured ways of survival in times of dearth. So clear are the links of *la guerrilla*, indeed, with the problem of rural poverty that a generation of Spanish Marxist historians has attempted to portray it as a conscious effort at social revolution. Such arguments cannot be substantiated, however. The insurgents may well have carried on a savage war against property, but they had no conscious political agenda and certainly did not identify themselves with progressive politics; indeed, not only does the traditional claim that they formed the bedrock of liberalism in the officer corps have little basis in fact, but many of their leaders went on to fight for the absolutist rebels who opposed the liberal revolution of 1820–23 (some, indeed, eventually became Carlists). That said, of course, neither do the guerrillas match the picture of patriotic heroism which has attached to them in the traditional historiography. Cause serious problems for the French though they did, the war in which they engaged was not just the product of blind and atavistic devotion to *dios, rey y patria*. Much research remains to be done on the subject, but it is all too clear that the isolated examples that can be found of areas – above all, northern Navarre – that do conform to the stereotype cannot be regarded as models for the whole of Spain.[26]

3. Portugal: the Ordenanças

Turning now to Portugal, it is clear that here, too, resistance was connected with factors other than simple loyalty to the Braganza dynasty. Governed from 1750 to 1777 by the enlightened reformer Pombal, Portugal had experienced a period of unprecedented upheaval which had had a very serious impact on the lower classes. Huge numbers of peasants were ruined, for example, when Pombal ordered the destruction of their vines in order to concentrate production in the hands of a small group of large landowners. In the same way, the favour afforded to great merchant houses proved disastrous for many small traders. Get rid of Pombal though the monarchy did in 1777, it did not reverse his policies and in fact continued to shower rewards on the wealthy families who had been his protégés. Growing still further in power, the resultant oligarchy began to acquire much land, particularly amongst the large estates of the south, the peasantry in the meantime continuing to suffer the most abject poverty. Meanwhile, insult was added to injury by the events of 1808 for, by escaping to Brazil, the royal family were perceived to have abandoned their unfortunate subjects. With as many as 10,000 nobles, merchants, landowners and officials joining them in exile and the remainder for the most part collaborating wholeheartedly with the invaders, when rebellion broke out in Spain there followed an explosion of social protest which the *notables* only succeeded in bringing under control by declaring war on Napoleon. Even then order was at best tenuous, the period 1808–1809 witnessing repeated disorders.[27]

Particularly worth discussing in this context was the actual method of Portuguese mobilisation against Napoleon. Effectively disbanded at the time of Junot's occupation of Lisbon in 1807, the regular army was reconstituted in the period 1808–10 by means of the Prussian-style system of conscription that had been in use since the previous century. However, only a minority of Portuguese mobilised against the French served with the regulars. For the bulk of those involved service was rather demanded of them through the provincial militia – a large force raised by conscription that was only mobilised in time of war – or the *ordenanças* – an irregular levy much akin to the Galician *alarmas*. Amongst these troops it is clear that discipline ranged from the lax to the non-existent and, while they conducted effective guerrilla operations against the French rear in the invasions of 1809 and 1810 and on occasion even tried to block the advance of entire French army corps, their general conduct left much to be desired. Provided, as in Spain, with an excellent pretext for excesses of all sorts in the claim that they were rooting out traitors, they murdered numerous army officers and officials and other local *notables* and engaged in frequent acts of pillage while cloaking their resentment and desire for vengeance in the affectation of much patriotic braggadocio. As one English resident who fled Oporto in February 1809 wrote, 'Many, many months before we left Portugal our life was a mixture of fear and anxiety, dreading what the morrow might produce.'[28] According to what she heard after she reached England, meanwhile, after Soult had marched on Oporto, everything had worked out precisely as she feared:

> For many successive days every horror was committed that can be imagined. Our servants had the good luck to escape with their lives. One young man that had married a servant in the family had set up his shop and was living happy and contented. In a few hours, what a change! A hasty flight . . . was the chance they had for safety. . . . All they possessed remained for the merciless savages, who pillaged the shop and house of everything.[29]

Clearly, then, in Portugal as much as Spain resistance to the French was accompanied by violence against the propertied classes. At the same time, too, there was at least as much resistance to conscription. However, the breakdown in authority never went as far as it did in Spain. As the French were only present intermittently, opportunity was lacking for the widespread irregular struggle experienced by the Spaniards. Meanwhile, the central authorities did not attempt to emulate the ambitious reformism of the Spanish liberals. Last but not least, the French themselves never had time to integrate Portugal into the Napoleonic Empire in the same manner as the rest of their conquests. The disruption to social relationships was therefore never as severe as in Spain or, for that matter, Calabria, but even so endemic poverty and wartime devastation ensured that brigandage survived long after the French had been driven out.[30]

4. Tyrol: the Schutzen

Turning now to the Tyrol, we again see a pattern of social and political disaffection that goes back to the eighteenth century. Thus, under the Habsburgs the Tyroleans had enjoyed a highly privileged status in that they were exempt from conscription – a privilege which they repaid by maintaining an irregular militia known as the *Schutzen* or sharpshooters – determined their own taxation, and were represented by a provincial assembly drawn largely from the peasantry. However, like so much else in the Empire, these privileges were eroded by the reforms of Joseph II (1780–90). Applied in the Tyrol, these reforms led to uproar, while the strongly Catholic province's feelings were further inflamed by Joseph's dissolution of lay brotherhoods, closure of many monasteries, 'purification' of traditional religious practices, emancipation of Protestants and Jews, and reorganisation of the Church's parishes and dioceses. When 1789 brought not only serious floods, but also a decree imposing retrospective restrictions on the ability to claim compensation for losses arising from the disappearance of the lay brotherhoods (which had come to function as friendly societies much patronised by the peasantry), the result was widespread rioting, encouraged by fierce protests in the Tyrolean estates. Confronted by even more tumultuous resistance elsewhere, Joseph revoked his military and administrative reforms, the Tyrol's freedoms therefore surviving into the Napoleonic age. As such, they could not but present an immediate challenge to the centralising policies of the Bavarian chief minister, Montgelas, when the Tyrol was ceded to Bavaria in 1806. The Tyrolean assembly was abolished, the province was split into three *kreise* – literally 'circles' – and its very name erased, moves were made to introduce conscription and the Bavarian system of taxation, large numbers of 'foreign' officials were appointed, and numerous petty steps were taken to reinforce the image of assimilation. Meanwhile, of course, the Tyroleans' Catholic sensibilities were being outraged by religious reforms based on the very Josephinian model that had caused such anger twenty years before. All this was accompanied by economic decline: Bavarian protectionism and the Continental System hit such native industry as there was very badly, trade was seriously disrupted – hence, perhaps, the prominence of innkeepers in the organisation and leadership of the uprising – while the poor exchange rates offered for Austrian paper money led to heavy financial losses.[31]

As a result of these factors, the Archduke John and other members of the war party which was now emerging in Vienna had no difficulty in fomenting a conspiracy in the Tyrol through a series of local *notables*, of whom the most famous was the innkeeper Andreas Hofer. Much encouraged by the small size of the Bavarian garrison and the appearance of Austrian troops upon the frontiers, when Austria went back to war in April 1809 the Tyrol duly rose against its oppressors.

As elsewhere, the ostensible rallying-point was loyalty to the established dynasty and the Catholic faith, but once again this legitimism was only a cloak for other interests. Many of those who had benefited from Josephinianism or Bavarian annexation were attacked, Jews were victimised, and a number of towns were pillaged, but the central focus of insurgent attention can be seen to have been the defence of the Tyrol's traditional way of life. During the planning that had preceded the insurrection, Hofer – who had been a member of the rebellious diet of 1789 – had been at great pains to impress upon the Viennese authorities the need to resurrect Tyrolean privileges in full; the peasant levies who sprang to arms did so under the flag of the Tyrol rather than that of the dynasty; and relations between the Tyroleans and the representatives of Vienna soon soured on account of disputes over taxation and the limits of imperial authority – not to mention Hofer's determination to overturn the anti-clerical measures implemented during the reign of Joseph II (unlike, say, the Emperor's abolition of Tyrolean political liberty, these had never been cancelled). Once the Austrians had been forced to make peace following the battle of Wagram, the split became even more apparent, the fact being that the Tyrol's identity was being asserted in the face not just of Bavaria but also of Austria.[32]

THE MYTH EXPLODED

To sum up, then, most of Napoleonic Europe suffered from common grievances under the Empire, but in very few areas did the resentment develop into outright revolt. Where it did, the key factors were a combination of suitable terrain, traditions of banditry or irregular warfare, and extreme socio-political tension. Often encouraged by exiled or defeated dynasties, or forces loyal to them, revolt everywhere assumed a legitimist outlook – as, indeed, did disorders of a less dramatic sort. This is clearly not the full story; while more research is needed, it seems likely that the peasant insurgents of Calabria, Spain, Portugal and the Tyrol were motivated above all by a combination of long-standing socio-economic grievances and a determination to preserve traditional ways of life. If that is so, then it is hardly surprising that even in reformist Prussia the response of the local authorities to ostensibly anti-French peasant unrest was to call on the occupation forces for help in maintaining order. As for any sense of modern nationalism, this was non-existent. Spaniards, Portuguese, Calabrians and Tyroleans had little concept of themselves as citizens of a modern nation, the most that can be said being that their resistance was fuelled by crude forms of xenophobia. To the extent that popular resistance was an issue, it therefore hardly marked the emergence of a new spirit in Europe. As its efficacy must also be doubted – armed popular resistance only survived in those places where it could be backed up by regular troops – it is clear that the whole subject is open to revision.

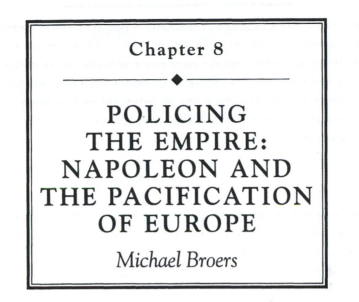

Chapter 8

◆

POLICING THE EMPIRE: NAPOLEON AND THE PACIFICATION OF EUROPE

Michael Broers

There are three important things which must always be remembered when thinking about the nature of the Napoleonic Empire. First, although Napoleon was always very clear in his own mind that he wanted to dominate Europe, he was never settled on the best way of so doing; he often hesitated before annexing 'foreign' territory or setting up one or other of his relatives as the ruler of a 'satellite kingdom'. Second, however confused Napoleon might have been about whether he wanted to rule Europe outside France directly, he had a very clear idea of how any region that was annexed – or converted into a satellite kingdom – ought to be governed; it should be ruled like France, or as closely as possible in local conditions. Finally, whenever and wherever a particular area came under Napoleonic rule, it had to be pacified – law and order as the French understood it had to be enforced – so that the basic institutions of the Napoleonic state could be installed, after which the region could be exploited efficiently in the French interest, and also so that the new regime might win a degree of support and admiration from the local population – or so it was hoped. This essay deals mainly with this third aspect of Napoleonic Europe, which is gaining in importance among contemporary historians in the field of Napoleonic studies. However, before delving into it in detail, it would be useful to look at some major points of the first and second aspects of the character of the Napoleonic Empire, to set Napoleon's campaign of 'internal pacification' in its wider context.

BUILDING THE EMPIRE

It must always be remembered that France had expanded its boundaries under the Directory (1795–99) as well. Some considerable time before Napoleon seized power in the coup of Brumaire in November 1799, the French revolutionaries had pushed French rule beyond the political borders they inherited from Louis XVI. This began with their doctrine of 'natural frontiers', which led the French to conquer Germany as far as the Rhine, Belgium, Savoy, Nice and all the 'foreign' enclaves within France, such as Avignon, which belonged to the Pope. As the revolutionary armies pushed forward, 'sister republics' were carved out of territories well beyond the 'natural frontiers', the most important being Napoleon's own 'Cispadane' and 'Cisalpine' republics around Milan, and the 'Ligurian Republic' centred on Genoa, all in northern Italy; the 'Batavian Republic' in the Netherlands; and the 'Helvetic Republic' in Switzerland, the only one among them still to bear the name given it by the French in the 1790s. But there were other, shorter-lived 'sister republics', notably the 'Parthenopean' in southern Italy, and there were abortive plans for others in south-western Germany – the 'Cisrhenian' – and even in Ireland, all of which failed when the French were driven back by the armies of the Third Coalition in 1798–99, this being the military crisis that provided the backdrop for Napoleon's seizure of power. Thus, when Napoleon reversed these defeats in his campaigns of 1799–1800, he was really recovering lost ground for France. More importantly in the present context, he was building on a previous tradition of 'imperial expansion' created during the French Revolution when he decided to keep most of these areas under French control; Napoleon finalised, rather than initiated, French imperial expansion in western Europe, through the re-annexation of Belgium and the west bank of the Rhine and the re-creation of the Batavian and Cisalpine republics. He 'filled in the gaps' left by the Directory with the annexation of the mainland territories of the House of Savoy, centred on Turin which stood between France and the Cisalpine Republic; and his shrewd, indir-ect assumption of control over Switzerland, when he was asked to be the 'Mediator' between the French- and German-speaking cantons. As will be seen, this was Napoleon's preferred method of dealing with territories he acquired beyond those listed above. The lands he re-took by 1800, most of which had already been under direct French rule or which came under the oldest, original 'sister republics', together with France, itself, became Napoleon's 'inner empire' – those lands he came to control most thoroughly, where French rule was best established and most secure, and where his campaign of internal pacification was most successful. Beyond it lay the vast tracts of Europe he went on to conquer, the results of his most famous military exploits.

It is a common assumption that Napoleon was constantly at war, and that while he ruled France, Europe knew no peace. The frequently quoted 'proof' of this is the misleading statistic that there were only eighteen months of peace between 1792 – when the French revolutionaries attacked Belgium – and Napoleon's first abdication, in April 1814; those eighteen months began with the peace of Amiens between Britain and France in 1801, and ended when these same two powers went back to war the following year. Technically, of course, this is true; but the niceties of diplomacy tell us very little about the reality of Europe in the first years of Napoleonic rule. The reality of the situation was very different. Between the peace of Campo Formio in 1800, which ended the war between France and the Habsburgs, and the resumption of war between France and the Russo–Austrian alliance in 1805, the Anglo–French conflict was the only war going on, and all the fighting connected with it took place either at sea or in the colonies. This meant that, in fact, continental Europe 'enjoyed' almost five years of general peace, between 1800 and 1805. 'Enjoyed' is a relative term because it was a very uneasy peace, but nevertheless it gave Napoleon the time he needed to confirm his grip on the lands of his 'inner empire', and to consolidate his rule. It was in this crucial, if often neglected, period that he perfected his system of government, the first stage of which was the process of pacification.

There was an almost perfect territorial continuity between Napoleon's inner empire and the conquests made under the Directory, and – to turn briefly to the second major aspect of the Napoleonic Empire, mentioned above – the basis of the French system of administration remained the same under the Consulate; France, its annexed – or 'reunited' – departments, to use the official euphemism of the time, and its resurrected 'sister republics', were all organised into departments and administered in accordance with the laws and statutes set out by the first great reforms of the French Revolution elaborated between 1789 and 1791. Nevertheless, there were important differences between the rule of the Napoleonic Consulate and its collaborators in the sister republics, and that of the Directory. On the one hand, the structures of Napoleonic rule were more authoritarian and more regular than those of its predecessor. Under Napoleon, departments were administered by a single official, the prefect, appointed by the central government rather than elected; mayors and justices of the peace were also no longer elected, but centrally appointed. The numerous statutes and laws issued by the revolutionary governments were compiled under Napoleon into the famous Civil Code which bears his name. All of this made local government more tightly controlled from the centre and less democratic, but it also made it more regular and efficient in its workings, a change, as will be seen, that had an important part to play in the process of pacification. It marked less a departure from the basic structures of the system of government created under the Revolution, than a tightening of those structures, to make public life more secure, regular and predictable for all concerned, as well as more controllable by Napoleon. This is probably typified by Napoleon's determination – only completed by Louis XVIII after his fall from power – to create a land register, the *cadastre*, for the whole of France. Its main function was to provide the government with the means to assess property of all kinds for tax purposes and – although its all-embracing nature made it appear a nosy, interfering measure – its most important consequence for the future was to place property taxation in France on a firm and fair footing, something that brought order and peace to these affairs as well as more solid, reliable sources of revenue for the state.[1] This particular project was but one part of a wider goal of the Napoleonic administration, of 'deciphering France' – of collecting statistical data about the French Empire and its inhabitants, to help the central government administer the country better. Again, this was work begun under the Directory, but that only really took off under the Consulate in the years of peace between 1800 and 1805; after this period, the demands of war slackened the pace and scope of these enquiries.[2] Nevertheless, the foundations laid in these years were very important for the regime.

THE GENDARMERIE: A NEW POLICE FORCE FOR A NEW STATE

There were other refinements of the work of the Directory in the first years of the Consulate that were to prove fundamental for Napoleon's campaign of pacification. Some were very striking and played a very prominent part in the struggle to impose law, order and central control on the Empire. Chief among them was the reorganisation and expansion of the Gendarmerie, a paramilitary police force set up early in the Revolution to protect the main highways and police rural areas. Napoleon tightened its regulations in an effort to create a well-disciplined, loyal and professional police force for those parts of the country – and of society – which had proved hardest to control throughout the history of western Europe: the countryside and the peasant communities who lived in it. Now, they were to have their own police force, garrisoned throughout the whole country in small brigades of six or seven men, all ex-soldiers – non-commissioned officers – with five years' combat experience, preferably tall, able to read, untainted by corruption and well armed. The fact that these brigades were established in small rural centres, and not just in the larger towns or along the main roads, gave the state a more direct, military and judicial presence in the very heart of society than had ever been the case before. When we remember that over 80 per cent of the people of western Europe were still peasants living in isolated villages connected by very poor roads to the outside world, the enormous importance surrounding the creation of the Gendarmerie starts to become more apparent. It ranks as the major advance made by the state into the lives of ordinary people during the years of the Napoleonic Empire. The state was present in force in places it had never before been able to reach in so permanent or powerful a fashion. Army patrols – such as the dreaded *dragonades* conducted by Louis XIV against the Protestant communities of the mountains of southern France in the seventeenth century – were ferocious, but transient affairs; once the forces of the state had dealt with the trouble, they pulled out, retiring to barracks in the large towns, leaving rural communities to themselves again. Not so the Gendarmerie, whose members lived among the people they policed all the time. Experience taught the French that, when they seized a region, establishing the Gendarmerie had to be their first priority. Just as General Wirion insisted on the primacy of organising the Gendarmerie in Belgium in 1796, in the Rhineland two years later and then in Piedmont in 1802, so the first steps the French took in Tuscany, in 1807 – even before formal annexation in 1808 – was to create a temporary, makeshift Gendarmerie under General Reille.[3] In 1811, they followed the same path in the newly annexed 'Hanseatic departments' along the North Sea coast of Germany.[4] This fact alone testifies to the central, basic role played by the Gendarmerie in the history of the Napoleonic Empire.

This force reinforced the power of Napoleon's regime to a very considerable degree, all the more so because, although his gendarmes were present in the midst of the populace, Napoleon's reforms took great care to ensure that his gendarmes did not mix with the locals or become directly involved in their affairs. The corps was housed in barracks, not lodged with locals, wherever possible – a policy which both insulated the gendarmes and ensured that they did not become a financial burden on those they policed. To further this end, they were paid by the army, not by local government; the corps was, indeed, a part of the French army, commanded by the Minister of War, and not in the least a civilian police force, despite the nature of its duties.

Marriage with local girls was firmly prohibited, and single men were definitely preferred for the corps. Finally, the government always preferred gendarmes to come from outside the areas they policed. Indeed, in the 'reunited' departments of Belgium, northern Italy and the Rhineland, two-thirds of each brigade, usually four out of six men, were drawn from France itself – 'the Interior' or 'old France' as contemporary officials called it – and two were local men to act as translators. It was a policy begun in the troubled western departments of France, centred on the Vendée, and extended for the first time to Belgium in 1798. Napoleon made it standard practice. When first extended beyond France to the Belgian departments, this policy had its idealistic side, as expressed by General Wirion, the man charged with its organisation, first in the Vendée, then in Belgium, and later in Piedmont. For Wirion, the mixture of Frenchmen and locals was 'an infallible method of cementing the spirit of concord and fraternity that we are trying to re-establish between the old and the new departments'.[5] In Piedmont, he dwelt more on the negative reasons behind this policy, chiefly the impossibility of entrusting law enforcement to partisan local men: 'In this way (with the inclusion of Frenchmen) I can stop the fears that might be raised among good citizens, that the guarding of their safety had been delegated to a corps incapable of inspiring their confidence, and also . . . incapable of winning it back.'[6] Either way, however, the end was the same: Wirion sought to create a professional, impartial police force.

It must be said that individual gendarmes seldom met the high standards set for them by the Napoleonic regulations. They were often too small, semi-literate and worse armed than the bandits or peasant rebels they had to con-front. Nor were they as well disciplined as was desired, and there were many nasty moments between civilian officials and the members of the corps about the mistreatment of suspects and ordinary people, especially in areas with a history of smuggling, rebellion, violent crime or – most often – all three. Nevertheless, they were all experienced soldiers, accustomed to mil-itary discipline, loyal to the Napoleonic regime and – almost invariably – remarkably brave in the face of danger. Local communities all over western Europe learned to loathe them for many reasons, which will be explored below, but they also came to see that, in the face of real danger to them, these same soldiers could be counted on to defend them, be it from bandits, thieves or even wolves. The most important point, however, was the simple fact that they were there.

Less spectacular than the creation of the Gendarmerie, but just as import-ant for the campaign of pacification, was the reform by Napoleon of a local unit of administration, the canton, together with the 'upgrading' of another, the military district. Napoleon abolished the canton as an electoral unit, as it had existed under the Directory, but then elections meant very little to the Consulate in any case, and this is not how its importance – or that of any administrative unit or public official – should be judged in a regime as authoritarian as the Napoleonic Empire. Henceforth, the canton became important as the joint headquarters of three very important, unelected arms of the state: the Gendarmerie, which has already been discussed; the justices of the peace, who comprised the lowest rung of the judicial ladder; and the police commissioners, who were civilian police appointed by the Minister of the Interior, and so quite separate from the Gendarmerie even though they worked closely with them. Each of these officials was, ultimately, independent of the prefects who ran the departments. While the prefect and his mayors were under the Ministry of the Interior, the gendarme answered to the Minister of War, the justice of the peace to the Minister of Justice and the police commissioner to the notorious, secretive and highly independent Minister of Police who, for most of the Napoleonic period, was the infamous and highly efficient Joseph Fouché. This made the canton a very flexible centre for policing operations and, in practice, meant that the prefects could do little directly to control such operations, an important fact that should qualify the somewhat standard view of the prefect as the most powerful figure in local government, for he is often seen as something akin to a 'mini-Napoleon' within the department.[7] At least in the early years of the Consulate, and in troubled areas for much longer, this was far from the case. Where policing, rather than routine administration, was the major concern of local officials, the canton and its set of 'enforcers' was the hub of activity, rather than the department. Indeed, the true test of the relative success of the Napoleonic process of pacification was when and whether the prefect and the departmental administration under him could assume a pre-eminent role in local affairs, a sure sign that the crisis was over.

The same was true at a regional, 'macro-level', with regard to the military division. These units grouped together several departments, and were headed by a military governor who could co-ordinate the work of the regular army and the Gendarmerie and had the authority to carry out policing operations beyond a single department, something prefects could not do. Operating in wider areas than the civilian administration, the commandants of the military divisions could group together several gendarme brigades into the feared 'mobile columns' which swept whole areas felt to be theatres of revolt or infested with bandits. These 'mobile columns' really had more in common with the old *dragonades*, at least in their methods, and it was another important sign of the success of pacification in a given area that the use of the Gendarmerie in this manner gave way to its normal pattern of service in permanent local brigades. In the Rhineland, Belgium, Piedmont and the Kingdom of Italy, this happened fairly quickly, although 'mobile columns' were always needed to enforce conscription. In most of southern Italy, and throughout the Napoleonic Kingdom of Spain, conditions were always too dangerous for 'the regular service of brigades' to take the place of the mobile columns, except along the main highways. Here, the Gendarmerie was confined to strong points – *blokhaus* – along the main roads, coming out only to defend the French supply lines from the Spanish guerrillas, surely the complete antithesis of its intended role.[8]

Military divisions were also coterminous with the jurisdictions of the highest of the Napoleonic judicial levels, the courts of appeal – and later with the larger, more powerful imperial courts – which mirrored the relationship between gendarme brigades and justices of the peace at the level of the canton. The courts of appeal were 'normal' bodies, however, and to supplement them, and give a harder edge to the judicial system in problem areas, criminal justice was often taken away from the normal courts and placed in the hands of special criminal courts whose judges were composed of a mixture of civilian magistrates – usually French rather than local in the reunited departments – and high-ranking officers of the Gendarmerie. In regions where these courts were installed, trial by jury was suspended in criminal cases until the need for such courts was felt to have passed too. Juries were felt to be either too easily intimidated by their communities, or their potential members too biased and 'politicised' to be relied upon, until true pacification was achieved in a particular region. Together, the special criminal courts, cantons and military divisions were the pivotal administrative units in the process of pacification. Indeed, they were its essence for they were the units of government which enabled Napoleon to over-ride his own administrative system in times of emergency, and there were always many such in the early years of French rule.

To sum up, then, the military divisions, cantons and special criminal courts were the chief administrative structures used by Napoleon to govern areas in need of pacification. Once pacification was felt to have been achieved, they gave way to the normal institutions based on the civilian courts and the departments. The chief arm of the process of pacification was the Gendarmerie, backed where necessary by regular troops, usually the reserve companies of veterans, which every department was obliged to maintain. It remains to be seen how Napoleon actually used these tools of policing and pacification, how successful they proved and, above all, why the Consulate felt western Europe – much of France included – had to be subjected to the intensive process of policing.

There were two main reasons why Napoleon invested so much time and effort in the process of pacification. One was to fulfil the promise he made when taking power: to be 'above faction' and restore ordinary law and order to the lands he controlled after the violence and disruption of the revolutionary years. The second was linked directly to the uneasy nature of the peace that prevailed in Europe between 1800 and 1805. Unlike all his former and future enemies, Napoleon took the chance he had in these years to forge a state powerful and efficient enough to enforce mass conscription on the peoples of western Europe. To do this, he first needed to create circumstances settled enough for his administration to operate normally. For the prefects, mayors, justices of the peace, and – above all – the Gendarmerie to be able to devote their efforts to this end, he created a massive imperial army, the *Grande Armée*, which could be replenished regularly and massively by the teeming peasant populations of the Empire.

The first imperative behind the process of pacification was largely a matter of the French trying to clean up a mess created, within France itself, by the divisive politics of the Revolution. In the reunited departments – the theatre of the major campaigns of the wars between 1792 and 1800 – it hinged on ending the social disruption caused by the fighting and on winning over these newly conquered peoples to French rule, only a few years after they had been subjected to invasion and occupation. This was where Napoleon's policies differed sharply from those of the Directory. Whereas the Directory had seen the conquered territories only in terms of economic exploitation to subsidise the French war effort, and showed scant regard for those occupied by the French, Napoleon took a different view, the needs of conscription notwithstanding. Life had to return to normal, property and persons had to be protected, disorder had to be quelled – and this meant more than stamping out overt, political resistance to French rule; it meant improving the standards of policing at all levels. It was a set of imperatives Napoleon applied inside and outside France, simultaneously, in these years; and he often met with greater success in the reunited departments and the sister republics than he did in parts of the 'Interior'. In the years before he returned to warmongering, it was on the success of this 'internal war' that Napoleon staked the standing and popularity of his new regime. It was as hard a campaign as any he would wage with the *Grande Armée* in the years ahead.

Napoleon and his advisers had already learnt much from the problems the Directory had faced in pacifying the Vendée, following the collapse and brutal repression of the great counter-revolutionary uprising in the west of France, 1793–94. Although large-scale resistance to the revolutionary regime was quelled by 1799, a fierce guerrilla war still raged over much of the west, mainly through the *Chouan* bands of Brittany and western Normandy, so called because their warning cries were imitations of sparrowhawks – 'chouans' in French. Napoleon turned to a true 'carrot-and-stick' policy in the region and, although it was never really considered pacified or loyal throughout the life of the regime, the approaches to pacification and policing he developed in the west of France became the models for what would follow elsewhere.

THE NAPOLEONIC POLICE IN ACTION

Many of Napoleon's preferred tactics were already put in place for him under the Directory, and the general view that Napoleon's seizure of power swept away a truly liberal regime, adverse to coercion, does not apply to its approach in regions like the Vendée or in the face of overt defiance elsewhere. As has been seen, it was in the Vendée that the French first learnt the need to deploy gendarmes from outside the area. It was also in the context of the Vendée, and in the first months of its rule, that the Directory created the dreaded Law of 10 Vendemiaire Year IV,[9] which it never repealed; even if it was phased out in certain areas, this dreaded law was never wholly abandoned under Napoleon. The Law of 10 Vendemiaire Year IV effectively reversed the principle that the Gendarmerie should never be a financial burden on the communities it policed. Where and when this law was invoked, a community was occupied by either a gendarme brigade or a unit of regular soldiers, or both, at the expense of that community, and a special tax was levied on its highest taxpayers; the troops were billeted on local families, at their expense, and the village or town was 'occupied' until the trouble was resolved.

What such 'trouble' might entail was given a very wide definition in law. The Law of 10 Vendemiaire Year IV was applied to a community designated as being 'in revolt' against the state, but 'revolt' could mean anything from a true armed rebellion involving a whole area to simply a violent fracas which involved resisting arrest by one or a handful of individuals. Three years after its creation – and less than a year before Napoleon took power – the Directory 'refined' the terms of revolt to embrace even tacit support for troublemakers, or even simple indifference to them: 'that, instead of confronting [the rebels] at the first sign of action, [where] it can be thought that several people even smiled maliciously and been present during the overthrow of public order . . . of having illegal hopes'.[10] Above all, it was meant to punish local officials, usually mayors of small villages and their municipal councillors who either collaborated with troublemakers, or were too afraid of them to do their civic duty. Napoleonic policing remained in its 'repressive' stage dominated by special criminal courts, military districts and the use of the Law of 10 Vendemiaire Year IV, not only because bandits infested the countryside or conscription was resisted by peasant communities, but also because – and for as long as – the local civilian authorities were regarded as unreliable, and their communities were disaffected by Napoleonic rule.

It was a policy Napoleon disliked but continued to use at the insistence of the local authorities until he felt it worse than useless. Indeed, some of the harsher aspects of the law were never actually applied under the Consulate or the Empire. The Directory had envisaged using the money raised in punitive taxes on rebellious communities to reimburse those in the area who had suffered for their loyalty to the government: 'Citizens who have been mistreated because of these riotous assemblies have the right to damages and compensation, including the widows and children of those who have been killed in such circumstances.'[11] Unlike the Directory, the Napoleonic regime knew a divisive policy when it saw one, and steered clear of this clause. It continued to levy 'punishment taxes' on communities to whom the Law of 10 Vendemiaire was applied, despite the protests of many prefects that some communities were simply too poor to pay them. A particularly repressive aspect of this law that was developed under Napoleon was to target the families of known bandits or of men defying conscription, and impose harsh fines on them. Firmness in the struggle against overt banditry and resistance to conscription never wavered among the police themselves, or at the top of the regime, even if civilian officials 'on the ground' sometimes threatened to 'go soft' during the process of pacification. In Tuscany in 1813, the prefect of Arno (the department based on Florence) came close to cracking in the face of a powerful bandit chief, Bonaccia, whose band was composed largely of deserters. When the prefect proposed an amnesty with Bonaccia which would accord his men a pardon – and their weapons – if they promised to fight for Napoleon in Spain, his superior in Paris turned on him in no uncertain terms: 'Such a state of affairs demands no illusions, and the proper means must be used to put an end to it; they must continue to be pursued until all these wrongdoers have been captured or driven beyond the borders of the Empire.'[12] It was not time to scale down the process of pacification in Tuscany, he concluded, but to send mobile columns into the area, and arrest the families of the bandit leaders.

However harsh Napoleonic repression could be – and many Napoleonic officials prided themselves on this to a degree that worried the policymakers in Paris – those at the helm of the regime never lost sight of the need for impartiality, or that the real goal of these policies was to end vendetta and the political divisions of the war period, not just to restore order for its own sake. Even in the midst of some of the worst moments – and one of the most unruly areas – of the Empire, it was always recognised, by some at least, that the best means of policing was with the support of local communities, however isolated, ignorant or seemingly weak their inhabitants might seem to Napoleonic officials. In the last months of French rule in Tuscany – a region of central Italy annexed only in 1808 which never really came under full French control – a gendarme could remark that 'If the line isn't taken of separating the interests of the peasants from those of the bandits, nothing will be got from the former, because the nature of the land favours the latter.'[13] The lands of the Napoleonic Empire were full of mountains and forests, and the technology of the period was little different from that at the disposal of Louis XIV, Charles V or the Medicis; these things remained inalterable for the gendarmes, prefects and their superiors; a set of circumstances which, when recalled, set the policing achievements of the Napoleonic state in their rightful context, as a great step forward, against steep odds – literally so, among the peasant (and bandit) communities of the Alps, Black Forest, Apennines, the Auvergne and the Pyrenees.

According to the ethos of the Napoleonic government, there was a time to 'crack down' and a time to stress the need for regular, civilian rule. Those at the top prided themselves on knowing when to shift their ground, and saw that moment as a source of pride. In the Piedmontese departments, for example, the order to end definitively the use of the Law of 10 Vendemiaire Year IV came in July 1807, shortly after the destruction of the last great bandits in the region, not least because Napoleon felt its application had come to show not the power of the police, but 'it seems to accuse the government of impotence in the repression of disorder', as well as the fact that it punished the innocent along with the guilty.[14] It was another way of saying that these departments – annexed in 1801 – were now pacified, and could get back to normal. Two years later, the Piedmontese were also granted the right to introduce juries for criminal trials, if they wished, a privilege they declined as being incompatible with their own legal traditions.[15]

Significantly, when Napoleon altered his policing policies, the men who enforced them moved on from those areas to the new trouble spots of the Empire. Two 'police teams' emerged during the Napoleonic period who specialised in the different stages of pacification. The 'first wave' was headed by General Wirion, as we have seen, and was concerned with setting up the basic institutions. It was usually followed, in the middle years of the Empire, by another, headed by General Menou, who had first come to prominence as the head of the military government in Egypt during Napoleon's occupation of Cairo in 1798, where he married the daughter of the owner of the Turkish Baths, converted to Islam and – for a wager as well as for love – was circumcised.[16] Menou was always a ferocious defender of the Gendarmerie against the complaints of the civilian administrators, and was known to despise even the special criminal courts as too soft on bandits, preferring his own *ad hoc* 'Extraordinary Military Tribunals'. He was the commandant of the 27 and 28 Military Divisions, which embraced north-western Italy until 1807, when he lost the argument over the use of the Law of 10 Vendemiaire Year IV, and over prolonging the life of the extraordinary military Commissions. What is important, however, is that this did not spell the end of his career. Menou was less sacked than transferred to Tuscany on its occupation by the French in 1808, where his methods were still deemed appropriate. Later, in 1810, he moved on to Venice, where he died the following year. In a very real sense, Menou's career path is a reflection of the growth and character of the Napoleonic Empire itself, and of how those who ruled it sought to evolve it. There was more than a little taste of the 'Wild West' about the pacification of Napoleonic Europe. The 'wild frontier' kept shifting farther away from the centre of the Empire – or, at least, that was the hope – and so the men who 'tamed' that frontier became unwelcome, moving on to the 'Indian country' of the new departments and territories. Menou is, probably, the major example of such men. He was colourful in the extreme, treated civilian officials with thinly disguised contempt while in Turin and did not change his ways after he went to Tuscany. Prince Eugene – Josephine's cold fish of a son and Napoleon's reliable viceroy in Milan – reported to Napoleon of Menou's conduct in Florence that 'he forgets his place a bit, neglects the business he doesn't understand, lives openly with a dancer, and in all these ways, he compromises his dignity and by this kind of conduct, he undermines the consideration and respect necessary for an official of his rank'.[17] Significantly, as long as a major rebellion threatened in Tuscany – as it did until 1810 – Napoleon kept Menou at the helm there. He was not alone. Menou's 'right-hand man', General Radet – who had been entrusted by Napoleon with the reorganisation of the Gendarmerie in the French interior in 1800 – went south from Tuscany to organise the Gendarmerie in the Papal States and the Kingdom of Naples when Menou headed north to Venice. He had a reputation for tough, effective policing, but there was little love lost between Radet and many civilian officials anxious to establish a more orderly, less aggressive form of imperial rule on 'the new frontier' of southern Italy. He drew real invective from Antoine Roederer, the prefect of the Trasimeno (Umbria): 'Radet is a rotten braggart who will finish badly, likely as not. I don't know how the Emperor doesn't still know about him or, if he does know, why he doesn't put him in his place. This man is dishonourable, real dirt, whatever his important position or his power.'[18] It must be said that Radet wrote a trenchant defence of himself, too controversial to be published in his lifetime, and even the sanitised version published by his family reflects his combative character.[19] This outburst came in the context of the prefect's complaints about corruption in the local Gendarmerie which seemed to interest Radet not at all. 'His place', however, continued to be at the forefront of the battle against brigandage, leading mobile columns all over southern Italy.

There were such men at all levels of the imperial police; they were not all French, but the 'Wild West' of the ever-expanding imperial frontier made room for those attracted to the power and danger offered by the process of pacification in its early stages. A Piedmontese police commissioner named Vendero – a civilian official under Fouché – followed in Menou's footsteps to a remarkable degree, the latter's distrust of the civilian police notwithstanding. He had been a pro-French republican since the Revolution, and served in the infamous Piedmontese *Gendarmeria* – a vicious local militia which Wirion had quickly disbanded in 1801 – before becoming the police commissioner of the Piedmontese town of Asti in 1802,[20] where he instigated a brutal but effective 'reign of Terror' which also had its spicier side. His own superior said of him that 'he abuses his official powers almost daily to give himself over to all sorts of excesses', among which was running a known troublemaker out of town – but then taking up with his wife and issuing dire threats against the man; 'His morals are so depraved that he has disrupted the lives of many honest families', the usual police euphemism for chasing young women. All the same, his superior in Turin had to admit of Vendero that '[he is] blessed with great courage and tremendous physical strength'.[21] His immediate superior, the prefect of Marengo, spoke of his 'intrepid' courage and noted that 'He made arrests of several very important, very formidable bandits', adding that 'I am persuaded that this is a man that the government can employ quite usefully.'[22] His director-general and his prefect wrote him honest, but glowing references for the post: 'I attest to his past services and his bravery . . . his courage and his intelligence and, above all, his severity. It was his unwise entanglements with women that led him into trouble. . . . Vandero will be a good policeman . . . because he has spirit and courage', according to his director-general.[23] His prefect charted his future with canny accuracy:

> It would be better to get him out of an area where his habits now have appeared a little scandalous, and I think that employed in one of the southern cities of the newly conquered ex-Roman states . . . this man, who has been blessed by nature with a bodily strength and a rare firmity of arm could give great service to a government to which he has always been very loyal.[24]

It was probably no coincidence that Vendero's rough-hewn reign of Terror in Asti was found out and dealt with only in 1808 when the region was pacified. In the same year Menou moved on, so did Vendero. No one ever denied his misdeeds in Asti; he was simply transferred to Rome, where he became a police commissioner in the newly annexed city in 1810.

Menou, Radet and Vendero were all of a type, and they all followed the imperial frontier when the 'imperial heartland' became too tame, but there was never an opportunity for the Napoleonic regime to dispense with their services altogether. Perhaps their true home was Spain, where the war against the guerrillas made them indispensable to the regime. Alongside the marshals who effectively ruled most of occupied Spain was the infamous director of police of Barcelona, Casanova, who ruled through corruption and intimidation while maintaining a lively private life. His usefulness to the French was shown by his transfer to the strategically important port of Genoa, in northern Italy, at the end of the Empire. His misdeeds were legion, but his dismissal was never countenanced as long as he did his dirty work on the edge of the Empire.[25] The frontier – and a certain kind of 'frontier spirit' that would not have been out of place in a classic Western film – was an integral part of the Napoleonic Empire and, in time-honoured fashion, there was often little to distinguish the 'good, the bad and the ugly' among the police and the bandits they chased. Everywhere they advanced, the Napoleonic armies created havoc; in recompense, they then sent back their 'best' veterans to clean it up. Retirement for a French soldier often meant fighting bandits or irate peasants instead of Austrians; it was not a career path for the faint hearted.

Their task was made no easier by the role they had to play in the execution of French rule. The story of the impact of mass conscription has already been alluded to in the course of this essay, and is well told elsewhere. Nevertheless, it left a double-edged legacy to those who enforced it, just as it brought desperate, if transient misery to the common people of Napoleonic Europe. The need to collect the conscripts became the chief job of the Gendarmerie, but it denatured the very essence of the service in two ways. First, it maintained the need for mobile columns in areas long pacified in other ways, removing gendarmes from their normal posts up to five times a year, when the prefects did their tours of the cantons, to carry out the ballot for conscription, the *tirage*. Put another way, and seen from the perspective of men like Wirion and Menou, it came close to making a nonsense of everything they had worked for in the early stages of the pacification process – the establishment of a police force in permanent brigades scattered over the countryside; all too often, only 'skeleton brigades' remained in their barracks during the enforcement *levées*.

Second, although many historians have rightly insisted on the vital role played by the process of conscription in bringing the state closer to rural society,[26] others have – with equal reason – dwelt on the disruption this caused, and the resistance it provoked, in rural communities.[27] In this context, it is also worth remembering the extent to which its inextricable involvement with conscription undermined the real purpose of the whole Napoleonic police edifice, that it engendered banditry in areas where it was little known, that it set rural communities all over Europe against a force that Wirion, its true founding father, hoped would everywhere be 'respected because it will not be oppressive'[28] and, in the non-French parts of the Empire, 'will reforge the links of brotherhood and cement the reunion of these territories to the mother country, to associate (the non-French peoples) to the eldest children of liberty'.[29] He failed in this or, more correctly, the policy of conscription made him fail. The process of pacification did much to transform the face of rural Europe, something historians are only now beginning to realise. It brought order, stability and higher standards of public service – policing chief among them – to societies which had often tolerated violence and crime as endemic, but the demands of the Napoleonic war machine, together with the early modern infrastructures it encountered so often, left those fighting behind the lines with very real mountains to climb. Theirs was a thankless, but deeply significant war for peace and order – if often realised by rough justice – in an age of overglorified carnage.

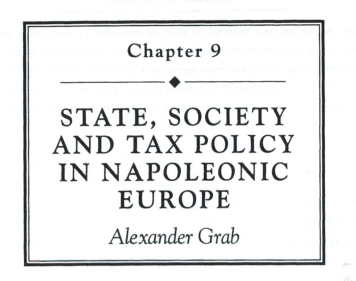

Chapter 9

◆

STATE, SOCIETY AND TAX POLICY IN NAPOLEONIC EUROPE

Alexander Grab

'Fiscal reform was the touchstone of Napoleonic modernization of the state.'[1] It was designed to place the state's fiscal system on a sound foundation and to generate steady revenues, without which the Napoleonic regime would have been unable to survive for very long or pursue its ambitious reform policy. Through financial reform and the increase in state income, Napoleon aimed to rid the state of burdensome public debt, so typical of the Ancien Regime. Financial restructuring also enhanced the state's power by establishing a new centralised and uniform financial administration, most notably a tax collection organisation that came under the state's control. The new tax system signified the elimination of the traditional fiscal privileges of the nobility and the Church, and enabled the state to create uniform and equitable taxation based on the citizens' ability to pay, thereby contributing to legal equality.

Most importantly, an efficient and lucrative financial system was indispensable for Napoleon's military campaigns and imperial expansion. Military costs constituted the largest expenditure of the Napoleonic regime and increased considerably during the imperial years. However, French taxation could not provide sufficient revenue to support the Napoleonic wars, and the Emperor needed to exact money and supplies from satellite states and vanquished enemies. The more resources Napoleon procured from those countries, the less he needed to secure from France, thereby reducing the risk of internal resistance to his policies. It is estimated that between 1804 and 1814 the conquered territories paid roughly half of Napoleon's military expenses.[2] Moreover, the French Emperor also forced the satellite states to maintain costly armies, which he integrated into the *Grande Armée*. Clearly, without substantial support from occupied Europe, Napoleon would have been incapable of maintaining and expanding his empire. To satisfy the onerous financial demands of Napoleon, the satellite regimes were forced to launch financial reforms to increase their revenues. Not surprisingly, many European countries adopted the French model of public finances, which in the long run laid the foundation for modern financial systems. They eliminated fiscal privileges, standardised and rationalised their tax system, launched uniform land *cadastres*, and set up efficient financial bureaucracies and tax collection. Those reforms constituted part of a broader set of innovations the governments launched to modernise their states and increase their power.

Despite the significance of the financial policies during the Napoleonic period, scholars have paid insufficient attention to this topic.[3] This article, which will explore the financial organisations and reforms in France, the Netherlands and northern Italy under Napoleon, and their impact on state and society, is designed to provide a modest contribution to fill this gap.

FRANCE

Napoleon Bonaparte inherited chaotic financial conditions from the Directory. In its four years in power (1795–99), the Directory faced a number of problems, including a growing public debt, budget deficits, inflation, depreciated paper money and a short supply of specie. Particularly burdensome was the rise in prices of basic necessities, which hurt the lower classes and provoked widespread discontent.[4]

To its credit, the Directory initiated several reforms in an effort to overcome the financial crisis. In February 1796, it stopped printing the *assignats* and began drawing them out of the market. The authorities replaced the *assignats* with new paper money called 'territorial mandates', redeemable for national lands, but those bills quickly depreciated to 1 per cent of their face value. In early 1797, the government abandoned them as well, and 'the revolutionary experiment with paper money was at an end'.[5] Reliance on coins also met with difficulty due to their scarcity caused by hoarding. The Directory tried to procure coins from conquered lands including Holland, Germany and Italy, but the war contributions from those countries supplied insufficient amounts of specie. To solve the national debt problem, the government reimbursed creditors two-thirds of the debt through bonds that could be used to purchase national property (30 September 1797). This constituted a drastic measure that, in practice, amounted to writing off two-thirds of the national debt, and exasperated creditors. The bonds quickly lost their value and eventually were unacceptable exchange for national property. To increase public revenues, the Directory proclaimed new indirect taxes, thereby provoking considerable dissatisfaction and increasing the regime's unpopularity. To improve the collection of direct taxes, the Directory created departmental collecting bodies, the *agences des contributions directes*, but to no avail. Property assessment was based on old, inaccurate surveys that rendered taxes arbitrary, hence tax arrears remained an ongoing problem. In its despair to augment its revenues, the government imposed a forced loan on the wealthiest citizens of France. The assessment of that contribution, however, was arbitrary and its collection faced serious opposition. Consequently, the government recovered only a fraction of the amount it had hoped to collect. The insufficient internal revenues meant that the Directory had to depend upon contributions from occupied lands, which financed more than one-fourth of the 1798–99 budgets.[6]

The unstable fiscal conditions and the unpopular financial policies weakened the Directory considerably and contributed to its collapse in the coup of Brumaire. With Bonaparte's rise to power, the state's coffers were virtually empty, holding a mere 16,000 francs. The First Consul understood that he needed to stabilise the fiscal conditions quickly in order to stay in power. Indeed, Napoleon's successful financial policies in the first two years of the Consulate (1800–1802) were as important as his triumph over the Second Coalition in explaining his ability to consolidate his authority. Napoleon's top financial aide was Martin Gaudin, the finance minister who held that position throughout the Consulate and Empire. Gaudin, a skilled and experienced technocrat, had served as a financial administrator under the Bourbons and the revolutionary governments. As finance minister, he was in charge of running the revenue side of the budget, particularly the oversight of tax collection and tax receivers. In 1801, Napoleon established a separate ministry of the treasury to manage the government's expenditures. Every payment by the authorities required the approval of the treasury minister. François Barbe-Marbois, another experienced financial official who had served under the Ancien Regime, filled that position until 1805, when he was replaced by Jacques Mollien, who served until Napoleon's fall in 1814.

Napoleon aimed at restoring public confidence in the financial system and at increasing public revenues in order to cover the growing expenses. A stable financial system was also necessary to gain the backing of the propertied classes, Napoleon's main base of support. The French ruler proceeded with considerable caution with his financial reform programme out of fear of repeating past mistakes; hence, he left part of the Directory's financial structure intact. The principal financial innovations under Napoleon pertained to the credit system, the establishment of a more rigorous financial administration, and greater centralisation and control by the state over fiscal policies and institutions.

Military expenses constituted the bulk of the budget. They amounted to more than half of the state's expenditure. Between 1805 and 1810 the military costs averaged 350 million francs annually, but in 1812, with the Russian campaign, they rose to 600 million.[8] In addition, marine expenses reached 100 million to 200 million a year. Public works increased from 25 million francs in 1803 to 154 million in 1811. The ministries of foreign relations, finance, treasury, interior, justice and religion had smaller budgets.

Taxes constituted the main source of the state's revenues. The First Consul devised no new direct taxes beyond the ones established during the revolutionary period. In fact, those taxes would last until the First World War. As for indirect taxes, Napoleon restored some of the Ancien Regime's levies that the revolutionary government had abolished. The establishment of a more efficient organisation of tax collection constituted the chief innovation of the Napoleonic tax policy.

Created in 1791, the land tax (*la contribution foncier*) was the principal direct tax. While it provided almost three-fourths of the government's income from direct taxes,[9] landowners complained that it was excessive and inequitably distributed. Napoleon, who viewed landowner support as crucial, gradually reduced the property tax rate. In 1803–1804, land tax brought the treasury 206 million francs, down from 240 million in 1791; in 1813, revenues rose back to 240 million, as a result of the expansion of France's territory.

Initially, property tax was assessed on the basis of agricultural income, but this provided inaccurate results and caused discontent. To establish the real-estate tax on an indisputable, equitable and uniform basis, Napoleon launched a national *cadastre* on 15 September 1807.[10] Through this significant reform, the authorities intended to survey and measure every plot of land throughout France, establish its value, and thereby calculate the land tax. The law stipulated that the value fixed by the assessment would last indefinitely. The French *cadastre* coincided with land surveys in two Napoleonic satellite states, the kingdoms of Holland and Italy. It was a gigantic operation that progressed slowly. In 1808, 1,248 communities were assessed; 5,243 were completed in 1811; and of 47,000 communities, 10,000 had been assessed by the end of the Empire.

The second direct tax, on personal property (*personnelle mobilière*), was paid primarily by urban residents for their domestic servants, horses, carriages and chimneys. It provoked much resentment among the well-to-do, who carried the main burden of that tax. The yield from personal property tax diminished substantially after September 1803, as more and more municipalities replaced it with higher duties on consumer goods entering the cities (*octroi*). Obviously, this substitution satisfied the interests of the wealthy. Taxes on doors and windows and the *patente*, a licence required from business-owners and merchants, completed the list of direct taxes, and amounted to less than 6 per cent of the annual income from direct taxes.[11]

The state's income from direct taxes was diminishing, and in 1813 amounted to a mere 29 per cent of the total revenues.[12] To compensate for the declining revenues from direct taxes, the Napoleonic authorities gradually increased existing indirect taxes and restored pre-revolutionary tributes. The augmentation of indirect taxes and the reduction of direct taxes, which started during the Consulate and continued during the Empire,[13] burdened primarily the popular classes. The regressive nature and unpopularity of indirect taxes did not deter Napoleon from increasing them, however. For the French ruler, 'the only quality of a good fiscal system was its yield. What had to be found were various taxes that were easy to apply and automatically productive. The indirect tax under these conditions became the ideal tax.'[14] Or as the First Consul himself stated, '[it was necessary] to establish a large number of indirect taxes, whose very moderate rate could be raised in proportion to need'. Indirect taxes were also advantageous to the state because taxpayers noticed them less than direct taxes.

The revolutionary government had abolished many unpopular indirect taxes, most notably the salt tax or *gabelle*. The Directory reintroduced the urban *octrois* on certain products in late 1798. It imposed duties on tobacco, playing cards, carriages, gold and silver ware, and alcoholic drinks. Revenues from the latter proved particularly lucrative. The Napoleonic government increased alcohol duties several times, thereby raising its income from 34.2 million francs in 1805–1806 to 116.3 million in 1812.[15] State officials were authorised to monitor the alcohol stocks of wholesalers and retailers periodically, provoking considerable popular resentment.

After his decisive victory at Austerlitz (December 1805), Napoleon felt secure enough to create new indirect taxes and increase the old ones. Particularly significant was the restoration of the hated salt tax (24 April 1806) that the French used to pay under the Bourbons. Tobacco duties constituted another rising source of income. The Napoleonic regime had increased tobacco fees annually from 1800 to 1806, and required tobacco producers to be licensed at a cost of 3,000 francs. On 29 December 1810, the government re-established another Bourbon policy when it proclaimed a state monopoly of the manufacture and trade of tobacco. Income from that tax rose from 25.5 million francs in 1810 to 43 million francs in 1812.[16] All those changes quadrupled indirect taxes between 1806 and 1812.[17] A third group of revenues consisted of customs, stamp fees, registry taxes, the lottery and post. The state also drew income from the sale of national property (*biens nationaux*), which had begun under the Revolution.

As stated earlier, the principal innovation of the Napoleonic tax policies was the establishment of an efficient tax collection apparatus.[18] Under the Directory, tax collection was largely ineffective due to the absence of specialised tax receivers and the lack of control by the central government. On 24 November 1799, soon after the coup of Brumaire, the government suppressed the previous direct-tax-collection administration, the Agency for Direct Contributions (*agence des contributions directes*), and created in every department an office for the collection of direct taxes (*direction du recouvrement des impositions directes*) composed of a director, an inspector and controllers – 840 for the whole of France. The new administration was responsible for the preparation of the taxpayer rolls and quickly accomplished this important task. Gaudin nominated a tax-collection hierarchy that included a general receiver for each department and a special receiver per *arrondissement*. Collectors in towns where contributions exceeded 15,000 francs were nominated by the First Consul, and their salary amounted to 4 per cent of the collected amounts. Receivers were required to pay a deposit (*cautionnement*) that amounted to one-twentieth (later it was augmented to one-twelfth) of the annual receipts. Soon, the government extended the *cautionnement* to other financial functionaries. This new measure provided the state's treasury with cash; equally significantly, it reserved the various positions to the bourgeoisie, the only class that could afford the *cautionnement*.[19] To accelerate the return of the direct contributions, Gaudin demanded that the general receivers remit every month the funds they had received. As for indirect taxes, the tax collection personnel were augmented by Napoleon with the increase in the number of taxes. In 1804, the authorities created the *regie des droits reunis* to levy the duties on alcohol, tobacco, playing cards, carriages and gold and silver ware.

Monetary reforms constituted a second area of Napoleonic innovation, and were designed to place the French currency on a uniform and solid basis. In April 1795, the Directory had established the franc as the national currency and had fixed its metallic composition. Yet monetary disorder persisted; the old *livre* and foreign coins continued to circulate along with the new franc, and shortage of species was rampant. Napoleon drew a lesson from the disastrous experience of the *assignats* and refused to issue paper money, basing the French monetary system on metallic currency.[20] This was paradoxical, given the widespread hoarding of coins and the difficulties in finding sufficient sources of metal for minting coins. On 28 March 1803, the authorities established a new monetary standard. They created the *franc de germinal* and established the ratio between gold and silver at 1:15.5. The decree regulated the content, size and weight of the new gold, silver and copper coins. For the first time, France possessed a currency whose real and face values matched. The new French currency became one of the strongest in Europe and would last for the next 125 years. Later decrees ordered the withdrawal of old money from circulation.

Tied up with the monetary stabilisation were the Napoleonic reforms in the area of public credit. The French ruler refused to borrow since he feared repeating the ruinous experience of the Ancien Regime.[21] At the same time, Napoleon could not ignore the issue of credit for two reasons. First, the tax increase and the improvement in the tax collection were insufficient to cover all the regime's expenses. Second, the Napoleonic government inherited the previous governments' debt that had to be paid off in order to guarantee public confidence.

The foundation of the Bank of France constituted the most important reform in the area of credit.[22] The First Consul aimed at establishing a national bank that would furnish credit to the state and to entrepreneurs, who had complained about the shortage of sources of loans. Formed on 16 February 1800, the Bank of France was privately owned and possessed an initial capital of 30 million francs in shares of 1,000 francs each. The top two hundred shareholders elected fifteen governors and three directors to run the bank. In April 1803, following a period of financial instability, the government strengthened the bank's position, by increasing its capital to 45 million francs and by granting it the exclusive right to issue bank notes of 500 and 1,000 francs. Those reforms proved inadequate when another fiscal crisis, stemming from speculations by top financiers, broke out and resulted in a run on the bank and the consequent near-depletion of its cash reserve. The bank's announcement that it would redeem only 1,000 francs per person caused its notes to lose 10 per cent of their value. In April 1806, Napoleon intervened, placing the Bank of France under stricter government control and appointing new officials to manage it. The authorities doubled the bank's capital to 90 million francs and extended its privileged position until 1843. In 1808, the Bank of France was authorised to set up branches in other cities in order to transform it into a truly national bank, but the branches in Lyons, Rouen and Lille remained small and unimportant. With the growing military expenses under the Empire, the treasury constantly resorted to short-term loans from the bank. For example, at the end of 1808, the Bank of France covered one-third of the projected deficit of 120 million francs for the following year.[23]

The Sinking Fund, established on 27 November 1800, constituted another new credit institution originally designed to relieve the regime's debt problems.[24] Despite its name, however, the Sinking Fund never served to pay off the public debt. Instead, it was used for other important fiscal purposes, most notably as a depository for tax receivers' security bonds and, through a massive purchase of government obligations, as a means to keep the interest rate at a relatively low level (5 per cent). The fund also provided much of the original capital for the Bank of France. The fund's capital consisted of public securities and cash deposits from the tax receivers. In April 1806 the government extended the Sinking Fund's resources by authorising it to issue bonds carrying 6–7 per cent interest. During the years 1806–12, the fund issued bonds that totalled 224 million francs,[25] capital that enabled the treasury to reduce the budget deficit. On 16 July 1806, the authorities established the Service Fund, a second credit institution designed to assist the treasury. The government ordered the departmental receivers-general to pay the tax amounts they collected into that fund, and encouraged them to hand in the sums before they were actually due by allowing them to open an interest-bearing account. The government also authorised the Service Fund to issue bonds based on expected revenues and to make those sums available to the treasury.

Yet the improvement in the French financial organisation and the increase in revenues were insufficient to cover all the public expenses, particularly in the later imperial years when military costs were escalating fast. Napoleon believed that 'war should pay for war [la guerre devait nourrir la guerre]', and indeed, 'It was solely thanks to conquests and permanent war contributions that the deficit remained moderate.'[26] Taxes from territories annexed to the French Empire such as the Netherlands, Belgium and Piedmont – along with impositions on satellite states and war contributions paid by vanquished enemies – added substantial revenues to the treasury. Those payments included hundreds of millions of francs paid by Austria following its defeats in 1805 and 1809, and by Prussia after its crushing rout in 1806. Pillaging and requisitions also helped to maintain the Napoleonic armies in occupied lands. In sum, the Napoleonic financial edifice could have survived only through conquests and exploitation of conquered enemies and vassal states.[27] In the following pages, we shall explore the fiscal conditions and policies in two of the Napoleonic satellite states, the Netherlands and northern Italy.

THE NETHERLANDS

In February 1793, the French Convention declared war on the Netherlands and Britain, thus ushering in the period of the coalition wars. For the next twenty years, until the fall of Napoleon in 1814, the Netherlands constituted a part of the French sphere of influence and underwent several changes of regime. In 1795, Dutch revolutionaries founded the Batavian Republic, which lasted until 1805. In 1806, Napoleon transformed the republic into the Kingdom of Holland, naming his brother Louis as its king. The Emperor then annexed the kingdom to the French Empire in 1810, where it stayed until the Netherlands regained its independence in 1813. Along with the changes in the state's political, institutional, legal and economic conditions, Dutch finances also underwent important transformations during the French period. The Dutch financial sector was beset by constant hardships, largely due to high military expenses and onerous French impositions. To cover the growing expenses, the Dutch government increased the demands on its citizens and introduced reform programmes designed to rationalise and unify the financial system, hoping to increase public revenues.[28]

The Batavian Republic, France's first 'sister' republic, was immersed in financial difficulties and rising deficits. It inherited a stagnant financial system from its predecessor, the Dutch Republic, which had failed to introduce the necessary financial innovations throughout the eighteenth century. The absence of reform finally took its toll in the 1790s when the war broke out, quickly increasing military expenses and French demands. In May 1795, the Batavian Republic signed the treaty of the Hague with the French Republic. Under this treaty, the Batavian Republic was obliged to pay France 100 million guilders in return for the latter's recognition, and provide France with ships and an army of 30,000–40,000 men. A secret clause compelled the Dutch to maintain 25,000 French troops on their soil.[29] Naval costs were also huge, since the Dutch government had to rebuild its fleet three times between 1796 and 1799. In sum, annual expenses rose faster than public revenues. Since the beginning of the war in 1793, expenditures ran between 40 and 55 million guilders while the annual average income of the Republic of Holland amounted to a mere 28 to 35 millions.[30] The national debt mushroomed and interest payments rose dramatically, causing fear that the republic would be unable to meet the payments to its creditors. In 1798, to pay for the mounting costs, the republic's authorities imposed a special levy on incomes. Such a measure could not be a long-term solution, however, in a small nation of 1.8 million inhabitants who had already been heavily taxed. Clearly, the Dutch government had to reorganise its tax system and find ways to increase its revenues.

Lack of financial unity constituted the main problem of the fiscal system in the Netherlands. This situation reflected the political reality during the pre-revolutionary years when the Dutch Republic constituted a loose confederation of seven provinces, each possessing a large degree of self-government, including financial autonomy. Since the late sixteenth century, each province had to provide the state's treasury with a quota of the general revenue. The various provinces were free to collect their taxes as they saw fit. Consequently, the Dutch Republic was covered by an abundance of direct and indirect taxes, dues and levies.[31] The leadership of the Batavian Republic was divided between 'unitarists' and 'federalists'. The former advocated a strong central state and the elimination of the traditional sovereignty of the provinces, while the federalists wanted to maintain a more decentralised system. Fiscal organisation constituted a major bone of contention in this struggle. A principal goal of the unitarists was to establish a national fiscal system that would merge the debts of the various provinces into a single national debt and establish a uniform system of taxation. The formation of a national debt favoured the heavily indebted provinces, like Holland; while a united tax system, the unitarists believed, would increase revenues and help the republic pay for its rising expenses. The inland provinces, which were only lightly indebted, opposed the amalgamation of the debt, thereby strengthening the federalist position. Following the destruction of the Dutch fleet at Camperdown in October 1797, the unitarists accelerated their campaign to establish a national tax system and increase public revenues in order to re-build the fleet. In January 1798 the unitarists carried the day when the assembly voted to implement a national tax.[32] This victory went hand in hand with the ratification of a new constitution in April 1798 that endorsed both the dissolution of the old federal system and the formation of a centralised state, and ratified the new taxation policy. A directory served as the executive, and appointed ministerial 'agencies' including an 'agency of finance'.

Isaac Gogel, the 'Agent for Finance', was the main architect behind the reorganisation of the fiscal system along national lines. Gogel, who would also serve as finance minister in the Kingdom of Holland, welcomed the French invasion into his country and had enthusiastically supported the formation of the Batavian Republic. A man of democratic conviction, he saw himself as a defender of the interests of the common citizen against the power of the rich, and wished to eliminate the extremes of poverty and wealth. Gogel opposed the old loose federation and provincial autonomy and aimed at building financial unity and an equitable tax system in the new Dutch Republic.

The reform project Gogel submitted to the republic's authorities aimed at replacing local taxes and dues with a uniform national tax system that would shift the fiscal burden from indirect to direct taxes, thereby placing a greater financial burden on the well-to-do, and raising the annual revenues to about 50 million guilders.[33] Much of the revenues in Gogel's programme derived from the *personeel* tax on rental income and the *verponding*, the property tax. Gogel proposed to replace the various provincial land taxes with a national *verponding*. He suggested an increase in the tax rate on luxury products and recommended that the stamp tax imposed on commercial and legal documents in the province of Holland be extended to the rest of the republic. Gogel's programme also included the elimination of tax farming and the creation of a new, uniform bureaucracy of assessors, tax collectors and auditors with clearly defined functions and accountability to the government. Gogel's programme faced strong opposition from legislators, who resented the imposition of stamp tax on their commercial and banking enterprises, and feared that it would weaken their control over the financial system. Appelius, a young representative from Zeeland, drafted a counter-proposal, more lenient toward the well-off. After a long battle coupled with procedural delays, the legislature finally approved Gogel's plan on 25 March 1801. A change in political circumstances, however, prevented the programme from going into effect. Three of the directors, with the help of the French General Augereau, dissolved the precarious unitary republican structure and restored provincial autonomy and administrative decentralisation. The pre-revolutionary ruling forces regained control over finances and the agency of finance was abolished.

Gogel would have to wait five more years before another programme he authored would be approved. In the meantime, the financial conditions of the republic deteriorated drastically. Rising military, naval, and debt-servicing expenses caused a succession of very high deficits after 1800. The resumption of hostilities between France and England in 1803 prevented a revival of Dutch commerce and deepened the economic crisis, thereby diminishing the republic's ability to recover financially. Indifferent to the Dutch fiscal hardships, Napoleon increased his impositions on the Batavian Republic. In 1804 the republic's expenses rose to over 70 million guilders with an estimated deficit of 38.2 million.[34] Interest payments for 1806 were projected at 35 million guilders, while the accumulated national debt swelled to 1,200 million guilders. Measures like loans, lotteries and extraordinary levies were both insufficient and politically unacceptable.

Structural tax reforms were essential to the republic's survival. On 14 July 1805, Gogel submitted a new general taxation plan to the legislature.[35] Similar to his former programme, Gogel's new plan aimed at replacing the financial autonomy of each province with a national tax structure. He meant to assure tax payments based on one's ability to pay, and stressed public accountability and savings in tax-collection costs. Gogel hoped ultimately to raise the state's income from 35 million guilders to 50 million. The plan faced opposition mostly from inland provinces, while the maritime provinces, including Holland, supported it. The legislature approved Gogel's programme. In June 1806, Louis Bonaparte became the king of the Kingdom of Holland. Gogel would serve as Louis' finance minister until 1809.

The main innovations of Gogel's new programme were in the area of direct taxation. The *verponding* constituted the most important direct tax. Historically, the *verponding* was assessed differently in various provinces. Each province had its own assessors, tax receivers and auditors. Often, discrepancies also existed within provinces. To set up a unified land assessment, the government created the Cadastre Commission that measured and evaluated the land according to uniform criteria.[36] The commission began its work in late 1807 and completed it in November 1808, despite opposition from landowners and local officials. The goal was to establish a just property tax, proportionate to one's ability to pay. Gogel's programme imposed other direct taxes including the *personeel,* which was assessed on rent and was paid by tenants, and luxury consumption tax on carriages and horses, expensive furniture, jewellery, tapestry, linen and servants. In an effort to encourage investments, Gogel proposed no tax on mercantile, industrial or financial capital other than the stamp tax. Those branches of the economy were undergoing a period of crisis, in large part due to the Continental Blockade, and Gogel wished to stimulate their development. As for indirect taxes, Gogel reduced their number by removing the most onerous duties on articles such as butter, sugar, tea and coffee. To make up for the losses, he substantially increased the duty on spirits. The new programme also abolished the large number of local tariffs, which typified the old federal system and constituted barriers to free internal trade.

Administratively, Gogel replaced the old tax bureaucracy with a simpler and cheaper national system designed to render tax collection more efficient. The central government appointed tax officials, who consisted of collectors, *verponding* assessors and regulators, inspectors and a corps of functionaries who heard taxpayers' complaints against financial bureaucrats. Gogel reduced the number of tax officials and achieved his goal of cutting administrative expenses. Altogether, the administration comprised 600 officials and the costs reached 3.8 million, a mere 8 per cent of the revenues.

The new property assessment met with landowners' protests, and managing the new tax collection faced the opposition of the local authorities. Problems were compounded by the incompetence and lack of experience of the tax receivers. Economic hardships also made it difficult for many to meet their tax payments. Gogel rejected the complaints by landowners. He succeeded in generating more revenues, reaching the target of 50 million in 1809, and in compiling the *cadastre*. Yet state income remained insufficient to cover the high military expenses, and high deficits lingered. This required the authorities to borrow, thereby increasing interest payments.

In May 1809, Gogel resigned due to disagreements with Louis over his tax programme. With the annexation of the Kingdom of Holland to France in 1810, Napoleon promised to replace the Dutch fiscal system with the French one. The French system was in part lighter. For example, the French land tax amounted to 70 per cent of the *verponding*. The stamp tax was eliminated and the *personeel* was reduced. However, other taxes were as onerous as the Dutch impositions. The Dutch public debt was added to the French debt, but Napoleon repudiated two-thirds of the interest on the national debt, a move that alienated the Dutch from the new ruler.[37] Also, French customs officials in the centre of the cities were heavy handed and were loathed by the population. Clearly, the French period signified a major financial burden for the Dutch, who did not master the resources to sustain the Napoleonic financial demands, no matter how innovative and enterprising they were.[38]

ITALY

In 1796, General Bonaparte crossed the Alps and, after defeating the Austrians, occupied northern Italy. For most of the next eighteen years (1796–1814) northern Italy remained under French domination. In 1802 Napoleon established the Republic of Italy and in 1805 he transformed it into the Kingdom of Italy, which lasted until the fall of the Napoleonic Empire. The geographical core of the Italian state, which at its peak had 6.7 million inhabitants, consisted of Lombardy, the Veneto and the provinces of Modena, Bologna and Ferrara.

Northern Italy constituted an important source of revenue for Napoleonic France,[39] and Napoleon was convinced that it was capable of supporting his financial needs. 'You have the most prosperous finances in the world', he wrote to Eugene de Beauharnais, his viceroy in Milan.[40] During the years 1802–11, public expenditure doubled from 70 million lire to 142 million. The combined costs of the Italian army, which reached 70,000 men in 1812, and the upkeep of the French troops stationed in the Kingdom of Italy amounted to more than half of the state's expenditure. Other expenses included the viceroy's court, servicing the public debt, the development of roads and waterways, judicial costs and bureaucratic expenses of the various ministries.

To satisfy the growing Napoleonic demands, the Italian authorities had to reform the area of taxation, the main source of revenues. The chief architect behind the new tax programme was the Minister of Finance, Giuseppe Prina. Like his counterpart, Martin Gaudin, Prina kept his position for the entire Napoleonic period. A capable and energetic official, Prina demonstrated total dedication to Napoleon. Through hard work and numerous reforms, Prina modernised the financial system, rendering it more efficient, uniform and remunerative. The Emperor appreciated Prina's services considerably, and in 1805 wrote to Eugene: 'There is no person who is more essential than the finance minister; he is a hard worker who knows his field.'[41] Prina's efforts to expand state revenues were helped by the annexation of new territories to the kingdom that added thousands of new taxpayers. While meeting Napoleon's financial needs, Prina's zeal signified an increased burden on the Italian population, thereby provoking rising discontent and resentment towards the finance minister.

Prina raised existing taxes, restored taxes levied in Austrian Lombardy and devised new ones. The most important direct tax was land tax, comprising close to one-third of the state's income. In harmony with the Emperor's wishes, Prina exerted great effort to maintain the land tax at a relatively moderate level in order to secure the support of landowners, who constituted the most important social base of the Napoleonic regime. The rise in the number of taxpayers from the new territories and frequent increases in indirect taxes enabled Prina to maintain moderate levels of land tax. Land tax constituted between a quarter and a third of landowners' income, not an exorbitant burden according to a contemporary economist. High agricultural prices increased landowners' income, and facilitated the land tax payment. The absence of a uniform land assessment constituted a major flaw and created great inequalities among taxpayers in the various departments. Prina and Eugene agreed that a standardised land survey was necessary to establish equity among taxpayers and at the same time to augment the treasury's profits. Moreover, a new *cadastre* would give the state greater control over the tax system and would weaken the local elites, who had dominated the tax system. The landed classes opposed the *cadastre* and succeeded in blocking that change during the republican years. With the founding of the kingdom, the need to rationalise the property-tax system grew more urgent. In January 1807, the Emperor himself ordered that reform, and in April the government started the operation. Under the watchful eyes of Prina, this complex operation progressed quickly. By the end of 1812, Prina informed Napoleon that close to 50 per cent of the total territory had been assessed. He hoped to complete the entire operation by 1816 or 1817. Although the Napoleonic regime never concluded the land survey, it constituted a major reform that increased tax revenues, established greater uniformity and equality among taxpayers, and at the same time undermined the traditional autonomy of local elites.

The two other direct taxes were the personal tax and business tax. Both originated from Austrian Lombardy, and had been repealed during the revolutionary years (late 1790s). Prina reintroduced them in the first years of the kingdom in response to Napoleon's growing fiscal demands. Personal tax fell on rural male citizens aged between 14 and 60, and averaged 5.10 lire per person. The proceeds were divided between the *comuni* and the state. Collection of the personal tax met with some difficulties owing to taxpayers' opposition and the laxity of local officials. In 1812, personal tax yielded 5.1 million lire. The business tax was paid by merchants, artisans and professionals, and yielded the smallest amount among the direct taxes.

Indirect taxes were imposed on a long list of consumer goods, including the monopolies of salt and tobacco. The authorities gradually raised the indirect taxes, thereby aggravating the fiscal burden on the popular classes. The *gabelle* constituted the most profitable indirect tax and was the second most lucrative source of revenue after land tax. It was also a stable source of income, since it fell on a basic necessity whose consumption was inelastic. The *gabelle* had been a state monopoly in the various Italian states during the pre-Napoleonic period. In 1803 the republic's government confirmed the salt monopoly and prohibited the sale of salt except by permission. The government frequently increased salt prices to augment revenues. Violations of salt regulations, including smuggling and theft from salt mines, were frequent. Yet between 1802 and 1811 income from salt more than doubled from 11.5 million to 25.4 million lire. The Napoleonic state also preserved tobacco monopoly, owing to the fiscal value of that product and its widespread use. Prina tightened state control over tobacco cultivation and retail sale, requiring licences to grow, sell and ship tobacco. As with salt, the authorities raised tobacco prices several times to increase its income. Despite smuggling and lower tobacco consumption, both induced by higher prices, the state's income from the sale of tobacco rose from 5.4 million to 11.8 million lire between 1802 and 1812.

Consumption duties constituted another main group of indirect taxes. They consisted of two types: duties on goods such as wine, flour, meat, oil and hay that were imported to walled cities (*octroi*); and annual licence fees paid by vendors of bread, meat, wine and liquor in small, unwalled *comuni* that had no toll gates. The former fell on a larger array of products and was more profitable. In 1807, for example, a person in a large city paid an average of 18.15 lire, while an inhabitant of a small town paid less than 1 lira. Prina, who believed that the rural population could pay more, revised the tax system in small towns, increasing licence fees on millers, bakers and butchers. He also imposed additional duties on flour, wine and liquor and established a new milling fee. The new taxes provoked a major rural revolt (July 1809),[42] forcing Prina to abolish the milling fee and the new consumer taxes. Revenues from consumption duties steadily increased. Income in large cities doubled from 7.5 million to 15.4 million, and tripled in unwalled *comuni* from 2.8 million to 7 million lire between 1802 and 1812. The rise in the tax rates, the annexation of new territories, the extension of taxation to products previously exempt and the tightening of police measures, all helped to expand these revenues, demonstrating the tendency to raise indirect taxes, thereby increasing the burden on the lower classes.

The authorities also drew revenues from indirect taxes imposed on official and legal documents, newspapers and licences. They included a stamp tax on items such as newspapers, playing cards and commercial records; registration tax on property transfers; registration fees on mortgages; and levies on navigation, anchoring, tolls on bridges and fishing fees. Aside from tax revenues, the republic and the kingdom also collected income from the sale of national property, customs duties and a lottery.

As in France and the Netherlands, the Italian authorities reformed the financial administration. Prina was determined to form a central financial bureaucracy, loyal to the state and chosen on the basis of merit, which would be able to routinise tax collection, eliminate fiscal privileges and reduce administrative costs. Such a machinery was designed also to strengthen the central state and undermine the power of the provincial elites. The new fiscal system was based on the French model and, as in France, the ministers of treasury and finance ran the fiscal administration. Both ministries were staffed by professional bureaucrats. In June 1805, Prina created seven general departments (*direzioni generali*): customs; salt, tobacco and consumption duties; national property; land tax; the lottery; mints; and post office. The *direzioni* were represented by lower officials in various departments who carried out the instructions of the finance minister and sent reports to the *direzione*, who transferred them to the minister. Indeed, Prina was very well informed about the fiscal conditions of the state and dispatched detailed annual reports to Paris.

The formation of an efficient and reliable tax-collection hierarchy constituted Prina's most important achievement. Communal tax collectors were required to sign a three-year renewable contract, and were forbidden from suspending the collection except in case of war, flood or plague. The collector's heirs had to assume his duties in case of his death. Tax receivers had to transfer the tax amounts to departmental collectors even if they had not raised all of them. Departmental receivers delivered those taxes to the ministry of treasury. While the new system was largely dependable and economical, it was not without problems; numerous communities, particularly in remote mountainous areas, remained without a tax receiver. The government decreed that in those communities the prefect should appoint a temporary collector for one year.

Prina succeeded to a large degree in increasing public revenues and satisfying Napoleon's needs. Between 1802 and 1812, revenues rose from 81 million to 141.1 million lire. The authorities were able to collect 90 per cent of the taxes by the end of the fiscal year, and to raise most of the outstanding revenues within a year. Those revenues allowed the government to meet the rising expenses of the Italian army and to pay close to 300 million lire for the costs of the French army in Italy. Tax collection costs amounted to only 8.5 per cent of the total amount raised. Yet despite these positive results, the rising fiscal pressure increased the difficulties for the Italian authorities in the last years of Napoleonic rule. Deficits began to accumulate and, in April 1812, Prina warned that 'ordinary revenues can barely suffice for the current expenses'.[43] Eugene asked the Emperor to reduce the annual payment made to maintain the French army in Italy, but Napoleon rejected that request. In 1813 the government took desperate steps to increase state revenues, including demanding a contribution of 3 million lire to be paid by wealthy citizens. By now, however, the kingdom was no longer able to sustain any new tax measures without threatening social and political stability. Prina became the target of widespread resentment. On 20 April 1814, with the collapse of the Kingdom of Italy, a Milanese crowd, incited by a group of nobles, attacked the house of Prina and murdered him.

CONCLUSION

In conclusion, the Napoleonic regime left important legacies in France, the Netherlands and the Italian peninsula. In France, Napoleon consolidated a number of reforms initiated during the revolutionary governments by implementing them more effectively. Most importantly, he confirmed the end of fiscal privileges, strengthened the fiscal unification of France and consolidated state control over the financial system, thereby contributing to the expansion of state power. Napoleon established a national tax system that would last to the First World War, initiated a uniform land assessment, created an efficient tax-collection structure, formed a rigorous fiscal bureaucracy, overhauled the credit system, established the Bank of France and consolidated the franc as the national currency.

Not surprisingly, the French fiscal system served as a model throughout Napoleonic Europe. In the Netherlands and Italy the Napoleonic financial policies reflected the regime's Janus face of subordination and exploitation combined with innovation and progress. Both states came under heavy Napoleonic fiscal pressure, which was one of the most tangible signs of their subjugation to the French Empire. The Napoleonic demands aggravated the conditions of a large portion of the population and frustrated the efforts of the authorities to balance the budget. At the same time, the wars and the Napoleonic fiscal demands stimulated the authorities of both states to launch a modernisation of the financial system and render it more efficient. This meant the establishment of a uniform, more efficient and equitable tax system, the formation of a centralised fiscal bureaucracy including a more effective tax collection, and the consolidation of state control over finances. In this sense, the financial reforms and new institutions created under Napoleon helped to lay the foundation for the central state in both countries during the nineteenth century.

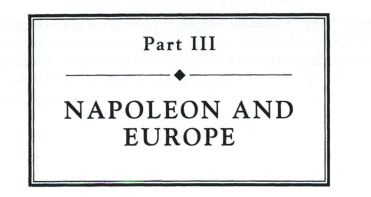

Part III

NAPOLEON AND
EUROPE

Chapter 10

BRITAIN AND NAPOLEON

Brendan Simms

Some sixty years ago, when the British faced an overwhelming continental adversary across the straits of Dover in the summer of 1940, it seemed natural to turn for inspiration to the great struggle with Napoleon 150 years earlier. Already in 1938, the refugee Paul Frischauer had published *England's Years of Danger*, a work with obvious presentist allusions.[1] In 1943 Carola Oman penned *Britain against Napoleon*.[2] Across the ocean, Frank J. Klingberg and Sigurd B. Hustvedt published *The Warning Drum*, a collected edition of British popular broadsides against the 'totalitarian' Napoleonic invasion scare of 1803.[3] Even Arthur Bryant, once susceptible to more modern Bonapartist sirens, contributed *The Years of Endurance, 1793–1802*, in which he suggested one might find 'many of the familiar phenomena of our own troubled time', and *The Years of Victory, 1802–1812*, works which were to establish his patriotic credentials beyond all peradventure.[4] But these publications were only part of a long and continuing British preoccupation with Napoleon. For more than a hundred years after his death he enjoyed the honour of being the subject of more English-language studies than any other leader, British or European. Nor has this interest shown much sign of abating recently; there have been more than a thousand books in English – to say nothing of articles – published in the past twenty-five years. In recent times, as one might expect, Napoleon has been overtaken by his successor, admirer and fellow failure, Adolf Hitler.

The contest between Britain and Napoleon has been seen as a struggle between universal monarchy and the balance of power, Carthage and Rome,[5] parliament and empire, Latin and Anglo-Saxon, revolutionary upheaval and

evolutionary change, hegemonic European integration and national particu-
larism, empiricism and rationality, Behemoth and Leviathan, Land and *Meer*,[6]
tiger and shark.[7] Its beginning and end dates are disputed. Did it begin with
the siege of Toulon in 1793, when the young Napoleon Bonaparte sustained
a life-threatening wound in the thigh from a British soldier while command-
ing the besieging revolutionary forces? Or in 1797, when Napoleon was
given command of the 'Army of England', but attacked Egypt instead? Or in
1799, when Napoleon became First Consul? Or even 1803, when an isolated
Britain faced the renewal of hostilities with France? Did it end with exile to
St Helena in 1815? Or in 1821 when his death brought a long cold war with
his jailor, Sir Hudson Lowe, to a close? The period 1793–1815 had seen
fewer than two years of precarious peace between Britain and France – in
1802–1803 and again in 1814–15.

Napoleon himself was obsessed by Britain and its part in his downfall. As
a school boy he had studied and made copious notes upon large sections of
English history before William III;[8] this selection, it will be noted, skipped
the salutary lesson of Louis XIV's contest with Britain. He was later to regret
his failure to invade England – perhaps via Ireland – in 1797–98; on St
Helena he claimed that he would have captured London within four days of
a landing and arrived as 'a liberator, a second William III, but more disinter-
ested and generous than he'.[9] Yet such benevolent fantasies were generally
crowded out by much harsher sentiments. In 1799 Napoleon described the
'English' – for a Corsican his sense of the nuances of British identity was
deplorably weak – as 'spirited, intriguing and active. Our government must
destroy the English monarchy or must expect to be destroyed by the corruption and intrigues of these active Islanders.' During the Third Coalition of
1805 he attacked the 'league which the hatred and gold of England has
woven', and spoke of 'This Russian army which English gold has transported
from the extremities of the universe.' The Russians – who boasted a much
more formidable and proximate army than anything Britain ever fielded on
land – were simply the 'hired servants of England'.[10] Throughout the contest
his state-controlled propaganda machine, even his servile clerical *Journal des
Curés*, poured fire and brimstone on England – an early example, as Geoffrey
Ellis has humorously suggested, of the *Gott strafe England* (or God punish
England) theme.[11] By 1808, he was calling England 'the enemy of the
world'.[12] In St Helena Napoleon claimed that 'With my France, England
should naturally have finished by being nothing more than an appendix.
Nature had made her one of our islands as much as those of Oleron or of
Corsica.'[13] Some island, some appendix!

British politicians – unsurprisingly – were a particular target. William Pitt, Prime Minister until 1801 and again from 1804 to 1806, was characterised as a 'real scourge, an evil genius', who 'set fire to the universe, and whose name will go down in history much as that of Erostratus has done amid flames, lamentations and tears'. Lord Castlereagh, Minister for War and Foreign Secretary in a number of wartime administrations, was a man who 'raised all kinds of turpitudes and immoralities to their highest pitch'.[14] Retrospectively, Napoleon was to describe 'England' as 'the agent of victory, the linch-pin around which all the intrigues of the continent had formed'.[15] The catch-phrase 'perfidious Albion' was first used – in its compound form – in a Napoleonic propaganda ditty in 1809. In 1813, after the defection of the Prussian General York von Wartenburg, Napoleon's Proclamation of Alost interpreted his treason as 'an action which only the intrigues and the corrupting gold of perfidious Albion could have woven'.[16] Yet Napoleon had never been to Britain and spoke no English.

The British were equally fascinated. William Pitt, his great adversary during the first half of the contest, famously saw 'various and opposite qualities – all the great and all the little passions unfavourable to public tranquillity – united in the breast of one man, unhappily, whose personal caprice can scarce fluctuate for an hour without affecting the destiny of Europe'.[17] Nor was this an elite preoccupation. Popular ballads and broadsides showered Napoleon with abuse and vied with each other in demonstrative patriotism. In the caricatures of Gillray, Cruickshank and many lesser talents, the Emperor was mercilessly lampooned, as if the existential threat he represented could be somehow diluted by ridicule. More mundanely still, mothers and nannies the length and breadth of Britain would cajole recalcitrant children to eat or sleep with threats of 'Boney'.

A small minority – mainly the literary avant-garde and Whig radicals – sympathised with Napoleon. Their motives were mixed, and E. Tangye Lean may well be right in identifying among them an 'acquired reversal which made [them] see the goodness outside and the evil at home',[18] the reverse being true of lesser mortals. At another level, it was part of the long affair between British radicals and foreign tyrants, preferably remote ones. For many long-standing critics of the crown, and Pitt's administration, the Napoleonic threat was a useful device to batter George III and his ministers. As Charles James Fox observed to his political ally Charles Grey in 1801, 'The triumph of the French government over the English does in fact afford me a degree of pleasure which it is very difficult for me to disguise.'[19] In 1802, he famously acclaimed Napoleon as the victor of the peace of Amiens, and suggested darkly that the English had already disposed of one king and elected another. For most 'Napoleonists', perhaps, it was a matter of striking poses, some of them contradictory. The Whig radical Lord Holland, for example, was an enthusiast for both Napoleon and the popular Spanish crusade against him.

A GLOBAL STRUGGLE?

The notion that the clash between Britain and France was a quintessential struggle between the sea and the dry land, between the imperial metropolis and a nest of corsairs went back to the revolutionary 1790s, and indeed to the Ancien Regime. Well before the advent of Napoleon, Britain was seen as the chief impediment to the imperial project of Jacobin rationalist expansionism. Danton urged the capture of the Netherlands with the words 'Take Holland and Carthage is ours.' The Prussian Jacobin Anarcharsis Clootz, visiting Paris, claimed that 'The mouth of the Rhine is essential to our well-being. It is in Holland that we shall destroy Carthage.'[20] But it was under Napoleon that the clash between French predominance on land and the British control of the seas took on its distinctive character. After the news of the destruction of his navy by Admiral Nelson at Aboukir off the Egyptian coast in 1798, Napoleon observed that 'On this occasion, as so often in the past, the fates seem to have decided to prove to us that, if they have granted us hegemony on land, they have made our rivals rulers of the seas.'[21]

This frustration – even resignation – in the face of British naval superiority was reflected in Napoleon's recourse to an old Bourbon gambit, which had been abandoned after 1763: an attack on the Electorate of Hanover, the German patrimony of the English monarch, George III. Whereas the revolutionary regimes had generally ignored the link – once a staple of eighteenth-century international constellations – Napoleon struck at least three times at what he believed to be Britain's weakest spot: in 1801, when he forced the Prussians to occupy the electorate as part of their obligations under the Armed Neutrality; in 1803, as a direct reprisal for the resumption of hostilities with Britain; and in 1806, when he made Hanover an object of the peace negotiations that year. As Napoleon observed wistfully in 1803, 'The English dominate the seas, are at this moment [1803] the premier power of Europe. . . . Before the fate of Europe is decided by the success or failure of an invasion of England, all I am left with is the territory of Hanover.'[22]

At the time, in fact, this resigned acceptance of British naval predominance might have been premature. After all, the combined tonnage of the

French, Russian, Dutch, Danish and Spanish navies just about matched that of Britain in 1800; and, as Richard Glover has pointed out, the notion that the victory at Trafalgar in 1805 established British superiority beyond per-adventure and banished the threat of invasion for good is not borne out by the facts.[23] A substantial French fleet in being was maintained to the very end, and the last years of the war saw a sustained attempt to build a new naval base at Antwerp, right on the Royal Navy's doorstep. Lord Melville, the First Lord of the Admiralty, later admitted that in time Napoleon could have 'sent forth such powerful fleets that our navy must eventually have been destroyed, since we could never have kept pace with him in building ships nor equipped numbers sufficient to cope with the tremendous power he could have brought against us'.[24] Nevertheless, it is true that by 1810, when French control over the Continent was at its height, British naval power was never stronger. In that year, the total British tonnage in large ships was a good one-third greater than that of all her potential European adversaries put together.[25] After 1806, in fact, the British lost more ships to inclement weather than to enemy action.[26]

The only way that Napoleon could hope to break Britain was through commercial warfare, partly on the high seas but particularly through the Continental Blockade. The Berlin decrees of November 1806 – issued after the Prussian defeats at Jena and Auerstedt – sought to exclude all British trade and thus starve her manufacturers of outlets. Napoleon's plan was to destroy Britain's export and re-export trade, reduce her revenue and thus undermine both her war-fighting capacity and her ability to fund continental coalitions. His aim, as he put it, was to 'conquer the sea by mastery of the land'.[27] It did not work; British trade with the Americas flourished, while smuggling and cor-ruption kept avenues to the Continent open. As Louis Napoleon, Bonaparte's long-suffering brother and King of Holland observed, one might as well try to prevent the skin from sweating as to stop continental trade with Britain.[28] The British response, on the other hand, was devastating. The orders in council of 1806 drastically reduced neutral trade with France and French-occupied Europe. Indeed, throughout the war the British stuck to their punitive maritime code, even at the risk of alienating European allies and undermin-ing peace efforts. As the Foreign Secretary, Lord Castlereagh, remarked to a colleague in December 1813, 'You know how acutely we feel upon all politi-cal subjects when our feelings have been long excited by animating events, but that, at all times, a maritime question touches us to the quick.'[29]

This British concern with naval security and predominance brought with it its own neuroses, ambitions and enmities. One by one, the colonies not merely of France, but of her (semi-voluntary) allies fell into British hands; by 1811 the French had lost, for the first time ever throughout the Second Hundred Years' War with Britain, all of her overseas possessions to the Royal Navy. Indeed, the clash between French pretensions to universal monarchy in Europe and British hegemony overseas explains the ambivalence with which other European states regarded the whole contest. They tended to equate the two – at least rhetorically – and at times they formed a common front with Napoleon against Britain. The Armed Neutrality of 1800–1801, which united Denmark, Sweden, Russia and Prussia in defiance of the British maritime code, was the most extreme example of this. But some such combination, in various permutations, was a latent threat throughout the period. It underlay a series of pre-emptive attacks on European powers in order to prevent the feared imminent capture of their navies by France. The Danes were subjected to this indignity twice, in 1801 and 1807; on the second occasion more than two thousand innocent civilians were killed in Copenhagen. The Spaniards had to put up with the pre-emptive seizure of their treasure fleet in 1804. Indeed, it is a curious fact that during the Napoleonic period Britain – supposedly fighting for the defence of European liberties against French hegemony – actually found herself at war with almost all of the major and many middling powers of Europe, at some point before 1815. War was declared, and in many cases waged against Russia, Prussia, Spain, Sweden, Denmark and Holland.

The resulting sense of British isolation was summed up by one Commander Inglis, who received news of the Armed Neutrality and the first attack on Copenhagen on his way to Egypt in 1801. 'I think we must have peace now,' he observed. 'We cannot fight the world.'[30] The idea that it was Britain, rather than Napoleon, which stood against the world had a wide currency, and was encouraged by Napoleonic propaganda.[31] But even Friedrich von Gentz, a committed political Anglophile and critic of French power, wrote in 1800 that 'The dominant principle of all the political theorists and writers at the present moment is – jealousy of British power.' Similarly, in 1807, after the second British attack on Copenhagen, William Augustus Miles, a former British diplomat, claimed that 'Our court must have been very badly informed of the tempers and feelings of the continent towards us if it has yet to learn that we are everywhere detested.'[32] Even amongst the Spaniards after 1808, and the French royalist émigrés, traditional suspicions of England were routine.

Much of this hostility, as we have seen, stemmed from British colonial ambitions, her arrogant application of the maritime code, and her high-handed destruction of potentially rival navies. But that was not all. European opinion and cabinets were also deeply suspicious of the British aim of maintaining a balance of power on the Continent, to which end they were believed willing to sacrifice the last Austrian, Prussian and Russian, while the Royal Navy swept up French colonies – and those of everyone else. By 1800, it is true, British colonial gains were and looked impressive: Tobago, St Pierre and Miquelon, Pondicherry in 1793, Martinique, St Lucia and Guadeloupe in 1794, Ceylon and the Cape of Good Hope in 1795, Trinidad in 1797, Minorca in 1798, Surinam in 1800, with more to come. After the prolonged haggling over subsidies in the 1790s and early 1800s, European powers were receptive to French propaganda about 'English gold'.[33] On three successive occasions, it might be argued, Britain had inveigled the powers into precarious coalitions, risking very few of her own resources on the mainland, only to abandon her allies for colonial gains when the going got rough – in the First Coalition of the 1790s, in the Second Coalition of 1798–1800, and in the Third Coalition of 1804–1805.

At first sight, this reserve seems justified. There was indeed a view within the British cabinet, and particularly the political nation at large, that the war against Napoleonic France should be waged by maritime means for imperial ends. The classic exponent of this 'blue-water' strategy, which had its roots in the great debates of colonialists versus continentalists in the eighteenth century, was Pitt's long-standing Secretary for War, Henry Dundas (later Viscount Melville). He formally set out his strategy in a famous series of memoranda penned in March and July 1800. Instead of fighting the enemy in Europe itself, a policy 'calculated beyond our means', Dundas demanded a new focus on expansion overseas, particularly the commercial penetration of a South America now only tenuously controlled by weak French-dominated Spain.[34] Instead of being hurled against the Continent in futile sorties, the Royal Navy and the land-striking forces should be deployed against the enemy's commerce and colonial possessions. After 1806, with the collapse of the Third Coalition, the defeat of Prussia and the Franco–Russian rapprochement, the 'blue-water' strategy appeared to gain wider currency as a cheap, profitable alternative to ruinous subsidies and land warfare.

Despite appearances, however, the continentalist orthodoxy with which Britain had entered the war was never displaced. In 1794, William Pitt had stated that 'This country had never so successfully combated [France] as when its maritime strength had been aided by the judicious application of a land force on the continent.'[35] Just over ten years later, Pitt still refused to be distracted by maritime chimeras when he expressed his 'resolve at this stage to husband all available strength for a potential contribution to a decisive result in Europe'.[36] Whenever Pitt pursued a 'blue-water' strategy, it was out of necessity, not choice; and, with the disastrous exception of the Ministry of All the Talents in 1806–1807, it was no different with his successors. As Piers Mackesy, the doyen of strategic historians of the war, has argued, 'limited warfare' was but 'a second best adopted because the initiative had been lost'.[37] British strategists could see that for every continental fiasco – such as the expedition to Holland, the expedition to northern Germany in 1805–1806, and the Walcheren catastrophe of 1809 – there was a matching quagmire overseas, be it the pestilential Sugar Islands, which did for more British troops in the 1790s than the French, or the spectacular failure in South America in 1806–1807.

There was, however, a discernible change of emphasis in British strategy after 1806–1807. This was most – and untypically – evident during the Ministry of All the Talents, perhaps the only time throughout the Napoleonic period when a genuinely 'blue-water' strategy was followed. The populist commitment to overseas expansion at the expense of continental expeditions and subsidies reflected not merely bitter recent experience, but also financial parsimony and a deep-seated suspicion of the other European powers. As the cabinet somewhat primly told the Austrians in 1807, 'If the great powers now at war, or threatened by France, cannot find in themselves the means of such exertion, it is vain to expect that this country, by any supplies which we could afford, would be able effectually to support them.'[38] Indeed, as the Secretary of State for War, William Windham, lamented, 'were we to be merely the great bank of Europe, on which the different nations of Europe should be empowered to draw on in defence of their own existence? Was not the result likely to be that they would make no spontaneous exertions?' This blend of resignation and strategic providentialism was summed up by the *Morning Chronicle* in October 1806, when it wrote that the Continent must be left in Napoleon's hands 'till his domination, aided by more favourable circumstances, shall excite a general effort of resistance, and work its own deliverance'.[39]

The unhappy interlude of the Ministry of All the Talents gave way to a return to the Pittite orthodoxy, albeit with a more cautious approach to continental commitments. The traditional rhetoric of European powers was now turned back on them; instead of taking the initiative in building coalitions against Napoleon, London sought to avoid giving the French pretexts for further expansion, and insisted that the Austrians, Russians and others go to war for their own ends and not at the pretended behest of Britain.

Nevertheless, the underlying aim of defeating Napoleon through direct or subsidised action on the Continent remained unchanged. This was summed up by George Canning – one of Pitt's most forthright heirs in foreign policy. Far from accepting a new order in which British maritime supremacy matched that of France on the dry land, Canning announced in October 1807:

> Our interest is that till there can be a final settlement that shall last, every thing should remain as unsettled as possible: that no usurper should feel sure of acknowledgement; no people confident of their new masters; no kingdom sure of its existence; no spoliator secure of his spoils; and even the plundered not acquiescent in their losses.[40]

Indeed, Canning explained a year later, 'We shall proceed from the principle, that any nation of Europe that starts up with a determination to oppose ... the common enemy of all nations ... becomes instantly our essential ally.'[41]

The primacy of Europe in British strategy throughout most of the Napoleonic period was to be demonstrated again and again. Whenever the opportunity presented itself, Britain engaged the French on land: in 1799 in Holland, in north Germany in 1805–1806, in Walcheren in 1809, in the peninsula after 1808 and, of course, in the Low Countries in 1815. The largest British expedition ever mounted so far – 40,000 men and 600 vessels – was sent to Walcheren and not on some imperial venture.[42] Only two major operations were mounted against colonial targets, those to the Cape of Good Hope in 1805 and South America in 1806–1807; the latter, it should be added, was simply an opportunist exploitation of an unauthorised initiative by Sir Home Popham, which ended in tears. It was no doubt to avoid such perils that Richard Wellesley in India was given strict instructions to undertake no further expansion and incur no new expenditures. Similarly, the powerful British presence in the Mediterranean, which had been confined to Gibraltar at the beginning of the period, did not correspond to any master plan, but resulted from cumulative strategic adhocery: Malta was secured to keep the French out, Sicily was occupied to protect and feed Malta, and much the same reasoning lay behind the presence in the Ionian Islands. Moreover, the great wave of colonial successes between 1808 and 1811 was not the result of a new strategy or fresh resources sent from London. Rather these gains were effected by local garrisons in response to immediate threats and opportunities. In so far as these were endorsed or prompted by London, the aim was to release ships to confront Napoleon in Europe, particularly his nascent fleet at Antwerp. For the most part, in fact, London saw colonial possessions as pawns with which to re-establish the European balance of power. Thus the Cape of Good Hope was, temporarily, restored to the Dutch in 1802.

It follows that for Britain, and indeed for Napoleon, the great confrontation was not – in any fundamental sense – a *Weltanschauungskrieg*, or irreconcilable clash of ideologies and political systems. Even in the 1790s, when French revolutionary fervour had been at its height, and the threat of domestic subversion the greatest, Britain had been more preoccupied with the fate of Flanders than with the internal government of France. Pitt, for one, denied any 'intention to wage war against opinion'.[43] If anything, the advent of Napoleon had eased the ideological tension. Some voices, such as Dundas, thought – in effect – that the resulting domestic stability would enable Paris to 'cut a deal' on the basis of British maritime and French continental supremacy.[44] Certainly, those – like William Wickham and William Windham – who saw the conflict as an ideological crusade were a minority. The British government never officially recognised the comte de Provence as king of France after Louis XVI's execution, and the restoration of the Bourbon *status quo ante* was never a war aim. At first, there was no hesitation in using royalist and other subversives to sap French power, but even this gambit was little used after 1803, largely because each rising proved more disastrous than the last, a fruitless drain on British resources which tended simply to strengthen Napoleon's domestic position. Castlereagh, then Minister for War, told the agent of Louis XVIII in 1807 that it was not consistent with either British or royalist interests 'to give any encouragement whatever to insurrectional movement'.[45] If Britain was unable to reach lasting agreement with Napoleon this had nothing to do with any social distaste for the 'usurper' and everything to do with his general unreliability and the lack of any obvious limits to his ambition.

Britain's aims were simple: to restore the broader European balance and, relatedly, to prevent the Low Countries from falling under French domination. It had entered the war in 1793 not to destroy the Revolution, but to keep the French out of Flanders. Even during the Second and Third Coalitions, restoring the Bourbons was not a declared aim of Pitt's, whereas the independence of the Low Countries and the creation of a credible barrier to French ambitions certainly was. As late as 1813, the British Lord President of the Council Lord Harrowby averred that 'Antwerp and Flushing out of the hands of France are worth twenty Martiniques in our own hands'.[46] To this end Britain was prepared time and again to try to tip the scales against Napoleon and to forgo maritime gains, if necessary. Napoleon's aims towards England, on the other hand, were less clear-cut, more modest and more grandiose at the same time. For Britain – despite the contemporary fears and subsequent fond imaginings of the British themselves and the dictator's own later remarks – was rarely Napoleon's first priority. He had inherited the struggle with Britain from the revolutionary governments, and his medium- to short-term focus rested firmly on his relations with the European great powers. Unlike Vergennes after 1763, Napoleon never committed the bulk of French resources to winning the naval and colonial struggle with Britain overseas.[47] The not inconsiderable navy he assembled in 1805 and again from 1809 was in addition to, not in place of, the *Grande Armée* and *Grand Empire*, with which it always had to compete for resources.

At one level, of course, Napoleon had global ambitions which clashed with those of Britain. These were manifested in his famous attack on Egypt in 1798, the projected joint Russo–French attack on India via Persia in 1801, and the less well-known plans for a Persian gambit in 1807, when Napoleon's negotiations with a delegation from the shah in a remote Pomeranian hunting lodge of Finkenstein was followed by the dispatch of an advance party under General Gardane to Teheran.[48] In fact, in the first fifteen years of the war – before Walcheren – the largest amphibious operations were launched by France: Hoche unsuccessfully to Ireland with 15,000 men in 1796 and the expedition to Egypt in 1798, with 300 vessels and 40,000 men, a veritable *corps d'Afrique*. Even as late as 1809 a French officer was captured as far afield as Sumatra in the Dutch East Indies – now Indonesia – and spoke of a planned descent of French frigates on the area.[49] Yet all this was less part of some imperial grand design than an attempt to carry the struggle to Britain in a more effective manner. The attack on Egypt was supposed to presage an assault on India and thus a hammer-blow against British power. In political terms, Michael Duffy claims that Napoleon's ambitions did not stretch much beyond the Levant.[50] Of course, had Napoleon been successful in Egypt and executed his design on Persia, his appetite might have grown with the eating.

The clash between Britain and Napoleon, therefore, may have taken on global characteristics, but its essence and virulence derived from Napoleon's limitless ambitions within Europe. This explains the breakdown of the peace of Amiens, concluded in 1802 on the basis of French continental and British maritime restraint. The immediate apparent cause of the breach was Britain's refusal to withdraw as agreed from Malta; Napoleon threatened the British envoy, Lord Whitworth, with 'a war of extermination' and 'Malta or war'. The British were indeed in violation of their treaty commitments in the narrow sense, and there has since been reasonable doubt – not just among French historians – about the blame for the resumption of hostilities in 1803. But Malta was not the real object of the quarrel. British hesitations derived not from any reluctance to surrender a maritime gain, but from real doubts about Napoleon's European intentions. As far as London was concerned, the treaty of Amiens was to be read together with the treaty of Lunéville (1801) between the French and Austrians, by which Napoleon had agreed to withdraw from Holland and restore the independence of Switzerland. By late 1802, he had shown no sign of doing so, nor were British suspicions allayed by the capture of French spies checking out England's coasts and ports.

Britain's part in Napoleon's downfall is difficult to assess. In narrowly military terms, the contribution was comparatively modest. Of course, it is true that British naval supremacy and various British expeditionary forces, particularly in Spain, helped to sap French power. But such peripheral strategies could only be peripheral to the eventual outcome. The *Grande Armée* was not bled to death by a thousand cuts, worn down by British-sponsored guerrillas or starved into submission by the Royal Navy; it was totally destroyed at great cost – in Russia in 1812–13 – and its successor was defeated by the Russians, Prussians and Austrians in 1813–14. It is widely accepted that had the Russian campaign been successful in 1812, the following year would have seen a reinforced French army across the Pyrenees to scotch Wellington's skilfully won gains. Even Waterloo in 1815, long hailed as the crowning British victory over Napoleon, owed much – as Peter Hofschröer has recently reminded us – to the Prussians (and indeed the Dutch and Belgians as well).[51]

In political terms, however, the role of Britain was crucial. Of course, it is not quite true that Britain 'stood alone' against Napoleon; for much of the period she had the dubious honour of being supported by the unhinged king of Sweden, Gustav IV. But it is certainly fair to say that, with the exception of the year of uneasy peace in 1802–1803 and perhaps the blue-water interlude of 1806–1807, Britain remained the focal point of European resistance to Napoleon. The winning formula of British gold and European coalitions eluded Pitt and his successors until 1813, but it was eventually found not only because of changes within Europe itself, but also because the British kept trying. And in 1813–14, it was not least Castlereagh's clever diplomacy and – as John M. Sherwig has shown – a more sensitive and generous use of subsidies, that prevented the final coalition from going the way of its three or four predecessors.[52]

THE HOME FRONT

It is sometimes noted that there is little trace of the contest with Napoleon in the novels of Jane Austen, the greatest contemporary English novelist. It is certainly true that Britain did not experience the same profound domestic transformations as Prussia, the *Rheinbund* states, Holland, the Italian and other European states did between 1792 and 1815. Napoleon was defeated, as Charles Esdaile has put it, 'without any fundamental reformation in either Britain's way of making war or her system of government'.[53]

At the level of high politics, the impact of the French wars was mixed. During the 1790s, the debate on the Revolution had torn the Whigs apart; a substantial group under Portland left to join Pitt in the war effort, the radical rump under Charles James Fox remained in sympathy with the Revolution and eventually seceded – temporarily – from the House of Commons. Nor did the advent of Napoleon bring any sense of national unity or political restraint. It is true that the decision to resume hostilities in May 1803 was overwhelmingly endorsed by about five-sixths of the House of Commons, but the conduct of the war remained a furious partisan issue throughout. The only remotely 'national' coalition – the Ministry of All the Talents, a bizarre blend of Whig sybarites, colonial opportunists, fiscal rectitudinarians, Bourbon restorationists and the occasional orphaned Pittite – was in fact neither inclusive nor particularly talented. Military–political failures such as Walcheren were dissected in the full glare of a public inquiry. Paradoxically, however, no government ever fell directly over a war-related crisis: Pitt and the Talents went in 1801 and 1807 over Catholic emancipation; Addington was brought down over his financial policies in 1804; Pitt's second administration ended with his death in 1806; Portland resigned due to ill-health in 1809; and Spencer Perceval's ministry was terminated by his assassination in 1812.

Despite all this, the impact of Napoleon on British society was considerable. For a start, the war required the most extensive mobilisation of British manpower yet seen. True, the available striking force was always small, particularly when large forces were committed to the peninsula. But by the late Napoleonic period about one-sixth of the population was available for military service in the army, navy, militia, volunteers and other formations – probably a higher proportion than in metropolitan France at that time.[54] In 1809, for example, the British could field some 240,000 regulars plus 100,000 seamen out of a population of 11 million; the French mustered 310,000 front-line troops out of a population more than twice that. The basis for this astonishing level of mobilisation was the British 'fiscal-military' state, as it had developed throughout the eighteenth century and was refined by the challenge of revolutionary and Napoleonic France. This implicit contract between the executive, the political nation and the financial elites for war, commerce and colonial expansion enabled Britain not merely to increase but also to access the national wealth for the great struggle.

Indeed, if we look more closely at the great domestic–political issues of the day, the link to the contest with Napoleon becomes immediately obvious. For when Pitt and the Talents unsuccessfully demanded the introduction of Catholic emancipation, they were not simply making a domestic point about the nature of toleration and the British Constitution. Rather, they had two war aims in mind. The first and more narrowly strategic was the desire to pacify Ireland and to prevent the French from opening up a new front there, as they had attempted to do in 1796 and 1798. The second and broader concern was to tap into the vast reservoir of untapped manpower and energies of disadvantaged British Catholics. Across Europe, the French challenge had led to the questioning of traditional hierarchies, beliefs and inequalities. It was no different in Britain, and if the impact on societal structures and attitudes was ultimately less profound, this not only reflected the tenacious rearguard action of the crown and other reactionary forces, but was a consequence of the relative remoteness of the threat. As it turned out, the British army was able to employ large numbers of Irish Catholic recruits even without the incentive of Catholic emancipation, which had to wait until 1829.

Britain's open contest with Napoleon – as opposed to the cold war he waged with Sir Hudson Lowe until his death on St Helena in 1821 – ended on an odd note. After the fiasco of the Hundred Days and the defeat at Waterloo, Napoleon made his famous public request for asylum in an appeal to the Prince Regent in July 1815. 'I come', he declaimed, 'like Themistocles to throw myself upon the hospitality of the British people. I put myself under the protection of their laws, which I claim from your Royal Highness as the most powerful, the most constant, and the most generous of my enemies.'[55] This was not the last such plea to be made by a defeated enemy – a very similar wish was expressed by the last German Emperor, William II, who dearly wanted to live out his retirement as a private gentleman in England. It would be tempting, therefore, to interpret Napoleon's gambit as a typical instance of an abject affection-loving foreigner seeking acceptance by the British, or the English even. But there is another explanation. For a start, the English option was always second best; Napoleon had originally wanted to go into exile in the United States, but dithered until cut off by the Royal Navy.[56]

Moreover, when giving himself up to HMS *Bellerophon*, Napoleon was well aware of the small but vocal and well-connected constituency he enjoyed in Britain. His final chance of avoiding banishment from Europe, or worse, lay in recruiting their not inconsiderable wealth and legal expertise to his cause. Once in England – and away from vengeful Prussians, Austrians and Russians – he could hope to turn the very constitutionality of Britain he had once despised to his advantage. This was also the hope of some Whig radicals, who busied themselves with plans to secure Napoleon's release on various technicalities. It may have been only the presence of mind of the captain of the *Bellerophon*, who prevented all attempts to serve Napoleon a subpoena to attend a court case in London, that prevented Napoleon from having the last laugh.

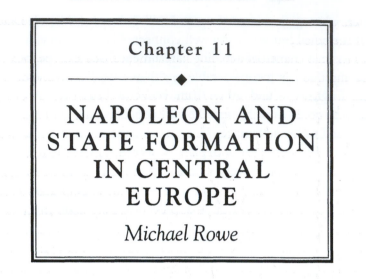

Chapter 11

NAPOLEON AND STATE FORMATION IN CENTRAL EUROPE

Michael Rowe

THE DESTRUCTION OF THE HOLY ROMAN EMPIRE

Thomas Nipperdey's bold assertion at the beginning of his magisterial synthesis of nineteenth-century German history – 'In the beginning was Napoleon' – is misleading in the sense that it underplays significant developments in central Europe in the last decades of the eighteenth century that come under the heading 'Enlightened Absolutism'.[1] Enlightened reform extended not only to the two biggest central European states, the Habsburg monarchy ruled by Maria Theresa (1740–80), Joseph II (1780–90) and Leopold II (1790–2) and the Prussian kingdom of Frederick II (the Great) (1740–86), but also to many of the smaller states into which the Holy Roman Empire was divided.[2] To an extent, these reforms prefigured those of the Napoleonic era, especially in terms of the development of the modern, bureaucratic, centralised, sovereign state. However, eighteenth-century reform was hampered by that thousand-year-old institution, the Holy Roman Empire, which covered the western (mainly German-speaking) part of the Habsburg monarchy and most of Prussia, as well as all the smaller German states. The Empire greatly restricted the scope of reforms which might impinge upon existing noble, clerical and urban privileges within the individual states. These privileges were protected by the imperial courts in Wetzlar and Vienna. Many Germans cherished the Empire as a guarantor of the peace in central Europe, and argued that it should be reformed and not abolished. Amongst the most prominent advocates of imperial reform in this period was the coadjutor of electoral Mainz, Karl Theodor von Dalberg, of whom more below.[3]

It was therefore a reforming, not stagnating, central Europe that received news of the French Revolution in 1789. The vast majority of educated Germans initially greeted the Revolution as the French finally catching up with the kind of reforms already implemented from above to the east of the Rhine. As the Revolution degenerated into Terror, opinion shifted from support to horror, with only a tiny minority – known somewhat misleadingly as the German Jacobins – remaining attached to the revolutionary cause after 1792. One often-overlooked response to the Revolution was the renewed assertiveness of the representative estates (normally composed of nobles, senior clerics and representatives of towns and cities) in parts of central Europe, including the Rhineland bordering France, Württemberg, Bavaria, Baden and Hesse, parts of the Habsburg monarchy, Prussia and Poland. These estates, which had emerged in the medieval period, had been pushed into the background in the seventeenth and eighteenth centuries by royal and then enlightened absolutism, which concentrated power in the hands of the monarchs, royal ministers and officials.[4]

A more dramatic consequence of the French Revolution was the outbreak of the revolutionary wars (divided into the war of the First Coalition (1792–97), and of the Second Coalition (1799–1801)). These wars transformed the map of central Europe. They coincided with the final partitions of Poland (1793 and 1795), which disappeared as an independent state. The consequence of the Polish partitions was not only the extension of Austrian, Prussian and Russian territory, but a growing fear amongst the smaller German states that they might share a similar fate. Some of the German princes even pondered whether or not revolutionary France might represent the best guarantee against the partition of the Holy Roman Empire between Austria and Prussia.

Decisive victories in the revolutionary wars gave France a dominant role in reshaping central Europe according to its own interests. The wars officially ended with the treaty of Lunéville (9 February 1801), signed by France (now governed by Napoleon) and the Habsburg ruler, Francis II (1792–1835), who was also Holy Roman Emperor. This agreement opened the final chapter in the dissolution of the Holy Roman Empire, which was forced to cede its territories west of the Rhine to France. The secular princes with possessions west of the Rhine, who included the rulers of Prussia and Bavaria, expected territorial compensation for their losses. It was generally accepted that this would come through the secularisation of the ecclesiastical states to the east of the Rhine. The details of this were subsequently decided by an imperial committee (*Reichsdeputation*) appointed by Francis II. France and Prussia favoured secularisation; the Habsburg monarchy, despite rhetoric, was by now more preoccupied with its interests in Italy. Russia, a co-guarantor of the integrity of the Holy Roman Empire, initially opposed revolutionary reform, but then reversed its policy (Franco–Russian treaty of 3 June 1802). Bilateral agreements between France and the more important German princes followed. With the diplomatic groundwork thus completed, the question of territorial reform was put to the *Reichsdeputation*, which consisted of the plenipotentiaries of the electors of Bavaria, Bohemia (Austria), Brandenburg (Prussia), Mainz and Saxony, the grand master of the Teutonic Order and the dukes of Württemberg and Hesse-Cassel. The decisive vote came on 8 September 1802, when Mainz joined Brandenburg, Bavaria, Württemberg and Hesse-Cassel in outvoting Bohemia, Saxony and the Teutonic Order in favour of secularisation. This decision was accepted by the imperial diet (*Reichstag*) on 24 March 1803 and received imperial ratification on 27 April. Accordingly, all the ecclesiastical states were secularised, and in addition, forty-five of the fifty-one independent free imperial cities were annexed to neighbouring territorial states. In all, 3.2 million souls – one-seventh of the Empire's population – and 10,000 square kilometres changed hands.[5]

The German Catholic Church emerged the big loser from the *Reichsdeputationshauptschluss*, as the settlement is known. Before secularisation, it had ruled 15 per cent of the Holy Roman Empire's territory and 11.4 per cent of its population. All this was lost, with the exception of the ecclesiastical electorate of Mainz, which was transformed into the Electorate of Aschaffenburg-Regensburg for the benefit of Dalberg. Pope Pius VII remained remarkably sanguine at the destruction of the old imperial Church not least because he had not forgotten the attempts of the German archbishops to break with the Holy See in the 1780s. Arguably, however, the loss of temporal power was one precondition for the long-term revival of the spiritual authority of the Catholic Church in nineteenth-century Germany.[6]

The Holy Roman Empire survived secularisation by three years, but was gravely weakened for two reasons: first, it lost its legitimacy as a legal order; second, the disappearance of the ecclesiastical states and imperial cities robbed it of its staunchest supporters. Nor did despoliation of the Catholic Church satisfy the appetite of the German princes who, having grown fat on secularisation, started illegally taking over the territories of the independent imperial nobility within their midst from October 1803 onwards. The

Prussians encouraged these actions, whilst the Habsburgs, whose traditional supporters the imperial nobles were, remained aloof. Dalberg, who remained *ex-officio* chancellor of the Holy Roman Empire, appealed to Napoleon to protect the imperial nobility. Dalberg now emerged as the leading proponent of a united 'third Germany' (Germany minus Austria and Prussia) under Napoleon's protection.[7]

The outbreak of the war of the Third Coalition (August 1805) between France and Austria, Britain and Russia ruined Dalberg's plans. For whilst Dalberg, as imperial chancellor, adopted a principled neutral stance during the war, the south German princes provided France with military support. Napoleon recognised that the newly enlarged individual German states rather than a reconstituted Holy Roman Empire would best serve his military needs. Therefore, following the defeat of the Third Coalition in December 1805, there was no chance that Napoleon would assist the imperial nobility against the princes. Instead, he gave the green light for the final wave of territorial consolidation with the elimination of the imperial nobility. German-speaking central Europe, previously fragmented into over three hundred quasi-sovereign entities, was now reduced to just over thirty states. Napoleon elevated the larger south German states, Bavaria and Württemberg, to the status of sovereign kingdoms in December 1805.

The Holy Roman Empire lingered on into 1806. There were even rumours that summer that Napoleon might crown himself Holy Roman Emperor. In reality, he had already decided to dissolve the Empire and replace it with a confederation of south German states. Napoleon's foreign minister, Talleyrand, had started preparing the necessary draft treaty as early as November 1805. Following the war of the Third Coalition, plans for a stronger confederation, as favoured by Dalberg, were modified in favour of a looser structure preferred by the south German princes. In May 1806, Napoleon approved the draft drawn up by Talleyrand for the creation of a military alliance encompassing sixteen southern and central German princes grouped within a confederation under French protection. Despite misgivings, the larger south German states wisely joined. The smaller states were more enthusiastic, viewing Napoleon's confederation as the best defence against the fate that had just befallen the ecclesiastical states and imperial nobles. Dalberg, as a consolation prize, was made 'prince-primate' (*Fürstprimas*) of the confederation and, after some hesitation, signed the Acts of Confederation (26 July 1806) and resigned as imperial chancellor (1 August). A week later, Francis II abdicated as Holy Roman Emperor, bringing the thousand-year *Reich* to an end.[8]

STATE FORMATION IN THE 'THIRD GERMANY'

The collapse of the Empire removed the last impediments to radical reform within the newly sovereign German states. The need of these states to incorporate secularised and 'mediatised' territories, with their different customs and laws, provided an added incentive for reform. Most of the reforms now implemented had been on the drawing board at the end of the eighteenth century. However, only the removal of the protection afforded to the privileged by imperial institutions allowed them to be put into practice. Once this occurred, far-reaching reforms were introduced with astonishing speed. In the largest state of the Confederation of the Rhine, Bavaria, the entire structure of the state was overhauled. In May 1808, a new constitution was introduced, both symbolising Bavaria's sovereignty and providing a framework for yet more reform. The preamble of the Constitution proclaimed the transformation of Bavaria from a 'simple aggregate of heterogeneous territories' into a single unit with natural borders. A series of executive decrees followed, the most significant being that of 21 June 1808. This replaced the old provincial governments with fifteen districts resembling French departments. In order to weaken provincial identities, these new administrative sub-divisions were named after geographical features, not historical entities. The Bavarian government also attempted to impose a new Bavarian identity throughout the state, which included many subjects – 'new Bavarians', as they were now called – previously subject to ecclesiastical rulers, imperial nobles or autonomous urban governments. Bureaucrats led the drive to turn the previously disparate territories into a whole. Representative institutions remained absent. Instead, reform was pushed through by a tiny number of bureaucrats – perhaps thirty in Munich and several hundred in the fifteen districts – recruited from a university-educated amalgamation of nobles and bourgeois, subordinate to the chief minister, Maximilian von Montgelas. These bureaucrats were Bavaria's primal citizens, the repository of Bavarian statehood and propagators of the new Bavarian state ideology.[9]

In Bavaria political power was concentrated in the hands of Montgelas and the bureaucracy rather than King Maximilian Joseph. In neighbouring Württemberg, the Holy Roman Empire's dissolution enabled the strong-willed King Frederick II to crush the estates and establish personal absolutism. The acquisition of secularised and 'mediatised' lands after 1803 had already tilted the balance in favour of Frederick, who exploited their fiscal resources to bypass the estates of the old duchy. The continued functioning of the imperial courts, however, prevented the complete abolition of the estates. This only came after Frederick's elevation to sovereign king, in recompense for support afforded Napoleon during the war against Austria in 1805. Napoleon now actively supported the abolition of representative estates, as he believed these hindered efficient administration. Frederick needed little prompting, dissolving them on the last day of 1805. Frederick also subsequently proceeded ruthlessly against 'mediatised' nobles within Württemberg's territory; their properties were invaded by Frederick's troops and bailiffs, their houses violated and anything not securely nailed down – furniture, pictures, silver, linen – carted off to Stuttgart.[10]

The Grand Duchy of Baden, the third main south German state, like Bavaria but unlike Württemberg, experienced reform driven by professional, tenured, university-educated bureaucrats who represented the only true citizens of the state (*Staatsbürger*) amidst a population still defined by its membership of an estate, city or home town. Following the Napoleonic re-ordering of Germany, Baden lost its Rhenish possessions but gained compensation that resulted in its quadrupling in size whilst its ruler, Karl Friedrich, was elevated to the status of grand duke. His grandson subsequently married Napoleon's step-daughter, Stephanie Beauharnais. Given the grand duke's age and increasing incapacity, political power devolved to reforming ministers, led by Friedrich Bauer and Sigismund von Reitzenstein. Following the collapse of the Holy Roman Empire, they issued a series of constitutional edicts that reduced the previously autonomous local towns and communities to the lowest administrative tier of the state, subjected the eight 'mediatised' noble estates (which enjoyed privileges over 20 per cent of the grand duchy's territory) annexed to Baden after 1803 to greater state supervision, and transformed a further hundred noble lords (*Grundherren*, who enjoyed rights over 10 per cent of Baden's population) into civil servants.[11]

South Germany was thus transformed after the war of the Third Coalition. The wave of upheaval and transformation spread north after the war of the Fourth Coalition in 1806. By 1805, Prussia – which had been neutral since 1795 – had become sufficiently alarmed at the expansion of French power eastwards to decide to join the Third Coalition. Napoleon's victory at Austerlitz on 2 December forced Berlin to change tack at the last minute, though Napoleon was not fooled. He now provocatively ignored Prussian interests.[12] After much goading, the Prussians presented Napoleon with an ultimatum on 26 September 1806, demanding the dissolution of the Rhenish confederation and the withdrawal of French troops from the right bank of the Rhine. Napoleon naturally refused, and hostilities commenced. Prussia's army was subsequently annihilated at the twin battles of Jena and Auerstädt

(14 October). Napoleon entered Berlin two weeks later. The Prussian court fled eastwards from where the Russians were marching in support, and a bitter campaign in the snowy wastes of eastern Prussia and Poland ensued in the early months of 1807. This culminated in Napoleon's crushing victory over the Russians at Friedland (14 June 1807). There followed the peace of Tilsit (7 July) between Napoleon and the Russian tsar, Alexander I. Northern central Europe was now securely within the French orbit.

In southern Germany, Napoleon could rely upon states under friendly native dynasties to support French interests against Austria. In the north, he needed to create something new, as the main existing states – Hanover, Hesse-Cassel and Brunswick – were hostile to France. The solution was the Kingdom of Westphalia, carved out of these territories plus Prussian possessions west of the Elbe ceded at Tilsit. The new kingdom served as a strategic French strong-point in Germany. It was also supposed to serve as a model of progressive, enlightened government, or so Napoleon informed his youngest brother, Jérôme, upon appointing him king of Westphalia. Westphalia's Constitution was drawn up with great care by leading French experts, some of whom were dispatched to set up and run the administration and judiciary of the new state. Westphalia became the first German state with a modern written constitution. On paper, this provided for a modicum of popular representation, with a state legislature composed of landowners, merchants, manufacturers and other worthies. In practice, the representative element proved a sham. Like the south German states, Westphalia instead became a model of bureaucratic state absolutism, governed (ostensibly) for but not by the people, but by a small number of native Westphalian and French bureaucrats who shared the same ideal of efficient administration.[13] Westphalia, along with all the other remaining German states (other than Austria and Prussia), joined the confederation. Most embarked upon reforms similar to those of the south German states and Westphalia: the strengthening of the centralised, bureaucratic structures of the state at the expense of previously privileged groups who had lost the protection afforded by the Holy Roman Empire. Only Saxony and the Mecklenburg duchies lagged behind the rest of Germany in this period, implementing few or no significant reforms in the Napoleonic era.

The Confederation of the Rhine and its states subsequently succeeded admirably in fulfilling their primary purpose, as defined by Napoleon: the mobilisation of resources in support of the French military machine. The military contribution of the confederation states was impressive. During the 1809 war against Austria, the Bavarians supplied a contingent of 47,000,

Saxony 23,380, Württemberg 19,700, Westphalia 8,000, Baden 7,600 and the smaller states 15,000 between them. In addition to this total of 120,680 came the sizeable contingents deployed in the Iberian peninsula.[14] Even greater numbers were supplied (and lost) during the Russian campaign of 1812. However, whilst conscription and taxation represented a heavy burden upon ordinary Germans, they contributed to the modernisation of the administrative structures of the state. In the short term, this encouraged centralisation and bureaucratic absolutism, not popular political participation. Over the longer term, it contributed to the emergence of constitutional government as a consequence of the need to manage vastly inflated state debts. For rising state debts encouraged the development of capital markets (notably, Frankfurt), replete with issuing houses, stock exchanges and specialised financial institutions, to meet the states' demands for loans. Over the longer term, such institutions were only prepared to lend at reasonable rates of interest to states whose constitutional structures provided guarantees. In practice, this meant representative assemblies holding the power of the purse previously held by the old estates. Thus the Napoleonic period, despite the elimination of the old estates in favour of streamlined bureaucratic government, laid the foundations of constitutional government that would emerge after 1815.[15]

In the shorter term, a greater potential Napoleonic contribution to the governance of western Germany came with the extension of the French *Code civil* of 1804, a document which enshrined the main principles of the French Revolution. In fact, recent research has stressed the success of the German princes and nobles in fending off or at least watering down the extension of the code's principles east of the Rhine. Like most Napoleonic creations, the Civil Code was an instrument of rule rather than a doctrine, and once it endangered French power by provoking large-scale resistance in the German states, Napoleon backtracked (in 1810–11), arguing pragmatically that the code did not suit German circumstances. Apart from some of the smaller territories, only the 'model states' of Berg and Westphalia introduced the code. Even then, this resulted in chaos, as the necessary structures and trained personnel did not exist to administer it. Furthermore, in practice, the Civil Code had the effect of reinforcing existing property relationships. Whilst in France this meant freezing the revolutionary land settlement, in Germany it resulted in the conversion of existing feudal bonds into equally oppressive commercial relationships, with peasants required to pay off their landlords with high redemption payments in compensation for lost dues. The confederation governments, as great landowners themselves (whose finances were groaning under the burdens of Napoleon's wars), naturally classified the widest possible range of feudal dues as commercial rather than personal, and therefore liable for compensation. The result was an added burden on the peasantry, which was itself already groaning under new taxes and conscription. Rural social discontent and state repression followed.[16]

DEFEAT AND REFORM IN PRUSSIA

The Confederation of the Rhine formed a buffer zone on the French Empire's eastern frontier, facing Prussia and Austria. Prussia, as we have seen, collapsed militarily in the face of Napoleon's *Grande Armée* in 1806. For a time, it seemed doubtful whether Prussia would survive, and it was Tsar Alexander's intervention at Tilsit that proved crucial in guaranteeing its continued existence as a state. As it was, Prussia's position was desperate. By the peace of Tilsit, its territory was cut by half, with the loss of everything west of the Elbe to Westphalia and a sizeable mass to the east that became the Grand Duchy of Warsaw. What remained was burdened with a massive reparations bill of 154.5 million francs, representing a third of the monarchy's revenues, plus a large French military presence for which the Prussians also needed to pay.

The scale of Prussia's defeat in 1806 persuaded even the cautious Frederick William III (1797–1840) of the need for change. Fortunately, a new generation of reform-minded bureaucrats had emerged over the previous decade and now stood ready with a raft of proposals for the overhaul of the state. Amongst them was Carl August von Hardenberg, who after 1797 had been head of the administration of the Prussian enclaves of Ansbach and Bayreuth. These were sufficiently remote from Berlin for Hardenberg to enjoy freedom in pushing through reforms he would later introduce throughout Prussia. Hardenberg subsequently bombarded the young Frederick William III with memoranda – in 1800, 1801 and 1806 – proposing an overhaul of government. Nothing came of these proposals at this stage, thanks to Frederick William's inability to take decisions.[17] Hardenberg, who was appointed foreign minister in 1804, seized the opportunity presented by Prussia's defeat to renew his calls for reform, but was then dismissed (3 July 1807) by Frederick William under pressure from Napoleon, who considered him Francophobe.

Instead, Frederick William III appointed (on 3 October 1807) Karl Freiherr vom Stein principal minister with wide-ranging powers to reform the state. Stein was an imperial knight from Nassau, and as such belonged to that class that had lost its quasi-sovereign status during the Napoleonic re-ordering of western Germany. He had entered Hohenzollern service in 1780 and subsequently distinguished himself as an able administrator. Often bad tempered and outspoken – even in his dealings with monarchs – Stein had been dismissed from office in January 1807 by Frederick William over differ-ences over the structure of government. In June 1807, Stein penned his famous 'Nassau memorandum', in which he repeated earlier suggestions for the replacement of unaccountable court favourites with accountable ministers.

Most pressing of all, however, following Stein's resumption of high office, was the question of peasant emancipation. Intellectual, social and economic developments *before* 1806 had been tending towards emancipation. Prussian agriculture during the decade of neutrality after 1795 had greatly expanded to meet a Europe-wide increase in demand. By 1805, Prussia's eastern provinces accounted for about half of Britain's grain imports. Against this context, the Scottish economist Adam Smith's writings found a particular resonance in the great grain-exporting harbour of Königsberg, especially amongst senior Prussian officials. Another conduit through which British ideas influenced Prussian agricultural theories was Göttingen University. Stein's chief adviser on agricultural reform, Albrecht Thaer, had previously studied there and developed his own ideas on the free market, the abolition of serfdom and enclosure. Commercial pressures made the prospect of a transformation of the landlord–peasant relationship, with its mutual obliga-tions, into one between employer and contractual labourer, increasingly attractive. On the eve of the 1806 war, Frederick William III had himself set an example by abolishing serfdom on royal domains.

By the time of Stein's appointment, a special commission for agricultural reform had already been set up and was busy thrashing out the details of what would become the 'October Edict'. Stein hoped peasant emancipation would not only encourage a more efficient agricultural sector, but also lead to the formation of a substantial class of English-style independent yeoman farmers. Divisions subsequently emerged within the Prussian bureaucracy between those who stressed the economic advantages of a free market and those who placed greater emphasis on a wider social agenda.[18] In the end, the Emancipation Edict (promulgated on 9 October 1807) favoured the nar-rower commercial objectives. Peasants gained their freedom but not the land. Stein, however, stuck to his wider social vision, and this inspired the ordin-ance of 14 February 1808. This undermined the free-market principle by stipulating that one-half of all land would remain perpetually in the hands of non-nobles. In practice, this ordinance did little to prevent the transformation of the Prussian peasantry into a class of landless agricultural labourers. The free-market principle was subsequently extended to the cities, where a series of edicts in 1808 abolished the many guild restrictions.

Apart from peasant emancipation, the edict reforming city government (19 November 1808) stands as the greatest monument of Stein's reform ministry. This measure established an uneasy balance between local self-government through councillors and mayors elected by property-owners, and central control through state-appointed police commissioners. Stein never fully recognised the difficulty in harmonising his ideal of an independent bureaucracy and the foundation of popular government. Subsequently, Stein sought to extend the urban synthesis between bureaucrats and *notables* to the provinces, through the establishment of administrations (*Regierungen*) for Prussia's four remaining provinces in which *notable* representatives would join civil servants at plenary meetings voting on policy. Stein's proposals for popular representation were less concerned with the principle of popular sovereignty, and more with making the bureaucracy run more efficiently.

As for the highest echelons of the state, Stein proposed (on 24 November 1808) the creation of a council of state composed of the king, members of the royal family, privy councillors and heads of ministerial departments. In addition, Stein commissioned a Silesian nobleman, Karl Nikolaus von Rehdiger, to draft a plan for the creation of a national representative body. Rehdiger was much influenced by the Napoleonic institutions he had encountered in Paris, favoured French-style electoral colleges rather than representation through the old estates, and wanted the university-trained bureaucratic elite to play a leading role. This Stein rejected, as he viewed the representational element – within which a reformed nobility would be the strongest element – as a means of checking a potentially overbearing bureaucracy.[19] Stein, unlike most other reform-minded bureaucrats, refused to admit that giving the nobility a powerful role would hinder future reform. In the event, proposals for national representation were never implemented. On 24 November 1808, Frederick William III dismissed Stein under pressure from Napoleon, who had discovered some incriminating correspondence of Stein's calling for a war of liberation against the French.

Stein's ministry was replaced by the Altenstein-Dohna government, which in turn was replaced (on 4 June 1810) by a government headed by Hardenberg, who received the new title of state chancellor. Hardenberg, unlike Stein, laid more emphasis on bureaucratic efficiency and uniformity, and less on representation. His Riga memorandum of 1807, for example, favoured the elimination of intermediate corporate bodies standing between the individual and the state. Representative bodies, if created at all, must be restricted to the local level. Rather than focus on these, the Hardenberg administration concentrated its efforts on those reforms that were the most urgent, notably state finance. This Frederick William III was prepared to countenance.

Military reform was also pressing. Military reform after 1806 owed much to the activities of the semi-official Military Society (*Militärische Gesellschaft*) that met in Berlin between 1801 and 1805. Head of the society was Gerhard von Scharnhorst, a native Hanoverian whose radical ideas horrified much of Prussia's military establishment, which he joined in 1801. The significance of the Military Society, which discussed new ideas, can be gauged from the fact that almost 60 per cent of the medium and junior-ranking officers who were members subsequently became generals; five became chiefs of the general staff and seven field marshals. Those few officers whose reputations were made rather than destroyed in 1806 were usually former members of the society, and it was they who dominated the military commission (chaired by Scharnhorst) established after the war to re-build the Prussian army.[20] This was done from scratch: all existing units bar a handful were abolished, the structure of the new infantry regiments completely changed, the artillery arm gradually reformed, the cavalry overhauled, greater stress laid on light infantry, and the so-called 'Krumper' system devised to circumvent restrictions placed on the size of the front-line army by the French by releasing men into the reserve as soon as they had been trained.

Despite reform, the prospects of the greatly reduced Prussian army – which under the provisions of Tilsit was restricted to 42,000 men – ever successfully challenging the French in the field appeared remote. Within this context, news of the popular Spanish uprising against French domination in May 1808, followed by the defeat of an entire French division at Bailén two months later, suggested the alternative of a national war of liberation in which the entire population might be mobilised. Stein was attracted to the idea, but foolish enough to commit himself in writing in letters intercepted by French agents. Another proponent of a popular rising was Scharnhorst's chief collaborator in the reform of the Prussian army, Neithardt von Gneisenau. Less impressed by talk of an apocalyptic people's war was King Frederick William, who became increasingly alarmed lest the military leadership involve Prussia in a suicidal war with Napoleon that would spell the end of his dynasty. In April 1809, he even received reports of a conspiracy, led by Scharnhorst, to replace him on the throne with Prince William – reports which proved to be false.[21] The following month, the Prussian Major von

Schill, acting on his own authority, led his hussar regiment out of Berlin in an attempt to organise a national German uprising against Napoleon in support of the Austrians, who were again fighting the French. The attempt was defeated and Schill killed, but the episode showed that some senior military officers now owed their allegiance to the abstract Prussian state and even to the German nation, however defined, and not to the Hohenzollern dynasty.

In the domestic field, Hardenberg's administration continued down the path of reform embarked upon by Stein. Amongst the more important measures pushed through in 1810 was the abolition of all remaining guild restrictions, thus creating a free market in the non-agricultural sector. In an attempt to alleviate Prussia's fiscal woes, Hardenberg abolished noble tax exemptions (27 to 28 October 1810) and introduced new taxes to cover reparations payments. The following year (on 14 September 1811), the Prussian government regulated peasant emancipation by making peasants free proprietors over two-thirds of their holdings, and transferring the other third to their former landlords in compensation for abolished dues.

Many of these measures were opposed by Prussia's conservative landowning nobility, the *Junkers*. Their most prominent spokesman was Friedrich August Ludwig von der Marwitz. Like many other opponents of reform, Marwitz had been temporarily silenced in the immediate aftermath of 1806, but re-emerged with renewed confidence during Hardenberg's chancellorship. Initially, Hardenberg attempted to placate and outmanoeuvre his conservative opponents by convening an assembly of *notables* to represent the interests of the nation. This proved a tactical error, as it simply gave the chancellor's opponents an institutional platform. Realising his mistake, Hardenberg quickly dissolved the assembly (September 1811), and even had Marwitz imprisoned. Hardenberg pressed on with his reforms, which culminated in the *Gendarmerie-Edikt* of 30 July 1812. This brought the lowest tier of administration, centred on local districts (*Kreise*), under the control of government-appointed officials, and amounted to a direct challenge to the authority of the nobility over their localities. Not surprisingly, there was a furious outburst of noble opposition to the measure. Hardenberg had now probed and discovered the limits of reform, for the *Gendarmerie-Edikt* was never implemented, but instead suspended (in 1814) and then superseded (in 1816) by a new measure that reinforced noble control over the countryside.

Ultimately, Frederick William shared the same social vision as his eighteenth-century predecessors: nobles remained the unique repository of honour, and were to be discouraged from entering demeaning bourgeois professions, just as the bourgeoisie were to be discouraged from acquiring noble estates. The Prussian law code of 1794, which enshrined these moral social inequalities in law, remained in force. Indeed, the Prussian nobility's status as an exclusive caste was reinforced rather than diminished after 1806; between 1807 and 1839 only 140 commoners were ennobled, the same number as for the period 1798 to 1806.[22] The Prussian nobility had weathered the storm.

THE HABSBURG MONARCHY AND THE NAPOLEONIC CHALLENGE

The Habsburg monarchy, unlike Prussia after 1806, remained a formidable power even after its defeats in 1797, 1801 and 1805. The fact that it did not find itself in the same desperate position as its northern rival diminished the necessity for far-reaching reform. The machinations of the so-called Austrian Jacobins – in reality, disaffected radical Josephist nobles, civil servants and officers – in the early 1790s, which were uncovered by Francis II's police in 1794, reinforced the Emperor's instinctive conservatism. A political freeze ensued that extended into the Napoleonic period. The main beneficiary of all this was the police ministry, which emerged from the 'Jacobin' trials with enhanced prestige and institutional importance. However, the regular civil service continued to act zealously in preserving Joseph II's reforms in non-controversial areas, such as the subordination of the Catholic Church to the state and codification of law (the penal code was promulgated in 1803 and the civil code in 1811), whilst avoiding initiatives on taboo subjects, such as peasant emancipation.[23]

Apart from legal codification, few reforms of note were implemented, even after the replacement of the old guard by the more dynamic Johann Philipp von Stadion (foreign minister from December 1805 to October 1809) and the Emperor's younger brother, Archduke Charles (appointed supreme military commander, or 'Generalissimus', on 10 February 1806), following defeat in the war of the Third Coalition. A major weakness was that the monarchy lacked any unified supreme decision-making body. The Council of State, originally established by Maria Theresa, was briefly re-established in 1801 at the Archduke Charles's prompting, but then abolished again. Francis, influenced by a clique of cabinet councillors, remained suspicious of anything resembling a responsible council of ministers. The only notable administrative reform of this entire period was a decree in 1808 ordering that mayors of towns would in future be appointed by the state rather than being elected by local councils.

Slightly more was achieved on the military front, where four important reforms were initiated after 1805: the introduction of corps, together with the necessary staff and support so that they could operate independently; the concentration of regimental guns into brigade batteries; the increase in the number of light infantry; and, finally and most controversially, plans to create a second and third layer of defensive reserves through the establishment of a 400,000-strong militia that would in addition bridge the chasm between the military caste and civilian population. In practice, not all these reforms were fully implemented. The lack of experienced corps commanders, capable of operating independently, meant that the reforms to the strategic structure of the army could not be profited from, whilst resistance from conservative elements at court limited the scope of reform with respect to the militia.

Stadion believed that the struggle against Napoleon would have to be conducted by the pen as well as the sword. Like Stein in Prussia, he was disgusted at the complete lack of popular patriotism, which he was determined to encourage. A brief thaw in Austria's intellectual life ensued. In January 1806, Francis issued a proclamation – which contemporaries ascribed to Stadion – calling on all people to assist in the regeneration of the state. The following month, Stadion announced his intention of encouraging a freer intellectual climate in the Empire. Later that year, the government founded a French-style polytechnic in Prague and drew up plans for a second in Vienna. Stadion, again like Stein in Prussia, strove to revive the noble estates as active participants in the regeneration of the monarchy, a role from which they had been excluded since the traumatic final years of Joseph II's reign. In addition, the government founded a number of newspapers to counter Napoleonic propaganda, whilst Stadion cultivated connections with Germany's cultural elite. Leading German writers, including notably Friedrich Gentz, were invited to Vienna in 1808 and 1809.[24]

Stadion, in whipping up popular patriotism, was playing with fire. For the Habsburg monarchy, to a far greater extent than Prussia or the Confederation of the Rhine, was distinguished by its multi-cultural flavour. Its estimated 5.6 million native-German speakers only made up about a third of a population of just under 20 million. Hungarians (or, more accurately, Magyars) made up the next largest group, numbering about 3.4 million, followed by the Czechs (2.6 million), Romanians (1.6 million) and Slovaks (1.3 million), with other Slav nationalities making up the rest.[25]

The Magyars were the most important nationality, not only in terms of size, but also historical awareness and institutional significance. In Hungary, the nobility, who accounted for just over 4 per cent of the population, regarded themselves as the embodiment of the nation. That this perception was not reinforced by the new concept of 'nation' that emerged from the French Revolution in a direction dangerous for Habsburg rule can in part be ascribed to the nobility's panic at the radical turn of events in Paris after 1792 and the retribution meted out to the Austrian and Hungarian 'Jacobin' conspirators in 1795. The 'feudal nationalist' Hungarian nobility was fundamentally hostile to social reform. The revolutionary/Napoleonic threat, if anything, increased support for the Habsburgs, and the personal popularity of the viceroy (or Palatine) throughout the Napoleonic period, Archduke Joseph (another brother of the Emperor), encouraged this. Those who favoured radical social reform remained a tiny, isolated minority until after the 1830s.[26] Nonetheless, the Magyar nobility demonstrated a growing interest in furthering the Hungarian language. This issue came to a head at the so-called 'Accursed Diet' in early 1808, and contributed to its dissolution amidst mutual recrimination – though, significantly, the diet voted additional reinforcements for the army. Yet there was never significant Hungarian support for Napoleon, who represented a potential threat to noble privileges. This sentiment, coupled with better political management, meant the next diet (the 'Handsome Diet', which convened on 31 June 1808) was a greater success, with the nobles voting 20,000 recruits to reinforce the Hungarian regiments in the Habsburg army and 60,000 militiamen for the territorial forces (an institution known as the 'Insurrection'). In return, Francis himself promised the Hungarian diet to further the cultural development of the nationalities under his rule. As for some of the other nationalities, Stadion attempted to appeal to them through the translation of patriotic songs into Polish, Czech and Slovenian; the foundation of a South Slav newspaper; and the exploitation of Napoleon's quarrel with Pope Pius VII to play on supranational Catholic sentiment.[27]

Napoleon's intervention in Spain and the subsequent uprising in May 1808 had an electrifying effect on governing circles in Vienna. For the Habsburgs, the consequences were threefold: first, Napoleon's deposition of the Spanish Bourbons revealed that no established dynasty was safe, even if it had allied itself with the French; second, the Spanish rising, and in particular, the Spanish victory at Bailén, suggested the French might be beaten by a combination of regular troops and popular patriotic enthusiasm; third, the developing Spanish ulcer forced Napoleon to transfer a considerable force from central Europe to the Iberian peninsula. These factors strengthened the hand of the war party in Vienna who, despite the warnings of Archduke Charles that the army was not ready, eventually pushed Francis into declaring war on 9 April

1809. The war ended in disaster for the monarchy; after initial advances into Poland, north Italy and Bavaria, the Austrian armies found themselves on the defensive on all fronts. Appeals to German nationalism met with no response in the confederation states, which, as already noted, supplied Napoleon with over 120,000 troops in the campaign. Despite the odds, the Austrian army performed surprisingly well, inflicting the first defeat on a French army led by Napoleon in person at the battle of Aspern-Essling (21 to 22 May 1809). This delayed rather than prevented defeat, which came at the climax of the campaign, the battle of Wagram (6 July), one of the bloodiest engagements of the Napoleonic wars.

The only area that responded to Habsburg calls for a patriotic rising was the mountainous Tyrol, an old dynastic possession that Napoleon had transferred to Bavaria following the 1805 war. The Tyrolese rising had nothing to do with German nationalism – the main targets were, after all, the Bavarians, not the French – but was one of several struggles waged by European peripheries against enlightened absolutism, be it of Josephist, Napoleonic or Bavarian stamp. The origins of resistance were partly geographical (the Tyrol's inaccessibility to regular forces), historical (the region had enjoyed numerous special privileges within the monarchy), military (the Tyrol's old and well-developed militia system) and sociological (the comparative absence of towns and nobles, and dominance of independent-minded farmers imbued with a culture of self-reliance). Given this combination, it was hardly surprising that the Tyrolese should react against the uncompromising centralisation imposed by Montgelas's bureaucrats, and news of the Austrian victory at Aspern provided the spark. The subsequent rising, led by Andreas Hofer (the son of an innkeeper), had no chance of success following Austria's defeat, when the French committed overwhelming numbers to finish the job previously botched by a Bavarian corps. Significantly, Napoleon's troops were viewed as liberators by many townspeople in the troubled region who had quickly turned against a rebel force dominated by peasants with little sympathy for urban culture. Napoleon finally crushed the rising in November 1809.[28]

Austria's defeat in 1809 represented a long-term disaster for the monarchy. Far from responding to defeat with more change, the whole reform agenda became discredited in Francis's eyes. Stadion was replaced as chief minister by Metternich, who would remain at the helm until 1848. Archduke Charles retired, and the Emperor's other able brothers were pushed into the background. Francis resorted to more tried-and-tested Habsburg survival strategies: the printing of paper money followed by a declaration of bankruptcy and a dynastic match, in the shape of the marriage of his daughter Marie-Louise to Napoleon.

THE END OF NAPOLEONIC HEGEMONY IN CENTRAL EUROPE

Napoleon's alliance with Europe's pre-eminent dynasty marked the high point of his power. Russia alone amongst the continental powers remained outside the fold. Napoleon's attempt to rectify this, and extend French power farther east still, resulted in defeat and the collapse of his hegemony within central Europe during what became known as the 'Wars of Liberation' of 1813. This phase of the Napoleonic wars began on 30 December 1812, when the commander of the Prussian auxiliary corps attached to the Napoleonic host that had invaded Russia the previous June, General Yorck von Wartenburg, signed an agreement with the Russians at Tauroggen, neutralising his force. What made this event extraordinary was that Yorck was acting without any authority from his king, Frederick William. As such, Tauroggen again demonstrated that at least some Prussian officers now served the higher abstract ideal of the state/nation rather than the dynasty.

Frederick William never forgave General Yorck for what was, in effect, an act of treason that may have endangered the survival of the Prussian state. It was only in March 1813 that he judged the time propitious to declare war on Napoleon and throw in his lot openly with the Russians, who had decided not to stop at their own frontiers but to liberate all Europe from the French yoke. On 17 March, he issued his famous patriotic proclamation to his people (*An mein Volk*). Over the following year the Prussian state engaged in a massive effort of resource mobilisation to win back its great-power status: 6 per cent of its entire population was called up; the army grew from 65,000 to 150,000 regulars plus 120,000 militia (*Landwehr*); and over 30,000 volunteered up to August 1814 for the Prussian forces. Few deserted. Between 20 per cent and 50 per cent of the student body in north German universities enlisted. This effort by Prussia was unmatched in *per capita* terms by any other power in this period, including France in 1793–94.[29]

The extent to which German nationalism contributed to this impressive effort remains debatable. The so-called Borussian school of the nineteenth and early twentieth centuries viewed the wars of liberation in terms of a modernised Prussian state leading a culturally revived and nationally aware German people against French oppression. Recent literature, in contrast, generally plays down the role of nationalism and instead sees the French defeat in central Europe in terms of great-power politics and regular armies rather than direct popular participation. In reality, the willingness of tens of thousands of Prussians to commit themselves to the war effort in a way they had singularly failed to do in 1806 had little to do with the reforms pushed through by Stein and Hardenberg in the interim. Nor was it part of a popular campaign in favour of a German nation state. Rather, it derived from simple hatred of the French, who had ruthlessly exploited Prussia over the previous seven years. Frederick William's government, far from fully exploiting this sentiment, watered down plans for a people's war in the summer of 1813, fearing the consequences of a Spanish-style uprising on Prussian soil.[30] Nor did popular hatred of the French in parts of the Confederation of the Rhine account for the ultimate defeat of Napoleon; nowhere did Francophobia determine the policy of the confederation princes. Indeed, fear of popular uprisings within their territories encouraged the princes to draw closer to Napoleon as the best guarantor of their sovereignty. What might be conceded is that popular hatred of Napoleon in northern Germany facilitated the coalition forces' advance in 1813, especially in Westphalia and Berg – new, artificial states that lacked native dynasties around which people might rally in times of crisis. The few thousand Cossacks who advanced on Westphalia's capital, Kassel, in September 1813, for example, encountered no serious resistance. Few, if any, 'Westphalians' were prepared to shed their blood for Napoleon's 'model' state.

The reluctance of the confederation princes to abandon Napoleon in 1813 stemmed from rational calculations concerning the preservation of their recently acquired sovereignty, something threatened by Prussian-backed German nationalists including Ernst Moritz Arndt and Joseph Görres. It was the Habsburg monarchy, and in particular its foreign minister Metternich, who created the conditions that facilitated the transfer of allegiance of the princes. Vienna's policy in 1813 was ultimately crucial in preserving the essence of the Napoleonic territorial settlement in Germany. This suited the key objective of Metternich, which was to re-create an independent European centre that could counter-balance the flanking powers, France and Russia, whilst simultaneously opposing Prussian attempts to carve out a hegemonic position in northern Germany. Metternich recognised many of the virtues of the Confederation of the Rhine. Indeed, he proposed its preservation in negotiations with Napoleon in the summer of 1813, though on condition that it came under the protection of all the great powers and not just France. This plan was threatened by Stein, who had re-emerged from exile in 1813 as an influential statesman within the coalition. Stein proposed substituting the 'arbitrary' rule of the thirty-six petty despots of the confederation with direct representation through the creation of a German national assembly, or *Reichstag*. More immediately, it was Napoleon's stubbornness and refusal to compromise that scuppered Metternich's attempts to mediate a settlement between France and the coalition over the summer of 1813 that would have re-established the European balance to Austria's advantage. Following the breakdown of negotiations, the Habsburg monarchy joined the war against France in August 1813.

From within the coalition, Metternich recognised that fear for their sovereignty was delaying the defection of the princes. To overcome this and thwart the nationalist agenda, he proceeded to sign separate treaties with the individual German states, guaranteeing their sovereignty in return for their adherence to the coalition. As the Emperor Francis had no intention of reviving the German imperial dignity abolished in 1806, Austria could now pose as the guarantor of the sovereignty of the confederation states. The most significant of Metternich's agreements was the treaty of Ried, concluded with Bavaria on 8 October 1813. The other German states rushed to sign similar agreements, lest they fall into the clutches of Stein, to whom the coalition powers had entrusted the administration of enemy territories occupied by their advancing armies. The only princes who failed to take advantage of Metternich's lifeline were Frederick Augustus of Saxony, Dalberg of Frankfurt and Karl of Isenberg-Birstein; all the others switched sides.[31] It was thus that the Napoleonic territorial order in Germany survived, in its essentials, until Bismarck's re-ordering in 1866 and Hitler's *Gleichschaltung* of 1934, only to re-emerge in the federalism of West Germany in 1949.

CONCLUSION

The Napoleonic period proved momentous for the development of central Europe. The temptation might arise to reduce the manifold ingredients of this development to the concept of 'modernisation', however defined. This would fail to do justice to the range of possibilities opened up by the impact of Napoleon, the unintended consequences of his actions and those of other leading players, and the extent to which seemingly progressive reforms in some areas coincided with or even reinforced existing institutions.

Despite the risk of oversimplification, some order can be imposed through the adoption of the familiar tripartite territorial division between the Habsburg monarchy, Prussia and the 'Third Germany'. For the Habsburg monarchy, the revolutionary and Napoleonic period stood at the boundary between the era of Maria Theresa and Joseph II, which was distinguished by reform, and the era of Metternich, a period of reaction. Prussia, at first glance, appears to provide a contrasting example of 'defensive modernisation' *par excellence*. No other great power experienced such a shattering defeat or dramatic diminution of status in the Napoleonic period, and no other great power rebounded from defeat so decisively. Yet, upon closer inspection, Prussia appears less an example of modernising reform than of the 'deficit in simultaneity' that arguably lies at the root of any German *Sonderweg* to modernity. The 'deficit in simultaneity' resulted from the rapid progress made towards a liberalised economy on the one hand and the stalling of socio-political reform on the other. As for the 'Third Germany', the impact of Napoleon on domestic development varied considerably. Those remotest from Napoleon geographically – notably, the Mecklenburgs and Saxony – experienced the least reform and were noted for their backwardness for much of the nineteenth century. At the other end of the spectrum stood the south German states, which enjoyed a reputation for 'liberalism' in the decades after 1815. At first sight this might appear odd, as during the Napoleonic period these states were characterised by bureaucratic state absolutism. Yet, in a prime example of unintended consequences, the resource mobilisation that was facilitated by bureaucratic government resulted in vastly inflated budget deficits and public debts that could only be sustained, over the longer term, through the promulgation of liberal constitutions. The experience of the south German states as compared to Prussia supports the argument that an effective transition to liberal constitutional government could only be achieved by an intervening period of bureaucratic absolutism that eliminated intermediate bodies standing between citizens and the state.

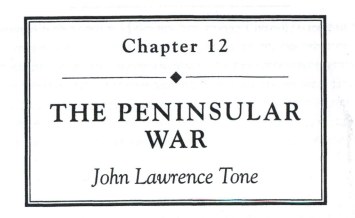

Chapter 12

◆

THE PENINSULAR WAR

John Lawrence Tone

From 1805 to 1807 Napoleon beat Austria into submission, dismantled Prussia and neutralised Russia. Then the Emperor cast his eyes upon Portugal and Spain, and in November 1807 he sent his armies there. Napoleon expected the conquest of Iberia to be easy, but it lasted six years, cost France 300,000 casualties, and wasted an enormous treasure before ending in failure. As Napoleon himself later lamented, the war in the Iberian peninsula was the beginning of the end for the Empire.[1]

It could be argued that the Peninsular War changed the world more dramatically than any other Napoleonic campaign. The destruction and chaos of the French occupation in Portugal and Spain created opportunities, however temporary, for new ideas and leaders to emerge there. Politicians adopted new practices and crafted a new language designed to mobilise large numbers of people, initiating in the Iberian countries, perhaps even prematurely, the nationalisation of the masses.[2] Moreover, the war created a space in which Latin Americans could begin to construct independent nations from the ruins of the Spanish and Portuguese empires.

Given the global impact of the war and Napoleon's own assessment of its central place in the failure of the French Empire, it is important to know why he sought to conquer Iberia in the first place and why the British, Portuguese and Spanish were able to defeat him there. With regard to the first question, both rational and irrational impulses lay behind Napoleon's decision to invade. However, it is also clear that the Emperor was not always a free agent and that the invasion of Portugal and Spain was a constrained decision determined in part by forces outside his control. Indeed, in a certain sense, the invasion of Iberia flowed from the nature of the Empire that Napoleon had created but that was not entirely his to command.

The second problem – explaining Napoleon's defeat – is more complex. The woeful state of the French economy, desertion by imperial conscripts, and the behaviour of poorly trained French officers and hastily mustered soldiers certainly did not help the occupation. At the same time, much of the credit for the allied victory must go to the resilient Portuguese, British and Spanish armies; to the British navy, which got supplies into Cádiz, Lisbon and other coastal centres of resistance; and to the skilled defensive campaign of the army commanded by Arthur Wellesley, later the duke of Wellington, who finally drove the French out of the peninsula in 1813.

However, the central problem for the French throughout the Peninsular War was their uneasy relationship to civil society, especially in Spain. A significant portion of the Spanish population refused to accept imperial tutelage, something that set Spain apart from most occupied territories in Europe and that lay at the root of all of the allied successes and imperial failures. Guerrilla warfare, in particular, occupied and wore down the bulk of Napoleon's forces in the peninsula before they could ever face allied concentrations. Thus, despite the neglect of the Spanish resistance as a subject for empirical research by historians, especially those working in the English language, the nature of Napoleon's defeat in Iberia can only be understood by examining the Spanish partisans. This chapter will explain the origins of the French invasion and explore the two most important and original components of the Spanish resistance – the urban revolutions of May and June 1808 and the subsequent guerrilla warfare that made the Spanish countryside ungovernable for imperial troops.[3]

THE INVASION OF IBERIA

Invading Portugal and Spain, Napoleon struck at Great Britain, the Empire's most dogged opponent. Napoleon had long toyed with the idea of a landing in Britain, but in 1805 he realised at last that he could never ferry an army across the Channel, so he turned instead to economic warfare. In 1806 he inaugurated the Continental Blockade, designed to isolate the British from the markets and raw materials of Europe. Following the victories of 1805–1807, most of the Continent lay under imperial control and had to adhere to the Blockade. Portugal, however, because of its economic and political dependence on Britain and its exiguous geo-political position, still enjoyed some latitude to operate outside the imperial orbit. Napoleon determined to eliminate this autonomy. By occupying Portugal, he planned to complete the Blockade that was supposed to bring Great Britain to its knees.

Scholars have long recognised that this explanation for Napoleon's actions is only part of the story. After all, at the last minute Portugal accepted French terms, agreeing to join the Blockade and to expel British subjects, yet Napoleon invaded anyway. The question is, why? And the answer, at least in part, is that the Emperor had by 1807 decided that he wanted Spain as well as Portugal, and he saw an attack on the Portuguese House of Braganza as a way to wrest Spain from the Bourbons, a family he particularly loathed. Bourbon loyalists in France still questioned Napoleon's legitimacy, and the Emperor repaid them by uprooting scions of the Bourbons wherever he could. In early 1804, Napoleon had the Bourbon duc d'Enghien kidnapped and killed, and in 1805 he dethroned the Neapolitan Bourbons, whose existence he pronounced incompatible with his honour. Only the Spanish Bourbons remained untouched. Though closely allied to France since 1795 and recommitted by the defence pact of January 1805 to aid Napoleon in his military ventures, the Spanish Bourbons nevertheless constituted an affront and a threat to the Bonaparte clan. Napoleon saw the invasion of Portugal as an opportunity to remove them.

Napoleon took a step towards this goal when, on 27 October 1807, France and Spain signed the treaty of Fontainebleau. The treaty required the Spanish government to participate in the assault on Portugal by providing passage and cantonment for French troops. In effect, by fulfilling the terms of the treaty, the Spanish Bourbons connived at their own destruction. Troops under Andoche Junot marched across Spain and occupied Lisbon on 30 November, forcing the Braganzas to flee to Brazil. But more French troops continued to cross the Pyrenees. In February, they seized key fortresses in northern Spain, and in March they entered Madrid, all under the guise of helping the Spanish Bourbons against the British threat. Napoleon believed that he was close to completing his design of taking Portugal, isolating Britain and eliminating the Spanish Bourbons, all virtually unopposed.

The Spanish Bourbons failed to respond to the French provocations of February and March, just as Napoleon expected they would. This was partly because the Spanish government reckoned imperial armies to be invincible, while Spain's own forces were in such a pitiable state that open resistance seemed suicidal.[4] In addition, a series of scandals and tumults had weakened and divided the Spanish royal family, making concerted action by the government difficult. King Charles IV and Queen María Luisa ruled Spain through a favourite, Manuel Godoy, who wielded nearly absolute power in the early years of the century.[5] Godoy was a reforming minister who had started out a common soldier, two facts that made him unpopular with envious social superiors who had been bypassed for preferment and whose wealth had in some cases been the object of Godoy's 'reform'. These men and their followers supported the more conservative heir to the throne, Ferdinand, and they blamed Godoy, Charles and Luisa for every conceivable ill, from bad harvests to the naval disaster at Trafalgar, where the Spanish fleet went down with the French.[6]

In October 1807 Ferdinand and his party decided to seize power from Godoy, but Charles discovered the plot and placed his son under house arrest. Each side looked to Napoleon for support. This 'Affair of the Escorial', as it was called, ended in a stalemate between Ferdinand and Charles, but it revealed the tawdry divisions within the Spanish royal household and provided the opening wedge Napoleon needed to insert himself into Spanish affairs. On 18 March 1808, the Bourbon family picture became even uglier when an uprising incited by Ferdinand's party at Aranjuez forced Charles, Luisa and Godoy to abdicate power. Such a change of government worried Napoleon very little, for he knew that Ferdinand was as servile as his parents. Indeed, all of them – Charles, Luisa, Godoy and Ferdinand – now sought the Emperor's protection and support, leaving no one in any official position to object when French troops began to occupy additional Spanish strong-points. When Napoleon called the Spanish royals to Bayonne for negotiations in April 1808, they dutifully attended and submitted to house arrest. Thus, to the list of underlying reasons for Napoleon's invasion of Iberia must be added the opportunity that Bourbon family squabbles gave the Emperor to become arbiter of Spain's fate. Just as empires are always drawn to power vacuums on their peripheries, so France and Napoleon were drawn to Spain.

Adherents of the 'liberal myth' of Napoleon have argued that France invaded Iberia at least in part to banish feudalism, foster economic growth, and bring enlightened, modern government to peoples straining under the chains of the old regime. This legend of Napoleon's good intentions originates, of course, in imperial propaganda, which at the time declared Spain in need of 'regeneration'. Reprising the republican discourse used to justify wars of conquest in the Vendée and elsewhere, Napoleon's supporters painted the Portuguese and Spanish as inferior fanatics led by monks and policed by the Inquisition.[7] Naturally, such a situation required French intervention to protect the Iberians from themselves, even at the cost of a long and bloody occupation.

Historians nowadays are careful not to adopt Bonapartist rhetoric when applied to the rest of Europe and to France itself, where the reputation of Napoleon as the saviour of the Revolution and founder of modern nations has been seriously questioned on a number of fronts.[8] Oddly, however, the notion of a liberal empire has found a last redoubt in histories of the Peninsular War, where even scholars otherwise critical of Napoleon sometimes condemn the Spanish resistance as a reactionary movement against the modernising tendencies of the Emperor.[9]

While it is true that certain reactionary elements in Spain rallied to Ferdinand, both the Bonapartist explanation for the invasion of Iberia and the tendency to see the Portuguese and Spanish resistance as anti-modern should be rejected for a variety of reasons. In the first place, Spain's and Portugal's greatest difficulty was not the old regime but the arrival from abroad of a newer, bloodier one. The French Revolution of 1789 and the generation of war that followed interrupted the slow work of reform and national construction that had begun under the enlightened ministers of the eighteenth century, delaying and even reversing moderate economic and political progress in the Iberian states, with tragic consequences for the future.[10] In short, if France and Napoleon represented a new order, it was one of economic ruination and dictatorship, not one of rationalism and progress. This fact reminds us that resisting France was not the same thing as resisting modernity, despite the tendency among some Napoleonic scholars to assert just such an equation.

The rhetoric of the liberal empire also ignores the fact that Napoleon could not have cared less about the people of Portugal and Spain. The administrations he set in place there drew upon opportunists among the old elite as much as they did upon anything approximating a 'rising bourgeoisie' or a reform party among the nobility and clergy. The occupation had as its purpose the extraction of wealth and the aggrandisement of the Bonaparte dynasty. Reforms only occurred as byproducts of schemes designed to raise money, requisition food, conscript soldiers, or secure other resources for the Empire. This was most obvious in Portugal. Napoleon initially projected a tripartite division of the country in order to reward Godoy and to provide himself with fiefs he could dispense to family members and close supporters. It should come as no surprise, therefore, that during the first occupation of Portugal, from November 1807 to August 1808, Junot reformed nothing and instituted nothing beyond pillage, taxation and state terror. Indeed, the harsh imperial reality, in Portugal as in many other places, was that the Emperor acted to end feudalism on paper but to shore up a kind of 'bastard feudalism' within which he could reward his followers with titles, properties and other compensations.[11] In any case, Napoleon's plan to eliminate Portugal from the map can hardly be construed as a step toward modernity for the Portuguese.

Similarly, Napoleon's liberal plans for Spain should be viewed with scepticism. Scholars sometimes identify the constitutional statute of Bayonne, 'ratified' by ninety hand-picked Spanish *notables* in June 1808, as the embodiment of Napoleonic reform. This Constitution, under which Napoleon's brother Joseph was supposed to govern Spain, included provisions, such as the elimination of internal tariffs, that would certainly have benefited the country, even if they were primarily designed to increase tax revenues. However, the Bayonne statute, undemocratic at its inception since it was imposed on Spain by the Emperor after he had deposed the Bourbons, did not really go very far, and it paled next to the more radical reforms championed at the time by some of the Spaniards fighting against France. In addition, the Bayonne statute was never enforced, partly because allied resistance made the establishment of any stable government in Spain impossible, but partly because Napoleon simply could not resist violating his own agreements whenever it was convenient.

More convincing as an underlying cause for the invasion of Iberia is the argument that by 1807 the state of France's economy and society required further conquest. Militarism was like an addictive drug, blocking certain economic channels and activities by redirecting resources to the armed forces. Under the Empire, government expenditure rose astronomically, and almost all of it went to the military. Increased taxes, the lack of government support for normal economic development and commercial warfare with Britain caused some of the most advanced sectors of the French economy to atrophy. In this environment, the spoliation of foreign resources replaced rational economic planning and growth as the road to financial solvency and created enormous pressure to expand further. In short, Napoleon was constrained by the very regime he had created to pursue dominion in Portugal and Spain.[12]

The invasion of Iberia, therefore, resulted from a combination of factors, including the nature of the French Empire, divisions within Spain, Napoleon's dynastic ambitions and the Emperor's vision for destroying Britain by completing the Continental Blockade. Ironically, the invasion served none of these interests. It threw old enemies – the British and the Spanish – together, opening up not only the peninsula but all of Ibero-America to British trade, which, in turn, benefited the British economy and attenuated the impact of the Continental Blockade. Meanwhile, the occupation of Portugal and Spain, far from providing resources to the Empire, proved to be a constant drain on

France, which discovered that imperialism did not always pay. Finally, the war in the peninsula produced disenchantment at home with the Bonaparte dynasty, for people understood quite well that the war mainly served Napoleon's family interests, something many Frenchmen refused to fight and die for with any kind of enthusiasm.[13]

NAPOLEON'S DEFEAT IN IBERIA

Napoleon failed to gain control over Portugal and Spain for many reasons. For one thing, most French generals turned out to possess none of their master's vision or luck. They loathed each other so thoroughly that they found they could not co-operate to achieve military objectives, instead devoting their energies to pillaging. French officials of all ranks proved more efficient at rousing Spanish and Portuguese civilians against France than at winning battles.[14]

Imperial conscripts were even less motivated than their officers. Particularly in Spain, the experience of war differed dramatically from anything that the French had faced, at least since Egypt, resulting in serious morale problems. Even soldiers inculcated into an ideology of cultural superiority and melded by the comradeship of arms may still occasionally baulk when ordered to subdue civilians, and this is what sometimes happened in Spain. During the siege of Gerona, for example, hundreds of imperial troops – French, Germans and Italians – deserted to the enemy, forcing the French to withdraw in order to prevent troops from fleeing to the encircled city. Sometimes conscripts deserted before they ever arrived in Spain. In one muster, 250 out of 295 recruits from the Loire deserted before they crossed the Pyrenees. High casualties also undermined morale. By January 1809, France had suffered more losses in the peninsula than in all of its battles between 1799 and 1808, making Spain the most dreaded destination for new recruits. And the worst of the fighting was still to come. If the war in the peninsula was a 'sideshow', as many military historians have insisted, then it was a deadly one that many imperial troops refused to join with their traditional élan.[15]

Napoleon's bid for Iberia also gave the British something they had been seeking – an ally on the European Continent that could be supplied by sea and that would remain active enough to allow a British expeditionary force to land and operate. The British had tried to establish such a connection in Calabria, but for a variety of reasons that effort had failed.[16] In Iberia, though, and particularly in Spain, the British found a place where aid and reinforcements to an indigenous resistance movement could tip the balance against the Empire. Behind the shield of the Spanish resistance, which occupied the bulk of imperial forces, Wellington was able to build Britain's best army in generations, while weathering the storm of successive but always partial French assaults from 1809 to 1811. By 1812, the British could go on the offensive. After securing or destroying fortified positions on the Portuguese–Spanish frontier, Wellington invaded Spain, briefly liberating Madrid in 1812. Temporarily forced back to Portugal, Wellington advanced in earnest during the following year, culminating in the victory at Vitoria, which finally forced the French to abandon Spain.

Thus, French blunders, Britain's ability to establish and supply a strong army in Portugal, and Wellington's astute use of that army were all critical to Napoleon's defeat. Above all, however, it was the surprising resistance by civilians in Spain that exposed the weaknesses of the French. The story of this resistance must lie at the heart of any account of France's defeat in the Peninsular War.

Spain's uprising began in the spring of 1808. The Escorial Affair in October 1807 and the coup at Aranjuez on 18 March 1808, when Ferdinand's supporters wrested the Spanish crown from Charles, had served Napoleon well as an excuse to intervene further in Spanish affairs. However, the Bourbon family dissensions, which seemed a sign of weakness to Napoleon, had also served as a mechanism for the creation of an important network of supporters for Ferdinand, both in Madrid and in various provincial capitals. These men began to agitate for a break with France. Some, such as the naval engineer, José Mor de Fuentes, and the artillery captain, Pedro Velarde, went so far as to formulate plans for armed resistance. Meanwhile, the rough behaviour of French troops had generated widespread disgust with the occupation. Ferdinand's friends did their utmost to mobilise these anti-French sentiments by promising that the new king, whom they dubbed 'the Desired One', would deliver Spain from the evils of the old administration and its French allies. All over the country, French troops became the object of popular wrath, and enthusiasm for Ferdinand seemed to grow.[17]

In Madrid Ferdinand's cabal tapped this anti-French sentiment and triggered the first uprising against the occupation. At 9 a.m. on the morning of 2 May, José Molina, Ferdinand's spy, rushed to the royal palace to stop a carriage about to transport the last Bourbon heir, Francisco de Paula, to exile and prison. A shoemaker and three women going to market were the only others present, so he gathered them into a little crowd. Shouting that the French had betrayed the royal family, Molina began to attract more people. A mob of some sixty men and women entered the palace and made Francisco de Paula agree to address the crowd from a balcony. Now hundreds of people gathered in front of the palace.

Led by Molina's cries of 'death to the French', the mob surged through nearby streets, killing an isolated French soldier and nearly killing another before returning to the palace. At 10 a.m. Murat had artillery placed before the palace and fired into the crowd. This action triggered an uprising in earnest. The crowd dispersed, only to rematerialise later in the Puerta del Sol, the great plaza in the heart of the city, while other nodes of resistance formed in other neighbourhoods. Madrileños fought with the weapons available to them – knives, tools and a few firearms – but Murat counter-attacked with overwhelming force and cleared the streets quickly. Only in the artillery park of Monteleón, where captains Pedro Velarde and Luis Daoiz led an organised resistance, did the French face any serious difficulties. And even this position fell to assault after an hour of intense combat. By early afternoon, the revolt known as the Dos de Mayo was over. The French had suffered 150 casualties, including 14 fatalities, while between 400 and 500 denizens of Madrid had died, together with hundreds of people from outlying villages.[18]

The Dos de Mayo failed to achieve any of its objectives, and no one followed the example of Madrid in the immediate aftermath of the rebellion. Still, the Dos de Mayo can help us to understand subsequent uprisings elsewhere in the country. The revolt in Madrid, often described as a popular, spontaneous uprising in defence of king and country, was actually a carefully prepared rebellion by some of Ferdinand's followers and by military officials. Hundreds of Madrileños participated in the fighting, but they were probably motivated by the violence of the French occupation rather than by any sense of nationalism.

Nevertheless, the men who would come to direct the Spanish resistance during the following months and years and who would become the founders of Spain's nationalist project in the nineteenth century gained a number of usable martyrs on 2 May. Among them were women and children, such as Manuela Malasaña, a working-class girl killed in the streets for carrying a pair of scissors as she returned home from her work as an embroiderer. Manuela was the unlucky victim of French fire, but legend placed her in the thick of the fighting, where her death served as a symbol of sacrifice and unity. In this and countless other ways, Spanish patriots re-invented the Dos de Mayo as a national uprising, creating a new patriotic rhetoric in which individual acts of courage and even senseless deaths like Manuela's became signs of national unity. It was in this ironic sense that the French occupation helped to recast

Spain as a modern nation. Indeed, Murat's exemplary violence in Madrid and the five years of violent struggle that followed constituted a much more effective 'modernising' influence in Spain than the unimplemented and unimpressive constitution of Bayonne and the 'regeneration' pursued unenthusiastically and sporadically by Joseph Bonaparte and the French military commanders.[19]

By the end of May resistance had emerged in the provinces, usually at the instigation of Ferdinand's supporters. In June 1808, revolutionary juntas took control in a number of unoccupied cities and declared war on France. Their first order of business was to raise armies from volunteers and from the remnants of royal regiments, which had melted away after Napoleon imprisoned the Spanish heads of state. The junta of Sevilla led the way in this task, and on 19 July at Bailén its army of 30,000 men, led by generals Francisco Castaños and Teodoro Reding, forced the surrender of 20,000 French under General Pierre Dupont. Meanwhile, the Spanish had seized French ships in Cádiz, Marshal Jean-Baptiste Bessiéres had become bogged down in his drive along the northern coast, and Marshal Jeannot de Moncey, startled by the scope of the Spanish resistance, abandoned his siege of Valencia and returned to Madrid. One of the most remarkable French defeats came at Zaragoza, where an armed population defended the poorly fortified city for two months, until the French were forced to abandon the siege in the general retreat of late summer.[20]

While this was going on in Spain, French troops in Portugal found that they were isolated, as peasants in the countryside withheld supplies and preyed upon French stragglers and requisition parties. After allowing Arthur Wellesley to land an expeditionary force at Mondego Bay unopposed, Junot met the British at Vimiero on 21 August. The French marshal attacked impetuously, trusting in the courage of his men to give him victory instead of developing a reasonable plan of battle. The result was yet another French defeat, and as Junot fled the field in a private coach, his army surrendered, to be shipped home by the British navy. Amid all of these disasters, the single French victory over Spanish forces at Medina de Río Seco on 14 July, followed by the murder of hundreds of Spanish prisoners, paled in significance. Joseph could not sustain the occupation, and he withdrew to a position north of the Ebro river in August.

This retreat critically damaged the French in at least four ways. First, in most of Europe, Napoleon had been able to rely on a significant collaboration. Lawyers, army officers, government officials and other professionals – both inside France and in the rest of occupied Europe – admired the Napoleonic order and perceived the Empire as their best chance for advancing their careers. These so-called *ralliés* formed the bedrock of Napoleon's regime. In Spain, many of these same careerists rallied at first to Joseph Bonaparte. It is even conceivable that, under different circumstances, these *afrancesados* might have formed the basis of a stable, conservative regime.[21] However, the French defeats of 1808 and the withdrawal of Joseph exposed these Spanish collaborators, and many of them abandoned Joseph or became cautious neutrals.

Second, the French withdrawal also gave a breathing space to the Portuguese and Spanish resistance. It was not enough time in which to build effective armies, but the respite did allow previously occupied territories to taste independence and to begin the process of mobilisation for war, a process that could not be entirely reversed, even when the French returned in force in November 1808. Third, the French retreat likewise allowed the British to consolidate their hold on Portugal and to prepare defensive positions around Lisbon.

A fourth effect of Joseph's retreat was to encourage resistance elsewhere in Europe. Suddenly, after Bailén and Zaragoza, the invincible French seemed less so, and Europeans began to think about imitating the Spanish. Austria, in particular, buzzed with a new kind of enthusiasm inspired by the Spanish example. In 1809 Austria went to war, and although the result was a French victory, the battles of Aspern-Essling and Wagram proved to be exceptionally bloody. The French preoccupation with Austria and Spain, moreover, encouraged opponents in Germany, Holland and even inside France to risk open rebellion. France was bleeding from many wounds in 1809.

The French situation in Spain actually appeared to improve in 1809. French armies rolled up the Spanish forces cobbled together by the revolutionary juntas and drove an English army into the sea, so that by 1810 the only effective centres of regular resistance were Valencia, Cádiz and, above all, the remaining Anglo–Portuguese army entrenched around Lisbon. However, even as regular allied armies collapsed or retreated before the French, a full-scale guerrilla war developed behind the lines, especially in rural areas in northern Spain. For the next four years, the Spanish guerrillas became Napoleon's most deadly opponents in Iberia.

Led by men such as Francisco Espoz y Mina and Juan Martín, 'el Empecinado',[22] the guerrillas proved ruinous to the French occupation. Guerrilla warfare served many purposes. The partisans seized mails, couriers and convoys, and generally made it impossible for the French ever to relax. The guerrillas caused the French enormous casualties, possibly as many as 180,000 over the course of the war, and certainly as many as were caused by allied regulars. Strategically, the guerrillas dispersed French forces and prevented them from concentrating upon Wellington and the other allied armies.[23]

As important as any of this, however, was the effect guerrilla warfare had on the occupation's ability to gain Spanish collaborators. The guerrillas punished collaborators ruthlessly the moment French troops were not present, making it difficult for the French to gain or keep adherents except in a few permanently garrisoned towns. The resulting lack of co-operation from local officials and landowners forced the French to extract taxes, livestock, grains and other goods almost entirely through extra-economic means. Yet, sending out armed requisition parties to every village and hamlet in the rugged rural landscape of northern Spain, aside from being costly, supplied the guerrillas with additional military targets. In short, the guerrillas were able to destroy or acquire the things the occupation needed to survive – collaborators, taxes, conscripts, horses, fodder, grains and the like. It was not the case that Spain was too poor to supply Napoleon's armies. On the contrary, guerrilla country in northern Castile, Navarre, Aragón and parts of Catalonia produced agricultural surpluses of all kinds. It was simply that the guerrillas had become the true masters of the countryside and were able to prevent the French from gaining access to any of these resources.

In guerrilla country, the French could not tell a partisan from a peasant, except during an actual battle, making reprisals either impossible or indiscriminate. In a state of permanent frustration and confusion, French soldiers, as they had in the Vendée and Egypt, assaulted neutral civilians and disguised enemies alike. This, of course, led to even greater disenchantment with the French regime and produced more recruits for the guerrillas. This dynamic of guerrilla warfare, in which irregulars prevent a foreign occupation or unpopular regime from gaining adherents and from peacefully exploiting the resources of the countryside, is familiar to anyone aware of the many guerrilla conflicts of the twentieth century. It was surprising, however, to Napoleon and to the rest of the world in 1808, and it was Spain's great contribution to the practice of war in the age of Napoleon. In symbiosis with the resistance of British, Portuguese and Spanish regulars, the guerrillas in Spain helped to destroy the French Empire. Long before Wellington prepared his final offensive to drive the French across the Pyrenees, the Empire had lost the war in Spain.

How should we understand the causes for this surprising Spanish resistance? Scholars sometimes invoke the formula that first appeared in Spanish wartime propaganda, where patriotic elites claimed that Spaniards fought for God, king and country. This formula contains some, but not all, of the truth.

Certainly, there are examples of resistance that seem to have been inspired by religious exaltation, loyalty to the person of Ferdinand, and even a sense of national outrage. Especially in the early months of the war, acts of resistance, usually organised or prompted by Ferdinand's cronies, often centred on persons or symbols associated with the Bourbons or with the Catholic Church. This is what happened, of course, around the royal carriage on 2 May in Madrid. In Zaragoza, the uprising seems to have been triggered by two bizarre rumours: that a crown had appeared in the sky with the inscription 'God loves Ferdinand' and that Ferdinand had returned to Spain in disguise in order, like Moses, to deliver his people from bondage. These rumours aside, we do know that a group of Ferdinand's close friends, led by José Palafox, organised and sustained the resistance in Zaragoza from the beginning and that they employed the personnel and rhetoric of the Catholic Church to help them. In another event rich with both religious and royal symbolism, a mob of women celebrating the feast day of St Ferdinand in El Ferrol threw open the arsenal and forced local leaders to declare Ferdinand king on 30 June, initiating the resistance in Galicia. Surely, these and other similar events must be understood as a reflection of the dynastic loyalties and religious sensibilities of at least some Spaniards.

The French had outraged these loyalties and sensibilities with reckless abandon, behaving with extraordinary brutality towards the clergy and cynical duplicity towards the Bourbons. The occupation regime closed Spain's monasteries and convents, seized church assets, turned places of worship into barracks and stables, and arrested and deported parish priests suspected of opposition. Indeed, the attack on the Spanish Church was so thorough and consistent that it leads one to wonder how the picture of the Emperor as a man indifferent to religion, except as a tool of social control, ever came into being. Perhaps Napoleon saw religion as one thing in France, where he had been able to win over much of the clergy, and as quite another thing in Spain, where his opponents were making use of it to mobilise people against him. Or perhaps Napoleon and his officers and troops were in fact deeply anticlerical and allowed a religious antipathy, which they had suppressed in France, to find expression in Spain. In either case, anti-clericalism, a weapon of great terror, proved to be a terrible tool of statecraft, for it clearly brought together at least some Spaniards in defence of the Church.

Napoleon also committed a grave error in his treatment of the Bourbons. Ferdinand VII, whose petty nature was as yet unknown to Spaniards in the spring of 1808, enjoyed immense popularity at the moment of his betrayal and arrest by Napoleon. When Spaniards learned of their king's treatment at

Bayonne, some, like the women in El Ferrol, were roused to take a stand against the Empire, even without prompting from Ferdinand's supporters. On the other hand, the guerrillas rarely expressed their motives in terms of religious or dynastic loyalty, and guerrilla armies often treated the properties of the Church as cavalierly as the French did. Some guerrilla chieftains even became noted liberals in the post-war period. In the end, it is probably fair to conclude that during the first few months of the war people in certain cities and towns were swept up in an orchestrated popular movement centred on the king and Church, but that the guerrillas who continued the fight in subsequent years were not notably moved by appeals to either.

The most doubtful element of the motivational triad – God, king and country – is the notion that Spaniards fought a 'people's war' in defence of the nation. Nationalism was a powerful force in the age of Napoleon. European political leaders, whether in imitation of 1789 or as a way of resisting the French tide, worked to eliminate legal, regional, economic and political barriers to the integration of individuals into national life and sought to rouse people with nationalist rhetoric. It should come as no surprise that Spanish elites also played the nationalist card in their effort to find a winning hand against Napoleon. In the revolutionary juntas and in the Cortes of Cádiz, which succeeded the juntas as the centre of Spanish political life during the war, politicians attempted to reform the Spanish state and to make it a more powerful instrument by widening political participation and by encouraging economic integration within Spain's borders. Spanish elites trumpeted the war as 'the will of the entire nation', contrasting the nationalism that animated Spaniards with the atomisation and apathy found in the rest of Europe. The question, however, is to what extent this nationalist reform agenda and its accompanying rhetoric reflected the experiences and beliefs of most Spaniards, rather than wishful thinking by elites. In particular, is there any sense in calling the Spanish resistance to Napoleon national in scope and nationalist in intent?

In fact, one of the striking things about the war in Spain was its parochialism. Spanish combatants almost always lacked a strategic vision for the entire peninsula, one of the many things Spain's British allies found frustrating. Regional juntas refused to co-operate with each other, sometimes even forbidding their armies to operate jointly. The junta of Extremadura expelled army recruiters from outside the province in order to prevent a 'loss' of manpower. The junta of Asturias refused to allow its levies to fight in León and Galicia. And the junta of Murcia fought constantly with Lorca, Cartagena and Mazarrán over conscription and supply issues.

Even the most famous guerrilleros, such as Juan Martín, were not exempt from this problem.[24] Early in 1811, Marshal Suchet's forces advanced on Valencia, where the captain-general conceived a plan of defence centred on the use of guerrilla tactics. He called upon Juan Martín, fighting under the auspices of the junta of Guadalajara, and General Villacampa, working for the junta of Aragón, to attack Suchet in the rear. However, their respective juntas refused to allow Villacampa or Martín to operate in distant Valencia, and the chance was lost. In June, Juan Martín received another order to attack Suchet in Valencia. Again the junta of Guadalajara was adamant that he should not remove any troops from the province and fomented a mutiny to make sure he would not. The rebellion resulted in the complete dissolution of Juan Martín's army of some 4,000 men.

The lesson of this disaster is that the junta and the volunteers of Guadalajara saw their mission as the protection of their homes and of their *patria chica*,[25] Guadalajara. They were not loyal to Juan Martín and were uninterested in pursuing the larger national strategy worked out by distant commanders in Valencia. As a result, the French captured hundreds of Martín's disorganised troops, and the four hundred men who remained with him proved not very good at regular operations away from home. Only when Juan Martín returned to Guadalajara and to guerrilla warfare on a local scale was he able to reconstitute his force.

Observers at the time criticised Juan Martín and the guerrilla campaign in general for its localism and lack of strategic vision. There is some justice in this complaint. However, it can also be argued that localism was what made Spain capable of defeating Napoleon. The ability of local resistance to continue, despite the collapse of national armies and central government, is one of the features that distinguished the Spanish theatre of war from the rest of Europe. Indeed, one could argue that one of the factors that aided the resistance in places like Guadalajara was the intensity of localism and the absence of an effective central state or national identity. Juan Martín's difficulties in 1811 arose from the attempt to use guerrilla forces as if they were regulars fighting a national war. His failure should not be blamed on the localism of the guerrillas but on his superiors' adoption of a national military strategy that was inappropriate to Spain at that time.

Events in Galicia also illustrate the motives of the men who fought Napoleon and the limits of their patriotism.[26] Galicia discovered guerrilla warfare in early 1809, and by June had raised an army of some 56,000 men, renamed the Division of the Miño. Galicia was mobilised by a combination of factors that had very little to do with king and nation and even less to do with God. The region had been traversed and occupied by a succession of Spanish, British and French armies in the winter of 1808–1809. In December, retreating Spanish forces under General Joaquín Blake looted Galicia to such an extent that the Spanish army had to shoot its own troops to save the province. Hard on the heels of the Spanish came General John Moore's British troops, who treated the province mercilessly as they fled headlong to the coast and evacuation. When the French passed into Galicia in early 1809, they were forced to requisition food from an abused and sullen population.

On 9 February 1809, near the town of Tuy, Marcelino Troncoso, the priest of Couto, raised a band of men who formed the kernel of Galicia's guerrilla army. Troncoso did not mobilise his compatriots through appeals to nationalism or piety, priest though he was. Rather, he enjoined them to fight the French in order to stop a new contribution announced by Marshal Soult. Soult had ordered the towns of Crecente and Alveos to supply him with horses, fodder and food for 20,000 rations. The towns struggled to comply, but Troncoso 'liberated' the rations before they could be delivered and recruited the towns' young men into a guerrilla band. That very day his new force killed fifteen French soldiers and captured fifty-one more. During the next two months Troncoso engaged in a classic guerrilla campaign. He cut the enemy off from the countryside, made tax collection impossible, forced Soult and Ney to send out requisition parties to feed their troops, ambushed these same requisition parties, and with the arms and supplies captured raised more troops. The Division of the Miño recaptured Vigo in March, Tuy in April, Santiago in May and La Coruña and El Ferrol in early June, driving the French out of Galicia after causing 47,000 casualties. A movement that began with resistance to requisitions in two exasperated towns ended with the liberation of Spain's largest province.

What happened after the French evacuated Galicia also tells us a great deal about why the Galicians fought. Instead of following Ney and Soult as they retreated into León and Castile, the Galicians disbanded. The truth is that in Galicia, as in Guadalajara and every other centre of guerrilla warfare, people were not terribly committed to liberating Spain. The objective of the junta of Galicia and of the soldiers in the Division of the Miño was to clear the province of French troops in order to prevent requisitions, tax collections and violence by French soldiery. As a result, attempts to rouse Galicia during the rest of the war, when France left the province alone, failed.

Indeed, tens of thousands of young men fled Galicia to northern Portugal in order to escape conscription into the Spanish army. The Spanish consul in Oporto tried to recruit these expatriates into the army anyway. The language that he used in proclamations to them is instructive. 'The defence of king, country and religion', he wrote, 'calls imperiously to all natives of Galicia in condition to take up arms to assemble with your compatriots to eject the cruel invaders of your country (in case your country is again invaded), and to defend your homes and families with all your might.'[27]

The key to understanding the consul's 'patriotic' appeal is the parenthetical phrase 'in case your country is again invaded', which could only apply to Galicia and not to Spain, since most of Spain was already occupied. The consul understood that the cause likely to arouse Galicians for a fight was their *patria chica*, Galicia, not Spain, and that defending one's home and family was the primary duty of the partisans. When, shortly after this appeal was issued, it became known that Galicia was safe from invasion, the consul's recruitment efforts collapsed. The junta of Galicia then tried its hand at raising men for a defence force, dispatching an agent, José Benito Munin, to gather volunteers in Portugal. In the end, however, he was able to recruit only 150 men, despite paying them liberally for joining the army. To make matters worse, of the 150 men who accepted Munin's bounty, 100 deserted before reaching the Spanish border, for they rightly suspected that they would be made to fight far from their homes. Munin's commentary shows that he realised what the problem was: Galicians could be made to fight only for Galicia.

These examples of localism from Galicia and Guadalajara can be duplicated in Aragón, Navarre and everywhere guerrilla warfare proved effective. The lesson from these examples is that the Spanish guerrillas did not fight for their nation, but for their homes, villages, valleys, districts and, at best, provinces. The Napoleonic era in Spain was one of nationalist rhetoric and the beginnings of national political life, all in the absence of widespread nationalist sentiment.

CONCLUSION

The urban revolutions and uprisings of May and June 1808, combined with the landing of a British expeditionary army in Portugal and the reconstitution of regular Spanish armies under the revolutionary juntas, secured a series of critical victories and forced the French to retreat northwards. When the French returned in November, they faced a new constellation of opponents and had to commit themselves to a long occupation or abandon plans to subjugate Iberia altogether, something that Napoleon and France found impossible to do. From 1808 to 1814 the French tried to live off of the occupied territory as required by Napoleon's strategic thinking and France's insolvency.

To do this, French troops had to be divided up into small units and flying columns whose sole purpose was to extract food and supplies from the rural population. This dispersion of French occupation forces made them vulnerable to piecemeal annihilation by guerrilla forces.

The skilful adoption of guerrilla strategies and tactics by leaders such as Juan Martín absorbed the French in counter-insurgency and occupation duties far from the so-called front lines around Cádiz and Lisbon. Regular British, Portuguese and Spanish forces were able to survive in these two defensive redoubts, and for a while in Valencia and elsewhere, because guerrilla resistance in other regions prevented the French from ever concentrating their forces for an all-out attack on regular allied formations. Finally, after years of exhausting themselves against the guerrillas, imperial troops – siphoned away in any case during 1812 by the needs of Napoleon's Russian campaign – became vulnerable to a counter-offensive spearheaded by Wellington and his British and Portuguese troops, who drove the French back across the Pyrenees in 1813 and brought a conclusion to what was, from the French perspective, already a hopeless war.

Spanish motives in the fight against Napoleon were complex. The formula 'God, king and country' is still serviceable, as long as one realises that for most Spaniards 'country' did not equate to nation but to province and sometimes to village, and that religious and dynastic loyalties played a clear role in the urban uprisings in the summer of 1808 but not in the guerrilla campaign that followed. Second, the peasants who made up Spain's guerrilla armies resisted, not because they were 'anti-modern', but because the survival of their families and communities was at stake. The French occupation generated conflicts centred on taxation and requisitions, conscription, sexual honour and other very personal and local matters. Guerrilla war was how rural communities responded to these pressures. Like residents of Madrid, Spanish peasants were goaded into fighting back by French provocations and, like the men of Alveos, they fought to protect their property from the tax collector and the requisition party. Like Spaniards everywhere, they tried to avoid fighting at any great distance from their homes, which is one sign that Spanish nationalism, loyalty to the Bourbons and religious piety had less to do with the war than scholars once surmised. Because guerrilla warfare was a defensive survival strategy, there was no military or political policy the French might have adopted to terminate the guerrilla war once it started, short of evacuating Spain or depopulating it.

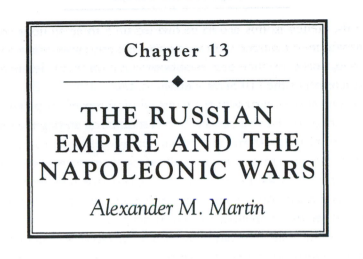

Chapter 13

◆

THE RUSSIAN EMPIRE AND THE NAPOLEONIC WARS

Alexander M. Martin

Like Great Britain, the Russian Empire was a foe that Napoleon could neither destroy nor co-opt.[1] Its sheer expanse and remoteness from France made it difficult to defeat, while its hostility to revolutionary ideology and its own pursuit of great-power status made it an irreconcilable enemy of French hegemony in Europe. However, the challenge of Napoleon also forced the Russian monarchy to make fundamental choices about its own future direction, choices that helped shape its subsequent history until it was destroyed in the revolution of 1917.

THE DYNAMICS OF RUSSIAN SOCIETY

The Russian response to the French Revolution and Napoleon was conditioned in part by the character of Russian society. The Russian Empire had 40 million inhabitants in 1800, a figure not dramatically greater than France's 29 million, the Habsburg Empire's 20 million or the British Isles' 16 million. European Russia alone, where most of the population lived, was equivalent in size to all other European countries combined, but was a sparsely settled and mostly rural country – only one out of every twenty-five Russians lived in a town, as against one in five people in France and fully one in three in England and Wales. Russia's advantages in population size and natural resources only partially compensated for the economic and military handicaps that resulted from the low population density, vast distances, harsh climate and long, vulnerable borders.

Over the centuries, Russia's rulers had pursued three strategies aimed at transforming their far-flung territories into a cohesive state. First, beginning in the tenth century, they had established Orthodox Christianity as the national religion of the east Slavs – Russians, Ukrainians and Belorussians – who made up three-quarters of the multi-ethnic Empire's population in the nineteenth century. This had created a common bond among their subjects, but also alienated them from the Catholics and Protestants to their west. The medieval habit among both western and eastern Christians of regarding one another as heretics gave rise to a mutual distrust that remained very much alive among the common people after 1800, when many Russians were prepared to believe that Napoleon was the Antichrist.

Second, owing to the difficulty of taxing a population of subsistence farmers who rarely used cash, the Russian government could not pay adequate salaries to its officials and soldiers. Instead, it relied on compulsory services and payments in kind by the population to support the nobles who served as officials and army officers. The legacy of this practice (the 'service state') by 1800 was that about half the population were serfs, owned by some 400,000 nobles who wielded powers comparable to those of American slave-owners; the remainder were mostly state peasants, in effect serfs of the monarch, and townspeople whose economic opportunities were limited by burdensome taxes and service obligations and whose local government was dominated by noble officials appointed by the imperial government. The oppressiveness of these arrangements was mitigated by the fact that underpaid officials were easy to bribe, and that absentee landlords had little day-to-day control over their serfs. Officials and serf-owners knew that they were vastly outnumbered by their social inferiors, so they demanded deference and occasionally inflicted savage punishment on obstreperous individuals but otherwise cooperated with village elders and other community leaders. A seamless web of authority extended from heads of households to noble landlords, imperial officials, the tsar and ultimately, it was believed, to God. People might detest particular authority figures, but most could not conceive of any fundamentally different system for governing society.

By the early eighteenth century, it was clear that the service state alone could not give Russia the military, economic, financial and intellectual tools needed to compete in the arena of European politics. So, beginning with Peter I ('the Great', reigned 1682–1725), an additional, third strategy was pursued: a bureaucracy and officer corps were created that were supposed to replicate the professionalism and efficiency found among Russia's European neighbours. The aim of this 'enlightened absolutism' was to force society to accept new (European) forms of education, administrative and military organisation, taxation, manufacturing and so forth. Since noble bureaucrats and officers were to be the executors of this policy, a special attempt was made to Europeanise the nobility's way of living and thinking.

Consequently, Russia by 1800 was a paradox. Its monarchs and many nobles had become indistinguishable from their western counterparts in dress, education and manners, and it was notorious that the most prominent among them spoke better French than Russian. To most, it was an article of faith that they were Europeans, and they shared the Enlightenment belief in the value of liberty and human dignity, though they mostly applied these notions only to themselves, not to the enserfed peasantry or the illiterate and impoverished townspeople. The lower classes, on the other hand, remained largely untouched by foreign influences since there was no education system or mass press to popularise them; few businesses that disseminated western goods at affordable prices; and few theatres, restaurants or other 'public spaces' where the lower classes might be exposed to western culture. Instead, most lived in a self-contained, illiterate village world that saw only the dark side of enlightened absolutism – high taxes, military recruitment, the arbitrariness of arrogant landlords and corrupt officials. Peter I and his successors transformed Russia into a great power, but in so doing they drove a deep wedge into the society. Russia's vibrant, Europeanised elite culture remained alien to the common people but soaked up the bulk of the country's wealth and its most educated and ambitious individuals. As a result, the population found itself isolated from the elite in a cultural ghetto that became increasingly conservative because it was deprived of oxygen by the competition of the dynamic and creative new imperial culture.[2] Under these conditions, it was very difficult for a modern sense of nationhood to form that might create a genuine sense of solidarity between government, elite and people. As one recent study argues:

> [d]uring the eighteenth and nineteenth centuries, the notions of authority, culture and community held by the imperial nobility and by the peasantry were diametrically opposed. . . . The result was that the two Russias weakened each other. The political, economic and cultural institutions of what might have become the Russian nation were destroyed or emasculated for the needs of the empire, while the state was enfeebled by the hollowness of its ethnic substance, its inability at most times to attract the deep loyalty of even its Russian, let alone its non-Russian subjects.[3]

Russia by 1800 faced no real threat of a revolution that could actually overturn the entire old regime and create something genuinely new. To begin with, Russians of all social classes continued to accept the religious and philosophical assumptions underlying the old regime. They had not yet experienced the intellectual revolution that led contemporaries in France and America to begin imagining a society in which all were equal citizens and where power was based on laws rather than on inherited social position or family status. Furthermore, the social base for a revolution on the French model was absent in Russia. Past uprisings by the lower classes had been sparked and led by Cossacks, warlike frontiersmen whose unruly, semi-independent communities lined the Russian Empire's southern borderlands; however, after the great revolt led by Emelian Pugachev in 1773–74, Catherine II ('the Great', reigned 1762–96) had brought them under tight government control. Likewise, the rebellious 'tribal peoples' along European Russia's eastern rim, such as the Bashkirs of the Ural mountains, were increasingly subdued by the growing imperial bureaucracy. On their own, the peasants in Russia (as in other countries) lacked the necessary leadership, organisation and political sophistication to go beyond sporadic, local protest. The same applied to Russia's townspeople, who in any case feared the anarchy of peasant revolt more than governmental tyranny; when urban riots did occur, as in Moscow during the terrible plague epidemic of 1771, there was no revolutionary political agenda. Serf-owners and officials, for their part, knew that they could neither persuade nor compel the people to tolerate their power and privileges without the aid of the monarch, who alone enjoyed the people's loyalty and could draw on moral support from the Orthodox clergy and military backing from the army. Businessmen and intellectuals in France and America may have felt that the monarchical system was increasingly anachronistic; to their Russian counterparts, on the contrary, the imperial regime was the bringer of progress in an otherwise backward and anarchic society. Thus, no major constituency in Russia was prepared to challenge the entire structure of the old regime.

Nevertheless, the state and nobility were deeply worried by developments in France in the 1790s to 1800s. To begin with, anyone who remembered the unrest of the 1770s understood the volatility of Russia's lower classes. What might happen, therefore, if Napoleon – with the world's most formidable military machine at his disposal – were to invade Russia and arouse the masses? Russian nobles believed that Napoleon was carrying forward the French Revolution's assault on the Ancien Regime, and the changes he wrought in the countries he occupied lent support to this view. It is impossible to know just what impact a revolutionary appeal by Napoleon would have had on the Russian peasantry, but clearly that was a nightmare scenario for many nobles. However, the system of enlightened absolutism that

Catherine II had perfected was threatened not only 'from below' (by the lower classes) and 'from without' (by Napoleon) but also 'from above', by the government itself. This was a result of a paradox embedded in the very nature of enlightened absolutism, in Russia as elsewhere.

On the one hand, the regime promoted the growth of a 'civil society' of people – mostly nobles – whose wealth, leisure, education and sense of personal security encouraged them to think critically about public issues and discuss their views in the increasingly popular masonic lodges, the growing book and periodical press, educational institutions, literary salons, scholarly societies and so on. Following the general European pattern, educated Russians' initial concern with moral and philosophical questions eventually expanded to include concrete socio-political problems, and the habit of talking, reading and writing about public issues created the expectation that the monarchy would begin to take note of civil society's opinions.

On the other hand, enlightened absolutism also advocated a bureaucratic system of government where decisions flowed efficiently from the top down and whose officials thought of themselves as a specialised profession distinct from other social groups. Bureaucracy, like civil society, was still in its infancy in Russia in 1800, and both an educated public and efficient government remained vital for Russia's future, but the experience of other countries suggested that conflicts lay ahead: civil society was made up mostly of nobles who wished to preserve their class's privileges but also acquire new freedoms and gain a voice in government; whereas the bureaucracy wanted to establish its control wherever possible, exclude all others from political decision-making and undermine class privileges that obstructed government policy. (Of course, the bureaucracy's defence of its own vested interests further complicated matters.)

Thus, noble privileges interfered with the monarchy's ability to raise taxes and recruit qualified officials. Peasants, whose surplus harvest was taken and sold by their tax-exempt landlords to help pay for foreign luxury goods, could not sell the surplus themselves to obtain cash that the crown might tax. Nobles also took advantage of the fact that peasants paid lower taxes than townspeople by encouraging their serfs to sell their wares in town at low prices; this undercut the manufacturing and commercial activities of the townspeople and stunted the growth of a bourgeoisie which, in other countries, provided the state with valuable tax revenues and business and technical skills. The interests of nobility and bureaucracy coincided in opposing government efforts to replace class origin and seniority with merit and education as criteria for appointment to official positions; as a result, the state's talent pool for critical posts remained limited to noblemen with many years in government service, while it was almost impossible to appoint non-nobles or non-career officials, however able they might be. While in France the Revolution had thrown even the highest positions open to qualified new-comers and thereby given the country a remarkable cadre of talented leaders, Russia's nobles and career bureaucrats retained their stranglehold on the state apparatus.

Even the absolute monarchy as an institution served the nobility's inter-ests at least as much as those of the monarch. If a constitution were adopted that transferred some of the monarch's authority to a council of state or to powerful bureaucrats, those top positions might become the fiefdoms of elite families that would promote only their own cronies, or they might fall into the hands of non-nobles who had little regard for noble class interests, whereas absolutism limited such influences and thereby protected the nobil-ity as a whole. From the government's standpoint, however, unfettered abso-lutism was more problematic. Of course, the monarchs did not wish to weaken their own power, but they could not govern without the aid of officials in any case, and the business of state might at least be conducted more effectively if it were governed by formal, predictable rules rather than the intrigues of their entourage. However, any formal limitation on the monarchs' power would also make it more difficult to force the nobles to part with some of their privileges, while anything that strengthened the bureaucracy also increased the bureaucrats' ability to manipulate both the information the tsar received and the way his decisions were implemented.

The major reforms under discussion after Catherine's death – reducing noble privileges, strengthening the bureaucracy and issuing a constitution – were therefore in conflict with each other. Enlightened absolutism, we know with hindsight, was by its very nature a transitional phenomenon, whose suc-cess at fostering simultaneously an assertive civil society and a powerful administration ensured that it would evolve either into a bureaucratic dic-tatorship or into an increasingly liberal order dominated by civil society.

RUSSIAN FOREIGN AND DOMESTIC POLICY IN THE ERA OF THE FRENCH REVOLUTION

To understand the evolution of Russia's relationship with France, we need to return to Catherine and her aggressive pursuit of territorial expansion in eastern Europe. Russia's principal targets were Sweden, Poland and the Ottoman Empire, all of which were on their last legs as major powers. When the French Revolution broke out, Catherine was of course appalled, but she did not believe that Russia's vital interests were directly threatened. Instead, her principal concern was Poland, Russia's ancient rival in eastern Europe, a sprawling country whose government – a weak monarchy held in check by a turbulent noble parliament – had in recent years fallen under Russian domination. When Poland (supported by Prussia, the ally of Great Britain) adopted a new constitution in 1791 that strengthened the monarchy and thereby threatened to make Russian interference more difficult, Catherine encouraged Poland's other neighbours, Prussia and Austria, to join the British, Spaniards and Swedes in the First Coalition against France in order to occupy them in western Europe and give herself a free hand in Poland. When war between France and the First Coalition erupted in 1792, her troops invaded Poland and in 1793 annexed large areas of it, leaving several other provinces to be taken by Prussia. At that point, after the execution of Louis XVI in France, her policy became much more overtly anti-French, but still she did not join the war against France; instead, after a pro-French revolution in 1794 in what remained of independent Poland, the country was partitioned by Russia, Prussia and Austria, not to reappear on the map of Europe as an independent state until the end of the First World War.[4]

Franco–Russian relations were driven by several forces. Russia was clearly hostile to revolutionary ideology but, unlike Great Britain or Austria, its security interests did not conflict directly with France's. However, a centuries-old rivalry between France and Austria had led France to ally itself with Austria's enemies in eastern Europe – Sweden, Poland and the Ottoman Empire. These were also Russia's enemies, so France's eighteenth-century foreign policy was anti-Russian as well. France also mattered to Russia because of its antagonism with Great Britain (Russia's major trading partner) and with Austria and Prussia (Russia's rivals for power in eastern Europe). A strong, menacing France could be useful to Russia by distracting the Prussians and Austrians, as it had in the early 1790s. However, total French victory over Prussia and Austria was not welcome to the Russians since it could draw France more deeply into east European power politics, encourage anti-Russian nationalism in Poland and spread revolution. After 1789, Catherine tightened police controls and censorship to limit the influence of French ideas in Russia, and fear of revolution – together with the pragmatic pursuit of state interests – shaped her foreign policy as well.

Her death in 1796 represents a watershed in Russian history, the end of a century of enlightened absolutism. The most immediate outward sign of the changing times was the attitude of the new tsar, her son Paul I, toward military things. Catherine II was at heart a civilian who preferred to avoid confrontation with her subjects and resorted to violence only when more indirect methods failed. Her son, on the contrary, like his father Peter III – Catherine's husband, whom the nobility had deeply disliked and who had been murdered in the 1762 coup that brought her to power – cultivated a passionate love for the military way of living and thinking that contemporaries derisively called 'paradomania', and devoted obsessive attention to the minutiae of military uniforms and ceremonies. At the imperial court, which modelled values and attitudes that nobles across Russia emulated, he sought to replace the sophistication and elegance of his mother's regime with a military spirit of gruff directness and authority. If the mother had been the refined salon hostess-in-chief of the Empire, the son intended to be the imperial drill sergeant, his country not a complex polity to be governed but an army to be commanded. Militarism and a chain-of-command conception of state and society, which had been largely absent from the Russian court in the eighteenth century (significantly, the Empire had been ruled almost exclusively by women in 1725–96), were henceforth a basic feature of the exclusively male-run monarchy of 1796–1917.

This shift reflected the monarchy's abandonment of the subtle blend of tolerance and repression, Enlightenment rhetoric and political cynicism that had characterised Catherine's rule. Paul – an idealistic, self-righteous, suspicious, vindictive and impulsive man – hated his mother and repudiated her legacy, which he regarded as both morally reprehensible and contaminated by Enlightenment notions that he associated with the French Revolution. Instead, he sought to articulate a clear ideological alternative to Enlightenment and revolution. Domestically, as the late Russian historian Natan Eidel'man pointed out, he sought to inspire the nobility with quasi-medieval notions of chivalry, honour, piety and service to the monarch. His militarism and irascibility – both of which found expression in the stupefying abruptness with which even the most blue-blooded army officer's career could be broken over minor details of his troops' performance on the parade ground – reflected his belief that a knight in the anti-revolutionary crusade must be an austere ascetic, not an easy-going epicurean. This ideology revealed itself in ways ominous to the nobles, who had never been thus treated by Paul's mother. The rights of their already feeble provincial assemblies were curtailed and the importation of western luxury goods that the tsar deemed subversive (ranging from sheet music and books to the newly fashionable round hats) was outlawed, while in the capital the tsar personally humiliated nobles in a way that had been completely unknown under Catherine. Though no enemy of serfdom – for instance, he continued Catherine's habit of giving away state peasants as serfs to nobles whom he wished to reward – Paul issued new laws to protect serfs from excessive labour demands by their noble masters, and common soldiers, themselves tormented by his parado-mania, nonetheless welcomed his crackdown on corrupt noble officers and gloated over the terror that the tsar inspired among them. Paul thus gave the impression of wanting to erode the crown's traditional, cosy alliance with the nobles and instead build a more despotic regime with support from other segments of the population. These policies may have generated sympathy for him among the common people, although documenting that is difficult. What is certain, however, is that he incurred the hostility of the nobles, both those who were concerned mainly about their class interests and those who believed in Enlightenment notions of freedom and progress.[5]

These ideological aspects of Paul's regime must be kept in mind when considering his foreign policy. France's place in his strategic calculations was ambiguous in the light of Russian policy toward Poland, Austria, Prussia and Great Britain. Catherine had attempted to have it both ways, declaring her hostility to France while taking advantage of Europe's disarray to carve up Poland. Paul, characteristically, was more blunt and forthright. Although he initially approached the European conflicts with a spirit of caution that con-trasted with his mother's more belligerent stance at the time of her death, he too was deeply troubled by the expansion of French power and viewed him-self as the supreme defender of the old regime across Europe. French expan-sion in Italy and the eastern Mediterranean, which threatened both Russian and Ottoman interests, made possible an unprecedented alliance of the two empires that drew Russia into the Second Coalition that formed in 1798 and also included Great Britain, Austria and Naples. The principal belligerents on the Continent were Russia and Austria. However, Austria was pursuing con-crete, limited territorial interests while Paul and his military commander, the brilliant if eccentric Aleksandr Suvorov, had ambitious notions of carrying the war into France and restoring the foreign monarchs overthrown by the French armies.[6] As a result of these differences, Suvorov's successful campaign against the French in Italy in 1799 was followed by a falling-out with the Austrians, who refused to restore various 'legitimate' Italian princes and reneged on their earlier support for an invasion of France. When the British sided with Vienna in the dispute, Paul angrily withdrew from the coalition in 1800.[7]

The consequence was a complete reversal of Russian policy, made pos-sible both by the tsar's mercurial personality and by a certain ambivalence in his and his entourage's assessment of the European situation. A powerful

France was not regarded as inherently incompatible with Russian interests, particularly given Paul's anger at Britain and Austria and the fearful neutrality of Prussia, the three powers most threatened by French might. In fact, the same Austrians and Prussians who blocked France's advance eastwards also hindered Russian expansion westwards, especially after the destruction of Poland had made them into neighbours. Strategically, therefore, an alliance of the two powers at the edge of the Continent (France and Russia) against those in the middle (Prussia and Austria) made sense, and indeed it was realised a hundred years later in the prelude to the First World War. There were, of course, ideological obstacles to an alliance between revolutionary Paris and absolutist St Petersburg, but the experience of the 1799 war had sobered Paul, while the dictatorship that Napoleon established in the same year gave the French regime a more conservative complexion and diminished Paul's animosity towards it; in fact, in their militaristic authoritarianism, Paul's and Napoleon's regimes rather resembled each other. Unable to achieve European stability and suppress revolution by co-operating with Austria and Great Britain, he sought it in an alliance with Napoleon. Some of his lieutenants, though, wished to give the relationship a more offensive character; thus, Paul's adviser Fedor Rostopchin proposed to him that Russia ally itself with France against Great Britain and undertake a partition of the Ottoman Empire in concert with Austria, Prussia and France.[8] There were even plans for a joint Franco–Russian military campaign across the vast lands of central Asia against India, the heart of Britain's colonial Empire.

In the end, however, Paul – like his father Peter III before him – incurred such hostility at home, particularly among the noble officers of the imperial guards regiments stationed in St Petersburg, that he was assassinated in March 1801 and replaced with his son Alexander. One contemporary reported that, among the nobility of St Petersburg, the glee at Paul's death 'exceeded the bounds of decency', and another recalled that 'people embraced each other as though it were Easter'.[9] Apparently, the city actually ran out of champagne before the day ended.[10]

ALEXANDER I AND RUSSIA'S ENCOUNTER WITH NAPOLEON

Alexander hated the tyranny of old-regime despots and serf-owners as well as the destructiveness of revolutionary radicals and, like the reformers in Prussia after 1806, he hoped that a reform-minded monarchy, aided by a progressive civil society and a more efficient bureaucracy, might find a middle way between them. In the same spirit, he saw a balance of power, not a close Russian alliance with either Napoleon or his enemies, as the key to peace in Europe.[11]

The 'magnificent dawn of Alexander's days', as the poet Aleksandr Pushkin described the beginning of his reign, was a time of great hopes. Whereas Paul had sought to strengthen his government through the despotic exercise of monarchical power, the youthful and charming Alexander hoped to achieve that goal by formalising the role and accountability of his official advisers – thereby breaking the shadowy influence traditionally wielded by imperial favourites and self-serving networks of powerful families – and by streamlining the bureaucracy that implemented his policies; officials at all levels were to become better educated, be promoted on merit rather than seniority, be better protected against unlawful pressures from powerful individuals outside the bureaucratic hierarchy, and hence be freer and better qualified to advise the monarch and carry out his policies. Professionalism, the rule of law and freedom within the bounds of legality – such were the watchwords of the day, in Russia just as in Napoleonic France and other early-nineteenth-century European monarchies. The same philosophy shaped policy in other areas: the education system was expanded, censorship was relaxed, the secret police was abolished, and there was talk of reducing the arbitrary powers of nobles over their serfs. Some of these ideas were instantly popular with civil society, but vital details remained to be worked out and were bound to be controversial, and implementing them required the monarch's undivided attention, so he could not afford to be distracted by foreign conflicts. As a result, Alexander mended fences with London, recalled the Cossack regiments that his father had dispatched to invade India, and put more distance between himself and Napoleon. His task was made easier by the fact that, with the Anglo–French peace treaty of 1802, Europe was at peace for the first time in a decade.[12]

These favourable circumstances proved short lived. Domestic reform proved extraordinarily difficult as Alexander found himself caught between opposing factions at court that each had many sympathisers among the nobility and bureaucracy.[13] Trapped in the crossfire of their conflicting proposals, he had to face fundamental political questions. If he ceded any of his autocratic powers, for example to the conservative senior officials who formed the Senate, might this not jeopardise future reforms? Might not a weakened monarchy ultimately strengthen the mutually antagonistic networks of elite families that already controlled a vast share of Russia's serfs and government offices, and thereby cause dissension within the regime and make the other nobles feel unfairly excluded? Could the rule of law – which assumed that individuals had legal rights in the first place – be reconciled with the reality that half the population were serfs and had no rights at all? On the other hand, would the noble civil servants, army officers and land-lords who actually governed the Russian people have any incentive to obey a tsar who threatened their most important social privilege, namely serfdom? If serfs were actually liberated, who would become the owner of the pres-ently noble-owned land on which they lived? And, given the bureaucracy's lack of funds and manpower, who would take over the landlords' current, unpaid function as judges and police among the peasants? In any case, might the peasants (who were perennially convinced that the tsar was secretly their ally against the hated nobility) not interpret any measures at all in their favour as a signal for a general attack on the nobles that would lead to social anar-chy? The cost of unwise choices was clear – both Alexander's father (Paul I) and grandfather (Peter III) had died at the hands of angry nobles, while the rage of the peasantry had given the Pugachev revolt its terrifying ferocity. Under the best of circumstances, reform was bound to be a gradual, halting process. But circumstances soon deteriorated.

In May 1803, war resumed between Great Britain and France, ending the European peace that Alexander had enjoyed as he was pursuing his reform efforts. During the twelve months that followed, Russo–French relations deteriorated. From a strategic point of view, Napoleon's expanding influence in Germany and in the Mediterranean, as well as his designs on the Ottoman Empire, led Alexander to see him as a threat to the balance of power. There were also matters of honour and principle: when the duc d'Enghien, a mem-ber of the ousted French royal family, was kidnapped on Napoleon's orders from his exile in the German Duchy of Baden (whose ruler was Alexander's father-in-law) and executed in March 1804, the Russian court and imperial family were outraged; and Napoleon's coronation as Emperor represented a further challenge to Alexander and other 'legitimate' monarchs. Meanwhile, one of Alexander's most trusted liberal advisers, Adam Czartoryski, urged him to pursue the creation of a European state system founded on the equal-ity and freedom of nations (including Czartoryski's Polish homeland) rather than Napoleonic hegemony. Like his conservative father, the more liberal Alexander was thus also influenced by ideology, and he understood in addi-tion that his credibility at home depended in part on the success of his for-eign policy. All of these circumstances drew the young tsar, who in any case was frustrated by his stalled domestic reform plans, into the Third Coalition that took shape by 1805.[14] When war broke out that year, reform was put on hold.

The combined Russian–Austrian armies were decisively defeated at Austerlitz on 2 December 1805, which forced the Austrians to accept the peace of Pressburg on 26 December. The ensuing expansion of Napoleon's influence brought Prussia into the war, but its forces were crushed at Jena and Auerstedt on 14 October 1806. The Russians were now alone. Defeated at Preussisch-Eylau (8 February 1807) and Friedland (14 June), and under attack from the south by the Ottomans since December 1806, Alexander agreed to the peace of Tilsit, a series of treaties signed on 7–9 July 1807. Napoleon was the victor, but his aim – as it had been in his dealings with Paul I – was to secure an alliance with Russia that would free him to deal with the German states and Great Britain, so his terms were not punitive for the Russians. However, Alexander had to accept the dismemberment of his Prussian allies, who lost their western territories and out of whose Polish provinces Napoleon formed a French satellite state on Russia's very doorstep (the Grand Duchy of Warsaw), and he was forced to join the Continental System, Napoleon's commercial embargo against Great Britain.[15]

Domestically, Tilsit was a political disaster for Alexander, and it antagonised every major group in Russian society. For the illiterate peasants, the main sources of news were imperial and ecclesiastical pronouncements read in church by their priests, and unverifiable rumours spread by travellers, all of which the peasants interpreted in the light of their own traditional religious worldview and their general hostility to the nobles and serfdom. Thus, tales circulated about a mythical letter from Napoleon to Alexander I in which the French Emperor allegedly vowed to continue the war until the Russian serfs received their freedom. Furthermore, when the tsar mobilised peasants in a temporary militia in 1806 to reinforce the army, many peasants incorrectly inferred that the military situation, and hence the position of the regime, must be desperate. Peasant alienation from, and distrust towards, government and nobles often went hand-in-hand with membership of illegal lower-class sects that viewed the official Orthodox Church with suspicion, rejected the authority of its learned bishops, and watched on their own for signs from God. When the Orthodox Church, acting on state instructions, declared in 1806–1807 that Napoleon was the precursor of the Antichrist, many peasants apparently concluded that he was indeed *the* Antichrist. This theory remained stubbornly alive among the population, and even revived in the 1812 war, even though the Church itself soon disavowed it in order to justify the Tilsit alliance and because it realised that the identification of Napoleon with the Antichrist inadvertently suggested – at least to scriptural literalists – that his victory was inevitable and would usher in the millennium. Similarly, when the peace of Tilsit became known, many believed that demonic forces had caused Russia's defeat.[16] Thus, like their counterparts in Spain, Russian peasants were prepared to see in Napoleon a mortal enemy of their faith. However, whereas the Spaniards usually followed the lead of the government-supported (Catholic) clergy, many Russians looked instead to sectarians whom state and Church considered subversive. As in other areas, the regime's authoritarianism and remoteness from the people's way of life prevented state and Church from acquiring deep popular roots and rendered the socio-political order exceedingly brittle in times of crisis.

The upper classes were equally dismayed over Tilsit. After the failure of his reform attempts, Alexander had now been humiliated on the battle-field as well, and much of the nobility was accordingly disillusioned with his leadership. Rostopchin, Paul I's erstwhile adviser who remained bitter over Alexander's involvement in the plot to kill Paul, remarked venomously after Austerlitz that 'God cannot protect the armies of a bad son', and the prominent writer Nikolai Karamzin added insult to injury by pointing out to Alexander that Russia had had nothing to gain from the war to begin with. At the same time, the Continental System disrupted Russia's highly profitable trade with Great Britain, thereby hurting both nobles (whose estates produced raw materials for export) and merchants. Hurt in their pocketbooks, frightened by the prospect of serf unrest, humiliated by their army's defeat and angered by the restoration of a Polish state (the Grand Duchy of Warsaw) that might lay claim to Russia's formerly Polish provinces, Russian nobles – from minor provincial landowners all the way to the imperial family – were bitter, perplexed and afraid. Many nobles came to see the conflict with Napoleon in both ideological and national terms. A wave of Francophobia swept the educated class in Russia, just as it did in the German states, which was all the more remarkable since in both countries fluency in speaking French and emulating French fashions and manners had until then been regarded as the hallmark of aristocratic breeding. This xenophobic mood co-incided with the beginnings of romantic nationalism in Russia. To a degree that was unprecedented, writers explored and glorified Russian history and folklore and condemned the speaking of French by Russian aristocrats. It became common to consider that Russia was distinct from the rest of Europe, that its greatness was inseparable from the institutions of absolutism and noble privilege, and that reform ideas from the west (especially France) were inherently un-Russian and tainted by their association with the French Revolution.[17]

These circumstances placed Alexander in a difficult position. Russia's defeat made reforms to strengthen the state seem more urgent than ever, and his distaste for the Russian old regime was unchanged. His new chief adviser, Mikhail Speranskii, was therefore entrusted with developing a programme of sweeping reforms. Yet the problems inherent in any reform effort remained undiminished; the nobility hated Speranskii, the upstart son of a mere country priest, who was thought to be an enemy of the noble class and who clearly drew inspiration from the Napoleonic regime – admittedly the most effective authoritarian state of the time; and Alexander could not make up his mind actually to implement Speranskii's ideas. In order to clamp down on opposition to the reforms and to the alliance with Napoleon, the tsar tightened censorship, restored the secret police and appointed one of his father's most brutal and hated lieutenants, Aleksei Arakcheev, to head the administration of the armed forces. Rumours circulated for years that a coup against Alexander was in the offing, and the St Petersburg aristocracy made its feelings known by refusing to invite Napoleon's ambassador to any of its magnificent balls even as it lionised the Prussian king and queen whom Napoleon had dispossessed.

Even as his domestic position thus deteriorated, Alexander privately concluded that the alliance with Napoleon was actually detrimental to Russia's interests, and began dragging his feet in fulfilling its terms even while publicly paying lip service to it. When Napoleon fought the Austrians in 1809, Russia provided only minimal assistance. When Napoleon proposed to marry one of Alexander's sisters, and thereby cement the alliance, he was turned down. Alexander was angry about France's treatment of the territories of his German relatives and was lackadaisical in enforcing the Continental Blockade. The aftermath of Tilsit thus antagonised domestic opinion in Russia without really winning Napoleon's friendship, but Alexander believed that he had no choice. He detested Napoleon's regime and could not accept French domination of Europe, yet open confrontation entailed grave risks.

By 1812, it was clear to Napoleon – who was already stymied in his efforts to defeat Britain and subdue Spain – that the Russians remained his enemies, so he decided to strike the first blow. The war was fraught with peril for Russia, whose forces were far weaker in numbers, experience and quality of leadership than the armies of France and its German, Polish and Italian satellites; any military setback that made the regime appear weak might encourage the peasants to revolt or prompt the nobles to stage a coup as they had in 1762 and 1801. At a minimum, Alexander needed the undivided loyalty of the nobles, and that required ending any talk of major reforms. Consequently, in March 1812, Speranskii was dismissed from his post and exiled to a remote provincial town, and high-level government positions were given to men known for their outspoken hostility to reforms. Then, on 24 June, the French attacked. Napoleon's central army group, 450,000 strong (out of a total of 655,000 mobilised for the campaign), marched eastwards towards Smolensk and, ultimately, Moscow, while other forces guarded their northern and southern flanks. Facing them were widely separated Russian armies that totalled only 220,000–240,000 troops.[18]

Reassured about their tsar's commitment to the traditional social order, the nobility rallied to the national cause, which was also the cause of their social class. However, they were uncertain of the loyalties of the population at large. Russia had experienced no major invasion in living memory, and the resulting stability of the power structure in its towns and villages had made social injustices appear, if not acceptable, then at least inevitable. However, no one could predict what might happen if and when that inertia was shattered by foreign troops who might come armed with revolutionary slogans of 'liberty, equality, fraternity'. Would the people remain passive bystanders, as the Prussian population had when their state was smashed by Napoleon in 1806? Would they organise guerrilla bands that attacked the French but could also challenge the authority of nobles and officials, as the peasants of northern Spain had since 1808? Or would they openly side with the enemy? The regime took what few preventive measures it could. Government proclamations argued that Russian national identity, the monarchy, the traditional social order and the Orthodox faith all represented a single whole that every Orthodox Russian was obligated to defend, that Napoleon was the enemy of God and intended to enslave Russia, and that any French promises of liberty and equality were nothing but lies. Some Russian leaders, such as General Mikhail Kutuzov, the immensely popular commander of the army, suggested that the war had to do with defending the Russian people's 'liberty'; propaganda of this sort helped encourage peasants to volunteer for the wartime militia in the (false) hope that serfs who fought for their country's freedom would receive their own as well. Other leaders, especially Rostopchin (the new governor-general of Moscow), took a different route by fanning popular xenophobia and launching demagogic witch-hunts against suspected traitors among foreign residents and Russians suspected of liberal sympathies.[19]

In the end, there was remarkably little popular unrest. The invasion began in June and was over by Christmas, so the occupation of any given area was too short lived to dissolve the existing social order. In contrast to the more

densely settled lands of western and central Europe, the typical Russian village was surrounded by woods, and when the enemy approached, the peasants – as in earlier centuries – took refuge deep in the forests. Similarly, most
people in Moscow came from villages to which they could return in times of
crisis; of the city's 275,000 inhabitants, it seems that only about 6,000
remained when Napoleon's army arrived. The population thus responded
less by either fighting the invader or collaborating with him (as in other countries) than by fleeing him as they might a deadly plague, leaving him to
occupy abandoned villages and towns where he found neither provisions nor
a population that he could try to enlist in his cause. Also, Napoleon did not
promise the Russian peasants freedom; his goal was to smash the Russian
army and force the tsar to recognise French supremacy, not unleash social
anarchy that would make Russia ungovernable. Just as in Spain, his army
antagonised the population through widespread looting and by desecrating
churches, which were used as barracks, stables, even latrines. Under these
circumstances, the Russian army was able to withdraw for 22 months and
600 miles without prompting popular unrest against the regime, even while
the arduous advance rapidly depleted Napoleon's forces. Before the bloody
battle of Borodino near Moscow (7 September), Napoleon's central army
group had already lost some 100,000 of its 450,000 troops, and thousands
more had to be diverted to garrison duty and other secondary functions.
Borodino claimed a further 40,000–60,000 Russian and as many French lives,
and while the Russians failed to halt the French advance, they did save their
army from the destruction that Napoleon had intended for it.[20]

Borodino allowed the French to occupy Moscow, the former capital and a
holy city to many Russians, where Napoleon hoped to spend the winter and
wait for the tsar to sue for peace. However, after being looted by both
Russian peasants and Napoleonic troops, the abandoned city was consumed
by a fire whose origins remain controversial; Napoleon obviously had no
rational interest in destroying his own winter quarters, but the fire was
nonetheless blamed on him by the Russians and completely discredited him
in the eyes of the population. Finally, on 19 October, with the Russian army
gaining strength with every passing day (the combined army, peasant militia
and irregulars by then outnumbered Napoleon's forces by a ratio of almost
5:2)[21] and Alexander unwilling to negotiate, the 100,000 men who by then
formed the central army group – decimated, hungry, demoralised, increasingly undisciplined and surrounded by a hostile population – withdrew from
the ruins of Moscow to return to their bases. On their long retreat through
the lands they had devastated during their advance just a few months earlier,

where they now found hardly any sustenance for men and horses, the starving soldiers of the *Grande Armée* perished by the tens of thousands – at the hands of pursuing Cossack cavalry and vengeful peasants, from cold as the harsh winter weather set in, or in the icy waters of the Berezina river when their army frantically rushed across to escape encirclement by the Russians.

Of the entire central army group, only 25,000 emaciated and frostbitten survivors straggled back to Poland in December 1812. Overall, Napoleon had brought 655,000 men with him to Russia; 370,000 of these perished during the campaign and another 200,000 were taken prisoner – of whom fewer than half survived. As for the Russians in 1812, their military losses were in the range of 110,000–150,000 dead, with roughly the same number of civilian victims; and an additional 250,000 Russian troops lost their lives in the other campaigns against Napoleon in 1805–14.[22] The devastation of 1812 was staggering: most buildings in Moscow and Smolensk had been destroyed, as had many villages and smaller towns, and even by the very conservative estimate of the Russian finance ministry the economic damage amounted to 200 million rubles (a sum equivalent to 40 million times the annual dues owed by a serf to his landlord, 500,000 times the annual salary of an army captain, or over 2 million times the market value of a serf woman).[23] Merely disposing of the dead soldiers, civilians and horses put the administration's resources to a severe test. In Moscow alone, 12,000 corpses were found after the French retreat, and conditions were no better in the countryside; for example, the district of Vereia, an area near Moscow no larger than a typical American county, had to deal with 2,871 corpses and 5,985 animal carcasses.[24]

RUSSIA AND THE LEGACY OF THE NAPOLEONIC WARS

War on so vast a scale made a profound impression on all who witnessed it, but Russians (like Germans and Spaniards) were deeply divided over its meaning. There were three principal interpretations. The peasants believed that, by fighting for Russia's freedom from foreign rule, they also gained a moral right to be free from serfdom. Many educated, liberal-minded Russians (especially junior army officers) similarly saw the mass support for the 'Patriotic War' of 1812 as proof that their nation had achieved civic maturity. The conclusion they drew, which most historians have since shared, was that the old authoritarian order – with its pervasive distrust towards the population and its efforts to enforce top-down controls – should make way for a more liberal one, modelled on what they had seen in Germany and France in

1813–15, in which all would enjoy personal liberty, the protection of the laws and the opportunity to participate in public life. Finally, conservative nobles and bureaucrats regarded the victory over Napoleon as a victory for absolutism, serfdom and noble privileges. The peasant hope for freedom was soon squelched: the wartime militia and guerrilla bands – both of them potentially rebellious forces of armed peasants – were quickly disarmed, and an imperial proclamation of 1814, after giving thanks to God for Russia's victory and promising specific new benefits to the clergy and nobility, added merely that the peasants ('our loyal people') would 'receive their reward from God'.[25] That, however, still left two possible routes for the post-war future. One pointed to a liberalisation of society, the other to a return to the old order. Caught between these options, and ambivalent about both, was Alexander I.

Alexander believed that the Enlightenment, by substituting religious scepticism and critical reasoning for Christian humility and morality, had encouraged the unrestrained pursuit of naked self-interest by monarchs and nobles, stoked the flames of lower-class hatred for the rich, and fuelled the utopian radicalism of the intellectuals. The outcome had been revolutionary terror, reactionary counter-terror and decades of warfare that finally ended only when the Russians and their allies swept through Germany and overthrew Napoleon in 1814. To ensure that the hard-won victory over Napoleon actually broke this vicious circle, it seemed necessary to replace the Enlightenment with alternative ideological principles that would reconcile all strata of society with each other and allow for both political stability and gradual, evolutionary social change. Alexander hoped to achieve this with the aid of a pietist form of Christianity – ostensibly non-denominational, yet basically Protestant in its focus on Bible reading and individual piety – which was introduced to Russia from Germany and Great Britain and to which Alexander himself became a fervent convert.[26]

This philosophy called for cautious reform efforts by the state regarding serfdom, education, industry and commerce, and the structure of government. To counter tensions between social classes and between society and government, civil society was to be involved in the reform effort through voluntary organisations that combated poverty, promoted literacy and otherwise advanced social justice; while a new Christian spirit was to be encouraged throughout the population by new school curricula, censorship policies, the mass distribution of cheap Bibles and other measures. Alexander sought to encourage similar policies by the governments of other countries. The new philosophy was most visibly articulated in the Holy Alliance treaty of 1815, a grand yet substantively vague document that committed the European monarchs to policies based on Christian brotherhood.

In the end, this programme failed. Reforms of serfdom and limitations on the absolute monarchy were stymied by the same forces as before 1812. The new associations for social and religious reform encountered little support, and sometimes outright hostility, from bureaucrats (who distrusted independent organisations of any sort) and conservative Orthodox clergymen (who resented their Protestant inspiration), while those who joined such groups as the Russian Bible Society and the Imperial Philanthropic Society often did so to demonstrate their loyalty to the regime more than out of genuine commitment. In contrast to Victorian England, where similar movements would later enjoy great success, Russia had too little tradition of independent activism by civil society. Some powerful officials further discredited the new piety in the eyes of civil society by cloaking their own brutality and careerist opportunism in displays of religious zeal that were as hypocritical as they were sanctimonious – for example, by persecuting university professors for allegedly paying insufficient heed to Christian teachings in their science lectures. In foreign policy as well, the dream of a 'Christian' alternative to revolution and reaction proved to be a mirage, and in the crises of the early 1820s, when revolution broke out across southern Europe, Alexander saw no other option than to side with the reactionary 'legitimate' monarchies.[27] Whereas, across Europe, progressive eighteenth-century *philosophes* as well as liberal enemies of Napoleon had idolised Catherine II and the young Alexander I, Russia after 1815 increasingly became identified in the minds of European liberals with reaction and 'obscurantism', that is, hostility to liberty and 'enlightenment'.[28] These same developments also disillusioned many young, aristocratic Russian officers, some of whom formed revolutionary groups similar to the ones that existed in Spain and elsewhere.[29] In December 1825, in the confused aftermath of Alexander's unexpected death, they made an unsuccessful attempt (the Decembrist revolt) to seize power in Russia.

Alexander's rule left a mixed legacy. In many areas – such as educational and economic policy – he had carried forward successful reforms in the authoritarian spirit of enlightened absolutism. Under his brother Nicholas I (reigned 1825–55), these policies were continued with considerable success; thus, Russia's laws were finally compiled in a single legal code, a key step towards the creation of a modern legal system. However, the various attempts at fundamental socio-political change – first the Catherinian version of the Enlightenment, then the brand of bureaucratic reform associated with Speranskii, and finally Alexander's post-1815 pietism – had failed to produce results, while the French Revolution, Europe's revolutionary crises of the 1820s to 1840s and the Decembrist revolt all suggested that liberalism was a deadly threat to the old regime. In response, Nicholas I muzzled civil society at home and used his army to crush revolutions abroad, while reforms of serfdom, though discussed secretly in government councils, were never carried out. As a result, the great wave of political and economic modernisation sweeping western and central Europe largely passed by a Russia that seemed frozen in the eighteenth century.

In retrospect, the Napoleonic wars appear as an important missed opportunity. Alexander's initial push for reforms was interrupted by war in 1805–1807. The humiliation of defeat aggravated the public hostility to Speranskii's reform plans but, unlike in Prussia after 1806, the defeat had not been disastrous enough to make reforms seem unavoidable. After 1812–14, when Alexander in any case was losing interest in the matter, victory removed the pressure for change. Fundamental reform therefore came to Russia only after 1855, when Nicholas I died and Russia suffered a catastrophic defeat in the Crimean War. By the time serfdom was abolished in 1861 and the idea of constitutional government was again under discussion, however, the passage of time had made the task of the reformers vastly more difficult than it would have been a half-century earlier.

SUGGESTIONS FOR
FURTHER READING

◆

The following list has been compiled from suggestions made by the contributors. Wherever possible, prominence is given to works in English, though foreign-language books and articles are cited when they are of particular importance or where no titles in English can be given.

The 'classic' writings on Napoleon which appeared between 1815 and the Second World War have been well distilled in Pieter Geyl's stimulating and long-serving study, *Napoleon: For and Against* (London, 1949). Geyl confined himself to French writers, but at least gave equal attention to the 'heroic' and 'black legends' recounted in their works. A shorter but wider statement, which includes coverage of the reactions to Napoleon by German, Italian and British contemporaries, is offered in chapter 7 of Geoffrey Ellis, *Napoleon* (London and New York, 1997). The over-riding emphasis in these earlier writings is on Napoleon the man, on how he saw himself and on how others saw him, and it also invites an exploration of the major primary sources available. Yet alas, it must be said that, in English at least, the literature is rather limited. We lack a full, modern and properly annotated translation of Count Emmanuel de Las Cases's *Mémorial de Sainte-Hélène*, 2 vols. (Paris, 1983), which was for so long the principal source for exponents of the Napoleonic legend. The English edition which immediately appeared (4 vols., London, 1823) has its own antique charm, but it is not now widely available outside major libraries. Much the same could be said of the copious letters of Napoleon, an estimated 32,000 in all. The crucial *Correspondance de Napoléon Ier publiée par ordre de l'empereur Napoléon III*, 32 vols. (Paris, 1858–69) has never appeared in an integrated English edition; nor have the collections in French of his correspondence with various contemporaries. A more accessible (if much briefer) introduction is available in the volume selected, translated and edited by J. M. Thompson, *Letters of Napoleon* (Oxford, 1934). These may be supplemented by the fascinating collection of items edited and translated by J. Christopher Herold, *The Mind of Napoleon: a Selection from his Written and Spoken Words* (New York, 1955).

On Corsica one can consult Dorothy Carrington, *The Dream-hunters of Corsica* (London, 1996), and *Granite Island: a Portrait of Corsica* (Harmondsworth,

1971). The only work in English on Napoleon's childhood and family background is the thoroughly researched study by Dorothy Carrington, *Napoleon and his Parents on the Threshold of History* (New York, 1988). Napoleon's elder brother, Joseph, is the object of a biography by Owen Connelly, *The Gentle Bonaparte: a Biography of Joseph, Napoleon's Elder Brother* (New York, 1968).

A number of articles on aspects of Napoleon's personality are available, although much is yet to be done. For his youth the most important is: Harold T. Parker, 'The formation of Napoleon's personality', *French Historical Studies* (hereafter *FHS*) 7 (1971), pp. 6–26. See also Harold T. Parker, 'Symposium – Napoleon: civil executive and revolutionary', *Consortium on Revolutionary Europe Proceedings* (hereafter *CREP*), (1972), pp. 18–49; 'Napoleon's changing self-image to 1812: a sketch', *CREP* (1983), pp. 448–463; 'Napoleon reconsidered', *FHS* 15 (1987), pp. 142–56; 'The writing of "The formation of Napoleon's Personality": a fruitful collaboration', *CREP* (1989), pp. 330–41; and 'Why did Napoleon invade Russia? A study in the motivation and the interrelation of personality and social structure', *Journal of Military History* 54 (1990), pp. 131–46. Useful also for the manner in which Napoleon developed a method of governing people is Parker's 'Napoleon and Conquered Territories, 1805–1807', *South Atlantic Quarterly* 51 (1952), pp. 70–84.

Material relating to the Bonaparte family's participation in Corsican politics during the French Revolution is for the most part in French. One can start with the entries in Jean Tulard's *Dictionnaire Napoléon* (Paris, 1987) by Jean Defranceschi on 'Bonaparte (Charles)', 'Corse', 'Paoli', 'Pozzo di Borgo' and 'Saliceti'. Defranceschi has also written *La Corse française 30 novembre 1789–15 juin 1794* (Paris, 1980), and *La Corse et la Révolution française* (Ajaccio, 1991). The nature of Corsican clan politics is explained in François Pomponi, 'Sentiment révolutionnaire et espirit de parti en Corse au temps de la Révolution', in *Problèmes d'histoire de la Corse (de l'Ancien Régime à 1815): Actes de Colloque d'Ajaccio 29 octobre 1969* (Paris, 1971). J. M. P. McErlean's *Napoleon and Pozzo di Borgo in Corsica and after, 1764–1821: Not Quite a Vendetta* (Lewiston, NY, 1996) is a study in the relationship between one of Napoleon's Corsican friends and eventual rivals, Pozzo di Borgo. The first chapters of the book deal with their political intriguing on Corsica.

The most accessible discussion of Napoleon's seizure of power at Brumaire is Malcolm Crook, *Napoleon Comes to Power: Democracy and Dictatorship in Revolutionary France, 1795–1804* (Cardiff, 1998). On the relations over time between Napoleon and his original supporters of Brumaire see Isser Woloch, *Napoleon and his Collaborators: the Making of a Dictatorship* (New York, 2001).

Napoleon was deeply conscious of the importance of the army to his own image and sought to envelop his person and his regime in a military mystique. This is already apparent in the bulletins he authorised from the front; texts can be found in Napoléon Bonaparte, *Proclamations, Ordres du jour, Bulletins de la Grande Armée* (Paris, 1964), an appreciation of their value in J. J. Matthews, 'Napoleon's military bulletins', *Journal of Modern History* (hereafter *JMH*) 22 (1950). The process of mythification is most clearly seen in the memoirs Napoleon supposedly dictated to Las Cases during his exile on St Helena (*Mémorial de Sainte-Hélène*). It is also apparent in his encouragement of history painting and his patronage of artists who depicted his military genius and his empathy with his troops. See Wayne Hanley, 'The genesis of Napoleonic propaganda, 1796–1799' (doctoral thesis, University of Missouri, 1998); Timothy Wilson-Smith, *Napoleon and his Artists* (London, 1996); Albert Boime, *A Social History of Modern Art, II: Art in an Age of Bonapartism* (London, 1993); and, as a somewhat atypical case-study, Christopher Prendergast, *Napoleon and History Painting: Antoine-Jean Gros's 'La Bataille d'Eylau'* (Oxford, 1997).

A succinct account of Napoleon's efforts to guarantee his place in history can be found in Annie Jourdan, *L'Empire de Napoléon* (Paris, 2000). Just how far he succeeded can be judged by the power of the Bonapartist myth in the nineteenth century and of the place of military imagery within it. A good starting point is Robert Gildea, *The Past in French History* (New Haven, Conn., 1994), especially chapter 2 and, across a broader canvas, Marcel Gauchet, 'Right and left', in Pierre Nora (ed.), *Realms of Memory*, vol. 1, ch. 7. Napoleon's role in shaping French popular imagination is discussed by Natalie Petiteau, *Napoléon de la mythologie à l'histoire* (Paris, 1999). For the lingering appeal of Napoleon in the countryside useful works in English include R. S. Alexander, *Bonapartism and Revolutionary Tradition in France: the Fédérés of 1815* (Cambridge, 1991), and Peter McPhee, *The Politics of Rural Life: Political Mobilisation in the French Countryside, 1846–1852* (Oxford, 1992). In French, see Bernard Ménager, *Les Napoléons du peuple* (Paris, 1988), which concentrates on the appeal of popular Bonapartism. The return of Napoleon's ashes for burial at the Invalides helped foster a cult of the Emperor during the nineteenth century, one which would be taken up by nationalists and even by many republicans in the years before the First World War. Military prowess and the thirst for national glory had entered the spirit of both right and left.

There is no shortage of scholarly material on the Napoleonic wars and on the armies that fought in them. There is also a great deal of popular military history which can tend to hagiography, presenting Bonaparte as a military genius who single-handedly took on Europe. Of recent general studies in English, both Charles Esdaile, *The Wars of Napoleon* (London, 1995) and David Gates, *The Napoleonic Wars, 1803–1815* (London, 1997) provide a good overview, and take care to link the wars to the more general political and economic context in which they were fought. So, across a broader canvas, does Geoffrey Best, *War and Society in Revolutionary Europe, 1770–1870* (London, 1982). Of the more narrowly military works, concentrating on battles and strategy, those of David Chandler are a mine of detail, especially his *Dictionary of the Napoleonic Wars* (London and New York, 1979) and *The Campaigns of Napoleon: the Mind and Method of History's Greatest Soldier* (London and New York, 1966). Owen Connelly's more concise work, *Blundering to Glory: Napoleon's Military Campaigns* (Wilmington, Del., 1987), provides a provocative antidote to the prevalent view of Napoleon's abilities as a commander. For an analysis of battlefield tactics and military hardware, see Gunther E. Rothenberg, *The Art of Warfare in the Age of Napoleon* (Bloomington, Ind., 1978). A brief discussion of the use which he made of the military to extend French imperium across Europe can be found in any general textbook; more specialised works include Stuart Woolf, *Napoleon's Integration of Europe* (London and New York, 1991), and Michael Broers, *Europe under Napoleon 1799–1815* (London, 1996). Both also give valuable bibliographies for further reading.

The culture of the army was inevitably affected by its revolutionary heritage. On the French revolutionary armies, the indispensable work is Jean-Paul Bertaud, *The Army of the French Revolution: from Citizen-Soldiers to Instrument of Power* (Princeton, NJ, 1988); more concise, and with a strong emphasis on the role of the individual soldier, is Alan Forrest, *The Soldiers of the French Revolution* (Durham, NC, 1990). The role of former Jacobins in the armies is discussed by Isser Woloch, *Jacobin Legacy: the Democratic Movement under the Directory* (Princeton, NJ, 1970), while the change in military values through the period of the Directory and Consulate is the subject of an important article by John Lynn, 'Towards an army of honour: the moral evolution of the French army, 1789–1815', *FHS* 16 (1989). Napoleon's own evolution from revolutionary general to First Consul is analysed by Martyn Lyons, *Napoleon Bonaparte and the Legacy of the French Revolution* (London, 1994); and the military image which he incarnated by Annie Jourdan, *Napoléon: héros, imperator, mécène* (Paris, 1998). For a discussion of the officer class, see Jean-Paul Bertaud, 'Napoleon's officers', *Past & Present* (hereafter *PP*) 112 (1986); and of the marshals David Chandler (ed.), *Napoleon's Marshals* (New York, 1987). A more general discussion of Napoleonic elites and of the spoils system that maintained them is to be found in Louis Bergeron, *France under Napoleon* (Princeton, NJ, 1981 transl.).

A more general discussion of Napoleonic elites and the spoils system that maintained them is to be found in Louis Bergeron, *France under Napoleon*, trans. R. R. Palmer (Princeton, NJ, 1981). Bergeron is also the most useful introduction to the social history of France during the Napoleonic era. Three other general works deal suggestively with social history: D. M. G. Sutherland, *France, 1789–1815: Revolution and Counter-Revolution* (London, 1985); M. Lyons, *Napoleon Bonaparte and the Legacy of the French Revolution* (London and New York, 1994); and J. Tulard, *La Vie quotidienne des Français sous Napoléon* (Paris, 1978), while several evocative documents are reprinted in J.-P. Bertaud, *Le Premier Empire, legs de la Révolution* (Paris, 1973). For the aftermath, see R. Price, *A Social History of Nineteenth-century France* (London, 1987), and Peter McPhee, *A Social History of France, 1780–1880* (London, 1994).

For the *notables*, as well as other aspects of social history, see the special number of the *Revue d'histoire moderne et contemporaine* (July 1970) devoted to La France à l'époque napoléonienne, and especially the article by Jean Tulard, 'Problèmes sociaux de la France impériale', pp. 639–63. The main work of synthesis is L. Bergeron and G. Chaussinand-Nogaret, *Les 'Masses de granit': cent mille notables du Premier Empire* (Paris, 1979). See also their biographical dictionary: *Grands notables du Premier Empire: notices de biographie sociale publiées sous la direction de Louis Bergeron et Guy Chaussinand-Nogaret* (Paris, 1978). Another stratum of official society is considered in M. Agulhon, L. Girard, et al., *Les Maires en France du Consulat à nos jours* (Paris, 1986), and in the work in progress by John Dunne. Jeff Horn's forthcoming work covers the elites of the Aude department. The Senate is covered in V. Azimi, *Les Premiers Sénateurs français: Consulat et Premier Empire, 1800–1814* (Paris, 2000). Finally, on the local *notables* who emerged under the Restoration and the July Monarchy see J. Tudesq, *La France des Notables, II: la vie de la nation, 1815–1848* (Paris, 1973). For the Napoleonic nobility a fine overview is provided by J. Tulard, *Napoléon et la noblesse d'Empire* (Paris, 1979). As to how the old nobility fared, see R. Forster, 'The survival of the French nobility', *Past & Present* (1967), pp. 71–86, and D. Higgs, *Nobles in Nineteenth-century France: the Practice of Inegalitarianism* (Baltimore, Md, 1987).

There is no general synthesis on the commercial elites of the Napoleonic era, but see L. Bergeron, *Banquiers, négociants et manufacturiers parisiens du Directoire à l'Empire* (Paris, 1978); P. Barral, *Les Périer dans l'Isère au XIXe siècle, d'après leur correspondance familiale* (Paris, 1964); and J.-P. Hirsch, *Les Deux rêves du commerce: entreprise et institution dans la région lilloise (1780–1860)* (Paris, 1991). One can also consult Jerffry Diefendorf, *Businessmen and Politics in the Rhineland, 1789–1834* (Princeton, NJ, 1980). For another kind of elite see M. Crosland, *The Society of Arcueil: a View of French Science at the Time of Napoleon I* (London, 1967). The position of lawyers is considered in Isser Woloch, *The New Regime: Transformations of the French Civic Order, 1789–1820s* (New York, 1994), ch. 12, and M. Fitzsimmons, *The Parisian Order of Barristers and the French Revolution* (Cambridge, Mass., 1987), chs. 6–7.

For the study of local society, a remarkably rich collection of source material is available consisting of over fifty departmental handbooks compiled under the direction of various prefects. They have been republished and introduced by J.-C. Perrot under the title *Sources statistiques de l'histoire de France: les enquêtes des préfets de l'Empire*, published by the Bibliothèque nationale in France and on microfiche by Clearwater Publishing Company in New York (1975). J.-C. Perrot and S. Woolf, *State and Statistics in France, 1789–1815* (New York, 1984) puts this valuable source in perspective. Few of the local monographs in which the French generally excel deal with Napoleonic social history, as opposed to administrative and political developments. The exceptions, to one degree or another, include M. Agulhon, *La Vie sociale en Provence intérieure au lendemain de la Révolution* (Paris, 1970); J.-P. Jessenne, *Pouvoir au village et Révolution: Artois, 1760–1848* (Lille, 1987); F. L'Huillier, *Recherches sur l'Alsace napoléonienne* (Paris, 1947); and Peter Jones, *Politics and Rural Society: the Southern Massif Central c. 1750–1880* (Cambridge, 1985). In a different vein the period's urbanism is explored by J. Tulard, *Nouvelle histoire de Paris: Le Consulat et l'Empire* (Paris, 1970). See also the unclassifiable Lanzac de Labourie, *Paris sous Napoléon*, 8 vols. (Paris, 1905–11).

Despite the central importance of public finance, historians have paid insufficient attention to this subject both in Napoleonic France and throughout the Napoleonic Empire. Issues like taxes, state expenditure, financial administration and public debt have not received the attention they deserve. Two useful works in French on the financial system are Marcel Marion, *Histoire financière de la France depuis 1715. Tome IV: 1797–1818. La Fin de la révolution, le consulat et l'Empire, la libération du territoire* (New York, 1925); and Réné Stourm, *Les finances du Consulat* (Paris, 1902). Three useful chapters which provide a good summary of the financial policies of the revolutionary and Napoleonic periods can be found in Jacques Godechot, *Les Institutions de la France sous la Révolution et l'Empire* (Paris, 1968). The late Ancien Regime and the revolutionary period have been explored in the excellent study by J. F. Bosher, *French Finances 1770–1795* (Cambridge, 1970). A more recent article by Jean Pierre Gross, 'Progressive taxation and social justice in eighteenth-century France', *PP* 140 (1993) contains material on finances in the revolutionary period. A number of books in English provide useful information on Napoleonic finances in France, although none devotes more than several pages. Those studies include Bergeron, *France under Napoleon*; Robert Holtman, *The Napoleonic Revolution* (Baton Rouge and London, 1967); and Ellis, *Napoleon*. Martyn Lyons, *France under the Directory* (Cambridge, 1975) includes important data on the fiscal policy under the Directory. There are also a few entries on financial issues in Owen Connelly (ed.), *Historical Dictionary of Napoleonic France 1799–1815* (Westport, Conn., 1985).

Several works discuss fiscal policies and financial conditions in Napoleonic Europe. General discussions on taxes, public debt, financial organisation and fiscal reform, with references to specific countries, can be found in Woolf, *Napoleon's Integration of Europe*. Owen Connelly provides useful information on finances in various Napoleonic satellites, including the kingdoms of Italy, Naples, Holland and Westphalia, in his work, *Napoleon's Satellite Kingdoms* (New York and London, 1965). Simon Schama provides a substantial analysis of the financial conditions in the Napoleonic Netherlands, within the overall context of its relations with France, in two studies: the voluminous *Patriots and Liberators: Revolution in the Netherlands, 1780–1813* (London, 1977); and his essay 'The exigencies of war and the politics of taxation in the Netherlands 1795–1810', in J. M. Winter (ed.), *War and Economic Development* (Cambridge, 1975). Alexander Grab, 'The politics of finance in Napoleonic Italy (1802–1814)', *Journal of Modern Italian Studies* 3 (1998), presents a discussion of the fiscal policies in the Republic and Kingdom of Italy on the basis of archival research.

In general, historians have tended to neglect the Napoleonic administration. However, a number of works in English illustrate the various approaches open to scholars. C. H. Church, *Revolution and Red Tape: the French Ministerial Bureaucracy, 1770–1850* (Oxford, 1981); Everett Dague, 'Henri Clarke, Minister of War, and the Malet Conspiracy', *CREP* (1996), and idem, 'Clarke and the defense of Paris', *CREP* (1997); H. T. Parker, 'Two administrative bureaus under the Directory and Napoleon', *FHS* (1965); Nathan Schur, *Napoleon in the Holy Land* (London, 1999); and E. A. Whitcomb, *Napoleon's Diplomatic Service* (Durham, NC, 1979), are all worth consulting.

There has therefore been relatively little published on the Napoleonic police in French and considerably less in English. While there are several fine studies of the Napoleonic police by English-speaking historians, it is worth noting that most of them are of pretty recent vintage. There is a real irony in the fact that, despite the traditional labeling of the Napoleonic regime as a 'police state', and over-frequent references to Fouché's ubiquitous network of spies and informers, it is only comparatively recently that scholars have turned to this aspect of the Napoleonic period in earnest. Peter de Polnay, *Napoleon's Police* (London, 1970), is a popular account of no academic value. Eric A. Arnold, Jr, *Fouché, Napoleon and the General Police* (Washington, DC, 1979) provides a competent analysis of the police bureaucracy, but unfortunately uses almost no archival sources. The history of the Gendarmerie, on the other hand, is well served by Clive Emsley, *Gendarmes and the State in Nineteenth-century Europe* (Oxford, 1999).

Many of the central problems of the period associated with policing were traced best by Colin Lucas in a series of seminal articles on the directorial period, most notably in 'The first French Directory and the rule of law', *FHS* 10 (1977), and 'The problem of the Midi in the French Revolution', *Transactions of the Royal Historical Society* (herefter *TRHS*) 28 (1978), works which have done much to set the agenda for those who followed. Building on this, is the perceptive article by Howard Brown, 'From organic society to security state: the war on brigandage in France, 1797–1802', *JMH* 69 (1997), which widens these issues beyond a regional perspective.

There are a number of interesting biographies of Fouché. The best of these is Hubert Cole, *Fouché: the Unprincipled Patriot* (New York and London, 1971), but students can also consult Stefan Zweig, *Joseph Fouché: Portrait of a Politician* (New York, 1930); Nils Forsell, *Fouché, the Man Napoleon Feared,* translated from the Swedish by Anna Barwell (New York, n.d.); and Ray Ellsworth Cubberly, *The Role of Fouché during the Hundred Days* (Madison, Wis., 1969). Fouché's fascinating memoirs exist in English in several nineteenth-century editions: *The Memoirs of Joseph Fouché, Duke of Otranto, Minister of the General Police of France* (Boston, Mass., and New York, 1825; and London, 1896) and *Memoirs Relating to Fouché, Minister of Police under Napoleon I*, translated by E. Jules Méras (New York, 1912). Pierre François Réal, *Indiscretions of a Prefect of Police: Anecdotes of Napoleon and the Bourbons from the Papers of Count Réal*, translated by Arthur L. Hayward (London, 1929) is an entertaining account by one of Fouché's closest collaborators. The memoirs of Fouché's successor have also been translated: *Memoirs of the Duke of Rovigo (M. Savary) Written by Himself, Illustative of the History of the Emperor Napoleon*, 4 vols. (London, 1828).

There is, surprisingly, almost nothing available on the opposition to the Napoleonic regime, except Louis de Villefoss and Janine Bouissonouse, *The Scourge of the Eagle: Napoleon and the Liberal Opposition*, translated by Michael

Ross (London, 1972). The only work on the many conspiracies against Napoleon is one article on the attempted assassination of Napoleon in 1800, Michael J. Sydenham, 'The Crime of 3 Nivôse (24 December 1800),' in J. F. Bosher (ed.), *French Government and Society, 1500–1850* (London, 1973) and one book (with no scholarly pretensions) on the Malet Conspiracy of 1812: Artom Guido, *Napoleon is Dead in Russia,* translated from the Italian by Muriel Grindrod (New York, 1970). Finally, Michael Sibalis has published two articles on police treatment of the regime's opponents: 'Prisoners by *Mesure de haute police* under Napoleon I: reviving the *Lettres de cachet*', *Proceedings of the Annual Meeting of the Western Society for French History* 18 (1991) and 'Internal exile in Napoleonic France, 1799–1815', *Proceedings of the Annual Meeting of the Western Society for French History* 20 (1993).

Law, order and policing in Napoleonic Europe were bound up inextricably with the problems of conscription, and there is no doubt that this subject has been the key that has done more than any other to open the door of the domestic history of the Napoleonic period to serious study. Conscription was to dominate so much of the political agenda and arouse much opposition among ordinary people. The most profound, seminal work has been done by Anglo-Saxon scholars, most notably by Alan Forrest in his indispensable *Conscripts and Deserters: the Army and French Society during the Revolution and Empire* (New York, 1989), and the crucial article by Isser Woloch: 'Napoleonic conscription: state power and civil society', *PP* 111 (1986). Forrest's work ranges over the whole revolutionary–Napoleonic period, and is based on intensive archival work in French departments, thus – almost for the first time – giving students a study of the regime 'on the ground', and yielding valuable insights into popular resistance to the state, at local level. By contrast, Woloch's article – later followed by his wider book-length study, *The New Regime* – view the history of conscription from the centre. Whereas Forrest senses that conscription sparked fierce, deeply rooted resistance to authority in many communities, Woloch sees it as a catalyst for change and the advance of the state into hitherto isolated, autonomous areas. Conscription also provoked wider dissent, in France and throughout the Empire. See Richard Cobb, *The Police and the People: French Popular Protest, 1789–1820* (Oxford, 1970); and, for northern Italy, Michael Broers, *Napoleonic Imperialism and the Savoyard Monarchy, 1773–1821: State-building in Piedmont* (Lampeter, 1997).

An analysis of the historiographical traditions in foreign policy can be found in Geyl's *Napoleon: For and Against,* and more recently Natalie Petiteau, *Napoléon, de la mythologie à l'histoire* (Paris, 1999). A cursory but not particularly inspiring overview of Napleonic foreign policy can be found in Jeremy Black, *From Louis XIV to Napoleon: the Fate of a Great Power* (London, 1999), ch. 7; and Roger Dufraisse and Michael Kerautret, *La France napoléonienne: Aspects extérieurs 1799–1815* (Paris, 1999). Harold C. Deutsch's *The Genesis of Napoleonic Imperialism* (Cambridge, MA, 1938), André Fugier's *La Révolution Française et l'empire* (Paris, 1954) and Edouard Driault's *Napoléon et L'Europe* (2 vols., Paris, 1910), although a little dated, are still worth consulting. Foreign policy is briefly treated in the relevant parts of Ellis, *The Napoleonic Empire* and his *Napoleon*, and in chapters 14 and 15 of Lyons, *Napoleon Bonaparte and the Legacy of the French Revolution*. They should be read in conjunction with Gates, *The Napoleonic Wars*. The most impressive recent survey of the Napoleonic wars from a foreign-political perspective can be found in Paul W. Schroeder, *The Transformation of European Politics, 1763–1848* (Oxford, 1994) which it offers time and again alternative perspectives to traditional interpretations. An important supplement to it is Esdaile, *The Wars of Napoleon*, which sets the military campaigns themselves in their broader political, diplomatic, social and economic context. Broers, *Europe under Napoleon*, provides an insightful analysis of French hegemony in Europe and introduces the notion of an 'inner' and an 'outer' empire. The last chapters of T. C. W. Blanning, *The French Revolutionary Wars, 1787–1802* (London, 1996), as well as being a wonderful summary of the foreign political events leading to the wars, deal with the impact of the French occupation in Italy and Germany as well as the much neglected naval campaign in the Mediterranean.

For the similarities between Ancien Regime and Napoleonic foreign policy, see Orville T. Murphy, 'Napoleon's international politics: how much did he owe to the past?', *Journal of Military History* 54 (1990), pp. 163–71. Harold T. Parker. 'Why did Napoleon invade Russia? A study in motivation and the interrelations of personality and social structure', *Journal of Military History* 54 (1990), pp. 131–46, suggests a number of tentative links between Napoleon's personality and foreign policy.

There was a time when the internal, domestic history of Europe featured hardly at all in studies of the Napoleonic period, but this has undergone great change in recent years, and now the study of 'the empire behind the lines', receives increasing attention in all serious academic works on the period. Even Charles Esdaile's essentially military study of the period – *The Wars of Napoleon* – gives considerable and considered attention to internal matters. The real break-through in the general literature came with Woolf's cerebral *Napoleon's Integration of Europe* and the succinct, perceptive work by Geoffrey Ellis, *The Napoleonic Empire* (Basingstake, London and New York, 1991).

Together, Woolf and Ellis shifted the focus of Napoleonic studies away from the sound and fury of battle, for the student. See also Broers, *Europe under Napoleon*.

In other respects, too, English readers are now much better provided for in this wider European field than they were even ten years ago. Of the earlier works, Connelly's *Napoleon's Satellite Kingdoms* has weathered best and remains a useful introduction. The aims, mechanisms and effects of French rule in the subject states of the 'Grand Empire' are briefly treated in the relevant parts of Ellis, *The Napoleonic Empire* and in chapters 4 and 5 of his *Napoleon*. Lyons, *Napoleon Bonaparte and the Legacy of the French Revolution* covers some of the same ground rather more expansively. Among the more comprehensive studies of Napoleonic rule in the annexed departments, and in the subject and allied states, as seen through the reactions of the ruled, Woolf, *Napoleon's Integration of Europe*, and Broers, *Europe under Napoleon* can be particularly recommended.

There is a growing literature in English on the non-French parts of the Empire and the satellite states, which should be read in conjunction with the works of Forrest and Woloch, who are both essentially interested in 'the French interior', as contemporaries called France. The Rhineland has been treated by Michael Rowe, 'Between Empire and home town: Napoleonic rule on the Rhine, 1799–1814', *HJ* 42 (1999). On the Napoleonic Kingdom of Italy, two key articles by the American scholar Alex Grab, which have appeared only recently, have added greatly to our understanding of the problems first explored by Forrest and Woloch in one of the most important parts of the Napoleonic state system: 'Army, state and society: conscription and desertion in Napoleonic Italy, 1802–1814', *JMH* 67 (1995), and the more wide-ranging 'State power, brigandage and rural resistance in Napoleonic Italy', *EHQ* 25 (1995). For the imperial departments of neighbouring Piedmont, there are the following works by M. Broers, all of which attempt to deal with similar questions: 'Policing Piedmont: "the well ordered police state" in the age of revolution, 1794–1821', *Criminal Justice History* 15 (1994), and the relevant chapters of *Napoleonic Imperialism and the Savoyard Monarchy, 1773–1821: State Building in Piedmont* (Lampeter, 1997). In the wider context of Napoleonic Italy as a whole, see M. Broers, 'The police and the *padroni*: Italian *notabili*, French gendarmes and the origins of the centralised state in Napoleonic Italy', *EHQ* 26 (1996). Above all, the well-established study by John Davis, *Conflict and Control: Law and Order in Nineteenth Century Italy* (London, 1988), sets the Napoleonic period in a wider chronological framework. The guerrilla war in northern Spain has also been approached, at least partly, in the context of law and order, by John Tone in *The Fatal Knot*, and in 'Napoleon's uncongenial sea: guerrilla warfare in Navarre during the Peninsular War, 1808–14', *EHQ* 26 (1996). It has also been studied for neighbouring Aragón, with less success, by D. Alexander in *Rod of Iron: French Counterinsurgency policy in Aragon during the Peninsular War* (Wilmington, Del., 1985).

Bibliographical material on popular resistance to the Napoleonic Empire is neither abundant nor particularly satisfactory, it only being in recent years that historians have begun to examine the problem in terms other than those of narrative military history. As a beginning, however, it is at least now possible to consult the introductions that are to be found in Woolf, *Napoleon's Integration of Europe*, Esdaile, *The Wars of Napoleon*, and Broers, *Europe under Napoleon*, all of which stress the importance of such issues as banditry, social unrest and resistance to enlightened reform, whether Napoleonic or absolutist. Beyond the necessarily brief treatments which these authors provide, however, there is little to be found of a generic nature, it being necessary instead to turn to works with a much narrower geographical focus.

Turning first of all to France herself, an excellent starting point is constituted by the relevant sections of D. M. G. Sutherland, *France, 1789–1815: Revolution and Counter-Revolution* (London, 1985). Beyond that, the question of draft evasion and desertion is covered most admirably by Forrest, *Conscripts and Deserters*, E. Arnold, 'Some observations on the French opposition to Napoleonic conscription, 1804–1806', *FHS* 4 (1966), and Woloch, 'Napoleonic conscription: state power and civil society', *PP* 111 (1986). Meanwhile, G. Lewis, 'Political brigandage and popular disaffection in the south east of France, 1795–1804', in G. Lewis and C. Lucas (eds.), *Beyond the Terror: Essays in French Regional and Social History 1794–1815* (Cambridge, 1983), and G. Lewis, *The Second Vendée: the Continuity of Counter-Revolution in the Department of the Gard, 1789–1815* (Oxford, 1978) between them constitute a helpful regional case-study.

Moving on to other areas of the Napoleonic Empire, the situation in the south is admirably dealt with in A. Grab, 'Popular risings in Napoleonic Italy', *CREP* (1990), idem; A. Grab, 'State power, brigandage and rural resistance in Napoleonic Italy', *EHQ* 25 (1995); and idem, 'Army, state and society: conscription and desertion in Napoleonic Italy, 1802–1814', *JMH* 67 (1995). Rather less helpful, at least in their approach, are M. Finley, 'Patriots or brigands? The Calabrian partisans, 1806–1812', *CREP* (1991); idem, 'The most monstrous of wars: suppression of Calabrian brigandage, 1806–1811', *CREP* (1989); and idem, *Most Monstruous of Wars: Napoleonic Guerrilla War in Southern Italy, 1806–1811* (Columbia, SC, 1994).

However scant, coverage of popular resistance in Italy is princely indeed besides that which has been accorded to Germany and the Tyrol. In so far as the former is concerned, there is almost nothing in English other than an extremely suggestive chapter in T. C. W. Blanning, *The French Revolution in Germany: Occupation and Resistance in the Rhineland, 1792–1802* (Oxford, 1983), whilst discussion of the latter is confined to the essentially narrative F. Eyck, *Loyal Rebels: Andreas Hofer and the Tyrolean Uprising of 1809* (Lanham, New York and London, 1986) and L. Harford, 'Napoleon and the subjugation of the Tyrol', *CREP* (1989). However, the 1980s saw a spate of German works on the Tyrol including W. Pfaundler and W. Kofler, *Der Tiroler Feiheitskampf unter Andreas Hofer* (Munich, 1984), D. Stutzer, *Andreas Hofer und die Bayern in Tirol* (Munich, 1983), and B. Wurzer, *Tiroler Freiheitskampf: Andreas Hofer und der Heldenhafte Aufstand eines Volkes 1809* (Nuremberg, 1984), and it may well be that these contain fresh insights.

Best covered of all is Spain although here, too, there is much room for improvement (Portugal, alas, has by contrast been absolutely ignored). Thirty-five years after its publication there is still no replacement for G. Lovett, *Napoleon and the Birth of Modern Spain* (New York, 1965) as a general introduction to the Spanish insurrection against Napoleon, but its views are now increasingly dated, and they should now be supplemented by the more nuanced ideas expressed in B. Hamnett, *La Política Española en una Edad Revolucionaria* (Mexico City, 1985), M. Moreno Alonso, *Los Españoles durante la Ocupación Napoleónica* (Málaga, 1997) and Charles Esdaile, *From Constitution to Civil War: Spain in the Liberal Age, 1808–1939* (Oxford, 2000). For the guerrillas in particular, the traditional view is stated by G. Lovett, 'The Spanish guerrillas and Napoleon', *CREP* (1975); and D. Chandler, 'Wellington and the guerrillas', in idem (ed.), *On the Napoleonic Wars: Collected Essays* (London, 1994), this being strongly questioned by C. Esdaile, 'Heroes or villains? The Spanish guerrillas and the Peninsular War', *History Today* 38 (1988) and C. Esdaile, ' "Heroes or villains" revisited: fresh thoughts on *la guerrilla*', in I. Fletcher (ed.), *The Peninsular War: Aspects of the Struggle for the Iberian Peninsula* (Staplehurst, 1998). Contrasting with Esdaile's critique of the guerrillas are the much more traditional J. Tone, *The Fatal Knot: the Guerrilla War in Navarre and the Defeat of Napoleon in Spain* (Chapel Hill, NC, 1994), idem, 'Napoleon's uncongenial sea: guerrilla warfare in Navarre during the Peninsular War, 1808–1814', *EHQ* 26 (1996), and D. Alexander, *Rod of Iron: French*

Counterinsurgency policy in Aragon during the Peninsular War (Wilmington, Del., 1985). For a work that focuses on the French side of the guerrilla conflict, see Alexander, *Rod of Iron*. However, one wishes that the essentially positive view which the authors concerned have of parts of the north could be supplemented in so far as the rest of Spain is concerned by something other than such more-or-less hagiographical studies of individual irregular commanders as A. Cassiniello Pérez, *Juan Martín, 'El Empecinado', o el Amor a la Libertad* (Madrid, 1995). Certainly, such modern regional studies as M. López Pérez and I. Lara Martín-Portugués, *Entre la Guerra y la Paz: Jaén, 1808–1814* (Granada, 1993) and M. Ardit Lucas, *Revolución Liberal y Revuelta Campesina: un Ensayo sobre la Desintegración del Régimen Feudal en el País Valenciano, 1793–1840* (Barcelona, 1977) tend to confirm the view of the sceptic rather than the believer. Two further works – J. Sánchez Fernández, *Nos Invaden! Guerrilla y Represión durante la Guerra de la Independencia Española, 1808–1814* (Valladolid, 2000), and idem, *La Guerilla Vallisoletana, 1808–1814* (Valladolid, 1997) – give an excellent picture of events in an area very different from Navarre.

The literature on Britain and Napoleon is large. An attempt to assess some recent work can be found in Brendan Simms, 'Britain and Napoleon', *HJ* 41 (1998). Curiously, there is no modern large-scale scholarly account of Britain's contest with Napoleon which covers the entire period from the late 1790s to the battle of Waterloo. P. Coquelle, *Napoleon and England 1803–1813* (London, 1904), a study from unprinted documents translated by Gordon D. Knox, with an introduction by J. Holland Rose, is by no means an apologia for Napoleon but short and very dated. J. B. Fortescue's *British Statesmen of the Great War, 1793–1814* (Oxford, 1911) is much broader than its title suggests and can still be read with pleasure. Jean Trani and J. C. Carmigiani, *Napoléon et l'Angleterre: vingt-deux ans d'affrontements sur terre et sur mer, 1793–1815* (Paris, 1994), with a preface by Jean Tulard, is essentially a picture book, though not an unserious one. Emma Vincent Macleod, *A War of Ideas: British Attitudes to the Wars Against Revolutionary France 1792–1802* (Aldershot, Ashgate, 1998), makes a balanced case for a *Weltanschauungskrieg*, but is chiefly focused on the 1790s and says relatively little about Napoleon. Rory Muir's *Britain and the Defeat of Napoleon, 1807–1815* (New Haven, Conn., 1996) perforce covers only half the story; a 'prequel' is needed. The short *British Strategy in the Napoleonic War 1803–1815* by Christopher D. Hall is occasionally laboured and, especially towards the end, rushed, but provides a sound synthesis. The best overall, thematic treatment is probably still the ten-year old collection edited by H. T. Dickinson, *Britain and the French Revolution, 1789–1815* (London and Basingstoke, 1989), which contains extremely pertinent contributions on politics, society, strategy, ideas and economics by the relevant experts. For a most welcome view of Britain in the overall European context see Esdaile, *The Wars of Napoleon*, ch. 5. For a diverting, florid and eccentric interpretation of Napoleon's 'vendetta' with Britain see B. Fortescue, *Napoleon's Heritage: an Ethnic Reconstruction which Explains his Mortal Duel with England* (London, 1934).

Specific periods of the struggle between Britain and France have been well covered. Piers Mackesy, the predominant strategic historian of the war, has published *The War in the Mediterranean, 1803–1810* (London, 1957), *The Strategy of Overthrow, 1798–1799* (London, 1974), *War without Victory: the Downfall of Pitt, 1799–1802* (Oxford, 1984), and, most recently, *British Victory in Egypt, 1801: the End of Napoleon's Conquest* (London and New York, 1995). His works may be supplemented by A. B. Rodger's *The War of the Second Coalition, 1798–1801: a Strategic Commentary* (Oxford, 1964); Oscar Browning's dated *England and Napoleon in 1803* (London, 1887), which covers the breakdown of the peace of Amiens, and by Muir's *Britain and the Defeat of Napoleon*, which takes the story from 1807. Naval issues and home defence are well covered in Richard Glover, *Britain at Bay: Defence against Bonaparte, 1803–1814* (London and New York, 1973). British subsidy policy is well covered in John M. Sherwig, *Guineas and Gunpowder: British Foreign Aid in the Wars with France* (Cambridge, Mass., 1969). For fascinating accounts of the embarrassment Napoleon's arrival off the British coast caused in 1815 see Jean Duhamel, *The Fifty Days: Napoleon in England*, trans. R. A. Hall (London, 1969) and Michael John Thornton, *Napoleon and the St Helena Decision* (Stanford, Calif., 1968).

On the biographical front the third volume of John Ehrman's biography of Pitt *The Consuming Struggle*, is principally, though by no means exclusively, devoted to his subject's confrontation with Napoleon. Herbert Butterfield's 'Charles James Fox and Napoleon. The peace negotiations of 1806', *The Creighton Lecture in History 1961* (London 1962) is – as the title suggests – narrowly focused on the Franco–British negotiations in 1806. British enthusiasts for Napoleon are discussed in E. Tangye Lean's curious but stimulating *The Napoleonists: a Study in Political Disaffection 1760/1960* (Oxford, 1970). For the Napoleonic hold on the English Romantic imagination see Simon Bainbridge, *Napoleon and English Romanticism* (Cambridge, 1995).

The impact of Napoleon on British society has been intensively covered by Clive Emsley, most accessibly if not most recently in *British Society and the French Wars, 1793–1815* (London and Basingstoke, 1979). British military mobilisation is also discussed in considerable and fascinating detail by J. E. Cookson, *The British Armed Nation, 1793–1815* (Oxford, 1997). The radical response is covered in Peter Spence, *The Birth of Romantic Radicalism: War, Popular Politics and English Radical Reformism* (Aldershot, 1996). For an attempt to put the impact of Napoleon in a comparative perspective see Brendan Simms, 'Reform in Britain and Prussia, 1797–1815: (confessional) fiscal-military state and military-agrarian complex', *Proceedings of the British Academy* 100 (1999).

British attitudes are discussed in F. J. MacCunn's inevitably dated *The Contemporary English View of Napoleon* (London, 1914). Popular satirical and polemical engagement with Napoleon is well covered in John Ashton, *English Caricature and Satire on Napoleon I* (London, 1888, re-ed., 1968), H. F. B. Wheeler and A. M. Broadley, *Napoleon and the Invasion of England: the Story of the Great Terror with Numerous Illustrations from Contemporary Prints, Caricatures, etc.* (London, 1908), and in the useful collection in Frank J. Klingberg and Sigurd B. Hustvedt (eds.), *The Warning Drum: the British Home Front Faces Napoleon. Broadsides of 1803* (Berkeley and Los Angeles, Calif., 1944). The propaganda war is covered by Robert Holtman, *Napoleonic Propaganda* (Baton Rouge, La, 1950, re-ed., New York, 1969), A. D. Harvey, 'European attitudes to Britain during the French revolutionary and Napoleonic era', *History* 63 (1978) and Simon Burrows, 'The struggle for European opinion in the Napoleonic wars: British francophone propaganda, 1803–1814', *French History* 11 (1997).

The coverage of Napoleonic central Europe by works in English is substantial, but uneven. For reasons of space, this list is selective, especially in those areas which are well served. Two recent syntheses of nineteenth-century German history include substantial sections on the Napoleonic era: Thomas Nipperdey, *Germany from Napoleon to Bismarck, 1800–1866*, trans. Daniel Nolan (Dublin, 1996); and James J. Sheehan, *German History 1770–1866* (Oxford, 1989). Also useful are sections of David Blackbourn, *The Long Nineteenth Century: a History of Germany, 1780–1918* (New York and Oxford, 1998), and Brendan Simms, *The Struggle for Mastery in Germany, 1779–1850* (London and New York, 1998). Though dated, H. A. L. Fisher, *Studies in Napoleonic Statesmanship: Germany* (Oxford, 1903) remains useful in default of any more recent synthesis focused on the Napoleonic age.

The Holy Roman Empire in its final years is analysed by John G. Gagliardo, *Reich and Nation: the Holy Roman Empire as Idea and Reality, 1763–1806* (Bloomington, Ind., and London, 1980). For the urban dimension, see Mack Walker, *German Home Towns: Community, State, General Estate, 1648–1871* (Ithaca, NY, 1971), and for the military, Peter H. Wilson, *German Armies: War and German Politics 1648–1806* (London, 1998). Many publications are devoted to the French Revolution and Germany. A good place to start is T. C. W. Blanning, 'The French Revolution and the modernisation of Germany', *Central European History* (hereafter *CEH*) 2 (1989).

Napoleonic Prussia is well covered by works in English. For Prussian reforms before 1806, see Otto Hintze, 'Prussian reform movements before 1806', in Felix Gilbert (ed.), *The Historical Essays of Otto Hintze* (New York, 1975). For the post-1806 reforms: G. S. Ford, *Stein and the Era of Reform in Prussia, 1807–15* (Princeton, NJ, 1922); Marion W. Gray, *Prussia in Transition: Society and Politics under the Stein Reform Ministry of 1808* (Philadelphia, 1986); idem., 'Schroetter, Schon and society: aristocratic liberalism versus middle-class liberalism in Prussia, 1808', *CEH* 6 (1973); Friedrich Meinecke, *The Age of German Liberation 1795–1815* (Berkeley, Calif., 1977); R. C. Raack, *The Fall of Stein* (Cambridge, Mass., 1965); and W. M. Simon, *The Failure of the Prussian Reform Movement, 1807–19* (New York, 1971). Several publications are devoted to the *Junkers* and conservatism: Robert M. Berdahl, *The Politics of the Prussian Nobility: the Development of a Conservative Ideology, 1770–1848* (Princeton, NJ, 1988); F. L. Carsten, *A History of the Prussian Junkers* (Aldershot, 1989); G. A. Craig, 'The failure of reform: Stein and Marwitz', in idem. (ed.), *The End of Prussia* (Madison, Wis., 1984); and Klaus Epstein, *The Genesis of German Conservatism* (Princeton, NJ, 1966).

On the Hanoverian dimension see Philip G. Dwyer, 'Prussia and the Armed Neutrality: the decision to invade Hanover in 1801', *International History Review* 15 (1993), pp. 661–87; idem, 'Two definitions of neutrality: Prussia, the European states-system and the French invasion of Hanover in 1803', *International History Review* 19 (1997), pp. 522–40; and Brendan Simms, '"An odd question enough". Charles James Fox, the crown and British policy during the Hanoverian crisis of 1806', *HJ* 38 (1995), pp. 567–96.

For the Habsburg monarchy, see chapter 4 of C. A. Macartney, *The Habsburg Empire 1790–1918* (London, 1971), the final chapter of C. W. Ingrao, *The Habsburg Monarchy, 1618–1815* (Cambridge, 1994), and the first part of Robin Okey, *The Habsburg Monarchy: from Enlightenment to Eclipse, c. 1765–1918* (London and New York, 2000), plus P. G. M. Dickson, 'Monarchy and bureaucracy in late eighteenth century Austria', *European History Review* (1995). Ernst Wangermann, *From Joseph II to the Jacobin Trials: Government Policy and Public Opinion in the Habsburg Dominions in the Period of the French Revolution* (Oxford, 1965), provides a good account of the political 'freeze' following the 'Jacobin' conspiracies. Broader than its title suggests is K. Roider, 'The Habsburg foreign ministry and the political reform of 1800–1805', *CEH* 22 (1982). Also, James A. Vann, 'Habsburg policy and the Austrian war of 1809', *CEH* 7 (1974). Little exists on the non-German nationalities. For Hungary, see R. J. W. Evans, 'The Habsburgs and the Hungarian problem, 1790–1848', in *TRHS* 39 (1989), B. Kiraly, 'Napoleon's proclamation of 1809 and its Hungarian echo', in S. Winters and J. Held (eds.), *Intellectual and Social Developments in the Habsburg Empire from Maria Theresa to World War I* (New York, 1975), and Domokos Kosáry, *Napoléon et la Hongrie* (Budapest, 1979). For Bohemia, J. Zacek, 'Contemporary Czech popular sentiment towards the French Revolution and Napoleon', *CREP* (1989).

For an introduction to the 'Third Germany', consult H. Schmitt, 'Germany without Prussia: a closer look at the Confederation of the Rhine', *German Studies Review* 6 (1983). For Bavaria, A. Cronenberg, 'Montgelas and the reorganisation of Napoleonic Bavaria', *CREP* (1990). For Baden, Loyd E. Lee, *The Politics of Harmony: Civil Service, Liberalism, and Social Reform in Baden, 1800–1850* (Newark, 1980); also for Baden (again, Loyd E. Lee) as well as Nassau (Barbara Anderson) and Saxony (Lawrence J. Flockherzie) see the 'Symposium: state building in the "Third Germany"', *CEH* 24 (1991). For Jérôme's Westphalia, Owen Connelly, *Napoleon's Satellite Kingdoms* (New York and London, 1965), ch. 6. For Hessian nobles and the new Westphalian state, Gregory W. Pedlow, *The Survival of the Hessian Nobility 1770–1870* (Princeton, NJ, 1988). For the rapid proliferation of public debts and its constitutional implications, Hans-Peter Ullmann, 'The emergence of modern public debts in Bavaria and Baden between 1780 and 1820', in Peter-Christian Witt (ed.), *Wealth and Taxation in Central Europe: the History and Sociology of Public Finance* (Leamington Spa, Hamburg and New York, 1987).

For an overview of intellectual developments, see Reinhold Aris, *History of Political Thought in Germany from 1789 to 1815* (London, 1936), and Frederick C. Beiser, *Enlightenment, Revolution and Romanticism: the Genesis of Modern German Political Thought* (Cambridge, Mass., 1992). Also illuminating is G. A. Craig, 'German intellectuals and politics, 1789–1815: the case of Heinrich von Kleist', *CEH* 2 (1969), as is Golo Mann, *Secretary of Europe: the Life of Friedrich Gentz, Enemy of Napoleon* (New Haven, Conn., 1946). For nationalism, see Hagen Schulze, *The Course of German Nationalism: from Fichte to Bismarck, 1763–1867* (Cambridge, 1991), Marion W. Gray, 'The rise of German nationalism and the wars of liberation (1803–1814)', in Donald D. Howard (ed.), *Napoleonic Military History: a Bibliography* (New York and London, 1986), John Breuilly (ed.), *The State of Germany: the National Idea in the Making, Unmaking and Remaking of the Modern Nation-state* (London, 1992), and Robert M. Berdahl, 'New thoughts on German nationalism', *American Historical Review* 77/1 (1972). For the Austrian dimension, Walter Consuelo Langsam, *The Napoleonic Wars and German Nationalism in Austria* (New York, 1930), and (for the 1809 Tyrolean uprising), F. Gunther Eyck, *Loyal Rebels: Andreas Hofer and the Tyrolean Uprising of 1809* (Lanham, New York and London, 1986). For German nationalism focused on the Confederation of the Rhine, Robert D. Billinger Jr, 'Good and true Germans. The "nationalism" of the *Rheinbund* princes, 1806–1814', in Heinz Duchhardt and Andreas Kunz (eds.), *Reich oder Nation? Mitteleuropa 1780–1815* (Mainz, 1998), and W. O. Shanahan, 'A neglected source of German nationalism: the Confederation of the Rhine, 1806–13', in *Nationalism: Essays in Honour of Louis L. Snyder* (Westport, Conn., 1981). For romanticism, consult H. Reiss, *The Political Thought of the German Romantics, 1793–1815* (Oxford, 1955), and S. Heit, 'German Romanticism: an ideological response to Napoleon', *CREP* (1980).

For French policy towards Germany in the 1790s, see S. S. Biro, *The German Policy of Revolutionary France*, 2 vols. (Cambridge, Mass., 1957). Karl A. Roider Jr, *Baron Thugut and Austria's Response to the French Revolution* (Princeton, NJ, 1987), covers Austrian foreign policy up until 1801. For Prussia, see Brendan Simms, *The Impact of Napoleon: Prussian High Politics, Foreign Policy and the Crisis of the Executive, 1797–1806* (Cambridge, 1997), and Philip G. Dwyer 'Prussia during the French revolutionary and Napoleonic Wars', in idem (ed.), *The Rise of Prussia* (London, 2000). Levinger, *Enlightened Nationalism: The Transformation of Prussian Political Culture, 1806–1848* (Oxford, 2000). E. E. Kraehe, *Metternich's German Policy*, 2 vols. (Princeton, NJ, 1963 and 1983), and D. Klang, 'Bavaria and the War of Liberation, 1813–1814', *FHS* 4 (1965), cover the later period.

The best introduction to the military dimension re Central Europe is Best, *War and Society in Revolutionary Europe*, which contains chapters on Prussia and Austria. For military structures and orders of battle, see Ray Johnson, *Napoleonic Armies: a Wargamer's Campaign Directory, 1805–1815* (London, 1984). John H. Gill, *With Eagles to Glory: Napoleon and his German Allies in the 1809 Campaign* (London, 1992) covers the contribution of the confederation states to Napoleon's war machine. For the Prussian army and reform, see O. Büsch, *Military System and Social Life in Old Regime Prussia, 1713–1807* (Atlantic Highlands, 1997), Charles Edward White, *The Enlightened Soldier: Scharnhorst and the Militärische Gesellschaft in Berlin, 1801–1805* (New York, Westport Conn., and London, 1989), W. Shanahan, *Prussian Military Reforms, 1786–1813* (New York, 1945), and (especially for wider social implications) Peter Paret, *Yorck and the Era of Prussian Reform 1807/15* (Princeton, NJ, 1966). Also useful is D. Showalter, 'The Prussian *Landwehr* and its critics, 1813–19', *CEH* 4 (1971). The Austrian angle is covered by Gunther E. Rothenburg, *Napoleon's Great Adversary: Archduke Charles and the Austrian Army, 1792–1814* (London,

1982). There is no good summary in English on the military history of the wars of liberation.

The most complete military history of the Peninsular War in English is still Charles Oman's seven-volume *A History of the Peninsular War* (London, 1902–30). Students can be grateful that Greenhill Books republished the work in 1995, later adding two new volumes, including a useful but uneven collection of recent essays on the war.

Oman dramatically revised the earlier standard in English, William Napier's tendentious five-volume *History of the War in the Peninsula and in the South of France* (London, 1834–40). Oman worked extensively in archives, and he even bothered to use a few Spanish sources, mainly letters and memoirs, to give at least the semblance of balance to his account. He replaced Napier's oddly wistful memories of Napoleon and the Empire with a more critical attitude toward the French regime.

Naturally, the work is now dated and flawed, especially as an entry point for understanding the Peninsular War in its Spanish context. Oman was expansive in his first volume, where he allowed himself to treat important subjects like the siege of Zaragoza, in which the British took no part. In later volumes, however, he focused almost exclusively and rarely critically on Wellington and the British expeditionary army. Oman was uncertain when dealing with Spanish affairs, unacquainted with important Spanish sources, and unsympathetic to Spanish perspectives. In an era given to measuring skulls and generalising about national character, Oman had no doubt of British superiority, not only over the French and Portuguese, but especially over the Spanish, whom he scorned only slightly less than Napier had. National, racial and class prejudices informed Oman's work at every turn, and incapacitated him for understanding Spanish politics or the nature, scope and power of the popular resistance in Spain.

Gabriel Lovett's more accessible two volume *Napoleon and the Birth of Modern Spain* (New York, 1965) is less complete as purely military history, but much more astute on important themes such as the nature of the urban revolutions of 1808. Students should read Lovett as a corrective to the accounts by Oman and Napier. However, Lovett went too far in uncritically accepting a romantic Spanish view of the guerrillas, a tendency found in certain other histories of popular resistance written in the 1960s.

On the subject of Spanish politics and the revolution of 1808, the best work is naturally in Spanish, including numerous memoirs and Count Toreno's classic *Historia del levantamiento, guerra y revolución de España* (Madrid, 1835). In English, the essays by Karl Marx on revolutionary Spain originally published in the *New York Daily Tribune* in 1854 are well worth reading. They were gathered in *Revolution in Spain* (London, 1939).

Richard Herr's 'Good, evil and Spain's rising against Napoleon', in Herr and Parker (eds.), *Ideas in History* (Durham, NC, 1965), has been the most influential work in English. Herr argued that popular resistance to France grew out of widespread hatred for Spain's reforming minister, Manuel Godoy, a hatred rooted in opposition to Godoy's liberal reforms and, more importantly, in the general economic malaise and suffering that affected Spain in the early nineteenth century. Herr overestimated the scale and spontaneity of popular involvement and underestimated the active role of elites in engineering various tumults and risings that initiated the resistance. He also borrowed too heavily on an imperial rhetoric that viewed the Spanish resistance as a reactionary defence of old ways against Godoy and, later, Joseph Bonaparte. But Herr's work was a great advance on earlier – and some later – accounts that stressed religious and nationalist motives for resistance.

On the subject of the French regime in Spain, students should begin with Joseph Bonaparte's memoirs as well as *The Confidential Correspondence of Napoleon Bonaparte with His Brother Joseph* (London, 1856). Owen Connelly's *The Gentle Bonaparte* (New York, 1968) and portions of his *Napoleon's Satellite Kingdoms* (New York and London, 1965) are the best biographical approaches in English. Other works that focus on French military problems are David Gates, *The Spanish Ulcer: a History of the Peninsular War* (London, 1986) and Donald Horward, *Napoleon and Iberia: the Twin Sieges of Ciudad Rodrigo and Almeida* (Tallahassee, Fla., 1984).

Charles Esdaile is the author of some of the best recent work on the Spanish war. *The Spanish Army in the Peninsular War* (Manchester, 1988) and *The Duke of Wellington and the Command of the Spanish Army* (London, 1990) are indispensable. These works together with his general survey *The Wars of Napoleon* (London, 1995) are invaluable for understanding the war in Spain.

The historiography of imperial Russia has traditionally subsumed the Napoleonic experience under the broader theme of the decline of enlightened absolutism and the emergence of a Europeanised elite culture and a distinctive social structure in the late eighteenth and early nineteenth century. Important works on Russian politics and enlightened absolutism include Marc Raeff, *The Well-ordered Police State: Social and Institutional Change through Law in the Germanies and Russia, 1600–1800* (New Haven, Conn., and London, 1983); Isabel de Madariaga, *Russia in the Age of Catherine the Great* (New Haven, Conn., and London, 1981); and John P. LeDonne, *Absolutism and Ruling Class: the Formation of the Russian Political Order 1700–1825* (New York and Oxford,

1991). The overarching issues of Russian social history have recently been explored by Elise Kimerling Wirtschafter in her books *Structures of Society: Imperial Russia's 'People of Various Ranks'* (DeKalb, Ill., 1994) and *Social Identity in Imperial Russia* (DeKalb, Ill., 1997). A good starting point for research on urban society is J. Michael Hittle's *The Service City: State and Townsmen in Russia, 1600–1800* (Cambridge, Mass., and London, 1979). An excellent discussion of rural society (both nobles and peasants) in a comparative context is Peter Kolchin, *Unfree Labor: American Slavery and Russian Serfdom* (Cambridge, Mass., and London, 1987).

The development of a civil society in Russia is discussed in Marc Raeff, *Origins of the Russian Intelligentsia: the Eighteenth-century Nobility* (New York, 1966); Douglas Smith, *Working the Rough Stone: Freemasonry and Society in Eighteenth-century Russia* (DeKalb, Ill., 1999); J. Laurence Black, *Citizens for the Fatherland: Education, Educators, and Pedagogical Ideals in Eighteenth-century Russia* (Boulder, Colo., and New York, 1979); and Gary Marker, *Publishing, Printing, and the Origins of Intellectual Life in Russia, 1700–1800* (Princeton, NJ, 1985).

The principal English-language works on Catherine II are Isabel de Madariaga's books *Russia in the Age of Catherine the Great* (cited above) and *Catherine the Great: a Short History* (New Haven, Conn., and London, 1990), and John T. Alexander's *Catherine the Great: Life and Legend* (Oxford, 1989). On Paul I, there is Roderick E. McGrew's *Paul I of Russia 1754–1801* (Oxford, 1992). Two good biographies of Alexander I are Janet M. Hartley, *Alexander I* (London and New York, 1994) and Allen McConnell, *Tsar Alexander I: Paternalistic Reformer* (New York, 1970). The politics of Alexander's court, with particular attention to domestic reforms, are the subject of Marc Raeff's *Michael Speransky: Statesman of Imperial Russia, 1772–1839* (The Hague, 1969); for an interpretation that differs from Raeff's, see David Christian, 'The political ideals of Michael Speransky', *Slavonic and East European Review* 54 (April 1976), pp. 192–213. Paul I's foreign policy is discussed in Hugh Ragsdale, *Détente in the Napoleonic Era: Bonaparte and the Russians* (Lawrence, Kans., 1980); Alexander I's foreign policy is studied by Patricia Kennedy Grimsted in *The Foreign Ministers of Alexander I: Political Attitudes and the Conduct of Russian Diplomacy, 1801–1825* (Berkeley and Los Angeles, Calif., 1969).

While there is a considerable literature on the 1812 campaign, often written by non-specialists and intended for a popular audience, there appear to be no scholarly, book-length studies in English of the Napoleonic campaigns from a Russian perspective and based on Russian sources. However, the interested reader might consult the following works, which rely almost exclusively on western sources: Alan Palmer, *Napoleon in Russia* (New York, 1967); Richard K. Riehn, *1812: Napoleon's Russian Campaign* (New York, 1990); Nigel Nicolson, *Napoleon 1812* (New York, 1985); and Curtis Cate, *The War of the Two Emperors: the Duel Between Napoleon and Alexander: Russia, 1812* (New York, 1985). Eugene Tarle, *Napoleon's Invasion of Russia 1812* (New York, 1942), is the English translation of a classic Soviet analysis of the war.

Two valuable studies of the 1812 invasion's effect on Russian society, written by specialists in the field, are: Janet Hartley, 'Russia in 1812, Part I: the French presence in the Gubernii of Smolensk and Mogilev', *Jahrbücher für Geschichte Osteuropas* 38 (1990), pp. 178–98, and 'Russia in 1812, Part II: the Russian administration of Kaluga *Gubernija*', *Jahrbücher für Geschichte Osteuropas* 38 (1990), pp. 399–416; and Yitzhak Y. Tarasulo, 'The Napoleonic invasion of 1812 and the political and social crisis in Russia' (ductoral thesis, Yale University, 1983). Primary sources include Nadezhda Durova, *The Cavalry Maiden: Journals of a Russian Officer in the Napoleonic Wars*, transl. by Mary Fleming Zirin (Bloomington, Ind., 1988), about a woman who served in the army in male disguise; *In the Service of the Tsar against Napoleon: the Memoirs of Denis Davidov, 1806–1814*, transl. and ed. by Gregory Troubetzkoy (London and Mechanicsburg, Pa., 1999); Sir Robert Thomas Wilson, *A Sketch of the Military and Political Power of Russia, in the Year 1817* (New York, 1817); *With Napoleon in Russia: the Memoirs of General de Caulaincourt, Duke of Vicenza* (New York, 1935), by one of Napoleon's leading generals and a former ambassador to Russia; M. de Fezensac, *The Russian Campaign, 1812*, transl. by Lee Kennett (Athens, Ga, 1970); Carl von Clausewitz, *The Campaign of 1812 in Russia*, transl. by Forrestt A. Miller (Hattiesburg, Miss., 1970); and Jakob Walter, *The Diary of a Napoleonic Foot Soldier*, ed. Marc Raeff (New York, 1991). The most important literary depiction of Russia in the Napoleonic wars is Leon Tolstoy's *War and Peace*.

Several books examine the political and ideological developments in Russian public opinion and government policy under Alexander I, including: James T. Flynn, *The University Reform of Tsar Alexander I 1802–1835* (Washington, 1988); Alexander M. Martin, *Romantics, Reformers, Reactionaries: Russian Conservative Thought and Politics in the Reign of Alexander I* (DeKalb, Ill., 1997); and Richard Pipes, *Karamzin's Memoir on Ancient and Modern Russia: a Translation and Analysis* (New York, 1964). A significant recent work on the connections between Russian domestic developments and international relations after 1815 is Theophilus C. Prousis's *Russian Society and the Greek Revolution* (DeKalb, Ill., 1994).

There is not, unfortunately, any up-to-date study of the Decembrist movement in English, so readers will have to make do with Anatole G. Mazour's rather dated *The First Russian Revolution, 1825: the Decembrist Movement, its Origins, Development, and Significance* (Stanford, Calif., 1937, reissued 1961). An alternative is a book by a very readable Soviet historian, which was published in the USSR in English translation: Natan Ia. Eidel'man, *Conspiracy against the Tsar* (Moscow, 1985). The reign of Nicholas I is studied in Nicholas Riasanovsky, *Nicholas I and Official Nationality in Russia, 1825–1855* (Berkeley and Los Angeles, Calif., 1959), and in W. Bruce Lincoln's books *Nicholas I: Emperor and Autocrat of All the Russias* (DeKalb, Ill., 1978) and *In the Vanguard of Reform: Russia's Enlightened Bureaucrats 1825–1861* (DeKalb, Ill., 1982).

There exists a variety of interesting primary sources, written or translated into English, on late eighteenth- and early nineteenth-century Russia. Among these are *Memoirs of Catherine the Great of Russia* (transl. by Katherine Anthony; New York, 1927); *The Memoirs of Princess Dashkova: Russia in the Time of Catherine the Great* (London and Durham, NC, 1995); *The Russian Journals of Martha and Catherine Wilmot* (London, 1934), which contains the letters of two British noblewomen who stayed in Russia in 1803–1808; Charles Francis Adams (ed.), *John Quincy Adams in Russia, Comprising Portions of the Diary of John Quincy Adams from 1809 to 1814* (New York and Washington, 1970) (Adams was US minister to the Russian court); and Sophie de Choiseul-Gouffier, *Historical Memoirs of the Emperor Alexander I and the Court of Russia* (transl. by Mary Bernice Patterson; Chicago, 1900). Two particularly thought-provoking primary sources are Robert Lyall, *The Character of the Russians and a Detailed History of Moscow* (London and Edinburgh, 1823), a rather critical account of Russian city life by a liberal Scotsman; and Sergei Aksakov, *A Russian Gentleman*, transl. by J. D. Duff (Oxford, 1994), which was written in the 1840s and describes, in nostalgic terms, life in rural Russia at the end of the eighteenth century. A more critical perspective on rural and small-town Russian life during the same period, written by the son of an Orthodox priest, is Dimitri I. Rostislavov, *A Memoir of Provincial Life in Russia from the 1760s to the 1820s*, transl. and edited by Alexander M. Martin (DeKalb, Ill., 2001). Essential reading for anyone using western primary sources and wishing to understand their concerns and biases is Martin Malia, *Russia under Western Eyes: from the Bronze Horseman to the Lenin Mausoleum* (Cambridge, Mass., and London, 1999).

The long-term legacy of Napoleonic imperialism in conquered Europe is now also well served in Michael Broers, *Europe after Napoleon: Revolution,*

Reaction, and Romanticism 1814–1848 (Manchester, 1996), and in the important collection of some fifteen conference papers recently published by David Laven and Lucy Riall (eds.), *Napoleon's Legacy: Problems of Government in Restoration Europe* (Oxford and New York, 2000). The latter, in spite of the brief format allowed to each of the individual contributors, covers a very wide arc across Napoleonic Europe, from various regional and topical angles, and is perhaps the most up-to-date index of the current state of research available in English.

NOTES

———— ◆ ————

Introduction

1. Gaspard Gourgaud, *Journal de Sainte-Hélène 1815–1818*, 2 vols. (Paris, n.d.), ii, pp. 107–108.
2. As well as the contribution in this volume by Harold T. Parker, one can also consult his article 'The formation of Napoleon's personality', *French Historical Studies* 7 (1971), pp. 6–26.
3. See Dorothy Carrington, *Napoleon and his Parents on the Threshold of History* (New York, 1988), pp. 113–40.
4. Geoffrey Ellis, 'The nature of Napoleonic imperialism', (in this volume), pp. 97–8.
5. On the importance of the family in Corsican society see François Pomponi, 'Sentiments révolutionnaire et esprit de parti en Corse au temps de la Révolution', in *Problèmes d'histoire de la Corse (de l'Ancien Régime à 1815): Actes de Colloque d'Ajaccio* (Paris, 1971), pp. 147–78; and, on the clan, idem, 'A la recherche d'un "invariant" historique: la structure clanique dans la société corse', in *Pieve e paesi. Communautés rurales corses* (Paris, 1978), pp. 7–30.
6. Alan Forrest, 'The military culture of Napoleonic France', (in this volume), pp. 43–59.
7. Annie Jourdan, *Napoléon: héros, imperator, mécène* (Paris, 1998), ch. 4.
8. Malcolm Crook, *Napoleon Comes to Power: Democracy and Dictatorship in Revolutionary France, 1795–1804* (Cardiff, 1998), p. 50.
9. Jean Tulard, *Napoléon, ou le mythe du sauveur* (Paris, 1977), pp. 115–29.
10. On the fraudulent plebiscite of the Year VIII see Claude Langlois, 'The voters', in Frank Kafker and James Laux (eds.), *Napoleon and his Times: Selected Interpretations* (Malabar, Fla, 1989), pp. 57–65.
11. Isser Woloch, 'The Napoleonic regime and French society', (in this volume), pp. 60–78; and idem, *The New Regime: Transformations of the French Civic Order, 1789–1820s* (New York, 1994), ch. 7.
12. For a discussion of the *notables* see the overview by Martyn Lyons, *Napoleon Bonaparte and the Legacy of the French Revolution* (London and New York, 1994), ch. 12.
13. Jean Tulard, *Napoléon et la noblesse d'Empire* (Paris, 1979), pp. 93–9, 146–54.
14. Lyons, *Napoleon and the French Revolution*, p. 167.
15. Forrest, 'Military culture', pp. 51–2.
16. Woloch, 'The Napoleonic regime', p. 73.
17. See Colin Lucas, 'Revolutionary violence and the Terror', in K. M. Baker (ed.), *The French Revolution and the Creation of Modern Political Culture* (Oxford, 1994), pp. 57–79.
18. Howard G. Brown, 'From organic society to security state: the war on brigandage in France, 1797–1802', *Journal of Modern History* 69 (1997), pp. 662, 677.
19. Ibid., p. 685.

20. *Correspondance de Napoléon Ier publiée par ordre de l'empereur Napoléon III*, 32 vols. (Paris, 1858–69), vi, nos. 4498, 4499.

21. Brown, 'From organic society to security state', pp. 685–8; idem, 'Domestic state violence: repression from the *Croquants* to the Commune', *Historical Journal* 42 (1999), p. 615.

22. Sibalis, 'The Napoleonic police state', (in this volume), pp. 79–83.

23. Michael Sibalis, 'Prisoners by *Mesure de haute police* under Napoleon I: reviving the *Lettres de cachet*', *Proceedings of the Annual Meeting of the Western Society for French History* 18 (1991), pp. 261–9.

24. Michael Sibalis, 'Internal exiles in Napoleonic France, 1799–1815', *Proceedings of the Annual Meeting of the Western Society for French History* 20 (1993), pp. 189–98.

25. Stuart Woolf, 'French civilization and ethnicity in the Napoleonic Empire', *Past & Present* 124 (1989), pp. 109–110.

26. Geoffrey Ellis, 'The nature of Napoleonic imperialism', (in this volume), pp. 97–117.

27. Michael Broers, 'Napoleon, Charlemagne and Lotharingia: acculturation and the borders of the Napoleonic Empire', *Historical Journal* 44 (2001), pp. 142–5.

28. Michael Broers, 'Policing the Empire: Napoleon and the pacification of Europe', (in this volume), pp. 153–4.

29. Philip G. Dwyer, 'Napoleon and the drive for glory: reflections on the making of French foreign policy', (in this volume), pp. 118–35.

30. Ellis, 'The nature of Napoleonic imperialism', (in this volume), pp. 108–13.

31. Paul W. Schroeder, *The Transformation of European Politics, 1763–1848* (Oxford, 1994), p. 376.

32. Alexander Grab, 'State, society and tax policy in Napoleonic Europe', (in this volume), pp. 169, 177 and 182. See also Jacques Wolff, 'Les insuffisantes finances napoléoniennes. Une des cause de l'échec de la tentative d'hégémonie européenne (1799–1814)', *Revue du Souvenir Napoléonien* 397 (1994), pp. 5–20.

33. For Napoleon's exactions in Italy, see Ferdinand Boyer, 'Les résponsabilités de Napoléon dans le transfert à Paris des oeuvres d'art de l'étranger', *Revue d'histoire moderne et contemporaine* 11 (1964), pp. 241–62.

34. Grab, 'State, society and tax policy', p. 185.

35. The most accurate calculations are those by Jacques Houdaille, 'Pertes de l'armée de terre sous le premier Empire, d'après les registres matricules', *Population* 27 (1972), pp. 27–50 (here pp. 42, 48–9).

36. Jean Tulard (ed.), *Dictionnaire Napoléon* (Paris, 1987), pp. 72, 828.

37. Woloch, *The New Regime*, pp. 418, 424; idem, 'Napoleonic conscription: state power and civil society', *Past & Present* 111 (1986), pp. 123–5.

38. Woloch, 'Napoleonic conscription', p. 101.

39. Alan Forrest, *Conscripts and Deserters: the Army and French Society during the Revolution and Empire* (New York, 1989), esp. ch. 10; Alexander Grab, 'Army, state and society: conscription and desertion in Napoleonic Italy, 1802–1814', *Journal of Modern History* 47 (1995), pp. 32–43.

40. Woolf, 'French civilization and ethnicity', pp. 105–106, 111–15.

41. Charles J. Esdaile, *The Wars of Napoleon* (London, 1995), pp. 117–35; idem, 'Popular resistance to the Napoleonic Empire', (in this volume), pp. 137, 142–52.

42. Broers, 'Policing the Empire', p.161. See also Clive Emsley, *Gendarmes and the State in Nineteenth-century Europe* (Oxford, 1999), ch. 4.

43. Emsley, *Gendarmes and the State*, pp. 70–2.

44. Michael Broers, 'The Napoleonic police and their legacy', *History Today* 49 (1999), p. 33.

45. Jean Tulard, *Le Grand Empire (1804–1815)* (Paris, 1982), p. 68; Roger Dufraisse, *Napoléon* (Paris, 1987), pp. 18, 36–7.

46. Simon Burrows, 'Culture and misperception: the law and the press in the outbreak of war in 1803', *International History Review* 18 (1996), pp. 793–818.

47. Brendan Simms, 'Britain and Napoleon', (in this volume), pp. 198, 199.

48. François Crouzet, 'The Second Hundred Years War: some reflections', *French History* 10 (1997), pp. 432–50.

49. John M. Sherwig, *Guineas and Gunpowder: British Foreign Aid in the Wars with France* (Cambridge, Mass., 1969).

50. A. D. Harvey, 'European attitudes to Britain during the French revolutionary and Napoleonic era', *History* 63 (1978), pp. 356–65.

51. Simms, 'Britain and Napoleon', pp. 201–2.

52. The most recent work on the impact of Napoleon on Europe is the collection of essays by David Laven and Lucy Riall (eds.), *Napoleon's Legacy: Problems of Government in Restoration Europe* (Oxford and New York, 2000).

53. A view propounded in Stuart Woolf, *Napoleon's Integration of Europe* (London, 1991).

54. See Ellis, 'The nature of Napoleonic imperialism', pp. 110–12, 115–17.

55. Michael Broers, 'Italy and the modern state: the experience of Napoleonic rule', in François Furet and Mona Ozouf (eds.), *The French Revolution and the Creation of Modern Political Culture*, vol. 3, *The Transformation of Political Culture 1789–1848* (Oxford, 1989), pp. 489–503, here p. 491.

56. As well as Michael Rowe, 'Napoleon and state formation in central Europe', (in this volume), pp. 208–11, see Matthew Levinger, 'The Prussian reform movement and the rise of enlightened nationalism', in Philip G. Dwyer (ed.), *The Rise of Prussia* (London, 2000), pp. 259–77.

57. Esdaile, *The Wars of Napoleon*, pp. 186–97.

58. See Mack Walker, *German Home Towns: Community, State, General Estate, 1648–1871* (Ithaca, NY, 1971), pp. 186–215.

59. Rowe, 'State formation in central Europe', pp. 207, 211; Tone, 'The Peninsular War', (in this volume), p. 229.

60. Ellis, 'The nature of Napoleonic imperialism', p. 111.

61. Tone, 'The Peninsular War', pp. 228–30, 236–41.

62. Esdaile, 'Popular resistance to the Napoleonic Empire', pp. 145–8.

63. Tone, 'The Peninsular War', p. 18.

64. Alexander M. Martin, 'The Russian Empire and the Napoleonic wars', (in this volume), pp. 253 and 255.

65. Esdaile, *The Wars of Napoleon*, p. 201.

66. Martin, 'The Russian Empire', pp. 260–3.

67. David Laven and Lucy Riall, 'Restoration government and the legacy of Napoleon', in idem, *Napoleon's Legacy*, pp. 10–14.

1 Napoleon's Youth and Rise to Power

1. Dorothy Carrington, 'The achievement of Pasquale Paoli (1755–1769) and its consequences', in *Consortium on Revolutionary Europe Proceedings* (1987), pp. 56–69; R. Le Mée, 'Un Dénombrement des Corses en 1770', *Problèmes d'histoire de la Corse (de l'Ancien Régime à 1815) – Actes du Colloque d'Ajaccio (29 Octobre 1969)* (Paris, 1971), p. 34.

2. Dorothy Carrington, *Napoleon and his Parents on the Threshold of History* (New York, 1988), pp. 13–22; Frédéric Masson and Guido Biagi, *Napoléon inconnu: papiers inédits (1786–1793)*, 3 vols. (Paris, 1895), i, pp. 8–9.

3. Hippolyte Larrey, *Madame Mère (Napoleonis Mater)*, 2 vols. (Paris, 1892), i, pp. 42–7, 58–9, 65.

4. 'Souvenirs de Madame Mère, dictés par elle-même', in Larrey, *Madame Mère*, ii, pp. 528–30.

5. François Antommachi, *Les Derniers moments de Napoléon* (Paris, 1975), pp. 159–60.

6. Dorothy Carrington, *Napoleon and his Parents*, p. 150.

7. Owen Connelly, *The Gentle Bonaparte: a Biography of Joseph, Napoleon's Elder Brother* (New York, 1968), p. xiii.

8. Ibid., p. 8.

9. This is based on Louis Villat, *La Corse de 1768 à 1789*, 2 vols. (Besançon, 1924); see also Thad Hall, 'Thought and practice of enlightened government in French Corsica', *American Historical Review* 74 (1969), pp. 886–905.

10. Arthur Chuquet, *La Jeunesse de Napoléon*, 3 vols. (Paris, 1897), i, pp. 117, 262–3; F. Ettori, 'Pascal Paoli: modèle du Jeune Bonaparte', *Actes du Colloque d'Ajaccio 29 Octobre 1969*, pp. 89–99; Masson and Biagi, *Napoléon inconnu*, i, p. 83.

11. Barry E. O'Meara, *Napoleon in Exile; or a Voice from St Helena*, 2 vols. (London, 1888), ii, p. 155.

12. André Corvisier, *L'Armée française de la fin du XVIIe siècle au ministère de Choiseul: le soldat*, 2 vols. (Paris, 1964), i, pp. 84, 104, 105, 107, 109, 136; ii, pp. 786–7, 801–802, 850, 867–88, 893–4, 942, 944, 952–4, 972, 977, 980, 985.

13. Masson and Biagi, *Napoléon inconnu*, i, pp. 165–6.

14. Ibid., i, pp. 185–94.

15. Ibid., i, pp. 281–509; ii, pp. 1–52, 216–74.

16. F. Pomponi, 'Sentiments révolutionnaires et esprit de parti en Corse au temps de la Révolution', in *Problèmes d'histoire de la Corse (de l'Ancien Régime à 1815)*, pp. 155, 165, 171, 175, 177; Villat, *La Corse de 1768 à 1789*, ii, pp. 370–2, 380.

17. The story is told in Jean Defranceschi, *La Corse française 30 novembre 1789–15 juin 1794* (Paris, 1980), pp. 33–194; Leonard A. Macaluso, 'Between clan and nation: Antoine Christophe Saliceti, 1789–1793', *Consortium on Revolutionary Europe Proceedings* (1994), pp. 10–18; J. M. P. McErlean, *Napoleon and Pozzo di Borgo in Corsica and after, 1764–1821: Not Quite a Vendetta* (Lewiston, NY, 1996), pp. 1–142; Marcel Mirtil, *Napoléon d'Ajaccio* (Paris, n.d.), pp. 50, 111–13, 171–2, 179.

18. Defranceschi, 'Corse', 'Pozzo di Borgo, Charles-André' and 'Saliceti, Antoine Christophe', in Jean Tulard (ed.), *Dictionnaire Napoléon* (Paris, 1987); and idem, 'Bonaparte, lieutenant-colonel des volontaires nationaux de la Corse – mythe et réalité', *Consortium on Revolutionary Europe Proceedings* (1999); McErlean, *Napoleon and Pozzo di*

Borgo, pp. 91–102; Masson and Biagi, *Napoléon inconnu*, ii, p. 397; Mirtil, *Napoléon d'Ajaccio*, pp. 117–59.

19. Masson and Biagi, *Napoléon inconnu*, i, p. 397.
20. Quoted in Felix Markham, *Napoleon* (New York, 1963), p. 27.
21. Auguste-Frédéric-Louis Viesse de Marmont, *Mémoires du duc de Raguse de 1792 à 1832*, 9 vols. (Paris, 1857), i, p. 178. André François Miot de Melito, *Mémoires du comte Miot de Melito*, 3 vols. (Paris, 1880), i, p. 154. Jean Defranceschi, 'Bonaparte, lieutenant-colonel des volontaires nationaux'.

2 The Military Culture of Napoleonic France

1. I developed part of the argument which follows in a paper to a conference on 'Immaginario napoleonico e luoghi della memoria', held in the Cittadella di Alessandria in June 2000. I should like to thank the organisers for permission to draw on that paper in the preparation of this chapter.
2. David Gates, *The Napoleonic Wars, 1803–1815* (London, 1997), pp. 4–5.
3. Charles J. Esdaile, *The Wars of Napoleon* (London, 1995), p. 66.
4. David Chandler, *Dictionary of the Napoleonic Wars* (New York, 1993), p. 297.
5. The military career of Carnot, artillery officer, mathematician and future Jacobin Minister of War, is dissected by Jean and Nicole Dhombres, *Lazare Carnot* (Paris, 1997). For the problems he faced in establishing himself as a military officer, see especially pp. 96ff.
6. Geoffrey Ellis, *The Napoleonic Empire* (Basingstoke and London, 1991), pp. 9–11.
7. Jacques Bainville, 'Préface' to Napoléon Bonaparte, *Souper de Beaucaire* (re-ed., Paris, 1930), p. 7.
8. Napoléon Bonaparte, *Souper de Beaucaire*, p. 45.
9. Jean-Paul Bertaud, *La Révolution armée: les soldats-citoyens et la Révolution Française* (Paris, 1979), p. 194.
10. Albert Meynier, 'L'Armée en France sous la Révolution et le Premier Empire', *Revue d'études militaires* (1932), pp. 17–23.
11. Isser Woloch, *Jacobin Legacy: the Democratic Movement under the Directory* (Princeton, NJ, 1970), p. 70.
12. John Lynn, 'Towards an army of honour: the moral evolution of the French army, 1789–1815', *French Historical Studies* 16 (1989), pp. 153–4.
13. Malcolm Crook, *Napoleon Comes to Power: Democracy and Dictatorship in Revolutionary France, 1795–1804* (Cardiff, 1998), pp. 42–3.
14. Josiane Bourguet-Rouveyre, 'Bonaparte vu par les mémorialistes français', *Annales historiques de la Révolution Française* 318 (1999), p. 610.
15. Archives départementales du Finistère, 35J11, letter from François Avril in Kelbruk, 16 Frimaire XIII.
16. Archives départementales de l'Oise, series R (unclassified), letter from Danserville to his uncle, 20 December 1807.
17. Owen Connelly, *Blundering to Glory: Napoleon's Military Campaigns* (Wilmington, Del., 1987), p. 72.
18. Bernard Ménager, *Les Napoléon du peuple* (Paris, 1988), p. 7.

19. Emmanuel de Las Cases, *Le Mémorial de Sainte-Hélène*, 2 vols., Marcel Dunan (ed.) (Paris, 1930), ii, p. 2.

20. Louis Bergeron, *France under Napoleon* (Princeton, NJ, 1981 transl.), p. 63.

21. Annie Jourdan, *L'Empire de Napoléon* (Paris, 2000), p. 255.

22. Ibid., p. 64.

23. Jean-Paul Bertaud, 'Napoleon's officers', *Past & Present* 112 (1986), p. 98.

24. Georges Six, *Les Généraux de la Révolution et de l'Empire*, p. 250; quoted in Jean Tulard, 'Problèmes sociaux de la France impériale', *Revue d'histoire moderne et contemporaine* 17 (1970), p. 654.

25. Georges Carrot, 'Gardes d'honneur', in Jean Tulard (ed.), *Dictionnaire Napoléon* (Paris, 1987), pp. 778–9.

26. Henry Laurens, *L'expédition d'Egypte, 1798–1801* (Paris, 1989), pp. 16ff.

27. Napoléon Bonaparte, *Proclamations, Ordres du Jour, Bulletins de la Grande Armée* (Paris, 1964), p. 148.

28. Ibid., p. 36.

29. Ibid., p. 14.

30. Las Cases, *Mémorial*, i, pp. 769–70.

31. Timothy Wilson-Smith, *Napoleon and his Artists* (London, 1996), p. 161.

32. Isser Woloch, *The French Veteran from the Revolution to the Restoration* (Chapel Hill, NC, 1979), pp. 196–7.

33. Archives départementales du Puy-de-Dôme, M122, programme of the Fête du 1er Vendémiaire VIII in Clermont-Ferrand.

34. Archives municipales de Lille, 18243, accounts of the principal festivals celebrated in Lille during 1799.

35. Christopher Prendergast, *Napoleon and History Painting: Antoine-Jean Gros's 'La Bataille d'Eylau'* (Oxford, 1997), pp. 199–201.

36. Timothy Wilson-Smith, *Napoleon and his Artists*, p. 150.

37. René Perrout, *Trésors des images d'Epinal* (Paris, 1985), p. 165.

38. Martyn Lyons, *Napoleon Bonaparte and the Legacy of the French Revolution* (London and New York, 1994), pp. 111–12.

39. Louis Bergeron, *France Under Napoleon*, p. 34.

40. Isser Woloch, 'Napoleonic conscription: state power and civil society', *Past & Present* 111 (1986), p. 101.

41. Alan Forrest, *Conscripts and Deserters: the Army and French Society during the Revolution and Empire* (New York, 1989), pp. 219–37.

3 The Napoleonic Regime and French Society

1. On the fight against brigandage see the contrasting views of H. G. Brown, 'From organic society to security state: the war on brigandage in France, 1797–1802', *Journal of Modern History* 69 (1997), pp. 661–95; and S. Clay, 'Ordre et désordre au temps de Brumaire: le test du brigandage en Provence', in *Du Directoire au Consulat: Brumaire dans l'histoire du lien politique et de l'Etat-Nation* [Colloque de Rouen] (Rouen, 2001).

2. Archives nationales, F1c III Seine Inférieure 8: Year X.

3. See F. Rocquain (ed.), *L'Etat de la France au 18 Brumaire* (Paris, 1874). On elections during the Directory, see M. Crook, *Elections in the French Revolution: an Apprenticeship in Democracy, 1789–1799* (Cambridge, 1996), ch. 6.

4. J.-P. Jessenne, *Pouvoir au village et Révolution: Artois, 1760–1848* (Lille, 1987), pp. 44–89 (a study of the Pas-de-Calais); P. M. Jones, *Politics and rural society: the southern Massif Central c.1750–1880* (Cambridge, 1985), chs. 4–6 (a study of the Aveyron). For a concise overview of rural society see M. Lyons, *Napoleon Bonaparte and the Legacy of the French Revolution* (London and New York, 1994), ch. 11. On the Napoleonic mayors see J. Dunne, 'Les Maires de Brumaire: notables ruraux ou "gens de passage"?', Colloque de Rouen: *Du Directoire au Consulat* (in press).

5. On the neo-Jacobins see I. Woloch, *Jacobin Legacy: the Democratic Movement under the Directory* (Princeton, NJ, 1970); and B. Gainot, 'Le Mouvement Neo-Jacobin à la fin du Directoire', 2 vols. (doctoral thesis, University of Paris I, 1993).

6. See I. Woloch, *The New Regime: Transformations of the French Civic Order, 1789–1820s* (New York, 1994), ch. 6.

7. Ibid., ch. 7; R. R. Palmer, *The Improvement of Humanity: Education and the French Revolution* (Princeton, NJ, 1985), ch. 7.

8. I. Woloch, 'Republican institutions, 1797–99', in C. Lucas (ed.), *The Political Culture of the French Revolution* (Oxford, 1988), pp. 371–87.

9. M. Agulhon, *La Vie sociale en Provence intérieur au lendemain de la Révolution* (Paris, 1970), p. 405; Jessenne, *Pouvoir au village*, p. 120; and especially L. Brassart, 'Réception et acceptation du coup d'état du 18 Brumaire dans l'Asine', Colloque de Rouen: *Du Directoire au Consulat*.

10. Woloch, *The New Regime*, pp. 397–404.

11. See Alan Forrest, *Conscripts and Deserters: the Army and French Society during the Revolution and Empire* (New York, 1989); and Woloch, *The New Regime*, ch. 13, which develops the author's notion of a Napoleonic 'conscription machine'.

12. J.-P. Bertaud, 'Napoleon's officers', *Past & Present* 112 (1986), pp. 91–111.

13. In fact, as he made clear in a private memo, Roederer would have liked to know a good deal about their opinions, such as whether they bothered to vote in the plebiscite and which newspapers they read. See Archives nationales, 29 AP 75 (Roederer Papers): circular from Roederer to the Prefects, 15 Prairial X; and memo, n.d., but dating from shortly thereafter.

14. Archives nationales, AF IV 1424. See also Archives nationales, F1c II 31/2: *Décisions donnés par le Ministre sur divers questions . . . sur les Assemblées cantonales et les Collèges électoraux* (January 1807), and *Modele général de listes* (1807).

15. See Archives nationales, AF IV 1429, dossier 4, especially Minister of Interior circular to prefects, Year XI. For the 'electoral charade' of the Napoleonic era in general see J. Y. Coppolani, *Les Elections en France à l'époque napoléonienne* (Paris, 1980).

16. L. Bergeron and G. Chaussinand-Nogaret, *Les 'Masses de granit': cent mille notables du Premier Empire* (Paris, 1979), and G. Chaussinand-Nogaret, L. Bergeron and R. Forster, 'Les notables du "Grand Empire" en 1810', *Annales – économie, sociétés, civilisations* (1971), pp. 1052–75.

17. Bergeron and Chaussinand-Nogaret, *Masses de granit*, p. 43.

18. Ibid., pp. 63–4. For further discussions of the *notables* see the seminal overview by L. Bergeron, *France under Napoleon* (Princeton, NJ, 1981 transl.), chs. 3 and 6; and the recent synthesis by M. Lyons, *Napoleon and the Legacy of the Revolution*, chs. 6 and 12.

19. Bergeron, *France under Napoleon*, pp. 125–33.

20. See, e.g., Marquis de Noailles, *Le Comte Molé, 1781–1855: sa vie, ses mémoires* (Paris, 1922 edn), pp. 41–52.

21. See the insightful article by R. Blaufarb, 'The Ancien Regime origins of Napoleonic social reconstruction', *French History* 14 (2001), pp. 408–23.

22. *Archives parlementaires* (2ème série), x, p. 12.

23. J. Tulard, *Napoléon et la noblesse d'Empire* (Paris, 1979), pp. 75–8.

24. Ibid., pp. 93–8, 146–54.

25. For a list of the imperial dignitaries see Bergeron, *France under Napoleon*, pp. 76–9.

26. T. Berlier, *Précis de la vie politique de Théophile Berlier écrit par lui-même, et adressé à ses enfans et petits-enfans* (Dijon, 1838), pp. 108–109.

27. Berlier Papers, Archives départementales du Côte d'Or (Dijon), 30F 7: Majorat and Dotation; Berlier, *Précis de la vie*, pp. 109–10.

28. A. M. Roederer (ed.), *Oeuvres du Comte P.-L. Roederer*, 7 vols. (Paris, 1854), iii, pp. 507–10; and Roederer Papers, Archives nationales, 29 AP 78: Ms. Notes for the senatorial deliberation on the creation of the Empire.

29. See the complaints about this tendency by one 'man of the Revolution' and early Napoleonic collaborator, A.-C. Thibaudeau, *Mémoires de A.-C. Thibaudeau, 1799–1815* (Paris, 1913 edn), p. 263. On the relations over time between Napoleon and his original supporters of Brumaire see Isser Woloch, *Napoleon and his Collaborators: the Making of a Dictatorship* (New York, 2001).

30. J.-J.-R. Cambacérès, *Mémoires inédits*, 2 vols. (Paris, 1999), L. Chatel de Brancion (ed.), i, pp. 684–5.

31. J. Bourdon, ed., *Napoléon au Conseil d'Etat* (Paris, 1963), pp. 62–3.

32. Imperial decree of 26 December 1809 in *Bulletin des Lois*, No. 254; Archives nationales, BB I 138: Conseil d'Etat, Nominations: *Auditeurs*, 1810.

33. Archives nationales, BB I 138, Nominations 1810. For a general study see C. Durand, *Les Auditeurs au Conseil d'état de 1803 à 1814* (Paris, 1958).

34. See the succinct introduction by the legal historian Jean Imbert in J. Tulard (ed.), *Dictionnaire Napoléon* (Paris, 1987). The debates over various sections of the code are reproduced and creatively organised in F. Ewald et al. (eds.), *Naissance du Code Civil: la raison du législateur* (Paris, 1989). See also J. Carbonnier, 'Le Code Civil', in P. Nora (ed.), *Les Lieux de mémoire*, Vol. II: La Nation (Paris, 1986).

35. On the conflicting reactions to innovations in family law see S. Desan, 'Reconstituting the social after the Terror: family, property, and the law in popular politics', *Past & Present*, 164 (1999), pp. 81–121.

36. See M. Darrow, *Revolution in the House: Family, Class, and Inheritance in Southern France, 1775–1825* (Princeton, NJ, 1989), focusing on a region where it was customary to favour the eldest son and more or less remained so, despite changes in the law.

37. The standard case study is R. Phillips, *Family Breakdown in late 18th-century France: Divorce in Rouen, 1792–1803* (Oxford, 1980).

38. See Woloch, *The New Regime*, chs. 11–12.

39. See J. R. Munson, 'Businessman, business conduct and the civic organization of commercial life under the Directory and Napoleon' (doctoral thesis, Columbia University, 1992) on various issues in the Code de Commerce.

40. F. Fortunet, 'Le Code Rural ou l'impossible codification', *Annales historiques de la Révolution française* 247 (1982).

4 The Napoleonic Police State

1. Howard G. Brown, 'From organic society to security state: the war on brigandage in France, 1797–1802', *Journal of Modern History* 69 (1997), pp. 661–95; idem, 'Domestic state violence: repression from the *Croquants* to the Commune', *Historical Journal* 42 (1999), pp. 597–622.

2. Quoted in Artaud de Montor, *Histoire de la vie et des travaux de comte d'Hauterive*, 2nd edn (Paris, 1839), p. 267.

3. Louis Madelin, *Fouché 1759–1820*, 2 vols. (Paris, 1901); Hubert Cole, *Fouché: the Unprincipled Patriot* (New York and London, 1971); Jean Tulard, *Joseph Fouché* (Paris, 1998).

4. Peter de Polnay, *Napoleon's Police* (London, 1970), p. 40.

5. Thierry Lentz, *Savary: le séide de Napoléon (1774–1833)* (Paris, 1993).

6. See Louis Madelin, 'La Police Générale de l'Empire', *Revue des Deux Mondes* 60 (1940), pp. 241–67; idem, *Fouché*, i, pp. 461–520; Eric A. Arnold, Jr, *Fouché, Napoleon, and the General Police* (Washington, DC, 1979).

7. Archives nationales, F^7 4257, 'Etat des employés du ministère, leurs grades et le traitement . . . au 1er août 1813'.

8. Ibid., F^7 8550, dossier 12,658-P2, Balguerie, *Le Préfet du département du Gers . . . à MM. les Maires, Adjoints et Commissaires de police de son département* [Auch, March 1810].

9. Jean Rigotard, *La police parisienne de Napoléon: la préfecture de police* (Paris, 1990).

10. Quoted in Tulard, *Fouché*, p. 132.

11. Quoted in Cole, *Fouché*, p. 140.

12. Henri Welschinger, *La Censure sous le Premier Empire* (Paris, 1882).

13. Henri Gaubert, *Conspirateurs au temps de Napoléon Ier* (Paris, 1962); Frédéric Masson, 'Le Complot des libelles', *La Revue hebdomadaire* 30 (1921), pp. 249–63, 399–411; Christian Bonnet, 'La Conspiration du Midi', in Jean Tulard (ed.), *Dictionnaire Napoléon* (Paris, 1987), pp. 488–9.

14. Jean Tulard, 'Quelques aspects du brigandage sous l'Empire', *Revue de l'Institut Napoléon* 98 (1966), pp. 31–6; Laurent Ripart, 'Pour une histoire des barbets des Alpes-Maritime', in Laboratoire d'analyse spatiale Raoul Blanchard, *Mélanges Paul Gonnet* (Nice, 1989), pp. 257–68.

15. Ernest d'Hauterive (ed.), *La Police secrète de premier Empire: Bulletins quotidiens adressés par Fouché à l'Empereur*, 3 vols. (Paris, 1908–22) and Jean Grassion (ed.), 2 vols. (Paris, 1963–64); Nicole Gotteri (ed.), *La Police secrète de premier Empire: Bulletins quotidiens adressés par Savary à l'Empereur* (Paris, 1997–). The quotation is by Gotteri in ii, pp. 17–18.

16. Jean Savant, *Les Espions de Napoléon* (Paris, 1957); Michael Broers, 'The Napoleonic police and their legacy', *History Today* 49 (1999), pp. 27–33; Georges Carrot, 'Gendarmerie Impériale', in *Dictionnaire Napoléon*, pp. 785–6 (for quotation about

gendarmerie); Joseph Fouché, *Les Mémoires de Fouché*, Michelle Vovelle (ed.) (Paris, 1992), p. 151; Etienne-Denis Pasquier, *Histoire de mon temps, Mémoires du chancelier Pasquier*, 6 vols. (Paris, 1893–95), i, p. 430.

17. Madelin, 'La Police Général', p. 260.
18. *Mémoires de Fouché*, pp. 221, 267.
19. Archives nationales, F[7] 8408, dossier 7819-P, prefect of Aude to Pelet, 31 March 1806.
20. Ibid., F[7] 6433, dossier 8933, letter by Ravelinghan Montmirel, 8 Prairial Year XII (28 May 1804).
21. Ibid., F[7] 8087, dossier 1879-R, prefect of Seine-et-Oise to Minister of General Police, 8 July 1813.
22. Ibid., F[7] 8279, dossier 9918-R2, decree, 5 February 1811; F[7] 6324, dossier 6861-BP, prefect of Seine-et-Oise to Minister of Justice, 21 Vendémiaire Year XI (13 October 1802); F[7] 8087, dossier 1879-R, correspondence, Year XIII-1813.
23. Ibid., F[7] 8139, dossier 8191-R, prefect of Loiret to Réal, 26 July 1811.
24. Ibid., F[7] 8495, dossier 1-P, general police commissioner (Toulon) to Desmarest, 4 Prairial Year XII (24 May 1804).
25. Ibid., F[7] 8684, dossier 6549-P3, prefect of Puy-de-Dôme to Pelet, 14 November 1812.
26. Ibid., F[7] 8684, dossier 6417-P5, reports, 1812–13.
27. Ibid., F[7] 3248, dossier Doubs, correspondence, 1809–10; F[7] 8634, dossier 353-P3, prefect of Doubs to Pelet, 21 April 1812.
28. Ibid., F[7] 8651, dossier 1927-P3, prefect of Meurthe to Minister of General Police, 16 December 1813.
29. Ibid., F[7] 6525, dossier 1435-Série 2, note, March 1807.
30. Ibid., F[7] 6555, dossier 2227-Série 2, report, 9 November 1810; F[7] 6434, dossier 8957, report, 27 Prairial Year XII (16 June 1804), prefect of Cher to Minister of Justice, 2 Prairial Year XII (22 May 1804); Archives départementales Gard, 1 M 516, mayor of Nîmes to prefect of Gard, 6 June 1809.
31. Archives nationales, F[7] 8707, dossier 316-M, report to Minister of General Police, 1e jour complémentaire Year XII (18 September 1804).
32. Ibid., F[7] 8234, dossier 7083-R2, prefect of Moselle to Réal, 7 June 1809.
33. Ibid., F[7] 8149, dossier 9279-R, prefect of Haute-Vienne to Réal, 21 August 1806; F[7] 8530, dossier 14431-P2, general police commissioner to Pélet, 12 October 1810; Archives départementales Loire-Atlantique, 1M 491, dossier 'Placards incendiaires 1813', police commissioner to mayor, 4 October 1813.
34. Archives nationales, F[7] 6227, dossier Bouches-du-Rhône, general police commissioner to Minister of General Police, 30 Vendémiaire Year IX (22 October 1800).
35. Archives départementales Maine-et-Loire, 1 M6/2, Réal to prefect, 3 Nivôse Year XIII (24 December 1804); Archives départementales Vienne, M4 12, ministry to prefect, 25 July 1812. On censorship of the theatre, see Odile Krakovitch, 'La Censeur théâtrale sous le Premier Empire (1800–1815)', *Revue de l'Institut Napoléon* 158–9 (1992), pp. 9–105.
36. Archives nationales, F[7] 8555, dossier 10,433-P2, police report, 15 June 1809.

37. Jean Destrem, *Les Déportations du Consulat et de l'Empire* (Paris, 1883); G. Lenôtre, *Les Derniers terroristes* (Paris, 1932); Michael J. Sydenham, 'The crime of 3 Nivôse (24 December 1800)', in J. F. Bosher (ed.), *French Government and Society, 1500–1850* (London, 1973), pp. 295–320.

38. Armand Dayot, 'La Justice et les prisons d'état sous le premier Empire', *Revue du Palais* 5 (1898), pp. 338–59; Jean-Claude Vimont, *La Prison politique en France* (Paris, 1993), ch. 3.

39. Archives nationales, BB30* 188, 'Prisonniers d'Etat'; F^7 6998, report to Emperor, n.d.; BB^{30} 189, dossier 2, Minister of General Police to Minister of Justice, 1 June 1812. See also Michael Sibalis, 'Prisoners by *Mesure de haute police* under Napoleon I: reviving the *Lettres de cachet*', *Proceedings of the Annual Meeting of the Western Society for French History* 18 (1991), pp. 261–9.

40. Archives nationales, O^2 1432, dossier 243 (Marin).

41. Ibid., F^7 8235, dossier 7211-R2 (Gachot).

42. Ibid., F^7 8073, dossier 146-R.

43. Ibid., F^7 6469A, dossier 155-Série 2 (Coney); F^7 6500, plaq. 3, # 232-55 (Caamano); F^7 6571, dossier 2817-Série 2 (Dumont).

44. Antoine François Eve, *Tableau historique des prisons d'état sous le règne de Buonaparte* (Paris, 1814), pp. 8–9.

45. A. Nemours, *Histoire de la captivité et de la mort de Toussaint-Louverture* (Paris, 1929), esp. pp. 201–209.

46. Michael Sibalis, 'Un aspect de la légende noire de Napoléon: le mythe de l'enfermement des opposants comme fous', *Revue de l'Institut Napoléon* 156 (1991), pp. 9–24; Archives nationales, F^7 8508, dossier 1655-P2, reports by prefect of Hautes-Alpes, May–June 1807.

47. Michael Sibalis, 'La Côte-d'Or, terre d'exil', *Annales de Bourgogne* 64 (1992), pp. 39–51; idem, 'Internal exiles in Napoleonic France, 1799–1815', *Proceedings of the Annual Meeting of the Western Society for French History* 20 (1993), pp. 189–98.

48. Archives nationales, F^7 8535, dossier 8803-P2.

49. Archives départementales Côte-d'Or, 20 M 1015, report on Caillebot, 19 June 1813; 20 M 148, mayor of Châtillon to sub-prefect, 26 May 1813; 20 M 1004, 1005, 1006, scattered reports on Lenoble; Archives nationales, F^7 3247, dossier Côte-d'Or; F^7 6400, plaq. 6–7, pièces 599–722 (Lenoble); F^7 9118, dossier 22,385 (Lenoble).

50. Antoine-Clair Thibaudeau, *Mémoires de A.-C. Thibaudeau, 1799–1815* (Paris, 1913), pp. 355–6.

51. Ibid., p. 287.

5 The Nature of Napoleonic Imperialism

1. Pieter Geyl, *Napoleon: For and Against* (London, 1986 edn).

2. Throughout this essay, the terms 'Empire' and 'Imperial' (with initial capital letters) refer to the formal delimitations of the French Empire from the date of its inauguration on 18 May 1804, or else to attributions of the Emperor Napoleon himself within that official context. The terms 'imperial' and 'imperialism' (with initial letters in lower case) refer to the process of empire-building in a more general sense, whether in relation to France or other states.

3. The major themes of Napoleonic historiography from 1815 to the Second World War are discussed in detail in ch. 7 of my *Napoleon* (London and New York, 1997).

4. Frédéric Masson, *Napoléon et sa famille (1769–1821)*, 13 vols. (Paris, 1897–1919).

5. J. Christopher Herold (ed.), *The Mind of Napoleon: A Selection from his Written and Spoken Words* (New York, 1955), p. 276.

6. Quoted in ibid., p. 47.

7. Quoted in Harold T. Parker, 'Napoleon's changing self-image to 1812: a sketch', *Consortium on Revolutionary Europe Proceedings* (1983), pp. 457, 463 n. 26.

8. Emmanuel de Las Cases, *Mémorial de Sainte-Hélène. Journal of the Private Life and Conversations of the Emperor Napoleon at Saint Helena*, 4 vols. (London, 1823), ii, pp. 197–8.

9. *Correspondance de Napoléon Ier publiée par ordre de l'empereur Napoléon III*, 32 vols. (Paris, 1858–69).

10. Harold T. Parker, 'Toward understanding Napoleon, or Did Napoleon have a conscience?', *Consortium on Revolutionary Europe, Selected Papers* (1997), pp. 201–208.

11. Stuart Woolf, *Napoleon's Integration of Europe* (London and New York, 1991).

12. Ibid., p. 4.

13. Stuart Woolf, 'French civilization and ethnicity in the Napoleonic Empire', *Past & Present* 124 (1989), pp. 96–120.

14. Ibid., p. 107.

15. Ibid., p. 109.

16. The details of all these administrative extensions into the annexed departments of the Empire are set out, with accompanying maps, in François de Dainville and Jean Tulard, *Atlas administratif de l'Empire Français* (Geneva and Paris, 1973).

17. Michael Broers, *Europe under Napoleon 1799–1815* (London and New York, 1996), *passim*, but esp. pp. 99 ff., and the map on p. 181.

18. Edward Said, *Culture & Imperialism* (London, 1994).

19. For a detailed account of the various regional effects of the Continental Blockade, see my published doctoral thesis, *Napoleon's Continental Blockade: the Case of Alsace* (Oxford, 1981). Shorter statements on the same subject are given in ch. 6 of my booklet, *The Napoleonic Empire* (Basingstoke and London, 1991); and on pp. 101–12 of my *Napoleon* cited in n. 3 above.

20. Michael Broers, 'Italy and the modern state: the experience of Napoleonic rule', in François Furet and Mona Ozouf (eds.), *The French Revolution and the Creation of Modern Political Culture*, vol. 3, *The Transformation of Political Culture 1789–1848* (Oxford, 1989), p. 495.

21. Elisabeth Fehrenbach, *Der Kampf um die Einführung des Code Napoléon in den Rheinbundstaaten* (Wiesbaden, 1973); and *Traditionale Gesellschaft und revolutionäres Recht: Die Einführung des Code Napoléon in den Rheinbundstaaten* (Göttingen, 1974).

22. Michael Rowe, 'Between empire and home town: Napoleonic rule on the Rhine, 1799–1814', *The Historical Journal* 42 (1999), pp. 673–4; Brendan Simms, *The Struggle for Mastery in Germany, 1779–1850* (Basingstoke and London, 1998), pp. 131–2.

23. Helmut Berding, *Napoleonische Herrschafts- und Gesellschaftspolitik im Königreich Westfalen 1807–1813* (Göttingen, 1973).

24. Monika Senkowska-Gluck, 'Les Majorats français dans le duché de Varsovie (1807–1813)', *Annales historiques de la Révolution française* 36 (1964), pp. 373–86; and

'Le Duché de Varsovie', in *Occupants–Occupés, 1792–1815. Colloque de Bruxelles, 29 et 30 janvier 1968* (Brussels, 1969), pp. 391–402.

25. Christof Dipper, Wolfgang Schieder and Reiner Schulze (eds.), *Napoleonische Herrschaft in Deutschland und Italien – Verwaltung und Justiz* (Berlin, 1995).

26. Helmut Berding, 'Le Royaume de Westphalie, Etat-modèle', *Francia* 10 (1982), pp. 345–58.

27. Quoted in Herold, *Mind of Napoleon*, pp. 178–9.

28. Quoted in ibid., p. 243.

29. See, for example, the relevant passages in ibid., pp. 178–202 (in the section entitled 'Nations and Peoples'), and pp. 239–56 (in that entitled 'Projects and Prophecies').

30. Napoleon, *Correspondance*, xxi, p. 70.

31. Bertrand de Jouvenel, *Napoléon et l'économie dirigée: le Blocus continental* (Paris and Brussels, 1942), p. 191.

32. Jean Gabillard, 'Le Financement des guerres napoléoniennes et la conjoncture du premier Empire', *Revue économique* 4 (1953), pp. 558–9.

33. David Laven and Lucy Riall (eds.), *Napoleon's Legacy: Problems of Government in Restoration Europe* (Oxford and New York, 2000).

34. Louis Bergeron, *France under Napoleon* (Princeton, NJ, 1981 transl.), p. xiv.

6 Napoleon and the Drive for Glory: Reflections on the Making of French Foreign Policy

My thanks to Charles Esdaile, Mike Broers, Harold Parker, Geoffrey Ellis, Frederick Schneid and Wayne Reynolds for their useful comments on drafts of this chapter.

1. Emmanuel de Las Cases, *Le Mémorial de Sainte-Hélène*, 2 vols. (Paris, 1983), ii, p. 143.

2. Albert Sorel, *L'Europe et la Révolution française*, 8 vols. (Paris, 1885–1904), v, p. 283; vi, p. 31; viii, pp. 494–7. Sorel refers to the *conquête des 'limites'*.

3. François Furet, 'Bonaparte', in François Furet and Mona Ozouf (eds.), *Dictionnaire Critique de la Révolution Française* (Paris, 1988), p. 226.

4. François Crouzet, 'The Second Hundred Years War: some reflections', *French History* 10 (1997), pp. 432–50.

5. Paul Kennedy, *The Rise and Fall of the Great Powers: Economic Change and Military Conflict from 1500 to 2000* (London, 1988), pp. 163–4.

6. Paul W. Schroeder, *The Transformation of European Politics, 1763–1848* (Oxford, 1994), p. 309.

7. Charles Esdaile, *The Wars of Napoleon* (London, 1995), pp. 10, 29, 35, 36 (my emphasis).

8. Gunther E. Rothenberg, 'The origins, causes, and extension of the wars of the French Revolution and Napoleon', *Journal of Interdisciplinary Studies* 18 (1988), pp. 771–93 (here p. 792).

9. Schroeder, *Transformation of European Politics*, pp. xi, 230, 284, 393; and idem, 'Napoleon's foreign policy: a criminal enterprise', *Journal of Military History* 54 (1990), pp. 147–61.

10. Schroeder, *Transformation of European Politics*, pp. 213–14, 224–5, 228–9, 323.

11. See Broers, 'Policing the Empire' (in this volume), p. 153.

12. Stuart Woolf, *Napoleon's Integration of Europe* (London, 1991), p. 15.

13. A distinction is made here between the Continental System and the Continental Blockade, often treated as one and the same by historians. In fact, they are two

distinct policies. The 'System' was an attempt to assure the supremacy of the French economy, and hence of France, by reserving a monopoly for itself with regard to continental markets. The 'Blockade', on the other hand, was associated with the war against Britain and was aimed at forcing that country to make peace with France by closing the coasts of Europe to British trade.

14. Henry Laurens, *L'Expédition d'Egypte, 1798–1801* (Paris, 1989), pp. 20–36.
15. Orville T. Murphy, 'Napoleon's international politics: how much did he owe to the past?', *Journal of Military History* 54 (1990), p. 167.
16. T. C. W. Blanning, *The French Revolutionary Wars, 1787–1802* (London, 1996), p. 261; George Lefebvre, *Napoléon* (Paris, 1969), p. 70; Schroeder, 'Napoleon's foreign policy', pp. 155–7.
17. Las Cases, *Mémorial*, ii, p. 49.
18. Emile Dard, *Napoléon et Talleyrand* (Paris, 1935), pp. 95–103.
19. Paul Bailleu (ed.), *Preußen und Frankreich von 1795 bis 1807. Diplomatische Correspondenzen*, 2 vols. (Leipzig, 1881 and 1887), i, pp. 363, 427; ii, pp. 51, 326–7.
20. Cited in Dard, *Napoléon et Talleyrand*, p. 301.
21. *Correspondance de Napoléon Ier publiée par ordre de l'empereur Napoléon III*, 32 vols. (Paris, 1858–69), xxiv, n. 19213; Jean Hanoteau, ed., *With Napoleon in Russia: the Memoirs of General de Caulaincourt, Duke de Vicenza*, 3 vols. (New York, 1935), i, pp. 284–5.
22. Schroeder, *Transformation of European Politics*, pp. 403–5.
23. The concept is taken from Hans-Ulrich Wehler's analysis of Germany's bid for colonial power in the late nineteenth century: *Bismarck und der Imperialismus* (Cologne and Berlin, 1969), pp. 112–26.
24. J. Lovie and A. Palluel-Guillard, *L'Épisode napoléonien. Aspects extérieurs 1799–1815* (Paris, 1972), pp. 168–71.
25. François Fugier, *La Révolution française et l'empire* (Paris, 1954), pp. 160–3; Lefebvre, *Napoléon*, p. 89.
26. Jean-Jacques Cambacérès, *Mémoires inédits*, 2 vols. (Paris, 1999), L. Chatel de Brancion (ed.), ii, p. 97; Jean Tulard, 'Le Fonctionnement des institutions impériales en l'absence de Napoléon d'après les lettres inédites de Cambacérès', *Revue des travaux de l'Académie des sciences morales et politiques*, (1973), pp. 231–46. For an interesting reflection on Napoleonic centralisation, see Stefano Mannoni, '"Administratio mediatrix": sur la centralisation napoléonienne', *Revue historique de droit français et etranger* 75 (1997), pp. 447–61.
27. Janet Hartley, *Alexander I* (London, 1994), p. 120.
28. What follows is (very loosely) based upon the model set out by Karen Horney, *Neurosis and Human Growth: the Struggle Towards Self-realization* (re-ed., New York, 1991), pp. 24–8.
29. See Annie Jourdan, *Napoléon: Héros, Imperator, Mécène* (Paris, 1998), pp. 85–92.
30. See Geoffrey Ellis, *Napoleon* (London and New York, 1997), pp. 193–4; the author points out that three elements are at play: destiny, fate and luck.
31. Gaspard Gourgaud, *Journal de Sainte Hélène, 1815–1818*, 2 vols. (Paris, n.d.), ii, p. 94.
32. Napoléon, *Correspondance*, v, n. 3785.
33. Maximilien Vox, *Correspondance de Napoléon. Six cents lettres de travail (1806–1810)* (Paris, 1948), pp. 277, 289.

34. 'Le discours de Lyon', in Frédéric Masson and Guido Biagi (eds.), *Napoléon, manuscrits inédits, 1786–1791* (Paris, 1907), pp. 279–80; Las Cases, *Mémorial*, i, p. 340: 'Oui, l'imagination gouverne le monde.'

35. Napoléon, *Correspondance*, iii, n. 2307.

36. Cited in Parker, 'Napoleon's changing self-image to 1812: a sketch', *Consortium on Revolutionary Europe Proceedings* (1983), p. 454.

37. Napoléon, *Correspondance*, iv, n. 3259; xvi, nos. 13736–8, and Napoleon to Alexander, 2 February 1808, pp. 586–7; xvii, nos. 13779, 13828, 13835, 13852, 13873, 13937, 13952, 13965, 13998. For Napoleon's Latin-American ambitions see William Spence Robertson, *France and Latin-American Independence* (Baltimore, Md, 1939), p. 39; Hanoteau, *Memoirs of Caulaincourt*, ii, pp. 213–14. On Napoleon's plans to partition the Ottoman Empire see Prince Richard de Metternich (ed.), *Mémoires documents et ecrits divers laissés par le Prince de Metternich*, 8 vols. (Paris, 1881–83), ii, pp. 144–66; Louis Antoine de Bourrienne, *The Life of Napoleon Bonaparte* (London, 1831), i, p. 208; Paul F. Shupp, *The European Powers and the Near Eastern Question, 1806–1807* (New York, 1931), pp. 542–6.

38. Cited in Jean Tulard, *Napoléon. Le Pouvoir, la nation, la légende* (Paris, 1997), pp. 137–8.

39. J. Christopher Herold (ed.), *The Mind of Napoleon: a Selection from his Written and Spoken Words* (New York, 1955), p. 47; Paul de Rémusat, ed., *Mémoires of Madame de Rémusat, 1802–1808* (London, 1880), i, p. 148.

40. Murphy, 'Napoleon's international politics', p. 168.

41. Comtesse de Boigne, *Mémoires de la comtesse de Boigne, née Osmond* (Paris, 1982), i, p. 211.

42. Hanoteau, *Memoirs of Caulaincourt*, i, pp. 129–30; Bailleu, *Preußen und Frankreich*, ii, p. 51; Schroeder, *Transformation of European Politics*, p. 427.

43. Cited in Albert Vandal, *Napoléon et Alexandre Ier*, 3 vols. (Paris, 1900), iii, p. 311.

44. Cited in E. E. Y. Hales, *Napoleon and the Pope: the Story of Napoleon and Pius VII* (London, 1962), p. 94.

45. *Mémoires de la comtesse de Boigne*, i, p. 211.

46. Bailleu, *Preußen und Frankreich*, ii, pp. 348–9.

47. Bailleu, *Preußen und Frankreich*, ii, p. 51; Dard, *Napoléon et Talleyrand*, p. 272.

48. See Bourrienne, *Life of Napoleon Bonaparte*, i, p. 212.

49. Hales, *Napoleon and the Pope*, p. 180.

50. Las Cases, *Mémorial*, ii, pp. 304–5.

51. Letters to Junot, in Vox, *Correspondance de Napoléon*, pp. 312–14; Napoléon, *Correspondance*, v, n. 3539; vi, nos. 4498, 4499; xii, n. 10657; Bailleu, *Preußen und Frankreich*, ii, p. 51.

52. Schroeder, 'Napoleon's foreign policy', p. 154; idem, *Transformation of European Politics*, pp. 286, 289.

7 Popular Resistance to the Napoleonic Empire

1. Cf. C. J. Esdaile, *The Wars of Napoleon* (London, 1995), pp. 108–42.

2. Cf. M. Broers, *Europe under Napoleon, 1799–1815* (London, 1996), pp. 99–120; C. J. Esdaile, 'Rebeldía, reticencia y resistencia: el caso gallego de 1808', *Trienio*, 35 (May 2000), pp. 57–80.

3. For general introductions to the subject of conscription in the eighteenth century, cf. M. S. Anderson, *War and Society in Europe of the Old Régime, 1648–1789* (London, 1988), pp. 111–24; J. Childs, *Armies and Warfare in Europe, 1648–1789* (Manchester, 1982), pp. 45–57.

4. For a discussion of the impact of conscription in one area of Europe that was particularly heavily affected, cf. F. C. Schneid, *Soldiers of Napoleon's Kingdom of Italy: Army, State and Society, 1800–1815* (Boulder, Colo., 1995), pp. 79–89, and A. Grab, 'Army, state and society: conscription and desertion in Napoleonic Italy, 1802–1814', *Journal of Modern History* 67 (1995), pp. 30–2.

5. The experience of French occupation is a subject that has yet to be examined on a Continent-wide basis. However, for a representative local study, see L. Lorente Toledo, 'Coyuntura económica y presión social en la España ocupada: el modelo tributario francés en Toledo, 1811–1813', in E. de Diego et al. (eds.), *Repercusiones de la Revolución Francesa en España* (Madrid, 1990), pp. 403–19.

6. For a general introduction to the economic impact of the Napoleonic wars, see F. Crouzet, 'Wars, blockade and economic change in Europe, 1792–1815', *Journal of Economic History* 24 (1964), pp. 567–90.

7. For the Dutch example, see S. Schama, *Patriots and Liberators: Revolution in the Netherlands, 1780–1813* (London, 1977), pp. 494–518.

8. For a local study of the implications of French rule in this respect, see L. Macaluso, 'Policing the people: Genoa under the Empire', *Consortium on Revolutionary Europe Proceedings*, 2 vols. (1989), ii, pp. 558–76.

9. Cited in J. Elting, *Swords around a Throne: Napoleon's Grande Armée* (London, 1988), p. 593.

10. For a discussion of Napoleonic policy towards the Catholic Church, see Broers, *Europe under Napoleon*, pp. 81–6, and S. Woolf, *Napoleon's Integration of Europe* (London and New York, 1991), pp. 206–11.

11. See Woolf, *Napoleon's Integration of Europe*, pp. 196–206.

12. For a good example of passive resistance, see the discussion of the French *petite église* in D. M. G. Sutherland, *France, 1789–1815: Revolution and Counter-Revolution* (London, 1986), pp. 394–6.

13. For a discussion of the peasant revolts in Lombardy in 1809, see A. Grab, 'Popular risings in Napoleonic Italy', *Consortium on Revolutionary Europe Proceedings* (1990), pp. 112–19.

14. Cf. Grab, 'Army, state and society', pp. 32–9; E. Arnold, 'Some observations on the French opposition to Napoleonic conscription, 1804–1806', *French Historical Studies* 4 (1966), pp. 453–62; A. Forrest, *Conscripts and Deserters: the Army and French Society during the Revolution and Empire* (New York, 1989), pp. 169–86.

15. Cf. I. Woloch, 'Napoleonic conscription: state power and civil society', *Past & Present* 111 (1986), pp. 101–29; A. Grab, 'State power, brigandage and rural resistance in Napoleonic Italy', *European History Quarterly* 25 (1995), pp. 39–70.

16. Cf. J. Rambaud (ed.), *Memoirs of the Comte Roger de Damas, 1787–1806* (London, 1913), p. 401; H. Bunbury, *Narratives of Some Passages in the Great War with France from 1799 to 1810* (London, 1854), pp. 216–19.

17. For some interesting reflections on the Calabrian revolt, see Moore to Gordon, 11 and 31 October 1806, British Library, Additional Manuscript 49482, ff. 39–43 and

44–6; and Bunbury, *Great War with France*, pp. 269–73, 437. The only modern study is M. Finley, *Most Monstruous of Wars: Napoleonic Guerrilla War in Southern Italy, 1806–1811* (Columbia, SC, 1994).

18. For a discussion of the background to the uprising, cf. C. J. Esdaile, *Spain in the Liberal Age: from Constitution to Civil War, 1808–1939* (Oxford, 2000), pp. 1–20; R. Herr, 'Good, evil and Spain's rising against Napoleon', in R. Herr and H. Parker (eds.), *Ideas in History: Essays Presented to Louis Gottschalk by his Former Students* (Durham, NC, 1965), pp. 157–81; and B. Hamnett, *La Política Española en una Edad Revolucionaria* (Mexico City, 1985), pp. 31–68.

19. Many of these issues are addressed in Esdaile, 'Rebeldía, reticencia y resistencia'; for desertion in particular, see E. Canales Gili, 'La deserción en España durante la Guerra de la Independencia', in L. Roura (ed.), *Le Jacobinisme: Bicentenari de la Revolució Francesa, 1789–1989* (Barcelona, 1990), pp. 211–30.

20. *Alarma* and *somatén* defy exact translation. Both were home-guards composed of all men of military age that were expected to turn out in times of invasion under the command of local *notables*. *Alarma* comes from *alarmar* – 'to warn' – and is probably best rendered by the archaic 'watch', whilst *somatén* is derived from the Catalan verb meaning to be alert, the inference being that the militia had to turn out at a moment's notice.

21. For two revisionist articles on the guerrillas, see C. J. Esdaile, 'Heroes or villains? The Spanish guerrillas in the Peninsular War', *History Today* 38 (April, 1988), pp. 29–35, and C. J. Esdaile, ' "Heroes or villains" revisited: fresh thoughts on *la guerrilla*', in I. Fletcher (ed.), *The Peninsular War: Aspects of the Struggle for the Iberian Peninsula* (Staplehurst, 1998), pp. 93–114.

22. For the activities of the guerrillas in 1813, see C. J. Esdaile, 'The Duke of Wellington and the Spanish Revolution', in C. M. Woolgar (ed.), *Wellington Studies, II* (Southampton, 1999), pp. 163–87.

23. Considerable information on the *josefino* militia may be found in J. S. Pérez Garzón, *Milicia Nacional y Revolución Burguesa: el Protótipo Madrileño, 1808–1874* (Madrid, 1978), pp. 33–59.

24. Sydenham to H. Wellesley, 12 September 1812, University of Southampton, Wellington Papers 1/361.

25. J. Kincaid, *Adventures in the Rifle Brigade* (London, 1909), p. 86.

26. Discussions of the links between the guerrillas, poverty and social tension may be found in M. Ardit Lucas, *Revolución Liberal y Revuelta Campesina: un Ensayo sobre la Desintegración del Régimen Feudal en el País Valenciano, 1793–1840* (Barcelona, 1977), pp. 211–25; Pérez Garzón, *Milicia Nacional y Revolución Burguesa*, pp. 80–4; Hamnett, *Política Española*, pp. 92–3 and M. Moreno Alonso, *Los Españoles durante la Ocupación Napoleónica* (Málaga, 1997), pp. 159–67. The example of Navarre is addressed by J. Tone, *The Fatal Knot: the Guerrilla War in Navarre and the Defeat of Napoleon in Spain* (Chapel Hill, NC, 1994).

27. For a brief introduction to Pombal and his policies, see K. Maxwell, 'Pombal: the paradox of enlightenment and despotism', in H. M. Scott (ed.), *Enlightened Absolutism: Reform and Reformism in Twentieth-century Europe* (London, 1990), pp. 75–118. Also helpful is J. F. Labourdette, *Le Portugal de 1780 à 1802* (Paris, 1985).

28. Peninsular-War Portugal awaits its historian. However, suggestive remarks may be found in a number of British memoirs, e.g. A. Hayter (ed.), *The Backbone: Diaries of a Military Family in the Napoleonic Wars* (Edinburgh, 1993), and E. Warre (ed.), *Letters from the Peninsula, 1808–1812, by Lieut. Gen. Sir William Warre, CB, KTS* (London, 1909).

29. Diary of Harriet Slessor, 21 February 1809, cit. Hayter, *The Backbone*, p. 212. For details of the military system of Portugal and the activities of her irregulars in 1809 and 1810, see C. Oman, *A History of the Peninsular War*, 7 vols. (Oxford, 1902–30), ii, pp. 211–49, and iii, pp. 179–83.

30. Diary of Harriet Slessor, n.d., cit. ibid., p. 219.

31. For Joseph II, cf. T. C. W. Blanning, *Joseph II and Enlightened Despotism* (London, 1970). Montgelas, meanwhile, is discussed in A. Cronenberg, 'Montgelas and the reorganisation of Napoleonic Bavaria', *Consortium on Revolutionary Europe Proceedings* (1990), pp. 712–19, and the impact of Bavarian rule on the Tyrol in F. G. Eyck, *Loyal Rebels: Andreas Hofer and the Tyrolean Uprising of 1809* (Lanham, New York and London, 1986), pp. 27–43.

32. For the Tyrolean revolt, see Eyck, *Loyal Rebels*, pp. 45–78.

8 Policing the Empire:
Napoleon and the Pacification of Europe

1. On the *cadastre* in Napoleonic France see R. J. P. Kain and E. Baignet, *The Cadastral Map in the Service of the State: a History of Property Mapping* (Chicago, 1992), especially pp. 228–31.

2. In English, see the good overview in S. J. Woolf, 'French civilization and ethnicity in the Napoleonic Empire', *Past & Present* 124 (1989), pp. 96–120.

3. General Reille to Napoleon, 9 December 1807, Archives de la Guerre, Vincennes (AG), C/4 (Armée d'Italie), dossier 'Correspondence du Général Reille pendant sa mission en Toscane (1807–1808)'.

4. J. Vidalenc, 'Les départments hanséatiques et l'administration napoléonienne', *Francia* 2 (1973), p. 420.

5. General Wirion to the Administrator-General, Brussels, 22 Pluviose Year IV (11 February 1796), Archives Nationales de Paris (ANP), F^{1e} 10 (Pays et Départements Réunis, Belgique), dossier 'Organisation de la Gendarmerie. Papiers communs aux neuf départements'.

6. Wirion to the Minister of War, 19 Thermidor Year IX (7 August 1801), AG X^f 150 (Gendarmerie).

7. See especially, E. A. Whitcomb, 'Napoleon's prefects', *American Historical Review* 69 (1974), pp. 1089–1118.

8. E. Martin, *La Gendarmerie française en Espagne et en Portugal (Campagnes de 1807 à 1813)* (Paris, 1898).

9. The date of the Revolutionary Calendar when it became law: 2 October 1795.

10. ANP F^{1e} 27, 'Extrait des Registres des Délibérations du Directoire Exécutif', 14 Brumaire Year VII (3 November 1798).

11. Ibid.

12. Minister, troisième arrondissement de police, to the prefect, dépt de l'Arno, 18 August 1813, ANP F⁷ 8809 (Police-Générale, dépt Arno).

13. Captain Thilorier to the Director-General of Police, Florence, 12 August 1813, ANP F⁷ 8809 (Police-Générale, dépt Arno).

14. Minister of the Interior to General Menou, 9 July 1807, ANP F⁷ 3690 (Police-Générale, dépt de la Sture).

15. G. S. Pene Vidari, 'Studi e prospettivi recente di storia giuridica sul Piemonte della Restaurazione', *Studi Piemontesi* 12 (1983), p. 7.

16. See G. Rigault, *Le Général Abdallah Menou et la dernière phase de l'expédition d'Egypte* (Paris, 1911).

17. Eugene to Napoleon, 28 December 1808, AG C3-6 (Ordres et Correspondance du Prince Eugène, 1805–10).

18. A. Roederer to P.-L. Roederer, 15 March 1812, ANP, Archives Privées, Fonds Roederer, 29-AP-15.

19. A. Combier (ed.), *Mémoires du Général Radet* (St Cloud, 1892).

20. Petition of Vendero to Fouché, Minister of Police-Générale, Paris, 7 March 1810, ANP F⁷ 9832 (Police-Générale, Statistique Morale, Commissaires de Police, dépt Rome). On the *Gendarmeria Piemontese* the account in M. Broers, *Napoleonic Imperialism and the Savoyard Monarchy, 1773–1821: State Building in Piedmont* (Lampeter, 1997), pp. 281–3, draws together the archival sources.

21. Director-General of Police, Turin, to Fouché, Minister of Police-Générale, Paris, 29 September 1808, ANP F⁷ 8578 (Police-Générale, dépt Marengo).

22. Prefect, Apennines, to Minister, troisième arrondissement de police, Paris, 16 March 1810, ANP F⁷ 9832 (Police-Générale, Statistique Morale, Commissaires de Police, dépt Rome).

23. Director-General of Police, Turin, to Minister, troisième arrondissement de police, Paris, 27 March 1810, ANP F⁷ 9832 (Police-Générale, Statistique Morale, Commissaires de Police, dépt Rome).

24. Prefect of dépt Marengo, to Minister, troisième arrondissement de police, Paris, 16 August 1809, ANP F⁷ 9832 (Police-Générale, Statistique Morale, Commissaires de Police, dépt Rome).

25. J. Mercador Riba, *Barcelona durante la occupacion francesca, 1808–1814* (Madrid, 1946), pp. 219–95.

26. See especially I. Woloch, *The New Regime: Transformations of the French Civic Order, 1789–1820s* (New York, 1994), pp. 380–426; and idem, 'Napoleonic conscription: state power and civil society', *Past & Present* 111 (1986), pp. 101–29.

27. A. Forrest, *Conscripts and Deserters: the Army and French Society during the Revolution and Empire* (New York, 1989); Broers, *Napoleonic Imperialism and the Savoyard Monarchy*, pp. 313–49; A. Grab, 'Army, state and society: conscription and desertion in Napoleonic Italy, 1802–1814', *Journal of Modern History* 67 (1995), pp. 25–54.

28. Wirion to General Jourdan, Administrator-General, Turin, 19 Thermidor Year IX (7 August 1801), AG Xᶠ 150 (Gendarmerie).

29. Wirion to the Minister of the Interior, 2 Vendemiaire Year VI (23 September 1797), ANP F¹ᶜ 27.

9 State, Society and Tax Policy in Napoleonic Europe

I should like to thank Suzanne Moulton for reading this article and making stylistic improvements.

1. Stuart Woolf, *Napoleon's Integration of Europe* (London and New York, 1991), p. 104.
2. D. M. G. Sutherland, *France, 1789–1815: Revolution and Counterrevolution* (London, 1985), p. 413; see also Jacques Godechot, *Les institutions de la France sous la Révolution et l'Empire* (Paris, 1968), p. 647.
3. The most comprehensive study of finances in Napoleonic France appeared more than seventy years ago: Marcel Marion, *Histoire financière de la France depuis 1715. Tome IV: 1797–1818. La fin de la Révolution, le Consulat et l'Empire, la libération du territoire* (Paris, 1925). For most of the Napoleonic satellites studies on the financial policies have yet to be written.
4. On the financial conditions under the Directory, see Martyn Lyons, *France under the Directory* (Cambridge, 1975), pp. 167–71; Godechot, *Les institutions*, pp. 506–15.
5. William Doyle, *The Oxford History of the French Revolution* (Oxford, 1990), p. 324.
6. Godechot, *Les institutions*, p. 514.
7. Jean Tulard, *Napoléon, ou le mythe du sauveur* (Paris, 1977), p. 124.
8. Marion, *Histoire financière*, pp. 324–5.
9. Louis Bergeron, *France under Napoleon* (Princeton, NJ, 1981 transl.), p. 38.
10. Marion, *Histoire financière*, pp. 307–12.
11. Bergeron, *France under Napoleon*, p. 38.
12. Ibid., p. 39.
13. Marion, *Histoire financière*, p. 298.
14. Bergeron, *France under Napoleon*, p. 39.
15. Godechot, *Les institutions*, p. 646.
16. Marion, *Histoire financière*, pp. 302–304.
17. Bergeron, *France under Napoleon*, p. 39.
18. On tax collection reforms in France see Godechot, *Les institutions*, pp. 640–2.
19. Ibid., p. 641.
20. Ibid., pp. 648–9; Bergeron, *France under Napoleon*, pp. 42–3.
21. Ibid., p. 41.
22. On the Bank of France see Marion, *Histoire financière*, pp. 206–12; Godechot, *Les institutions*, pp. 650–2; Geoffrey Ellis, *Napoleon* (London and New York, 1997), pp. 71–3.
23. Bergeron, *France under Napoleon*, p. 49.
24. Ibid., pp. 44–6.
25. Godechot, *Les Institutions*, p. 650.
26. Ibid., p. 655.
27. Ibid.; Ellis, *Napoleon*, p. 73.
28. Unless otherwise indicated, the following is based on Simon Schama's *Patriots and Liberators: Revolutions in the Netherlands, 1780–1813* (London, 1977).
29. Simon Schama, 'The exigencies of war and the politics of taxation in the Netherlands 1795–1810', in J. M. Winter (ed.), *War and Economic Development: Essays in Memory of David Joslin* (Cambridge, 1975), p. 111.
30. Simon Schama, *Patriots and Liberators*, p. 384.

31. Jonathan Israel, *The Dutch Republic: its Rise, Greatness, and Fall 1477–1806* (Oxford, 1995), pp. 285–91; Schama, 'The exigencies of war', pp. 107–108.

32. Schama, 'The exigencies of war', p. 115.

33. Schama, *Patriots and Liberators*, pp. 385–8.

34. Ibid., p. 497.

35. Ibid., pp. 501–12.

36. On the Dutch *cadastre*, see ibid., p. 506; R. J. P. Kain and E. Baignet, *The Cadastral Map in the Service of the State: a History of Property Mapping* (Chicago, 1992), pp. 32–6.

37. Schama, *Patriots and Liberators*, p. 615.

38. Schama, 'The exigencies of war', p. 128.

39. On the fiscal conditions in northern Italy under Napoleon, see Alexander Grab, 'The politics of finance in Napoleonic Italy (1802–1814)', *Journal of Modern Italian Studies* 3 (1998), pp. 127–43.

40. Napoleon to Eugene de Beauharnais, 25 April 1806, *Correspondance de Napoléon Ier publiée par ordre de l'empereur Napoléon III*, 32 vols. (Paris, 1858–69), xii, p. 307.

41. Napoleon to Eugene de Beauharnais, 7 June 1805, *Correspondance*, x, p. 490.

42. On the revolt see Alexander Grab, 'State power, brigandage and rural resistance in Napoleonic Italy', *European History Quarterly* 25 (1995), pp. 39–70.

43. Archivio storico di Milano, *Aldini*, cartella 103, 19 April 1812.

10 Britain and Napoleon

1. Paul Frischauer, *England's Years of Danger: a New History of the World War 1792–1815 Dramatised in Documents* (London, 1938).

2. Carola Oman, *Britain against Napoleon* (London, 1943).

3. Frank J. Klingberg and Sigurd B. Hustvedt (eds.), *The Warning Drum: the British Home Front Faces Napoleon. Broadsides of 1803* (Berkeley and Los Angeles, Calif., 1944), p. 4.

4. Arthur Bryant, *The Years of Endurance, 1793–1802* (London, 1942); idem, *The Years of Victory, 1802–1812* (London, 1944).

5. See Emmanuel Berl, 'Denn wie Karthago muß auch England zerstört werden!', in Heinz-Otto Sieburg (ed.), *Napoleon und Europa* (Cologne and Berlin, 1971), pp. 161–70.

6. See Roman Schnur, 'Land und Meer – Napoleon gegen England. Ein Kapitel der Geschichte internationaler Politik', in idem, *Revolution und Weltbürgerkrieg. Studien zur Ouverture nach 1789* (Berlin, 1983), pp. 33–58.

7. See Brendan Simms, 'Fra Land e Mear. La Gran Bretagna, la Prussia e il problemo del decisionismo (1804–1806)', *Ricerche di Storia Politica* 6 (1991), pp. 5–34.

8. See Henry Foljambe Hall (ed.), *Napoleon's Notes on English History* (London, 1905).

9. Cited in E. Tangye Lean, *The Napoleonists: a Study in Political Disaffection 1760/1960* (Oxford, 1970), p. 7.

10. Cited in A. D. Harvey, 'European attitudes to Britain during the French revolutionary and Napoleonic era', *History* 63 (1978), p. 358.

11. Geoffrey Ellis, *Napoleon* (London and New York, 1997), p. 170.

12. Cited in François Crouzet, 'Great Britain's response to the French Revolution and to Napoleon', in idem, *Britain Ascendant: Comparative Studies in Franco–British Economic History* (Cambridge, 1990), p. 285.

13. Cited in Jean Trani and J. C. Carmigiani, *Napoléon et l'Angleterre: vingt-deux ans d'affrontements sur terre et sur mer, 1793–1815* (Paris, 1994), p. 11.

14. Cited in Crouzet, 'Great Britain's response', p. 287.

15. Cited in ibid., p. 285.

16. See H. D. Schmidt, 'The idea and slogan of "perfidious Albion"', *History* 14 (1953), pp. 612–13.

17. Cited in John Ehrman, *The Younger Pitt. Vol. III: The Consuming Struggle* (London, 1996), p. 688.

18. See Lean, *The Napoleonists*, p. 209.

19. Cited in Herbert Butterfield, 'Charles James Fox and Napoleon. The peace negotiations of 1806', *The Creighton Lecture in History 1961* (London, 1962), p. 2.

20. Both cited in Karl Goldmann, *Die preussisch-britischen Beziehungen in den Jahren 1812–1815* (Würzburg, 1934), p. 34.

21. T. C. W. Blanning, *The French Revolutionary Wars, 1787–1802* (London, 1996), p. 196.

22. Cited in Paul Bailleu (ed.), *Preußen und Frankreich von 1795 bis 1807. Diplomatische Correspondenzen*, 2 vols. (Leipzig, 1881 and 1887), ii, pp. 215–16.

23. See Richard Glover, *Britain at Bay: Defence against Bonaparte, 1803–1814* (London and New York, 1973), p. 13.

24. Cited in Glover, *Britain at Bay*, p. 19.

25. See the table in Michael Duffy, 'World-wide war and British expansion, 1793–1815', in P. J. Marshall (ed.), *The Oxford History of the British Empire. Vol. III: The Eighteenth Century* (Oxford, 1998), p. 204.

26. Rory Muir, *Britain and the Defeat of Napoleon, 1807–1815* (New Haven, Conn., 1996), p. 17.

27. Cited in Geoffrey Ellis, *The Napoleonic Empire* (Basingstoke and London, 1991), p. 97.

28. See Herbert Butterfield, *Napoleon* (London, 1939), p. 91.

29. Cited in Goldmann, *Die preussisch-britischen Beziehungen*, p. 37.

30. Cited in Piers Mackesy, *British Victory in Egypt, 1801: the End of Napoleon's Conquest* (London and New York, 1995), p. 52.

31. See Therese Ebbinghaus, *Napoleon, England und die Presse, 1800–1803* (Munich and Berlin, 1914), pp. 123–43.

32. Both cited in Harvey, 'European attitudes', p. 356.

33. See Robert Holtman, *Napoleonic Propaganda* (New York, 1969 edn), pp. 3–6.

34. See Ehrman, *Consuming Struggle*, pp. 354–67.

35. Cited in ibid., p. 4.

36. Cited in ibid., p. 796.

37. Piers Mackesy, 'Strategic problems of the British war effort', in H. T. Dickinson (ed.), *Britain and the French Revolution, 1789–1815* (London and Basingstoke, 1989), p. 159.

38. Cited in Christopher D. Hall, *British Strategy in the Napoleonic War, 1803–1815* (Manchester and New York, 1992), p. 137.

39. Cited in Hartmut Gembries, 'Das Thema Preußen in der politischen Diskussion Englands zwischen 1792 und 1807' (doctoral thesis, University of Freiburg, 1988), p. 154.

40. Cited in Muir, *Britain and the Defeat of Napoleon*, p. 6.

41. Cited in ibid., p. 39.
42. Ibid., p. 101.
43. Cited in Ehrman, *Consuming Struggle*, p. 228.
44. See Mackesy, 'Strategic problems', p. 161.
45. Cited in Michael Duffy, 'British diplomacy and the French Wars 1789–1815', in Dickinson (ed.), *Britain and the French Revolution*, p. 136.
46. Cited in Muir, *Britain and the Defeat of Napoleon*, p. 309.
47. A point made by Crouzet, 'Great Britain's response', p. 287.
48. Iradji Amini, *Napoleon and Persia: Franco–Persian Relations under the First Empire* (London, 1999).
49. See Hall, *British Strategy in the Napoleonic War*, p. 189.
50. See Duffy, 'World-wide empire', p. 196.
51. See Peter Hofschröer, *1815: the Waterloo Campaign, Wellington, his German Allies and the Battles of Ligny and Quatre Bras* (London, 1998).
52. See J. M. Sherwig, *Guineas and Gunpowder: British Foreign Aid in the Wars with France* (Cambridge, Mass., 1969).
53. Charles J. Esdaile, *The Wars of Napoleon* (London, 1995), p. 143.
54. So Esdaile in ibid., p. 144.
55. Cited in Muir, *Britain and the Defeat of Napoleon*, pp. 367–8.
56. See Michael John Thornton, *Napoleon and the St Helena Decision* (Stanford, Calif., 1968), pp. 14–15.

11 Napoleon and State Formation in Central Europe

1. Thomas Nipperdey, *Germany from Napoleon to Bismarck, 1800–1866*, trans. Daniel Nolan (Dublin, 1996), p. 1. For the purposes of this chapter, central Europe refers to Prussia, the Habsburg monarchy and the states of the Confederation of the Rhine. The left bank of the Rhine, which was incorporated into the French Empire, and the Grand Duchy of Warsaw are excluded.
2. H. M. Scott (ed.), *Enlightened Absolutism: Reform and Reformers in Later Eighteenth-century Europe* (London, 1990).
3. Michael Hughes, 'Fiat justitia, pereat Germania? The imperial supreme jurisdiction and imperial reform in the later Holy Roman Empire', in John Breuilly (ed.), *The State of Germany* (London and New York, 1992), pp. 29–46.
4. Michael Stolleis, 'Verwaltungslehre und Verwaltungswissenschaft 1803–1866', in Kurt G. A. Jeserich, Hans Pohl, Georg-Christoph von Unruh (eds.), *Deutsche Verwaltungsgeschichte*, 6 vols. (Stuttgart, 1983–88), Vol. 2: *Vom Reichsdeputationshauptschluß bis zur Auflösung des Deutschen Bundes*, pp. 58–62. Wolfgang Neugebauer, 'Landstände im Heiligen Römischen Reich an der Schwelle der Moderne. Zum Problem von Kontinuität und Diskontinuität um 1800', in Heinz Duchhardt and Andreas Kunz (eds.), *Reich oder Nation? Mitteleuropa 1780–1815* (Mainz, 1998), pp. 51–86.
5. John G. Gagliardo, *Reich and Nation: the Holy Roman Empire as Idea and Reality, 1763–1806* (Bloomington, Ind., and London, 1980), pp. 187–289.
6. For this Catholic revival, see Jonathan Sperber, *Popular Catholicism in Nineteenth-century Germany* (Princeton, NJ, 1984).

7. Konrad M. Färber, *Kaiser und Erzkanzler: Carl von Dalberg und Napoleon* (Regensburg, 1994), pp. 41–9.

8. Georg Schmidt, 'Der napoleonische Rheinbund – ein erneuertes Altes Reich?', in Volker Press (ed.), *Alternativen zur Reichsverfassung in der Frühen Neuzeit* (Munich, 1995), pp. 228–31. Francis II now became Francis I, Emperor of Austria, a title he had created for himself in August 1804 after Napoleon's creation of the French imperial dignity.

9. Walter Demel, *Der Bayerische Staatsabsolutismus 1806/08–1817. Staats- und gesellschafts-politische Motivationen und Hintergründe der Reformära in der ersten Phase des Königreichs Bayern* (Munich, 1983), *passim*. Bernd Wunder, *Privilegierung und disziplinierung: die Entstehung des Berufsbeamtentums in Bayern und Württemburg (1780–1825)* (Munich, 1978), *passim*.

10. Paul Sauer, *Napoleon's Adler über Württemberg, Baden und Hohenzollern. Südwestdeutsch-land in der Rheinbundzeit* (Stuttgart, Berlin, Cologne and Mainz, 1987), pp. 58–9, 67–9, 105–109, 170–8.

11. Loyd E. Lee, *The Politics of Harmony: Civil Service, Liberalism, and Social Reform in Baden, 1800–1850* (Newark, 1980), pp. 18–36.

12. Brendan Simms, *The Impact of Napoleon: Prussian High Politics, Foreign Policy and the Crisis of the Executive, 1797–1806* (Cambridge, 1997), pp. 230–65.

13. Owen Connelly, *Napoleon's Satellite Kingdoms* (New York and London, 1965), pp. 176–222.

14. John H. Gill, *With Eagles to Glory: Napoleon and his German Allies in the 1809 Campaign* (London, 1992), p. 23.

15. Hans-Peter Ullmann, 'The emergence of modern public debts in Bavaria and Baden between 1780 and 1820', in Peter-Christian Witt (ed.), *Wealth and Taxation in Central Europe: the History and Sociology of Public Finance* (Leamington Spa, Hamburg and New York, 1987), pp. 63–78.

16. Elisabeth Fehrenbach, *Der Kampf um die Einführung des Code Napoleon in den Rheinbundstaaten* (Wiesbaden, 1973), *passim*.

17. Thomas Stamm-Kuhlmann, *König in Preußens großer Zeit. Friedrich Wilhelm III. Der Melancholiker auf dem Thron* (Berlin, 1992), pp. 158ff., 207ff.

18. Marion W. Gray, *Prussia in Transition: Society and Politics under the Stein Reform Ministry of 1808* (Philadelphia, 1986), pp. 122ff.

19. Gray, *Prussia in Transition*, pp. 113–18.

20. Charles Edward White, *The Enlightened Soldier: Scharnhorst and the Militärische Gesellschaft in Berlin, 1801–1805* (New York, Westport, Conn., and London, 1989).

21. Stamm-Kuhlmann, *Friedrich Wilhelm III*, pp. 298–306.

22. Stamm-Kuhlmann, *Friedrich Wilhelm III*, pp. 160–2.

23. Waltraud Heindl, *Gehorsame Rebellen. Bürokratie und Beamte in Österreich 1780 bis 1848* (Vienna, 1991), pp. 21–37, 44–5, 59, 64–5, 71–2, 80–7.

24. Hellmuth Rössler, *Graf Johann Philipp Stadion. Napoleons deutscher Gegenspieler*, 2 vols. (Vienna and Munich, 1966), i, pp. 23–50, 226–9, 232, 234–8, 287–8. Walter Consuelo Langsam, *The Napoleonic Wars and German Nationalism in Austria* (New York, 1930), pp. 32–8, 43, 58–61, 66ff., 94ff.

25. These figures are based upon those provided by Macartney for 1780, but rounded up to reflect population growth and with significant deductions for some nationalities to reflect the loss of possessions during the revolutionary and Napoleonic wars. C. A. Macartney, *The Habsburg Empire 1790–1918* (London, 1971 reprint), pp. 76–82.

26. Domokos Kosáry, *Napoleon et la Hongrie* (Budapest, 1979), *passim*.

27. Macartney, *Habsburg Empire*, pp. 138, 174, 177–8, 184–6; Rössler, *Stadion*, i, pp. 296, 299.

28. F. Gunther Eyck, *Loyal Rebels: Andreas Hofer and the Tyrolean Uprising of 1809* (Lanham, New York, London, 1986), pp. 1–17, 27–35, 37–41, 68–9, 109, 158–9.

29. Rudolf Ibbeken, *Preußen 1807–1813* (Cologne and Berlin, 1970), pp. 398ff.

30. Ibbeken, *Preußen 1807–1813*, pp. 397–400.

31. Michael Hundt, *Die mindermächtigen deutschen Staaten auf dem Wiener Kongress* (Mainz, 1996), pp. 35–7, 43–4, 61–2.

12 The Peninsular War

1. Emmanuel de Las Cases, *Mémorial de Sainte-Hélène*, 2 vols. (Paris, 1823), i, pp. 609–10.

2. A good orientation to the literature on this subject may be found in Stuart Woolf, *Nationalism in Europe: 1815 to the Present* (London, 1996); E. J. Hobsbawm, *Nations and Nationalism since 1780* (Cambridge, 1990); and Ernest Gellner, *Nations and Nationalism* (Oxford, 1983).

3. The best general account is José María Toreno, *Historia del levantamiento, guerra, y revolución de España*, 3 vols. (Paris, 1851). See also Gabriel Lovett, *Napoleon and the Birth of Modern Spain*, 2 vols. (New York, 1965). For the military history see José Gómez de Arteche y Moro, *La Guerra de la Independencia*, 14 vols. (Madrid, 1868); and Charles Oman, *A History of the Peninsular War*, 7 vols. (London, 1902–30).

4. Charles Esdaile, *The Spanish Army in the Peninsular War* (Manchester, 1988).

5. See Manuel Godoy, *Memorias* in *Biblioteca de autores españoles*, vols. 88–9 (Madrid, 1965); and Douglas Hilt, *The Troubled Trinity: Godoy and the Spanish Monarchs* (Tuscaloosa, Ala., 1987).

6. Pedro Cevallos, *Exposición de los hechos y maquinaciones que han preparado la usurpación de la corona de España y los medios que el Emperador de los franceses ha puesto en obra para realizarla* (Cádiz, 1808); Richard Herr, 'Good, evil and Spain's rising against Napoleon', in Richard Herr and Harold T. Parker (eds.), *Ideas in History: Essays Presented to Louis Gottschalk by his Former Students* (Durham, NC, 1965), pp. 157–81.

7. This imperial rhetoric may be sampled in works by veterans of the wars, including that of Maximilién Sébastien Foy, who blamed the Spanish for failing to recognise that the French were 'a more civilised people' simply trying to do Spain a good turn. Foy, *Histoire de la guerre de la péninsule*, 4 vols. (Paris, 1827), iv, p. 25.

8. Louis Bergeron, *L'Épisode napoléonien. Aspects intérieurs, 1799–1815* (Paris, 1972); Jean Tulard, *Napoléon, ou le mythe du sauveur* (Paris, 1977); and for a critical biography, Alan Schom, *Napoleon Bonaparte* (New York, 1997).

9. For example, Charles Esdaile, *The Wars of Napoleon* (London, 1995), pp. 29–30, 122–30. For a view of the Spanish resistance as 'heroic and retrograde', see Roger Dufraisse, *Napoleon* (New York, 1992), p. 105.

10. A suggestive essay on this subject is Julián Marías, *La España posible en tiempo de Carlos III* (Barcelona, 1988). See also Richard Herr, *The Eighteenth Century Revolution in Spain* (Princeton, NJ, 1958).

11. Geoffrey Ellis, *The Napoleonic Empire* (Basingstoke and London, 1991), p. 92.

12. For this perspective, see the works already cited by Ellis, Bergeron and Schom.

13. Tulard, *Napoléon*, p. 336. On resistance to conscription in this period, Isser Woloch, *The New Regime: Transformations of the French Civic Order, 1789–1820s* (New York, 1994), ch. 13.

14. On the evolution of the French army see Jean-Paul Bertaud, *The Army of the French Revolution: from Citizen-Soldiers to Instrument of Power* (Princeton, NJ, 1988).

15. Schom, *Napoleon*, p. 486. For an interesting account of the siege of Gerona, Pedro Espraeckmans, *Diario del sitio de Gerona en el año de 1809 por el séptimo cuerpo del ejército francés* (Olot, Catalonia, 1909).

16. Milton Finley, *The Most Monstruous of Wars: The Napoleonic Guerrilla War in Southern Italy, 1806–1811* (Columbia, SC, 1994).

17. Juan Escoiquiz, *Idea sencilla de las razones que motivaron el viaje del Rey Fernando VII a Bayona en el més de abril de 1808, dada al público de España y de Europa* (Madrid, 1808); and Juan Antonio Llorente, (pseud. Juan Nellerto), *Memoria para la historia de la revolución española* (Paris, 1814).

18. A good starting point for understanding Madrid's uprising is the excellent collection, *Madrid, el 2 de Mayo de 1808, viaje a un día en la historia de España* (Madrid, 1992).

19. Jesusmaría Alía y Plana, 'El primer lunes de Mayo de 1808 en Madrid', in *Madrid, el 2 de Mayo de 1808*, pp. 105–38.

20. The best sources for the basic military history of the period are Arteche y Moro, *La Guerra*, and Oman, *A History of the Peninsular War*.

21. The term *afrancesados* refers to Spaniards who were attracted in one way or another to French culture and who collaborated with the French regime.

22. There is no English equivalent. Juan Martín's nickname originally described anyone from the Castrillo de Duero, a region characterised by lots of *pecinas* – that is, silty, detritus-laden mud found at the bottom of the still pools commonly found around Castrillo. It carried a slightly pejorative connotation, and this is how people understood the word when Juan Martín, who was born near Castrillo, adopted it as his *nomme de guerre*. Later, because of Juan Martín's fame, the word came to describe any guerrilla fighter or, indeed, any young man with an impetuous, obstinate, tenacious character. Like the modern meaning of the word 'guerrilla', the word 'empecinado' is forever linked to Spanish resistance to Napoleon.

23. John Lawrence Tone, *The Fatal Knot: the Guerrilla War in Navarre and the Defeat of Napoleon in Spain* (Chapel Hill, NC, 1994). This work was expanded in a Spanish language edition, *La guerrilla española y la derrota de Napoleón* (Madrid, 1999).

24. On Juan Martín, see Andrés Cassinello Pérez, *Juan Martín, 'El Empecinado', o el Amor a la Libertad* (Madrid, 1995).

25. In Spain, local and regional identity has always been strong, at times trumping nationalism. The term *patria chica*, or 'little country', captures this characteristic of Spanish political culture.

26. On Galicia, see Ramón Artaza Malvarez, *Reconquista de Santiago en 1809* (Madrid, 1909); Andrés Martínez Salazar, *De la Guerra de la Independencia en Galicia* (Buenos Aires, 1908); and Manuel Pardo de Andrade, *Los guerrilleros gallegos de 1809* (La Coruña, 1892).

27. María Cruz Figueroa Lalinde, *La Guerra de Independencia en Galicia* (Vigo, 1993), pp. 136–7.

13 The Russian Empire and the Napoleonic Wars

1. I should like to thank Marc Raeff and Theophilus Prousis for their generous comments and advice. Of course, the responsibility for the content of the chapter is mine alone.

2. Marc Raeff, *Comprendre l'ancien régime russe: Etat et société en Russie impériale* (Paris, 1982), pp. 67–8 (English edition: *Understanding Imperial Russia: State and Society in the Old Regime* (New York, 1984)).

3. Geoffrey Hosking, *Russia: People and Empire 1552–1917* (Cambridge, Mass., 1997), pp. xxv–xxvi.

4. Isabel de Madariaga, *Russia in the Age of Catherine the Great* (New Haven, Conn., London, 1981), pp. 187–236, 377–451.

5. Natan Ia. Eidel'man, *Gran' vekov: Politicheskaia bor'ba v Rossii, konets XVIII-nachalo XIX stoletiia*, in *V bor'be za vlast': Stranitsy politicheskoi istorii Rossii XVIII veka* (Moscow, 1988), pp. 71–85, 120–1, 130–5, 149.

6. Roderick McGrew, *Paul I of Russia 1754–1801* (Oxford, 1992), pp. 289–96.

7. Hugh Ragsdale, *Détente in the Napoleonic Era: Bonaparte and the Russians* (Lawrence, Kans., 1980), pp. 26–8.

8. Ibid., pp. 34–40, 113, 118.

9. Dmitrii Obolenskii (ed.), *Khronika nedavnei stariny. Iz arkhiva kniazia Obolenskago-Neledinskago-Meletskago* (St Petersburg, 1876), p. 90. Filip F. Vigel', *Zapiski*, ed. S. Ia. Shtraikh, 2 vols. (Moscow, 1928; repr. Cambridge, England, 1974), i, p. 121.

10. Eidel'man, *Gran' vekov*, p. 577.

11. Patricia Kennedy Grimsted, *The Foreign Ministers of Alexander I: Political Attitudes and the Conduct of Russian Diplomacy, 1801–1825* (Berkeley, Calif., 1969), pp. 45–6, 56, 67–8, 75.

12. Ibid., pp. 66–8.

13. Janet M. Hartley, *Alexander I* (London and New York, 1994), pp. 30–49.

14. Grimsted, *Foreign Ministers of Alexander I*, pp. 104–50.

15. Hartley, *Alexander I*, pp. 72–8.

16. Evgenii V. Tarle, *Otechestvennaia voina 1812 goda. Izbrannye proizvedeniia* (Moscow, 1994), pp. 213, 241–2.

17. Alexander M. Martin, *Romantics, Reformers, Reactionaries: Russian Conservative Thought and Politics in the Reign of Alexander I* (DeKalb, Ill., 1997), pp. 39–56.

18. David Chandler, *The Campaigns of Napoleon* (London and New York, 1966), reproduced in Frank A. Kafker and James M. Laux (eds.), *Napoleon and his Times: Selected Interpretations* (Malabar, Fla., 1989), p. 246. P. A. Zhilin et al., *Borodino 1812* (Moscow, 1987), p. 41.

19. Martin, *Romantics, Reformers, Reactionaries*, pp. 123–42.

20. Scholars disagree substantially on the casualty figures. See Zhilin, *Borodino*, p. 216; D. M. G. Sutherland, *France, 1789–1815: Revolution and Counterrevolution* (London, 1986), p. 418; Tarle, *Otechestvennaia voina 1812 goda*, pp. 167, 501; Boris S. Abalikhin and Vladimir A. Dunaevskii, *1812 god na perekrestkakh mnenii sovetskikh istorikov 1917–1987* (Moscow, 1990), p. 167.

21. Zhilin, *Borodino*, p. 248.

22. Chandler, *The Campaigns of Napoleon*, pp. 246–7, estimates their 1812 military casualties at 150,000. The Soviet demographer B. Ts. Urlanis calculates that Russia lost a total of 360,000 soldiers in the wars after 1805, including 111,000 in 1812. P. A. Zhilin, *Otechestvennaia voina 1812 goda* (Moscow, 1988), p. 416. Others have estimated the total Russian losses (civilian and military) for 1812 at 250,000. Boris N. Mironov, *Russkii gorod v 1740–1860e gody: Demograficheskoe, sotsial'noe i ekonomicheskoe razvitie* (Leningrad, 1990), p. 60.

23. Ibid., p. 416. Heinrich Storch, *Historisch-statistisches Gemälde des Russischen Reichs am Ende des achtzehnten Jahrhunderts*, 8 vols. (Riga, Leipzig, 1797–1803), ii, p. 361. Idem, *Russland unter Alexander dem Ersten: Eine historische Zeitschrift*, 9 vols. (St Petersburg, Leipzig, 1804–1808), iii, p. 92. Friedrich Raupach, *Reise von St Petersburg nach dem Gesundbrunnen zu Lipezk am Don. Nebst einem Beitrage zur Charakteristik der Russen* (Breslau, 1809), p. 250.

24. Zhilin, *Borodino*, p. 257. Petr I. Shchukin (ed.), *Bumagi otnosiashchiiasia do Otechestvennoi voiny 1812 goda*, 10 vols. (Moscow, 1897–1908), i, p. 77.

25. Martin, *Romantics, Reformers, Reactionaries*, p. 141.

26. See Francis Ley, *Alexandre Ier et sa Sainte-Alliance (1811–1825) avec des documents inédits* (Paris, 1975).

27. Martin, *Romantics, Reformers, Reactionaries*, pp. 143–202.

28. Martin Malia, *Russia under Western Eyes: from the Bronze Horseman to the Lenin Mausoleum* (Cambridge, Mass., and London, 1999), pp. 91–4.

29. The links and similarities between the coup attempts by liberal officers in Spain (1820) and Russia (1825) are discussed by Isabel de Madariaga in 'Spain and the Decembrists', *European Studies Review* 3 (1973), pp. 141–56.

INDEX

———— ◆ ————